Guru English

TRANSLATION | TRANSNATION

EDITED BY EMILY APTER

Guru English

SOUTH ASIAN RELIGION
IN A COSMOPOLITAN LANGUAGE

Srinivas Aravamudan

PRINCETON UNIVERSITY PRESS

PRINCETON AND OXFORD

Published by Princeton University Press, 41 William Street, Princeton, New Jersey 08540

In the United Kingdom: Princeton University Press, 3 Market Place, Woodstock, Oxfordshire OX20 1SY

Library of Congress Cataloging-in-Publication Data

Aravamudan, Srinivas.
  Guru English : South Asian religion in a cosmopolitan language / Srinivas Aravamudan.
    p.   cm.   — (Translation/transnation)
  Includes bibliographical references and index.
  ISBN-13: 978-0-691-11827-7 (cl. : alk. paper)—ISBN-13: 978-0-691-11828-4
  (pb. : alk. paper)
  ISBN-10: 0-691-11827-2 (cl. : alk. paper)—ISBN-10: 0-691-11828-0 (pb. : alk. paper)
    1. English language—Religious aspects—South Asia. 2. English language—Social
  aspects—South Asia. 3. South Asia—Religion—Study and teaching. 4. Religion
  and culture. 5. Cosmopolitanism—India. I. Title. II. Series.

PE3502.G87A73 2005
420'.954—dc22   2004062907

British Library Cataloging-in-Publication Data is available

This book has been composed in Palatino

pup.princeton.edu

Printed in the United States of America

10 9 8 7 6 5 4 3 2 1

For Prema Srinivasan

Contents

Acknowledgments

This book combines autobiographical accident with scholarly necessity. Let me begin with the autobiographical antecedents. I was brought up in urban middle-class Indian surroundings and given an English education. My family circumstances also emphasized exposure to South Asian religious and cultural heritage. Although my early education was in Catholic-run "convent" schools with names such as St. Aloysius (Kanpur), St. Columba's (New Delhi), and St. Joseph's (Allahabad), I completed high school in two different Krishnamurti schools. The first of these, Rishi Valley, is set in the arid beauty of the Madanapalle Hills in Andhra Pradesh, India. The second of these, Brockwood Park, is located in the idyllic countryside of Hampshire, England. My youth was spent learning about the cadences of English literature as well as those of Vedic chanting in contexts other than that of formal education. I was aware of a variety of religious practices and doctrines running a gamut from the Brahmanical orthopraxy of diet and daily rituals to skeptical atheism and materialism as expressed by friends, family, and acquaintances. I became acquainted with the teachings of Ramakrishna Paramahansa and Swami Vivekananda as a result of my mother's volunteer involvement with the Ramakrishna Mission when I was a child. Following four years in Krishnamurti schools that fostered vegetarianism, yoga, and meditation even as they inculcated the founder's strictures against all organized religions, I earned my bachelor's degree in English literature from Loyola College in Madras (now Chennai), returning me to a Jesuit educational environment that I recognized from earlier years.

These first acknowledgments are therefore to an entire background, and indeed a rich worldview, generated by the contingencies of family history, scholarly trajectory, and chance encounter. Even as a child, I was dimly aware that Hinduism meant very different things to different people; that Tibetan Buddhism was not the same as Ambedkar's; and that Sufis were Muslims, but arguably so. I thank my parents, Dorai and Srimathi; my aunt, Prema Srinivasan; and my cousin, Malini Srinivasan, for many of these earlier contacts and influences that are impossible to measure accurately, but that undoubtedly inspired the questions behind this project. Continuing conversations and dialogue with my father, Dorai, and my uncle, Rangaswami Mukundan, further sharpened these thoughts. Pupul Jayakar was an amazing interlocutor of my youth, as was David Bohm. These are some of the indirect debts to the original ground that predisposed me. It is necessary to record here that my own religious views are somewhere between agnosticism and atheism, combined with strong objections to religiously sanctioned social oppression, violence, and identity politics.

The scholarly basis of this book comes from my having recognized that the autobiographical details I sketched were indeed not as accidental as they originally seemed. *Guru English* crystallizes the anglophone discourses of South Asian religion in terms of an academic nomenclature, but as is typical of such projects, scholarship became a belated recognition and an objectified reconstruction and reinterpretation of earlier lived experience. Now it would be more accurate to render this understanding as groundedly historical rather than just accidentally autobiographical. What came to be at stake in this project was the ongoing legacy of English education within and beyond South Asia, in an expanded sense from the colonialist late eighteenth century of Europe to the diasporic and neotraditionalist challenges of the twenty-first-century United States and the world. The themes under examination in this book have also been inflected by my ongoing interest in colonialism, orientalism, empire, agency, and sovereignty. I have benefited greatly from my familiarity with eighteenth-century studies, contemporary literary theory, and postcolonial cultural studies. A more recent turn in my work to interdisciplinary humanistic research and the comparative general study of imperialism and sovereignty also helps situate this study.

Guru English was not a book project to start with—I had previously explored ideas regarding South Asian religion and anglophone postcolonial literature in essayistic form—but became one when I was approached by Emily Apter, the series editor. I am very grateful to Emily and also therefore delighted to present this book within Princeton University Press's Translation/Transnation series. Following Emily's encouragement, Mary Murrell, then literature editor at Princeton University Press, and three anonymous readers gave me much feedback and advice about the manuscript. The book is much better as a result of their interventions, and I thank them. I also thank Hanne Winarsky, who replaced Mary Murrell toward the final stages of this project, as well as my able copyeditor, Beth Gianfagna. The book expanded to address significant suggestions made by the readers, as well as other aspects of the topic that had been revealed as worthy of more involved discussion once I began imagining this venture as a book. Producing the manuscript involved early editorial assistance by Amardeep Singh. However, in the crucial intermediate stages from manuscript to book, I relied immensely on the savvy editorial, research, and bibliographical support given by Mandakini Dubey. I am deeply grateful for her humor and intellectual verve, which contributed a great deal toward developing aspects of the project that I may not otherwise have explored. I am appreciative of the good humor expressed by the staff at the India Office reading rooms of the British Library. Many thanks to Jennifer Howes for guiding me through the Mackenzie collection.

Grant Farred, Bruce Lawrence, and Susan Willis, my colleagues at Duke University, gave me plenty of suggestions after reading an early version of the complete manuscript. I thank all three of them for the most generous form of collegial labor that can ever be donated to another. I would also like to thank Ken Wissoker, editor in chief of Duke University Press, for inviting me to be on Duke University Press's Editorial Advisory Board in 2001—an ongoing labor that nonetheless gave me a broader perspective on current scholarly publishing and that undoubtedly helps make this a better book. I know Ken will forgive my decision to take the book elsewhere—for the simple reason that Princeton had asked me first and already had it under contract.

Other colleagues at Duke University have also been amazingly helpful. I would especially like to thank David Aers, Cathy Davidson, Barbara Herrnstein Smith, Fredric Jameson, Walter Mignolo, Ebrahim Moosa, Maureen Quilligan, Marianna Torgovnick, and Priscilla Wald for engaging me on specific aspects of the project. In addition, I want to thank my cohort at Duke University's Franklin Humanities Institute with whom I co-convened a faculty seminar on "Race, Justice, and the Politics of Memory" in 2002–3. Charlie Piot was a wonderful person with whom to host this seminar. I also want to thank other fellows who discussed the book with me that year: Ian Baucom, J. Kameron Carter, Grant Farred, Alessandro Fornazzari, Thavolia Glymph, Evelyn Brooks Higginbotham, Leigh Raiford, Stephane Robolin, and Susan Thorne. At a late stage in the project, I benefited from conversations about several aspects of this book's topic with Romila Thapar. I thank her for her generosity and feedback after reading the entire manuscript.

Here I should mention that this book was also vastly improved by presenting its arguments to a number of institutions and in a number of locations. Again, my first thanks go to Emily Apter for inviting me to UCLA in 2001 to present from this project. Gayatri Chakravorty Spivak honored me by asking for a lecture on Kipling drawn from this project, which I presented to the English Institute at Harvard University in September 2003. I thank Barbara Johnson, Marjorie Garber, Luke Menand, Michael Moon, Homi Bhabha, and others for their questions. I would also like to thank Frank Conlon and Paul Brass at the University of Washington for inviting me to give a talk at the South Asian Canadian Pacific Area Network conference at the University of British Columbia in 1999, when the project first began to coalesce around the notion of "Guru English." I thank Bruce Robbins for soliciting the article version for *Social Text*. I am also grateful to Henry Staten at the University of Washington for his early skepticism that helped me refine the concept. I thank my friend Paavo Pyllkänen, who invited me to give a talk on "Guru English" at the University of Skövde in Sweden. Even earlier, Karen Lawrence invited me to the Joyce conference at Seville, Spain, in 1996, where I gave a version of what became my reading of Theosophy, Joyce, and Desani in chapter 3. Peggy Battin and Brooke Hopkins, former colleagues and friends at the University of Utah, discussed this project in great earnest with me at Cambridge University in 2000. I thank them for their continued camaraderie. Earliest of all, I should thank Richard Klein of Cornell University for soliciting my first scholarly publication, on Salman Rushdie's *The Satanic Verses* in 1988, and sustaining my interest in "nuclear criticism" with his brilliant interventions. Some of the contours of that much earlier argument on Rushdie and nuclear criticism are discernible in chapter 5.

As I write these acknowledgments I am sadly aware of the recent death of Jacques Derrida, for whose seminar in Paris the reading of Rushdie was initially prepared as a presentation. My scholarly writing continues to exhibit several traces of Derrida's deconstructionist influence that I gratefully acknowledge. I gave as a public presentation a version of chapter 4 while I was the DeRoy Distinguished Visiting Lecturer at Wayne State University in 2001. I thank Dick Grusin, Donna Landry, and Gerald MacLean for that invitation. I also spoke about nuclear rhetoric to audiences at the University of Virginia, the University of Minnesota, the University of North Carolina at Chapel Hill, Florida State University, the University of California at Berkeley, and the University of Utah in the past few years. I thank Eleanor Kaufman, Daniel Brewer, Kevin Parker, Rip Lhamon, Priya Joshi, and Jim Lehning for those invitations. Thanks to Russ Leo for so sweetly reminding me about Pynchon. I lectured about Aurobindo in the South Asia Conference at the University of Wisconsin on the invitation of Amardeep Singh. I express much gratitude here to various hosts, audience members, colleagues, and students who questioned me at these presentations, all of whom I cannot acknowledge by name. For invaluable assistance at the proofreading stage, I am deeply grateful to Hollianna Bryan, Sara Lerner, and Sunthar Visuvalingam.

Roughly a third of the material in this book is drawn from earlier forays. As is also usual, many of these earlier arguments have been modified, revised, embedded in others, or even reversed. All the same, I would like to acknowledge gratis permissions from copyright holders Johns Hopkins University Press, Duke University Press, and Cambridge University Press that have allowed me to draw on my own previously published material. " 'Being God's Postman Is No Fun, Yaar!': Salman Rushdie's *The Satanic Verses*," was published in the pages of *Diacritics* 19, no. 2 (Summer 1989, Johns Hopkins University Press). "Postcolonial Affiliations: G. V. Desani's *All about H. Hatterr*," was published in *Transculturing Joyce*, ed. Karen Lawrence (New York: Cambridge University Press, 1998). "Guru English" was published in *Social Text* 19, no. 1 (Spring 2001, Duke University Press). "The Colonial Logic of Late Romanticism" was published in *South Atlantic Quarterly* 102, no. 1 (Fall 2003, special issue on "The Afterlives of Romanticism," ed. Ian Baucom and Jennifer Kennedy, Duke University Press).

I am grateful to Preethi Krishna and Ram Sundaram for providing me a home away from home in New York and much besides. In London, I thank Shyam Khanna, Mona Khanna-Chander, Sunil Chander, and Aditya and Shefali for being my in-laws and my family. In India, I thank Krishna, Seetu, and Aditi.

Most of the material in this book is the result of an ongoing intellectual and personal partnership with Ranji Khanna. I am deeply grateful to her for sustaining me in many ways over the past fifteen years.

I dedicate this book to my aunt, Prema Srinivasan. Almost a mother to me, and an inveterate seeker, she did more to expose me to the guru phenomenon in my formative years than any other single person. While that would be reason alone, there are many other reasons why this book is dedicated to her.

Guru English

INTRODUCTION

> Imbued with a knowledge of objective sciences by English
> education, our people will be able to comprehend subjective
> truths.
>
> —Bankimchandra Chatterjee, *Anandamath*

IT IS A TRUISM, universally acknowledged, that English dominates the globe today as no language ever has in the recorded history of humanity. Despite the linguistic diversity of a world that features more than five thousand natural languages by some counts, a mere one hundred languages account for the mother tongue of 95 percent of the world's population, twenty-five languages for about 75 percent, and just twelve languages for about 60 percent.[1] Second in terms of total number of speakers, English dominates by virtue of its stranglehold on global organizations as an international auxiliary or link language. Barring theories of the monolinguistic origin of the species that can never be proven, the observer can only look at existing examples of linguistic globalization in recorded history in order to glean the evidence.

A comparison of the current dominance of English with that of other languages at different times leads to the discovery that empires and religions have been the two most obvious vehicles of linguistic universalism. Sometimes a universalizing religion inherited a language-vehicle from a successful empire, as the Catholic Church did from the Romans, thereby establishing Latin as an administrative and scholarly medium of communication across Europe for a millennium and a half. In the case of Arabic, the situation developed the other way around, whereby the political ambitions of the caliphs spread it around the Mediterranean and West Asia from Spain to Persia and India for at least half a millennium, even though various political empires had actually inherited the language from Islam's humble origins as an iconoclastic desert religion. Pan-Arabism has still kept modern Arabic alive as a viable lingua franca throughout western Asia and northern Africa, and to a limited extent in other places where Islam is a presence. Mandarin Chinese, demonstrably the tongue with the greatest number of speakers today, remains one of the stable legacies of Han imperial suzerainty, even if there is no significant religious impulse to spread it beyond familiar ethnic confines. The case of Sanskrit reveals a pattern of survival that is exactly opposite to that of Chinese. A largely sacerdotal language with only sporadic instances of political backup, Sanskrit has neverthe-less survived for well over three millennia. Although still very much in use for ritual and religious instruction throughout South Asia and wherever Hinduism has a foothold, from Bali to Trinidad, Sanskrit is now largely a dead, classical language imbued with symbolic meaning. Hindi and Bengali, two of Sanskrit's many descendants, are counted among the top ten spoken languages in the world, but there is con-siderable resistance in India to Hindi as a national language. German and Russian had correspondingly greater and lesser roles—now vastly diminishing—because of their histories of joint political dominance in central and eastern Europe, and for the latter, also in central Asia. Japan-ese is important in east and southeast Asia, but is becoming less so with the importance of English as an international auxiliary language. The role of Swahili, initially promoted by Pan-Africanists, has declined along with the other political goals of the movement. All the same, francophone Africa and the hispanophone Americas continue to sound their different imperial and postcolonial legacies. Spanish is certainly one plausible transcontinental alternative still competing with English.

Turning to the case of English, it is obvious that events have conspired (although by no means as irreversibly as some might assume) to give it its current status. That the world has moved from the dominance of the British Empire in the late nineteenth century to the United States as unilateralist hyperpower by the twenty-first century without having to change the language of imperial dominance (save dialectal differences from British to American English) is perhaps a fortunate (depending on already acquired English proficiency) or unfortunate turn of events for the new rulers as well as the ruled. It is not merely the political dis-pensation at hand that ensures English supremacy at this point: the cultural and technical vocabularies of science and technology, capital-ist business economics, and television and media have instituted an even more important role for English to play as the ultimate knowl-edge base from which other languages can be launched or situated in relation to each other. English is still a minority elite language in the world, as any imperial or religious language always has been, to a lesser or greater extent. But English's strong connection with comput-ers, medicine, business, media, higher education, and communications—well before all these areas exploded globally—makes its dominance even greater than did the twentieth century's handover of global po-litical supremacy to the Americans. It is arguable whether a future Chi-nese domination of the globe (as some futurologists predict) would, if it did occur, nonetheless maintain the highly differentiated and spe-cialized functions that English has already come to play, with ramifica-tions that are legal, technical, and communicational.

While the simple abstraction of English-in-general has potentially a very long history ahead of it, there are also differentiations that occur within the language as it spreads itself. Languages do not always remain unified, as the history of Latin's or Sanskrit's multiple offspring demonstrates. This book focuses on the global impact of Indian English in the spirit of identifying a discrepant cosmopolitanism within it. Much has already been made of the peculiarities of English in South Asia, as a dialect and lingua franca with considerable cosmopolitan appeal. In terms of the total numbers of English speakers, India now ranks third in the world, after the United States and Great Britain. In India, maybe 3 to 5 percent of the population speaks English fluently (approximately 30 million to 50 million speakers), an especially significant minority constituting most of the elite and a section of the urban upper middle classes. If passive comprehension of English vocabulary were included, the figures would increase considerably. While such class parameters suggest that the language remains an acrolect—or a language spoken largely by elites—studying this language's iterations and performances leads to new and interesting discoveries. Before positing a historical essence (whether postcolonial, bureaucratic, or technological) bound up with English's role, significance, and global outcome, it would be best to track the many anomalous refashionings of the language and reflect on their variety.[2]

First introduced in South Asia by Christian missionaries in the seventeenth century, English made few inroads until the expansion of the activities of the East India Company. While Western colonialism and Christian evangelism often went hand in hand around the globe in the last few centuries, it is well known that the record in South Asia is especially complicated; from the outset, important conflicts arose between missionary and commercial agendas. The English Bible was one of the first texts to be translated into a number of South Asian vernaculars. Several outstanding discussions of the impact of the Bible in colonial South Asia have transformed our understanding of the consolidation of national identities as well as the elaboration of transcultural differences.[3] By 1823, learned natives such as Raja Rammohun Roy were petitioning the company's authorities to make English education, especially of the scientific and secular variety, more widely available. The culmination of this process was the much-discussed Macaulay Minute that was approved on March 7, 1835, a document that declared in the voice of the British rulers that they needed "a class who may be interpreters between us and the millions whom we govern—a class of persons, Indians in blood and colour, but English in taste, in opinion, in morals and in intellect." The same document also disparages native learning with the phrase that "a single shelf of a good European library [is] worth the whole native literature of India and Arabia." British imperial rule therefore unapologetically replaced Persian, the prestige language under the Mughals, with a new one, English.[4]

An Indian form of English—and therefore its development as a new South Asian vernacular rather than just as an imperial echo—first acquired recognition, paradoxically, when representatives of high Victorian imperialism dismissed it as a bureaucratic cant of the native functionaries and interpreters of the Raj, a "Baboo English" or "Cheechee English," to be literally ridiculed and disparaged. Even lesser variants began to be recognized, such as Butler English, Bearer English, Box-Wallah English, Kitchen English, and Hinglish (Hindi-English).[5] By February 1830, the first issue of an English-language journal in Calcutta entitled *The Parthenon* called itself the voice of people who were "Hindu by birth, yet European by education"—in other words, the voice of those multilingual and bicultural intermediaries of imperial governance. While educational qualifications in the many vernacular languages conferred much less prestige, being a colonial functionary, or *baboo*, engendered considerable frustration and intellectual alienation from both the Anglo-Indian elite and indigenous traditions. The baboo began to be satirized as a volatile mixture of the dregs of imperialist culture and the heights of philosophical absurdity. The baboo stereotype—from Rudyard Kipling to Peter Sellars—features a singsong accent, clownish head-nodding, pretensions to erudition, credentializing anxieties, a moralistic tone, a liberal use of clichés and mixed metaphors, and incongruous literal translations into English from the vernacular. Baboo English (as Indian English) is also subject to interferences from typical features of South Asian languages that are uncommon in English—such as the function of word reduplication as an intensifier ("little little children"; "very very nice"). Recognizing this hybrid and ridiculous subject as an anomaly several decades later, in 1874 a writer in *Mukherjee's Magazine* would metaphorically wring his hands in an article entitled "Where Shall the Baboo Go?"[6] Baboo (or Babu) English eventually became the butt of Victorian satire and the prized linguistic object of colonial lexicographies such as Colonel Henry Yule's and A. C. Burnell's famous *Hobson-Jobson*.

Sociolinguistics has attempted to separate analytically distinct aspects of Indian English, such as the instrumental function (in establishing prestige and social hierarchy), the regulative function (in law, administration, and business), the interpersonal function (as a link language within modernity), and the innovative function (in literature or cultural production).[7] While the first three aspects have always been very important, in the last two centuries of the reception of English in South Asia—and hence the ubiquity of the baboo stereotype—it is only in recent decades that greater attention is being paid by the literati to the imaginative and innovative function of cultural production supported by dialectal—as well as political—independence. Post-independence writers from G. V. Desani to Salman Rushdie, and Indian cinema and media have since disseminated an Indian English dialect (with regional variants) that has gone global in its quest for new markets and audiences. India is among the ten largest book-producing countries in the world and the third-largest producer of English-language books after the United States and Great Britain. It produces more full-length feature films than any country in the world, in multiple languages, but frequently with significant English content. Even so, a recent comprehensive literary history of anglophone writing in India is scathing in its characterization of the imaginative literature, through its title, as *Babu Fictions*.[8] Old habits die hard, and older slurs find newer and more persuasive contexts for their justification: while from the British point of view, the indigenous speaker of English could never shed his "Indianness," now it has become fashionable to assert that anglophone Indians can never shed their compromised elite status. To the extent that the English language is seen reductively as the expression of upper-class status and perspective alone, its capacity to represent the larger social whole is found lacking. Appearing to its speakers as a combination of prestige and disparagement, English represents a complicated status for South Asians that linguists have called *diglossic differentiation*, or the continual awareness of a relationship between high and low variations. Therefore, Probal Dasgupta calls Indian English an "auntie" (as opposed to mother) tongue, because "the meaning of English in India is not an independent referential potential, but a cross-referential or anaphoric meaning." A dependent or diglossic relationship makes English in India refer itself either to non-English speaking natives (with implicit superiority), or non-native metropolitan speakers from Britain or the United States (with implicit inferiority). English nonetheless remains the pathway to modernity, science, and business opportunity. Even though India, Pakistan, Bangladesh, Sri Lanka, and other South Asian countries are in the sixth decade after formal independence from British suzerainty, Macaulay, it would appear, continues to have the last laugh.[9]

Following a specific line of inquiry arising from these more generalized literary and linguistic antecedents, this book explores Guru English as a language variant of South Asian origin. There are at least four major aspects of this phenomenon. First of all, in its most literal sense, Guru English is not so much a dialect (even though it might be linked to dialectal variations of Indian English) or a jargon (even though it might frequently possess an esoteric and technical vocabulary), as it is an example of what linguist Michael Halliday has called a *register*.[10] However, this definition would have to be applied in an expanded sense, as the notion of register is linked to the language of a clearly demarcated socioprofessional group (such as doctors, lawyers, or engineers), whereas Guru English does not function only within such parameters. Anglophone scholars and proselytizers of South Asian religions (especially Hinduism and Buddhism in their revivalist and cosmopolitan versions) use this register in search of audiences who can "only connect" via English. Aspects of free play and innovation within the syntax, vocabulary, and rhetoric of this specific register can be discerned through multiple examples cited by religious practitioners throughout the chapters that follow. As register, Guru English is a *theolinguistics*, generating new religious meanings. Analyzing religion through language, and language by religion, Guru English is a practice nourished by eighteenth-century orientalists and twenty-first-century gurus alike.

The second, more generalized, aspect of Guru English is as a literary *discourse*. This form uses multilingual puns, parody, and syncretism that tend to open-ended and indeterminable futures that can influence the religiously inclined and also entertain those not so disposed. While specialized registers might be standard to a speech community, in this case they will vary across communities and practitioners, especially as there is no centralized linguistic stock exchange or even swap meet of lexically innovative gurus and their followers. When it begins to accommodate multiple registers and innovations, Guru English expands into a free-floating literary discourse that can tolerate a high degree of ambivalence. At this point, if I may invoke Michel Foucault, the range of the discourse makes visible characteristics that are not directly linguistic but also institutional and practice-oriented, and contextual to the deployment and manipulation of language as a material phenomenon with corresponding effects within social networks of power. When the Jesuits in Pondicherry planted the spurious *Ezourvedam* among the natives in order to make for an easier transition to Christianity from a purportedly ancient Hindu deism, they could not have foreseen that Voltaire would use the rationalism of the same text to launch an attack on Christianity in Europe. (Although the original example was in French, the impact of its translated English version was also considerable.) The multiple outcomes of Theosophy through a series of literary innovations I term *theosophistries* were similarly surprising.

These aspects of register and discourse also make Guru English function in the third sense, as something of a *transidiomatic* environment—where Guru English is not the directly active participant, but the passive background that informs and enables other cultural or linguistic activity. More about this function will be discerned when Guru English sustains creative interpretations that weave history and politics around perceptions of science, weaponry, and technology—where J. Robert Oppenheimer quotes from the Bhagavadgītā at Los Alamos or when the Indian and Pakistani military establishments manipulate religious vocabularies into state-sponsored nuclear rhetoric while naming weapons systems or taunting each other during their recent nuclear standoff. As environment, Guru English can, therefore, be the ground for discursive reversal and secondary elaboration as much as it can be the extension of linguistic register into literary discourse.

If the notion of Guru English as environment is a deeper cultural materialist idea of the notion of register, its fourth aspect is a more aggressive version of its second variant as discourse, namely as a *commodifiable cosmopolitanism*. Discourses can also be doctrinally thematized as interested and motivated rhetoric. Producing transnational religious cosmopolitanism that retails a saleable commodity, as does Deepak Chopra, in this last sense, Guru English names a marketing device that connects various levels to each other and that extracts a surplus from its mastery of the transidiomatic environment. While it might initially be confusing to use the same phrase to characterize a (linguistic) register, a (literary) discourse, a (transidiomatic) environment, and a (commodifiable) cosmopolitanism, Guru English's trafficking between negative or passive poles (such as register and environment) and positive or active ones (such as discourse and cosmopolitanism) reveals a story of discrepant levels of engagement. It is hoped that the liquidity of the phrase, Guru English, also allows it to be used by the author and other critics as a tracking device or a depth charge that forces various elements for analysis to the surface for the reader's attention and critique. However, these four abstract definitions need some more explanation, following which Guru English also merits being situated historically as well as structurally.

In Guru English as register as I have defined it, the indeterminacy of the modifier is visible: there is no possessive finality of the definite article, as there is with *the* King's (or *the* Queen's) English. Issuing rival dicta, gurus are many, even if at any time there is just one British monarch. The Sanskrit etymology of *guru* presents this figure as "a dispeller of darkness." The guru's power is perceived to be spiritual even as the śiṣya or chela—the disciple in search of wisdom or enlightenment—can choose to pursue and is sometimes encouraged to perform an absolute surrender of his or her will to the will of the master. Etymologically, the male śiṣya might perform the funeral rites of a son for the guru, saving him from an afterlife in the underworld. Unlike the spiritual authority of the guru, that of the *ācārya* (preceptor or teacher) is understood to be that of a circumscribed pedagogic authority within accepted social conventions, whereas the figure of the guru, as Sudhir Kakar has also argued, features powerful parental and psychoanalytic functions for the disciple.[11] The guru's function for the disciple, within the framework of an open-ended religious transaction, is therefore potentially unlimited in the manner in which it could transgress personal and social boundaries. *Guru* is also the astronomical term for Brihaspati, the preceptor of the Hindu pantheon, and designates the largest planet of the solar system that under the Western nomenclature goes by the name of "Jupiter." This parallel Sanskrit etymology of *guru* as the planetary and astronomical "heavy" with considerable influence[12] may be just as relevant, even if ironically so, in relation to a history of complicity with, as well as antipathy for, gurus within the history of religion in South Asia.

For these reasons, before we assume too readily the spread of Guru English as lingua franca across the globe, a number of questions must be addressed: Whose (South Asian and Indian) Guru English?[13] What are the goals of this language's users? What happens when indigenous religious and cultural conceptions are translated and represented in terms of a language that is, relatively, a very recent presence on the subcontinent? What links various aspects of (South Asian and Indian) English, whether as international lingua franca or national official language, or even more as precise acrolects, sociolects, and idiolects?[14] When native religion and colonial language come together in Guru English, the double engine of religion and empire makes deeper inroads into global dominance and proselytization. Guru English, as register, discourse, environment, and cosmopolitanism, exceeds most other diasporic outcomes of Indian English whether as mother or "auntie" tongue.

The links between Guru English as literary discourse and linguistic register, and the larger questions of the role of English suggests multiple directions of inquiry. Argot almost immediately raises for interrogation various aspects of its profile and function and the goals of its users. Initially, the anglicization of colonial subjects, while eventually making its mark on a global scale, was conceived as crucially necessary for a South Asian audience. Writing to a positivist friend, Jogen Ghosh, in the late nineteenth century, the Bengali novelist Bankimchandra Chatterjee asserted, "anyone who wishes to address all Hindus must of necessity write in English."[15] Bankim's most famous novel of religious atavism, *Anandamath* [Abbey of bliss], ends with the proposition that "imbued with a knowledge of objective sciences by English education, our people will be able to comprehend subjective truths." The point made by Bankim's conclusion, even if a hopeful stretch given empirical realities, was that the English language would, as a means of international access and especially scientific technocracy, objectively create the conditions where pan-Indian cultural unity could be discovered as a kind of remaindered essence. This adoption of English as a *via negativa* to the literary discourse of "subjective truths" is quite different from other plausible choices, such as Persian, which in Bankim's context had greater historical precedent as the language of Mughal bureaucracy and government, or Sanskrit, the sacerdotal language of the Brahman-dominated religious and cultural elites of the Hindu majority. We now find that there is an anomalous afterlife to Bankim's recommendation that he may not have anticipated: the circulation of Hinduism through English was probably an early alternative means—and continues to be an important vehicle—for the religious discourse of middle-class urban Hindus in search of their "subjective truths." The global transmission of Hindu and Buddhist thought eventually led to the rise of the self-proclaimed ethno-religious nationalist as well as the detached and Asian-influenced cosmopolitan. It might be worth considering the most provocative version of Bankim's thesis, that the use of English was indispensable to the defining of Hinduism as a universalist "spirituality" at the outset. This new articulation of spirituality cohered around several general assumptions brought to it by colonial discourses and practices, even as it undoubtedly made good use of preexisting practices and doctrines. This necessarily modern presentation of ancient practices explains the constitutive contradiction of Hinduism's national and cosmopolitan roles far more effectively than various empirical accounts that map the contingent coming together of a number of loosely related practices and identities under the pressure of British colonial rule.[16]

Continuing to the third aspect discussed, Guru English is perhaps a perfect example of what linguist Marco Jacquemet has described as transidiomaticity. The notion of certain languages and discourses as constituting a transidiomatic environment allows us to understand how they might have considerable appeal with multiple audiences without necessarily having to posit the particular medium of communication as a coherent foundation. How is this language idiomatically dispersed, translated, and disseminated? Rather than focusing on the exclusively dystopian visions of language-death amidst linguistic imperialism as many linguists have done, Jacquemet urges us to consider languages as flow: mutant, recombinant, and morphing under the conditions of globalization.[17] A renewed appreciation of cultural interconnection by way of transidiomaticity leads to the question of translation. In one sense, transidiomaticity attempts to bypass the necessity for a more conscious or full-fledged translation. Ideas arrive in prepackaged ways that merge with their analogs or cousin-ideas in the host language, thereby preempting a self-conscious reflection on the matter and the manner of translation.

Guru English presents itself as already translated, even though a critical perspective on it would lead to the conclusion that it is very much in need of further translation and specification. The transnational aspect of Guru English mobilizes a South Asian spiritual superiority in search of hegemony. Critical attention to such ideas can dissolve them into particulars that are insufficiently transparent to all locations. To paraphrase translation theorist Naoki Sakai, translation is constitutive of its context only because it fixes two interpretive communities in terms of a stable relation.[18] Of course, these communities might themselves be in full mobility, and the relation is always a temporary one in danger of being broken. For this reason, while Sakai distinguishes sharply between a "homolingual" and "heterolingual" address of translation, it might be preferable to think that all translational situations—like all transnational situations—simultaneously involve homogeneity and heterogeneity, transidiomaticity and incommensurability. The partial nature of context, audience, and subject matter under translation makes for the simultaneous possibilities of communication and its failure. As the special case of a transnational translation currently under purview, Guru English could be at times innocuous, and at other times, noxious. On some occasions, Guru English leads to at least a partial understanding and a fulfilling New Age East-West encounter, whereas at other times this very production is in danger of becoming an explosive and dangerous misapprehension, nothing more than a dehistoricized and false claim to tradition, whether European or Asian. As recombinant, mutant, and simulacrum, Guru English is the sign of heterogeneity within the homogeneous, demonstrating that the imperial tongue can be reshaped internally even as English colonizes its linguistic others.

With respect to the fourth aspect—cosmopolitanism—its relationship to the volatile terrain of religion needs explanation to understand the function of Guru English as one such form. Such a relationship may appear counterintuitive, especially as the Voltairean-Kantian-Weberian legacy of Enlightenment modernity has depicted the dominant line of cosmopolitanism as resulting from the privatization of religion, and indeed, disenchantment with the world. Clichés of the sort that modernity resulted in the twilight of the idols, and the death of God(s), abound in this tradition, despite growing evidence that the news of religion's death was greatly exaggerated and that the history of Judeo-Christian monotheism and deism was rather conveniently collapsed with the itineraries of polytheistic and other faiths. Cosmopolitanism, according to this general Enlightenment doctrine, is a disposition that creates world fellowship, or at least passive membership, through the abandonment of religion for a (political) philosophy. The basis for this philosophy would have been a humanist recognition of the discrepant itineraries of individual lives. As Rammohun Roy put it in an 1831 letter to Talleyrand, pleading for the abolition of the passport system, such an act would be necessary "to promote the reciprocal advantage and enjoyment of the whole human race." According to Rammohun, "it is now generally admitted that not religion only but unbiased common sense as well as the accurate deductions of scientific research lead to the conclusion that all mankind are one great family of which numerous nations and tribes existing are only various branches."[19] Amid a generalized recognition of the rights of individual subjects and the dignity of all cultures, as well as affirmations of the freedom of individual and group expression as resistances to dominant forms, the cosmopolitan, as a mediator, eschews interested particularity for the role of spatial referee, sometimes turning into a crypto-universalist if not into a full-fledged one. However, others, by identifying earlier Christian and Renaissance humanisms as performing this universalistic task, have undercut grand narratives of the Enlightenment's romantic transformation of religious irrationalism into secular rationalities. As Tzvetan Todorov asserts, the doctrines of the world-proselytizing religions such as Christianity and Islam have done a great deal of the groundwork for modern transcultural dialogue. More specifically to South Asia, the neoreligious Right in India is promoting its own disturbing version of Hindu universalism. We have, therefore, a situation where a number of enchanting and enchanted modernities contest the disenchanted Enlightenment stereotype.[20]

Cosmopolitanism itself is undergoing something of a revival, and it is useful to identify Guru English as one amongst several alternative and popular forms of cosmopolitanism. While the disavowal of cosmopolitanism after 1968 could be explained in the context of the global Left's repudiation of Stalinism and the decline of internationalism following decolonization, responses to the failure of modernization theses and developmental agendas took several routes. One tendency was the repudiation of cosmopolitanism itself as a bourgeois, Western, or delocalized aesthetic aspiration, outmoded and tone-deaf to contemporary realities. A more tolerant (if patronizing) downgrading of cosmopolitanism represented it as a noble but idealist goal that could not respond to, or correspond with, the rootedness of local politics, interests, cultures, and perturbations. Thus cosmopolitanism was seen as politically ineffective but nonetheless tolerable in manifestoes, mission statements, and party congresses. However, after these reactions reached the dead end of extreme particularity with the fragmentary positions of subnationalisms, radical relativism, and the micropolitics of location, it appears that several thinkers have taken a step back in the direction of the general. We now see the return of die-hard cosmopolitanisms of the old kind, featuring Kantian projectors, World Bank economists, and religious universalists. Recent apologists for the grand normative scaffolding of Western liberalism and universalism include Martha Nussbaum, Tzvetan Todorov, or Julia Kristeva. There are, of course, those philosophers such as Richard Rorty who are willing to eschew universalism and embrace the charge of being ethnocentric, thereby actively separating the tradition of Western liberalism from that of science, rationality, and universal truth, but such pragmatism sacrifices global scruples for a blinkered chauvinism or cultural particularism.[21]

More cautious voices than these recommend a shuffle between globalization and localization that leads to a "glocalization" of uncertain consequence. Such a newly cautious cosmopolitanism attempts to rebuild and pluralize cosmopolitanism from below. Its theorists thereby describe the new cosmopolitanisms as "discrepant," "vernacular," and "actually existing" in place of the older forms, which were preformed, normative, and universalistic. This grass-roots version of cosmopolitanism—one that migrant workers, tourists, and refugees participate in as equally as transnational executives, academics, and diplomats—is represented by James Clifford, Homi Bhabha, and Bruce Robbins, who insist on the careful reconstruction of cosmopolitanism as an efficacious (but always provisional) lingua franca that dissolves the reifications of particularity. Cosmopolitics in general, however, runs the danger of being perceived as a vacuous idealization despite various qualifications. Like any other discourse, cosmopolitanism cannot be inherently stable in terms of its meaning but will shift semantically according to context, use, and function.[22]

While these debates have not resolved sticky cultural differences into an all-encompassing identity of contemporary cosmopolitanism, they increasingly suggest that we turn to the globalized particular, or to the particular generalization, with a heightened sense of their mutual relationship. The attempt of this book to characterize Guru English as one more such venture is not necessarily as positive in its outcomes as defenders of cosmopolitanism would want, or even recognize. Cosmopolitics is increasingly more effective as a rooted discourse rather than a free-floating one, just as much as border-crossing and nomadism appear to have greater purchase when anchored in relation to the specific ecologies and geographies where the crossings are taking place and where they acquire very specific forms of transgressive meaning. Guru English as cosmopolitanism, then, is the lived practice of which a universalism of some sort is often the theory—even if cosmopolitans might often disavow their universalist underpinnings. Understanding this perceived unity masking practical multiplicity in the case of the Englishes that are contained within the notion of a global English might also result in a reinterpretation of other universalisms and cosmopolitanisms, whether religious or secular. Étienne Balibar's notion of multiple universals echoes this idea of a cosmopolitanism under the conditions of transidiomaticity: the new universalism consists of "a temporal movement whose regulatory claims are iterative rather than imperative, translational rather than transcendental." This feature is especially visible in universalisms from below that enact themselves through performance and intercultural communication rather than from centralized directives.[23] Despite their ambivalences, will postcolonial cosmopolitans suffer the fate of being misunderstood as straightforward Western liberals (sometimes with validity)? There is no easy answer to these debates, as Rabindranath Tagore realized in his lectures on nationalism: "[N]either the colourless vagueness of cosmopolitanism, nor the fierce self-idolatry of nation-worship is the goal of human history." The postcolonial world has flirted with both prongs that Tagore criticizes and yet has found neither option ultimately rewarding for its inhabitants.[24]

Religious forms of affinity in late modernity have grown in proportion to the fact that state secularism and the politics of civil society have not delivered adequate forms of group vindication. The utter lack of a successful progressive politics under the global rule of the market has led to even obscurantists exploiting cosmopolitan strategies for gaining leverage. Notorious for the September 11, 2001, attack on the United States that shook the world, Osama bin Laden's Al-Qaeda network functioned through various shadowy electronic and transnational mechanisms. This right-wing Wahhabism—and its client group, the Taliban, which gave it sanctuary in Afghanistan—has been characterized as representing "a deracinated fanaticism—a kind of bleak Islamic cosmopolitanism."[25] Such developments arose partly because the postcolonial state, from which the gospel of diverse collectivity could have been preached (whether universalism, nonsectarian uniformitarianism, or multiculturalism), was exposed as ideologically bankrupt even as the double standards of the Western powers led to the First World's continued obliviousness and instrumentalization of the lives of the rest of the world as before. Hijacked by local elites for financial gain and ethnic domination, the postcolonial states survived—and continue to survive—as a homeostasis between the cynicism of global powers and the marketplace, and the great internal contradictions, corruption, political violence, and repression characteristic of the rule of the few in so many countries.

In a brilliant essay entitled "The Command of Language and the Language of Command," Bernard Cohn argues for the existence of a transmission process whereby Indians produced knowledge about themselves as a form of tribute, a knowledge that was subsequently recoded by Europeans. While orientalists took credit for discovering and cataloging the cultural riches of India, their labors would have been impossible without a vast retinue of translators, scribes, scholars, and informants. Guru English represents aspects of this recoding that began a life of its own as a supplement, even as "practical necessity" began to trump "scholarly curiosity" and Hindustani replaced Persian as the practical language of command within India. As Cohn suggests, "the Indians who increasingly became drawn into the process of transformation of their own traditions and modes of thought were . . . far from passive." Guru English is about the productivity, agency, and cumulative consequences of this original tribute exacted in a colonial situation, although it is never simply about the reasserted command of language by just Indian natives or British colonizers but, as we shall see, about eventually much more than just the initial parties to the historical quarrel.[26]

A beautiful watercolor from 1790 demonstrates a scene of instruction that can be read as a generative allegory for the origin of Guru English, in the context of the extraction of tribute through the various investigative modalities of colonial epistemology that Cohn outlines. And yet, there is the hint of something entirely different. One of the paintings in the voluminous Mackenzie collection of the India Office Library, "View of Dindigul, with an English officer, perhaps Colin Mackenzie, and an Indian in the foreground," poses several intriguing aspects of the religious knowledge transcreated in a colonial situation that anticipates future outcomes other than just the predictable one of empire. A Scot who joined the East India Company out of the desire to learn more about Hindu mathematics, Mackenzie became a military engineer who rose to surveyor general of the Madras Presidency and eventually to the post of the first surveyor general of India from 1815 until his death in 1821. Mackenzie was no conventional orientalist, however. He did not speak any Indian languages even though he was interested in antiquities, coins, engravings, archaeological sites, and any accounts of religious "contentions" and "establishments." He sketched constantly and also employed scribes, artists, fellow officials, and local informants to document visually what they saw, thereby accumulating a vast archive. Yet he died without being able to organize his vast collection into anything like the evidentiary materials for a full-fledged colonial sociology. That was to come after him.[27]

Mackenzie's vast collection contains some drawings of gurus, sannyasis, and itinerant holy men. However, "View of Dindigul" is unusual in its foregrounding of a dialogue between a British redcoat and a robed Indian. The native appears to be a Muslim religious teacher, possibly a Sufi. In the background is the impressive fort of Dindigul, built on the top of a rock formation in southern (the name *tintukkal* in Tamil means "bolster-shaped rock"). Looking like a Tuscan hilltown rendered through the techniques of the British school, the painting reveals several indeterminate structures within the walls of the fort, including possibly the temples to Mariamman, Vinayaka, and Muruga that are still extant there today. Tipu Sultan controlled this area and is said to have installed the Mariamman temple, although he was defeated by the British several years later at the battle of Seringapatam (Srirangapatna) in 1799.

However, the figures in the foreground are not engaged in a conversation about the fort, but yet another structure. They are both seated, with the North Briton as recipient of the information revealed by the authoritative indexical gesture made by the South Indian. The rock in the background resembles anything from a seated elephant to a gigantic conch shell—both iconographically more relevant for Hindu notions of the sacred than the local comparison of the rock to a bolster. Rather than gesturing to the magnificent rock, the obvious subject of the painting, the native points to the archaeological structures at the left (his right). These structures are likely Islamic, perhaps a mausoleum of a local Muslim chieftain or saint. There is an air of tranquil communion about the scene that does not suggest anything like the peremptory catalog description by Mildred Archer, "Colonel Mackenzie cross-examines a villager about a nearby tomb."[28] Imperial hindsight has clearly infected the catalog description with the suggestion of a quasi-judicial prosecution where the native is being held to account, but does a careful look at the image suggest, in part, the more lyrical portrait of a transculturated guru and chela, an Indian religious teacher and a European disciple? That might be too much of an interpretive stretch in the opposite direction. Although Mackenzie is clearly taller and unable to sit in the Indian's posture (appearing to balance on a rock with his feet disrespectfully pointing outward), he communicates a mixture of authority and deference toward his interlocutor, as does also the Indian. While the officer gazes curiously (and uncomfortably) at the monument, the fakir (entirely at ease in his surroundings) is the source of its meaningful relevance, and intent on communicating this (in no uncertain terms) to the officer. The suggestion is that neither figure can do without the other, and that both are needed for the scene's intended viewer. The slight disharmony between the two figures, with one expounding to the other, and the other rapt in the object rather than his interlocutor, allows a reflection on several outcomes.

While the zoomorphic rock-fort is the spectacular and arresting image in the background, suggesting the archaic and picturesque mysteries of monumentality expressed through paintings and etchings by William Hodges and Thomas and William Daniell during this period, the human interchange in the foreground is more prosaic. Evoking contemporary time, the figures in the foreground stage a moment of simple revelation. The conversation with the native elicits the topographical, architectural, and possibly religious information that Mackenzie was after. Yet, the color and pattern of the clothing of the Indian figure visually echo the rock in the background, connecting the "ancient" Hindu landscape to the "medieval" Muslim exponent, and through him to the British officer, emblem of the busy surveyor of "modern" India. In this manner, the painting becomes an anticipatory allegory of British historiography's tripartite periodization of Indian history that was still to follow.

In 1817, Mackenzie wrote lyrically about the Brahman informant who greatly assisted his Mysore survey several years later: "the connexion then formed with one person, a native and a Bramin, was the first step of my introduction into the portal of Indian knowledge; devoid of any knowledge of the languages myself, I owe to the happy genius of this individual, the encouragement and the means of obtaining what I so long sought. . . . From the moment the talents of the lamented Boria [by then deceased] were applied, a new avenue to Hindoo knowledge was opened."[29] As this quotation reveals, the linguistically incapable Mackenzie would need to have relied on the early locutions of Guru English to make sense of his environment, and he is deeply grateful to his native instructor. Perhaps the person strikingly present in the Dindigul image is a Muslim version of Boria, serving the role of the Brahmanical (all too Brahmanical) intermediary or translator. It is through such translations that Guru English will later become one of the primary modes of communicating Indian religion to outsiders.

A brief historical schema for the development of Guru English is necessary to explain the chronological sweep of the project, which ranges from the late eighteenth century of the image to the present. Taking stock of developments since the advent of the British in an early survey entitled *Modern Religious Movements in India*, J. N. Farquhar sees a great religious awakening beginning in India around 1800. Farquhar puts forward a threefold answer to the question of why the awakening began at that time rather than any other:

> The answer is that the Awakening is the result of the cooperation of two forces, both of which began their characteristic activity about the same time, and that it was quickened by a third which began to affect the Indian mind a little later. The two forces are the British government in India as it learned its task during the years at the close of the eighteenth and the beginning of the nineteenth centuries, and Protestant Missions as they were shaped by the Serampore men and Duff; and the third force is the work of the great Orientalists [Colebrooke, Wilson, and Tod]. The material elements of Western civilization have had their influence, but apart from the creative forces, they would have led to no awakening.[30]

Following from Farquhar's analysis of neoreligious awakening, but generating some different periodizations for the anglophone representations of Indian religions (and especially Hinduism), I see the evolution of Guru English as occurring in three distinct phases corresponding to the political rule of the subcontinent. These would be as follows: (a) the period of the East India Company (1757–1857); (b) the period of the British Raj (1858–1947); and (c) the postcolonial period (1947–the present). The first phase could be subdivided into two parts: (i) 1757–1805, when the work of the first-wave orientalists was consolidated; and (ii) 1806–57, when the rise of utilitarianism repudiated or sidelined orientalist agendas with the anglicists triumphing over the orientalists by 1835. However, it was in the heyday of anglicism that Raja Rammohun Roy provided the first sustained native voice in Guru English through his inception of the Brahmo Samaj while in dialogue with European and American Unitarians. The second phase, of the formal period of the British Raj, could also be subdivided into two parts. An important period was (i) 1858–1919, when first-wave nationalism as well as cosmopolitan syncretisms such as the Brahmo Samaj, Theosophy, and the Ramakrishna Mission reinterpreted and modernized Hinduism in English, even as orientalism was greatly revived as high Indo-European philology under scholars such as Max Müller and Monier Monier-Williams. The second part of this period, (ii) 1920–47, saw a partial disappearance of Guru English as the nationalist sway overwhelmed other religious-cosmopolitan agendas with the great success of political Gandhianism—even though these cosmopolitan agendas continued to exist below the surface. Theosophy made inroads in Asia, Europe, and the Americas at least until the late 1920s, even as it became more common for the first wave of gurus and yogis to proselytize in the United States. The third, and final, post-independence phase could again be split into two parts of dormant and active religious cosmopolitanism.

The immediate post-independence years, (i) 1947–65, were a period of religious intensification in South Asia (with the partition and its aftermath and significant territorial and military conflicts). Also underway was a subtler preparatory phase among individuals and movements for South Asian proselytization of the rest of the world alongside state-sponsored explorations of secularism. In the most recent period, of (ii) 1966–the present, the guru phenomenon exploded worldwide, after first forming a beachhead in the United States and becoming one accepted component of so-called New Age religions. It was in this final part (since the mid-1960s) when gurus became entirely commonplace in the West, whether it took the form of seeing Hare Krishnas distribute their literature in airports and on the street, learning about transcendental meditation techniques at the office, or encountering competing schools of yoga among the exercise choices at the local health club. Guru English ultimately took on the appearance of the "lifestyle" choice it has come to represent, as a form of domesticated xenotropia within the West and beyond, or what has also been called "the postcolonial exotic."[31]

Orientalist rediscoveries concerning Indian religion, and the religious syncretism and imperial cosmopolitanism of groups such as the Theosophists formed an important underlay of the Indian nationalist movement even when its goals were ostensibly secular. Annie Besant, longtime president of the Theosophical Society, also served for one year as the president of the Indian National Congress. The nationalist movement's two best-known leaders—Mahatma Gandhi and Jawaharlal Nehru—had both been exposed to Theosophy in their youth. While Nehru remained largely atheistic and secular throughout his life, Gandhi turned to his version of nonviolent Christianized Hinduism as a personalized politics when he returned to India from South Africa. But it is important to note that even "Bapu"—the acknowledged father of the modern Indian nation—developed his creed after being stimulated by initial encounters with Theosophy in England:

Towards the end of my second year in England I came across two Theosophists, brothers and both unmarried. They talked to me about the Gītā. They were reading Sir Edwin Arnold's translation—*The Song Celestial*—and they invited me to read the original with them. I felt ashamed, as I had read the divine poem neither in Sanskrit nor Gujarati. . . .

The brothers also recommended *The Light of Asia* by Sir Edwin Arnold . . . and I read it with even greater interest than I did the Bhagavat Gītā. Once I had begun it I could not leave off. They also took me on one occasion to the Blavatsky Lodge and introduced me to Madame Blavatsky and Mrs. Besant.[32]

While many historians see a double movement in Indian religion from colonial rule and orientalism to modernizing revivalism and nationalism, it is necessary to add to this account a third step: cosmopolitanism, diaspora, and the postnational futures of religious renewal. A language that was produced in the crucible of colonial contestation and modernizing transformation did not stay uniquely in the confines of the sphere within which it arose. The movement from (British) empire to (Indian) nation inexorably led also to and through (transnational) cosmopolitanism.

Enlightenment metanarrative, which proclaims the birth of modernity in the decline of religion, is put on the defensive when faced with religiously based collectivities. When religion reenters the political sphere (as for example, the European Christian Democrats), it is seen as a conservative social phenomenon that has made its peace with a secularized and democratized polity. However, the counterexamples are many. The entries of the Hindu Right into democratic politics in India, and the religious Right in the United States and Israel are also paralleled by the consolidation of Islamist neopatriarchies in several countries from Iran to Egypt to Indonesia. The outcome of religion's reentry into democracy (just as that of secularism's supposed defeat of religion) can never be stable or predictable. As Talal Asad has argued persuasively, the secular and the religious have always coexisted as constitutive forces of social order. While *secularity* as epistemic category exists everywhere alongside religious conceptions of the world, *secularism* is a more modern political phenomenon whose goal is to keep religion at bay and purge its role in precise areas such as civil law, politics, and governmental policymaking.[33] The embrace of secularism— after all, a kind of state religion especially since the French Revolution— has led to state-sponsored normative orthodoxies that are very much on the defensive against religious revivalism in countries as different as France, Turkey, or India. In the United States, constitutional history points to an oscillation between two different institutionalizations of secularism—one based on seventeenth-century notions of the passive toleration of religious difference and expression (the conservative approach) and the other similar to the more aggressive "French" idea of antireligious state policy that paradoxically validates by inversion the Christian religion that it has evacuated from that public sphere (the liberal approach). Various well-meaning secularists inadvertently recreate parodically what they most seem to combat, by putting their faith in reason, whereas religious believers had put their faith in the divine. To avoid this contradiction (whereby even atheism begins to resemble a religion), Gayatri Chakravorty Spivak suggests that we can find the secular that is not a secular*ism* only by adopting a deconstructive approach of "detranscendentalizing the radical other (of the divine) into figurative instrumentality"—in other words, by paying much closer attention to the idiom of religious belief, especially when this idiom is turned away from theological or divine performance into marking the boundary of the lived everyday.[34]

Debates about the relationship between nationalism and culture prove that, even when defined as secular, the category of culture is deeply inflected by latent religious markers that become manifest in particular situations—as can be seen the world over in the ideological battles concerned with religion in the schools or opposition to state-imposed normativity in areas of clothing, dress, and physical appearance (Sikh turbans, Muslim headscarves, Jewish yarmulkes, Christian crosses, and the like). Prescient in his critique of Benedict Anderson's modular and optimistically secular notion of postcolonial nationalism, Partha Chatterjee has argued that the postcolonial subject concedes modernity and progress narratives to the West but holds the nation dear as some kind of atavistic, premodern, and nostalgic religious form, which is then appropriately inflected with ethnic and regional markers. In this regard, it might appear that Partha Chatterjee's work is a long paraphrase of Bankim's dictum discussed earlier. While Chatterjee's criticism affords a better understanding of South Asia's religion-inflicted politics, its model of nationalism is perhaps unnecessarily pessimistic, even as Anderson's modular account of nationalism is perhaps optimistic about the triumph of nationalism as secularism and the ease of political transformation following that triumph. Anderson's revision of his own position is also an interesting development: now he characterizes popular pre-independence nationalisms as forms of unbounded seriality that are universalistically potent but which later become ethnic separatisms only when nationalisms acquire a state and exercise bounded serialities in the form of censuses, and also when long-distance nationalisms fuel reified forms of ethnic particularisms. However, if Anderson's description of nationalism helps us understand some of its secular bourgeois variants, and Chatterjee's model is best for mapping South Asian religious nationalism as the pathology of a permanently scarred outcome, neither of their approaches enables us to understand the extensive transnational outreach of South Asian religious cosmopolitanism. In any case, that would be faulting them for what is an epiphenomenon to their projects even though it is central to the concerns of this book.[35]

If we turn outside South Asia to a social-anthropological approach to the Hindu diaspora, such a shift is also only partially revealing. The spread of Guru English as a linguistic phenomenon is far in excess of its countable demographic collateral: according to one such study, there are about twelve million Hindus outside South Asia (and only over nine million if Indonesia were excluded). Other studies have delineated the diasporic impact of the recent rise of religious fundamentalism and the continuing impact of orientalism on the study of South Asian religion.[36] However, this book analyzes some of the consequences of the religious cosmopolitanism that originated in South Asia and that has managed to attain considerable global visibility before and alongside the developments of domestic South Asian politics. Focusing on this flow is not meant to preclude grounded analyses of South Asian religion which have specific purchase on their object of knowledge. This study can, however, be taken to be an important supplement to those that have drawn the picture of recent religious developments exclusively within South Asia. While it is helpful to study the sociology of Hindu, Muslim, Christian, Sikh, Buddhist, or Jaina identity within minority communities outside the sacred geography that anchors Hinduism as the majoritarian religion of a South Asian environment, such an approach is surely quite limited by its empiricist reconstruction of communities as stable objects of analysis, alongside their requisite complexity and transformation. Tracking a discourse is a more subtle, and potentially elusive venture, because this kind of flow doesn't always leave telltale signs or inhabit mental landscapes exclusively, or even predominantly. Of course, as these structures become subtler, mapping their agency likewise poses a harder task. Arjun Appadurai's cartographic metaphors regarding postmodern disjuncture and difference are also relevant to this issue. Guru English, while it participates in the ethnoscapes or population movements that are reshaping the globe, also marks an important presence in the mediascapes and the ideoscapes, or the representational and the ideological apparatuses. A set of images, representations, and vernacular expressions and colloquialisms, animated by Guru English, has considerable extranational impact and resonance. Movies, literature, and cultural forms using religious discourses synthesizing Asian religious themes have populated Western and global representational flows as never before. Guru English also participates in what Appadurai calls the technoscapes and the financescapes, as some of the later chapters in this book—on the South Asian nuclear standoff, the Rushdie affair, and the literary sociology of gurus—argue.[37]

The six chapters that follow can be characterized as describing instances of overlapping periodizations of Guru English. Provisionally, these categories could be named neoclassicism, Romanticism, modernism, nuclearism, postmodernism, and New Ageism respectively. While the chapters range chronologically, the first half of the book deals with legacies of the pre-independence period and the second half with independence and after. Two different models of periodization are implicit in the two halves—labels such as neoclassicism, Romanticism, and modernism recall to mind extant conventions of Western periodization, whereas the periodizations involved in the second half—nuclearism, postmodernism, and New Ageism are more controversial and contested as temporal markers, naming one kind of modern apocalyptic millenarianism and two distinct postmillenarian outcomes. The more compressed or telescoped character of the book as it approaches the present—given that the last three chapters deal with some aspects of the post–World War II period—also undoubtedly demonstrates the arbitrary nature of periodizing gestures. I propose these periodizing terms for heuristic reasons. While they cannot entirely be avoided, it is important to stress that these periodizations are speculative proposals rather than positings of deep ontological divisions between radical or discontinuous epistemes of historical temporality.

The first chapter explores the impact of the orientalists and the resultant reaction-formation of a number of indigenous voices with diasporic appeal, including Brahmos such as Rammohun Roy and Keshub Chunder Sen, Vedantists such as Vivekananda, and yoga exponents such as Yogananda. These figures are neoclassical in that they reinvent continuous tradition under the sign of the advent of modernity. Through some of these individual cases, I narrate the existence of the discourse of Guru English from the late eighteenth to the mid-twentieth century. It is indeed moot whether neoclassicism of this sort can ultimately be separated very carefully from Romantic nationalism.

More through a principle of convenience and slightly different philosophical emphasis rather than that of radical separation from the figures treated in the first, the second chapter examines the parallel implication of Guru English into a literary form of late colonial Romanticism. Writers such as Bankimchandra Chatterjee, Rudyard Kipling, Rabindranath Tagore, and Sri Aurobindo are shown to contribute richly to this enterprise, one that participates in the Janus-faced project of Romantic nationalism. Looking back atavistically, Romantic nationalism also generates a wholly modern idiom that is produced prosthetically. These important early figures are but the very beginning of a whole range of Indian and foreign romanticists and romanticizers of the subcontinent's religious wealth. The eternal rediscovery of Indian spiritual and religious mysteries continues unabated, whether in travelogues, tourist brochures, pulp fiction and media, or even occasionally in religious anthropology.

The third chapter focuses on Theosophy and its critique, taking two very important novels, James Joyce's *Ulysses* and G. V. Desani's *All about H. Hatterr*, as the vehicle for this investigation. This chapter shows how modernism helps these writers derive an ethics of destabilizing and satirical laughter when confronted with the creative obscurantism of religious innovators such as Helena Petrovna Blavatsky. However, rather than document Joyce's "influence" on Desani, or conversely, attack those who thereby produce assessments of Desani's diminished creativity, this chapter focuses on the transcultural dynamics of both Joyce's and Desani's attitudes toward Eastern religions. The use of Hinduism and Buddhism (especially through a Theosophical lens in Joyce's case) makes for other narratives of cultural filiation. Desani's relationship to Joyce is one of creative affiliation, as is Salman Rushdie's, and affiliations such as these—which are voluntary and cross-cultural— can best be understood within the postcolonial frameworks of Guru English.

Following these three chapters, the second half of the book shifts to modern techno-millenarianism and its aftermath. The fourth chapter features the sublime rhetoric of nuclear weaponry since 1945, within which Guru English is also deeply implicated. The organizing intelligence behind the Manhattan Project that produced the atom bomb, Robert Oppenheimer, relied extensively on the Bhagavadgītā—not just personally, but publicly—to ascribe meaning to the creation of the genocidal weapon that would usher in the nuclear age. Yet the Bhagavadgītā was also paradoxically the favorite text of various apostles of nonviolence, from Thoreau to Gandhi. How is this possible? A brief textual analysis of the relevant sections of this ancient text will situate it within its imperial and postcolonial contexts. These contexts are deeply informed by the histories of genocide and nuclearism. Perceptions of the weaponry of mass destruction are always connected to other cataclysmic experiences of political conflict and massacre. I analyze the corresponding fallback to the "deep time" of religious imagery by nuclear strategists and antinuclear opponents, by warmongers as well as peacemakers, and by the state as well as the individual. The language of nuclear holocaust, a potent cryptoreligious and cosmopolitan discourse, brings genocide, nationalism, and technology together in terms of an ultimate de-differentiation of the separate spheres that modernism, despite all its epic heroism and parodic syncretism, could not keep apart.

The fifth chapter takes a look at the multiple contexts—of controversy, hybridity, apostasy, and parody—that surround the vexed reception of Salman Rushdie's satire of South Asian Islam, *The Satanic Verses*. Treating this episode as one of postmodern crossed connections that renders visible a logic of escalation inherited from nuclearism, and to some extent also as an example of failed theosophistry, I emphasize the limits of Guru English (and indeed Mullah English as its parodic shadow-double). While some observers would want to make a more essentialist argument about Islam in relation to *The Satanic Verses*, I instead render visible the conceptual embedding of Rushdie's satire within South Asian syncretic religious contexts and identify the colonial legal apparatuses that he brings into our purview. This ludic relation to Islam is certainly a South Asian legacy Rushdie inherits, among others. While the notion of an Islam sitting within a Guru English might seem inadequate to those who want a fuller accounting of Islam (and the gamut of non-Hindu religions) in South Asia, I would argue that these overlaps are an important beginning to understand common lines of flight that are relevant for the cultural analysis being conducted through this book as a whole. Indeed, there is an immediate and valid objection to be addressed throughout about the "Hinduization" at work in Guru English that ought not to be symptomatically replicated in this critique, or collapse into just one particular form of culturalist accounting. However, as my discussion amply shows, Guru English is a conceptual umbrella that is more likely to be regarded as indiscriminate rather than exclusionary in terms of the religious phenomena it reassembles. In that respect, the concept may well be subject to the limitations and the perversions of the "Hindu Catholicity" that wryly characterize Mrs. Tulsi in V. S. Naipaul's *A House for Mr. Biswas*.

The sixth and final chapter turns to an analysis of several modern gurus and the fabrication of a new cosmopolitan lingua franca in New Age enterprises. Episodes in the ongoing saga of gurus in the West are taken up for investigation, including especially the cases of Maharishi Mahesh Yogi, Bhagwan Rajneesh (Osho), and Deepak Chopra. I deliberately pair these historical figures with their fictional counterparts from the works of V. S. Naipaul, John Updike, and Hanif Kureishi, in order to show how novelistic fiction and historical fact mutually anticipate and interrogate the meanings that circulate around these phenomena. Given the plethora of gurus and clients available for study, these particular instances—whether sociological or literary—are not held up as representative archetypes, but taken as provisional entry points into a whole range of populist trends. Gurus are to be studied more carefully for their transidiomatic suppleness, their rhetorical persuasiveness, their translatability, their commodifiability, and their consumability. Even a brief look at various "pitches" made by gurus at different historical moments, whether colonial or postcolonial, modern or postmodern, historical or literary, shows how versatile and mobile these discourses indeed are. Through Guru English, Madame Blavatsky claims to meet her Theosophical master at the great imperial exhibition at the Crystal Palace in 1851, Swami Vivekananda makes his global career by way of an uninvited bravura performance at the World Parliament of Religions in Chicago in 1893, and Deepak Chopra jockeys for new readers through full-page advertisements in the *New York Times* after the terrorist attacks of September 11, 2001. Observing gurus at work can provide us with very cogent insights into how religious vocabularies, market culture, and utopian desire intersect, in early, middle, and late modernity, and the dystopian futures of nuclearism are more than matched by the utopian projections of contemporary gurus. Or, is this distinction between utopia and dystopia no longer viable in a postapocalyptic world within which we observe the vacillations of economic, political, and religious phenomena?

A brief afterword rounds out the argument of the book, returning us to what is overall at stake, even as I make a few speculative observations on the directions that could not be taken given constraints of time, space, and personal interest. Ranging over two centuries, as well as barrelling on through religious practitioners, literary texts, and world-historical phenomena, this book has something for almost everyone. Such a venture resembles collections of insects in amber: a rendering into concrete of flights of fancy that nonetheless stay alive, in the air and through the brain, with the cadences of Guru English.

CHAPTER ONE

Theolinguistics: Orientalists, Brahmos, Vedantins, and Yogis

> Let the Persian or the Greek, or the Roman, or the Arab, or the
> Englishman march his battalions, conquer the world, and link
> the different nations together, and the philosophy and spiritu-
> ality of India is ready to flow along the new-made channels
> into the veins of the nations of the world. The calm Hindu's
> brain must pour out its own quota to give to the sum total of
> human progress. India's gift to the world is the light spiritual.
> —Swami Vivekananda, *Lectures from Colombo to Almora*

EUROPEAN COMPARATIVE FRAMEWORKS dominated the first attempts
to render South Asian religious practices into English. By resituating ancient Sanskrit texts and granting them greater performative force than
they had at that point in time, the British orientalists demonstrated a
neoclassical sensibility. The recent Mughal hegemony in northern India
was displaced by a convergent account of Hinduism as the religion of the
majority population. The textualism of such an approach also favored
Brahmanical interpreters of Hindu religion over popular practitioners.
An antiquarian idealization of texts and doctrines allowed for a rational-
izing account of the revelations behind Hindu practices and an etiological
narrative about historical distortions. The Christian and deist affiliations
of these investigators influenced the selection of texts and the objectives
of the first translations. The hired interlocutors of the orientalists had
ample indication of the kinds of texts and interpretations sought by their
employers and were most enterprising in finding appropriate originals—
and sometimes inventing them.

Such neoclassicism had a delayed impact when Hindu modernizers
took up the task of the religious rejuvenation of their peers and the
proselytization of others. Keeping with orientalist simplifications that
demonized Islam as a foreign entity and depicted the non-Islamic majority as civilized but disenfranchised, many Hindu revivalists built on
the deistic and monotheistic interpretation of Brahman-dominated Hinduism suggested by these recent interventions. One goal was to go beyond traditional Brahmanical ritual and decry the priestly stranglehold
on religion. A Hindu deism or (even a moderate monotheism) was the

foundational clearing to be carved out of a polytheistic forest. As indigenous religion consisted of orthopraxies rather than orthodoxies, and as only specific sects have linear histories, Romila Thapar has suggested that premodern Hinduism had never become "a uniform, monolithic religion," but had always remained "a flexible juxtaposition of religious sects." The modern construction of "syndicated Hinduism" is to be understood as an administrative reorganization of the "rest" under the sign of a renovated Brahmanism.[1]

In this chapter, I first discuss some of the early innovations of the orientalists and their linguistic imitators, followed by a section on the significant impact of Rammohun Roy's dialogue with Unitarianism. The continuation of Brahmo theism in place of Rammohun's deism under the syncretic experimentation of Keshub Chunder Sen's New Dispensation religion is the focus of the third section. The chapter is rounded off with an account of how neo-Advaita and yoga as espoused by spiritual entrepreneurs such as Vivekananda and Yogananda took up the mission of a rejuvenated Hinduism for the twentieth century, in place of the Christianized legacy of the Brahmos that had been crafted for a mid-Victorian audience. Such neoclassicism, disseminated through linguistic innovation and doctrinal suppleness, participates in and creates a representational framework for the part-orientalist, part-anglicist theolinguistics that is Guru English. This structure features Guru English as both specialized register and generalized discourse.

The brilliance of first-generation orientalists such as William Jones, Charles Wilkins, and Nathaniel Brassy Halhed, who went to India in the late eighteenth century, turned out to be no guarantee against the dismissal of South Asian pasts by anglicists such as William Bentinck, Charles Trevelyan, and Thomas Macaulay in the 1830s. Orientalist antiquarianism was quickly undermined by the values of modernizing utilitarianism. William Jones's intense Hinduphilia was countered by James Mill's virulent Hinduphobia: Mill's suspicion of India undergirding his *History of British India* was magisterially emphasized by his declaration that a trip there would be unwise. Such a trip would only compromise Mill's search for impartial objectivity and was therefore best avoided. A European vantage point was better, from which evidence could be sifted and judged. Knowledge of India was "singularly defective" because of "partial impressions" acquired by observers. Instead, a "cursory survey" by a writer who had never visited India and who had only elementary acquaintance with its languages would nonetheless approximate judicial neutrality.[2]

The reverence that some South Asianists still have for the orientalists is readily matched by modernizing attacks on the Indo-European civilizational myths propagated by a line of orientalists from Jones to Max

Müller, Mircea Eliade, and Louis Dumont.[3] Religion and philology once ruled supreme for orientalist erudition on South Asia, whereas more recent materialist approaches foregrounding economics or politics are skeptical of past disciplinary biases toward religion and culture. For every David Kopf who still defends orientalism, Susobhan Sarkar (or more recently, Javed Majeed) shows that utilitarians were not as dismissive of India as is sometimes made out. Earlier, Rammohun Roy or Syed Ahmed Khan more readily accepted criticism about their societies than later Indian and Pakistani nationalists would ever concede.[4] Framed in terms of identifying the hitherto excluded discontents of the colonial state formation, the discoveries of the influential historical journal *Subaltern Studies* in recent decades constitute a major advance. More recently, however, subalternist scholarship has fallen victim to its own success, becoming increasingly mired in theoretical disagreements about the relative weight to be accorded to Marxist versus postmodernist methodologies, and to political-economic indicators versus cultural-religious phenomena. Additionally, the historiographical exceptionalism of many Indian historians who ignore comparative frameworks has been roundly criticized.[5]

For these reasons, the battle between mythopoetic orientalism and antiorientalist critique continues in complex and displaced ways. Edward Said's disciplinary intervention into the contemporary politics of knowledge and his dressing-down of European orientalism as malevolent colonialist teleology has become a tenacious point of reference among a variety of South Asianist cultural scholars who wish to modify his insights to their object. Within India, the metanarrative around urban-educated middle-class nationalism that characterizes ruling-class hegemony is now under challenge by groups putting forward alternative histories, whether Dalit, tribal, or regional. Given these new disciplinary and political challenges, Ashis Nandy cannily suggests that there are still four kinds of stories that continue to be told about Indian modernity. While the first template is the progress narrative of Westernization and modernization familiar to early colonial historians and still popular among South Asianists in the era of globalization, the second is the opposing narrative, involving Hindu nationalist resurgence against British domination, as the next chapter discusses in relation to Bankimchandra Chatterjee and Sri Aurobindo. The third template involves the Gandhian departure from both the European thesis and the indigenous antithesis, one that includes considerable autocritique of Indian society even as it consolidates Brahmanical modernization by reference to asceticism, nonviolence, and self-denial. The fourth template, and only recently emergent according to Nandy, is a post-Gandhian set of popular political movements that rejects upper-caste leadership and questions hegemony and bourgeois consolidation from the standpoint of various subaltern groups representing a demographic majority that was hitherto silenced. It is this standpoint that was brought to the forefront of history and anthropology by *Subaltern Studies*, even though this is, properly speaking, not so much one standpoint for another nationalist narrative as a location from which multiple epistemic fractures and many other microhistories can be described from below.[6]

Although related to these four templates, Guru English marks a fifth strand, with a cosmopolitan and diasporic logic that articulates countercommunities and virtual spaces rather than just replicating the naturalized boundaries of national or regional imaginings. Guru English also takes off along with the early Western assimilationists, sometimes tests its mettle against Hindu revivalists, and at other times beds down with them. However, when compared with the third and fourth templates, Guru English eschews the groundedness of Gandhian nationalist politics, and has little connection with post-Gandhian regional populisms. Rather, Guru English heads for political futures that are still only partially realized by cosmopolitan deracination. Such theolinguistic outreach is a direct function of the cosmopolitan-national interface. Relying on modernized and often transnational mediation of supposedly traditional practices and doctrines, Guru English is sometimes vehicle and at other times fabricator.

Guru English has been hitherto ignored as a generalized theolinguistics, perhaps because it reveals the pattern of the "global popular" rather than that of a substantive historiography or discourse located in South Asian space. Frivolous and extraterritorial, Guru English can also be seen as unevenly or insufficiently globalized. The cultural consumerism of the global popular, which can, for instance, be discerned through the action-attraction movies produced by Hollywood, Bollywood, or Hong Kong cinema, suggests a series of related particularities and material practices rather than any grand narrative of cultural globalization.[7] The formation of the global popular—in its most expanded sense, which ought to include Guru English—is difficult to historicize because of the fragmentary and transcommunal nature of cosmopolitan religious thematics and dispositions. However, more recently there have been suggestions that the postcolonial is itself a globalizing version of the commodifiable and the exotic, in which case Guru English is an excellent specific instance of a more generalized phenomenon.[8]

Conventional histories of philosophy and religion are of little help here, although much can be gleaned from individual case studies that can be put together to designate a larger whole. Early movements that retail South Asian religion for an international audience—especially those featuring the orientalists, the Brahmos, the Theosophists, and the early Vedantists—form an important prehistory for Guru English and need to be studied more carefully in terms of the present as their eventual outcome.[9] Gauri Viswanathan's brilliant analysis of conversion as creating tension between civil society, religion, and political authority—and thereby deconstructing secular modernity—furnishes important pointers. However, Guru English is perhaps better understood as a medium of cosmopolitan expression or transidiomatic background rather than as the critical agency enacted by narratives of conversion. Along with the work done by theorists of relativism such as Bruno Latour and Barbara Herrnstein Smith, Viswanathan's book has suggested the adoption of more flexible approaches to the question of truth within pluralized and incommensurable contexts.[10] Rather than "meticulous[ly] construct[ing] ethnographic plots" of conversion in the manner of the colonial census as documented by Viswanathan, Guru English represents a transcommunal phantasm of global interactivity without a strong sociological basis—or doctrinal core—to underpin its claims. A number of religious universalisms and cosmopolitanisms come together through Guru English, allowing these mutants and recombinants to jostle, proliferate, and clash within the confines of a common theolinguistic frame.

Peter van der Veer's call for an interactional perspective in historical investigation can help mitigate the disciplinary proprietorship that field specialists exhibit toward those arguing for a thoroughly hybridized cultural history. While studying the joint impact of British Christianity and Indian Hinduism on each other, van der Veer uncovers a series of paradoxes concerning the manner in which secularity and religiosity were jointly constructed and policed by the modern colonial state apparatus and by each other. Critiquing both Marxist materialist and Weberian culturalist accounts of the rise of modernity, van der Veer demonstrates that the emergent public sphere in both the metropolis and the colony was strongly influenced by the rise of voluntary religious movements and also by the universalization of religion as a cultural category. Aided by comparative philology, nationalists were especially keen to find their own path to an alternative modernity that combined spirituality, science, and political progress, even as colonial officials were triangulating their secular rule against the mobilization of British Christian missionaries and South Asian neoreligious revival. It helped enormously that neophyte spiritual movements in the West (such as mesmerism, Theosophy, or paganism) could project intellectual affinities with analogs from ancient India, however fantasmatic these affinities might have seemed to skeptical observers then, or might still seem to us now.[11] Guru English operates within this hazy space of East-West interconnection, a theolinguistics amply enabled by the fuzzy logic of comparative philology and the dizzy identifications of colonial desire. A result of interactional, transnational, translational, and transidiomatic exchanges, Guru English sometimes produces the minimal amount of communicative noise and sometimes engenders substantial neoreligious movements that animate practitioners and their social worlds to the point of making recognizable history.

Orientalist Initiations

As Friedrich Max Müller, the dean of nineteenth-century orientalist comparative philology suggests, the proposal that Indo-European was a linguistic source of diverse languages and cultures created a notion of global community that had hitherto not existed. For Müller, who was in search of a Christian Vedanta, as were his British forbears, language could be a much greater unifier than blood or race: "while a so-called community of blood conveys really no definite meaning at all, a community of language that extended even to consonants, vowels, and accents, proved an intellectual fraternity far stronger than any merely genealogical relationship." Müller here chimes in with Ernest Renan, whose formulation of national consciousness as a daily plebiscite has been applied with considerable success more recently by Benedict Anderson, Homi Bhabha, and others. Of course, the highly speculative nature of comparative philology's theory of common linguistic origins did not deter those like Müller. Dugald Stewart, like many of his Scottish Enlightenment predecessors, highly valued conjectural reasoning as a scientific alternative to the indolent philosophy of religious miracles. As Stewart puts it, "when we cannot trace the process by which an event *has been* produced, it is often important to show how *it may have been* produced by natural causes."[12] This type of secularizing conjectural reasoning about colonial times has been exploited recently with brilliance by postcolonial novelists such as Amitav Ghosh in works such as *In an Antique Land* and *The Calcutta Chromosome*.[13]

Speculative and conjectural, Guru English as theolinguistics commences its activity by repositioning the secular and the religious within a common framework. Conventional religion draws the curtain on the further explanation of the mysteries. Ancient Hindu, Greco-Roman, Persian, and Nordic pasts constituted a free-floating combinatorium for a conjectural history, whence epic, law, religion, and literature could be beautifully synthesized and presented as the ur-tradition of all traditions. While it could be argued that the search for explanation leads to yet further mystification, this mystification is not of an older but a newer sort, a creative theolinguistics of secular modernity rather than a simple repetition of already elaborated theology. Putative translation creates a new discourse altogether, even if the transidiomaticity of this discourse makes multiple users believe that they are in contact with a functional translation. Comparative religion was the natural outcome of comparative linguistics, and theolinguistics similarly was a creative extension of the policy of English education fueled by native knowledges.[14]

While they produced an originary historical synthesis, the first-generation orientalists are even more significantly productive of future discourse for the way they exercised comparative methods while assessing Indian religious belief. Comparativism would become a mainstay of Guru English, and indeed the first attribute of modern South Asian theolinguistics. Attempts by several orientalists to present Hinduism as Protestantism or Unitarianism began just the first of several historical attempts of religious translation and transculturation outward from South Asia. In the famous inaugural orientalist text (not the first, but one of the first translations of a Hindu religious text in its entirety into a European language), Charles Wilkins already speculates that hegemonic consolidation and doctrinal synthesis are at work in ancient India.[15] In the translator's preface to the Bhagavadgītā, Wilkins speculates, "the principal design of these dialogues was to unite all the prevailing modes of worship of those days; and by setting up the doctrine of the unity of the Godhead, in opposition to idolatrous sacrifices, and the worship of images, to undermine the tenets inculcated by the Veds."[16]

Wilkins therefore suggests that "the most learned Brahmans of the present times are Unitarians according to the doctrines of Kreeshna; but at the same time that they believe but in one God, an universal spirit, they so far comply with the prejudices of the vulgar, as outwardly to perform all the ceremonies inculcated by the Veds, such as sacrifices, ablutions, &c."[17] The orientalists' broad delineation and separation of philosophical doctrine from popular religion—highbrow texts from lowbrow culture—is an early version of modern Hinduism already at work. An inevitable distillation occurs, separating doctrine from practice, and otherworldly truth from this-worldly necessity. Such sophisticated decontextualization rationalizes the myriad forms of later philosophical import-export. The justification of Hinduism in relation to a single divinely revealed text was itself very new, an analogical imposition originating from expectations formed through Judaism, Islam, and Christianity. Separating and reconstituting religious fundamentals, Wilkins shows the way toward much subsequent reappropriation and creative license. As we now know, various doctrinal and ritual elements are synthesized in multiple ways by many modern gurus who need both ideological cover for their ventures and fresh disciples for their missions. The strategy of synthesis had already been devised as a speculative aside by the time of Jones, and if not by him personally, perhaps by the frequently unidentified scribes, translators, and native scholars that constituted his cohort of informers.

It is on an instructive parallel that William Jones ends his essay "On the Gods of Greece, Italy, and India" by suggesting that Muslims and Hindus can be converted to Christianity most easily by planting representative samples of Christian wisdom within Hindu and Islamic scripture. The Christian missionary can prevail by simple fraud: "[T]he only human mode . . . of causing so great a revolution will be to translate into Sanscrit and Persian such chapters of the Prophets, particularly of Isaiah, as are indisputably Evangelical, together with one of the Gospels, and a plain prefatory discourse containing full evidence of the very distant ages, in which the predictions themselves, and the history of the divine person predicted, were severally made publick; and then quietly to disperse the work among the well-educated natives."[18] This wry thought is something of a wisecrack on Jones's part, as his work is known to be scrupulous, even if subsequently proven wrong. Perhaps unwittingly, the comment anticipates a more general truth: planting ideas, as well as the creative exploration of dubious etymologies, were fringe activities of Indology that soon took on greater significance. The most famous example of a spurious Sanskrit text was the one deliberately constructed by the French Jesuits in the eighteenth century entitled *Ezourvedam*, a fabrication that prefigures a Christianized deism akin to that which Wilkins propounded on the basis of the Bhagavadgītā, written with the objective of preparing the way for the Christian conversion of the polytheists found in India. Possessing a French manuscript version as early as 1760, Voltaire had found this piece of "Guru French," as it were, to be very useful for an attack on Christianity in toto. Such a surprising turnabout suggests the creative potential of counterdiscursive revisions on the basis of an earlier theolinguistics. Even the learned Anquetil Duperron was taken in by the forgery. Little could the Jesuits have imagined that a spurious French translation they invented as a semi-Christian halfway house to convert heathens would be used by their critics as evidence of a Vedic culture philosophically far superior to the theistic Christianity that they were trying to extend to the natives.[19] Direct appreciations of Indian religion were also well under way before the establishment of the Calcutta orientalists. Writing about the importance of John Zephaniah Holwell's *Interesting Historical Events, Relative to the Provinces of Bengal, and the Empire of Indostan* (1765–71) for British Indomania, Thomas Trautmann says "Hinduism, in Holwell, reads like Milton with transmigration." For Holwell, the Bible was rendered sublimely transparent only after reading ancient Hindu texts, classed by him at the same level as the scriptures of Moses and Christ.[20]

While comparative philology was abandoned when the anglicists took control of the imperial mission, it had a much longer and sustained impact on Indian self-definitions. The explosion of creative etymology through revivalist Aryanism and Hindu fundamentalism still continues unchecked. Contemporary creativity of this sort comes from mythistorians such as P. N. Oak, whose life's work can be summarized by the title of one of his books: *World Vedic Heritage: A History of Histories, Presenting a Unique Unified Field Theory of History that from the Beginning of Time the World Practised Vedic Culture and Spoke Sanskrit*. In this and multiple other books, Oak regales us with the deep punning of Vatican as *vatikā* (hermitage), Sistine Chapel as *śivasthāna* (Shiva's station), Scandinavia as *skandanāviya* or *skandanābhi* (the warrior-god Skanda's naval settlement, or Viking's navel), Russia as *ṛṣīya* (abode of sages), Moscow as *moksha* (salvation; surely the focus of a land of sages?), Canterbury as *śankarapuri* (the renowned Advaitin Sankara's town), England as *angulīsthāna* (fingerland, because fingerlike when compared with Europe as a palm), Nile as *nīla* (blue; hence the blue Nile), Australia as *astrālaya* (land of missiles where weapons used in the epic battles of the *Mahābhārata* were supposedly tested), America as *amaraka* (land of the immortals—surely this ought to be desired even if ultimately untrue!), Abraham as corruption of *brahma*, Pope (or Papa in Italian) as *pāpa-hā* (absolver of sins), Herodotus as *hari-dūta* (messenger of Vishnu), Socrates as *sukrutas* (of meritorious conduct), Alexander as *alakṣyendra* (the invisible god), and so on ad nauseam if not quite ad infinitum.

Oak, while certainly creative in proliferating these delusional etymologies, merely follows on the heels of some of the early numbers of the *Asiatic Researches*. Francis Wilford speculated about supposed Puranic references to England as *śveta-dvīpa* (white island), Egypt as *guptasthāna* (land of secrets), and Ethiopia as *kuśasthāna* (Cush in the Bible). Later, to his chagrin, Wilford discovered that the pandit in his employ had composed over twelve thousand fake "Puranic" verses as interpolations within existing texts, including a rousing account of Noah's sons Ham, Shem, and Japhet as Sharma, Karma, and Jyapati. Charles Vallancey, with a bee in his bonnet about common Celtic-Indian roots that would continue all the way to W. B. Yeats, Æ, and other Irish revivalists, speculated about the Albion theme as already present in Sanskrit, and thereby also found Scotland to be the golden island mentioned in the Puranas (*suvarṇa-dvīpa* or *sukuṭa*; hence near homonyms of Hibernia or Scotia) and Ireland as *pitṛsthāna* (land of the manes; but also Patrick's land).[21] The scientist Joseph Priestley, discoverer of oxygen ("phlogiston") and also a religious comparativist who wrote *Comparison of the Institutions of Moses with Those of the Hindoos* (1799), also focuses on general principles derived from Jones that reveal Indo-Aryan equivalents from the plausible to the utterly spurious, of Indra Divespiter (*dyaus pitṛ*) and Jupiter or Diespiter; Ganesha and Janus; Viswacarman and Vulcan; and Chrishnou and Vishnou.[22] While the inspired pun of Christ as Krishna and Christianity as *Krishnanīti* (or Krishna ethics) is an amusing one, we can add to such multilingual felicities the lines of Edward Pococke, who argued in his book *India in Greece* that Rajputs colonized Greece and named Macedonia after Magadha, and that Philip of Macedon was named after the central Indian tribal group, the Bheels.[23] Indeed, later in the nineteenth century, Monier Monier-Williams still holds out the prospect of using Sanskrit for Christian evangelism: "such, indeed, is the exuberance and flexibility of this language and its power of compounding words, that when it has been, so to speak, baptized, and thoroughly penetrated with the spirit of Christianity, it will probably be found to be, next to Hebrew and Greek, the most expressive vehicle of Christian truth."[24] Such theolinguistic lucubrations reconfirmed the privileged status accorded to Egyptian, Greek, and biblical antiquity by Europeans. These pedantries were the outcome of a desire for analogy, correspondence, and exact equivalence in the manner of what Michel Foucault describes as the Renaissance *epistēmē*. Even the arch-orientalist William Jones was wont to privately dismiss as "learned foolishness," the Celtic-Indian analogical speculations of Charles Vallancey, who equated the Irish writing of *Ogham* with the Babylonian *agam*, or the Sanskrit *āgama*. After studying Vallancey's book, Jones wrote, "[D]o you wish to laugh? Skim the book over. Do you wish to sleep? Read it regularly." Indeed, Jones's prescient dismissal could stand as an indictment of much that is being called Guru English here: humorous in small installments but soporific in large doses. Whatever his demurrals, Jones too had helped unleash the speculative mania. The convenient pick-and-choose attitude of some of his imitators lacks his characteristic restraint. However, even Jones had been taken in when he had translated some of the spurious Sanskrit verses passed along to him by Wilford, verses that had built on Jones's previous misidentification of the Sanskrit Satyavarman as the biblical Noah.[25]

One could indeed fill several more pages listing some of the most creative of these multilingual puns from the eighteenth to the twentieth centuries—some of which fill entire books—to demonstrate the efficacy of pseudo-philology run amok on the heels of the discipline of philology, but its entertainment value begins to diminish rapidly, even as the plausible and the unbelievable are mixed in equal measure. While such an enterprise could be seen as giving Joyce's *Finnegans Wake* a dreary run for its money, this word game acquires a more ominous function when it is linked with anti-Muslim and anti-Christian propaganda under a neofascist Hindutva banner.[26] Not only is most world geography deemed as being indebted to ancient Vedic culture, but also, predictably, science, religion, literature, and history on all the five continents can be traced back to the suppression of Sanskrit origins. Oak's unerring methodology finds coincidental assonance through multilingual word games. These ingenious discoveries are then revealed as deep etymology. A lame pun of this sort put out by Sai Baba literature suggests that *bābā* (colloquially, "father") as the reincarnation of Christ, is literally the Lamb of God, because lambs when they bleat, say "baa-baa." While the orientalists took upon themselves the cosmopolitan task of the critical comparison of pantheons, languages, and myths even while consigning popular religion to its South Asian particularity, the later burgeoning of Guru English was the outcome of finding a workable "global popular" equivalent.

In the very early phase, this might have taken a form that would now be hard to recognize as genealogically related. Consider, for instance, the case of the grammarian of Bengali, Nathaniel Brassey Halhed, the author of the *Gentoo Code* (1776) and *Grammar of the Bengal Language* (1778), who, even before Wilkins or William Jones, discussed the similarity, and grammatical superiority, of Sanskrit to Latin and Greek. Halhed, a member of Governor-General Warren Hastings's faction, returned with him to England in 1785 and, despite becoming a member of Parliament and participating in the nabob phenomenon of instant colonial riches, had lost a considerable fortune by 1795. At this point Halhed staked his personal reputation by becoming the advocate of a messianic prophet called Richard Brothers, going to the extent of publishing several pamphlets in his favor and imploring Parliament to heed his call.[27] Brothers claimed that he would shortly be revealed as the ruler of the world. As is the case with messianisms, the apocalyptic date came and went without the promised events, and Brothers was subsequently imprisoned as a criminal lunatic for various seditious utterances. Humiliated, and his reputation destroyed, Halhed subsequently led the life of a recluse, withdrawing from society and still waiting for the promised event. In search of a guru, Halhed followed another charismatic prophet, Joanna Southcott. In her biography of Halhed, Rosane Rocher speculates that Halhed's later fixation with Brothers's biblically based prophecies probably derived from his orientalist research in the 1780s, "primarily geared toward the discovery of a grand scheme of the world, divinely revealed to the people of the earth through their several scriptures. [Halhed] had been fascinated by the Hindu concept of cyclical time, with its periodic creations, destructions, and regenerations, and its elaborate computations of time."[28]

Rocher's suggestion of a psychoanalytically transferential relation is indeed provocative. While this episode might be one more workaday instance of turn-of-the-century Christian apocalypticism, it is poignantly anticipatory if we explore its family resemblance to later South Asian millenarianisms. While peasant revolts in the nineteenth century were transferential reactions to the apparatus of colonialism as it intersected with popular protest and an accompanying language of accommodation or resistance, Halhed's protest (if it was that) took place in the imperial metropolis. He was mostly solitary, verging on the certifiably insane. Of course, there are significant differences between Halhed's lunacy, peasant millenarianisms in nineteenth-century Bengal of the kind Ranajit Guha has discussed, and the cosmopolitan millenarianism of the Theosophical Society's predictions of the coming of a World Teacher in the 1910s and 1920s that coalesced around the extraordinary figures of Annie Besant, Jiddu Krishnamurti, and Rukmini Arundale.[29] Trivial and tangential though it might appear in relation to these later displacements, the Halhed episode is worth analyzing as an early symptom of an individual's pathological reaction to orientalist syncretism. Halhed's eccentricity contains an early glimmer of the global popular displacement of South Asian religion into European space. Guru English, spawned by orientalists, soon became a productive neoreligious discourse taken up by self-defining Indians, Indian-identified Europeans, and diasporic metropolitans, who also found in it a transidiomatic environment as well as materials for a responsive and discrepant cosmopolitanism.

UNITARIAN ENCOUNTERS

The Brahmo movement took off several decades after orientalists such as Jones and Halhed had made their initial forays, and within it can be found intriguing and fully developed cases of translational religious authority. A guru manqué because of his untimely death, Rammohun Roy as the initiator of the movement merits analysis, especially because of his success at triangulating American Unitarians, Hindu traditionalists, and British colonial reformers. Rammohun focused on social reform and doctrinal clarification in equal measure and served as a channel of communication between reformers in different locations.

Reviled by Hindu traditionalists as a colonial toadie and also as an Islamophile, Roy was attracted to a form of Unitarianism with universalistic appeal and Hindu affiliations while keeping straightforward Christianization at arm's length. Ultimately, however, the task of Rammohun as anglophone guru was to clarify and extol the virtues of Indian religion as meriting the European gaze. Twenty-five out of forty of his English publications were on religious issues. Rammohun's assertion in the preface to his *Translation of an Abridgment of the Vedant* (based on Sankara's *Brahmasūtrabhāṣya*) sounds plaintive: "I expect to prove to my European friends, that the superstitious practices, which deform the Hindoo religion have nothing to do with the pure spirit of its dictates."[30] In other works published in England, he is more doctrinaire: "the unity of the Supreme Being, as the sole Ruler of the Universe, is plainly inculcated, and the mode of worshipping him particularly directed. The doctrine of a plurality of Gods and Goddesses laid down in the preceding chapters, is not only controverted, but reasons assigned for its introduction."[31]

However, at this relatively early stage of modern Hinduism, promoting religious controversies while propagating Unitarianism was clearly a dangerous game to play, especially if the practitioner wanted to maintain credibility with multiple audiences. Here, it was important for Rammohun to claim translational authority on both sides of the colonial divide. Therefore, in his well-known polemics with B. Sankara Sastri, a traditionalist, Rammohun would astutely "beg to be allowed to express the disappointment I have felt, in receiving from a learned Brahman, controversial remarks on Hindoo theology, written in a foreign language."[32] The implication, of course, was that if Rammohun was being reviled for being more loyal than the King and more Christian than some missionaries, he could also make the counterassertion that his Sanskrit erudition was no less than that of any other learned Brahman, even if he had commenced a religious career later in life than had his adversaries. While Sanskrit discussion of theology is deemed by Rammohun to be until then the "invariable practice," he enters the lists as a respondent rather than as an initiator. Rammohun did not proselytize in Sanskrit—that would have reached a very small audience of only learned Brahmans anyway—even though he was attacked by works such as *Vedāntacandrikā*, translated in English as *An Apology for the Present State of Hindoo Worship*, to which he responded in English with *A Second Defence of the Monotheistical System of the Veds*. Some scholars deem Rammohun's Vedantic publications to be linguistically inadequate, but others come to his defense with the suggestion that he was adept at localizing his translations according to the audience he had in mind.[33]

Rammohun's turn to a religious career after a stint in East India Company service rendered him especially suspect to traditionalists. In an autobiographical letter, he would later claim to have received preliminary instruction in *vedānta darśana* from Pandit Mrityunjay Vidyalankar, a learned Brahman at the College of Fort William library. But such a retroactive self-credentialization was contested, especially as he had increasingly come into direct opposition with Calcutta's *śākta* theologians. It was rumored that Vidyalankar had authored *Vedāntacandrikā* to refute his erstwhile disciple, but in fact the work was the product of one Radhakant Dev. Fluent in Bengali, his mother tongue, Rammohun received initial training in Persian and Arabic in order to prepare him for a career in Mughal administration. He learned some Sanskrit and also Hindu customs from an observant mother, but the family context as a whole was that of worldly-wise and professionally oriented (*laukika*) rather than scripturally adept (*vaidika*) Brahmans. Rammohun was taken to be an *ashraf* (or Islamicized aristocratic hedonist) by many of his detractors. The entire *bhadralok* (the Bengali upper class) was often painted in that broad brush. All the same, Rammohun was greatly respected by the renowned French orientalist Eugène Burnouf, and the English orientalist Horace Hayman Wilson, even if the Calcutta orientalists would have no truck with him. He was refused a membership in the prestigious Asiatic Society, even while the French Société Asiatique gave him honorary membership in 1824.

Rammohun's first tract was written in Persian. Entitled *Tuhfatu'l-muwahhiddīn*, and published in 1803–4, it confirms to his biographers that a deep knowledge of Hindu texts was lacking at the beginning. The *Tuhfat* attacks religious charlatanry and simony, and therefore focuses on religious intermediaries such as brahmans, mullahs, or preachers, all of whom are deemed untrustworthy. Described by one scholar as expressing "a kind of untutored, eclectic latitudinarianism," the early *Tuhfat* already suggests some of the clarificatory directions taken by Rammohun's later anglophone cosmopolitanism.[34]

Rammohun's turn to disputational theolinguistics, first with his traditionalist and later with his Christian missionary detractors, was heavily mediated by his earlier encounters with colonial bureaucracy and late-Mughal class privilege. He was aware of at least two very split audiences of Bengali and British elites. The differing agendas of British colonial officials and missionaries on the one hand, and the rival demands made on the *bhadralok* by both reactive traditionalists and collaborationist modernizers (or at least moderns) on the other were difficult to juggle and simultaneously maintain credibility with all parties. But in the manner of many practitioners of Guru English who would come after him, Rammohun would claim during this particular controversy with Sankara Sastri that he was "not a reformer or a discoverer," but merely an accurate interpreter who was casting the net wider to include all those who would otherwise remain ignorant of Indian spiritual wisdom.[35]

Rammohun's attacks on Hinduism were celebrated in various Christian missionary circles, such as the *Missionary Register* and the *Evangel ical Magazine*, and associates such as William Ward suggested that his conversion to Christianity was just around the corner. The *North American Review* in Boston claimed that Rammohun was almost a Christian, and he corresponded widely with Unitarian leaders such as William Ellery Channing, Joseph Tuckerman, Lant Carpenter, and John Thornton Kirkland (then president of Harvard University). Rammohun was featured favorably in other North American Unitarian publications such as the *Christian Register* and the *Salem Courier*, even as Baptist journals such as the *Christian Watchman* fulminated against him. Emerson read him avidly, and his connection with Kirkland ensured that Andover-Harvard Theological Library at Harvard Divinity School still contains some of the most important Rammohun papers and literature.[36] Furthermore, Adrienne Moore's study suggests, with the aid of a comprehensive quantitative bibliographical investigation of North American religious journals, that Rammohun was the main Hindu influence on the American Transcendentalists from 1816 to 1840.[37]

At the same time as his star was on the rise across the Atlantic, in Calcutta attempts were made on his life. His charisma had increased amongst the Indian intelligentsia, and he was perceived as a threat to different religious factions. By the early 1820s, Rammohun wrote *Precepts of Jesus: The Guide to Peace and Happiness*, revealing to the chagrin of his Christian associates that he was a proponent of the Arian heresy that God and Christ were not consubstantial, as also argued the American Unitarians. Perhaps he was as religiously radical as the British Unitarians, who were Socinians, or those who denied Christ's divinity altogether. This rejection of the Athanasian creed, and the Trinitarianism that went along with it, was characteristic of many Hindus who could come closest only to a Unitarian form of Christianity. Rammohun's position that Jesus was human, and all too human, left the Baptist missionaries (who were themselves split into rival Serampore and Calcutta factions till 1837) furious with disappointment. They had expected him to convert, and this turn of events resulted in a pamphlet controversy with Joshua Marshman. To add insult to injury, Rammohun introduced the line of thought, to be taken up later by Keshub Chunder Sen, that Jesus was more oriental than occidental.[38] Meanwhile, Rammohun's associates defended Vedanta from Christian attacks in a journal entitled the *Brahmunical Magazine: The Missionary and the Brahmun*. At the forefront of the petitioners who advocated the outlawing of sati, or widow self-immolation, that eventually happened under Lord Bentinck in 1828, Rammohun earned the ire of Hindu traditionalists jealous of British interference in local customs. Rammohun was ultimately an anglicist, or an orientalist modernizer, depending upon one's interpretation. It is notable that he preferred Western-style modern education rather than instruction in Sanksrit or Persian for Indians. In a brief letter on English education addressed to Governor-General Amherst that anticipates and foreshadows Macaulay's Minute, Rammohun opposes the proposal for a Sanskrit college in Calcutta on the grounds that such an establishment "can only be expected to land the minds of youth with grammatical niceties and metaphysical distinctions of little or no practical use to the possessors or to society." Just as Baconian philosophy replaced the schoolmen in England, so, Rammohun thought, English education would displace Sanskrit metaphysics in India. In works such as *Remarks on Settlement in India by Europeans* (1832), Rammohun anticipated a largely English-speaking India as the eventual outcome, and positioned this future anglicized India as the enlightener of Asia.[39]

Rammohun's flirtation with conversion suggests that he was aware of the possibility of identitarian displacements and the multiple affiliations that Gauri Viswanathan has credited with conversion in nineteenth-century India and Britain. Propagating a modernized indigenous religion with the early Brahmo doctrines he favored, Rammohun's Guru English became a cosmopolitan religious supplement to English education. It is perhaps fitting that Rammohun is credited with the first use of that English nominalization, "Hindu*ism*." Much more cut-and-dried with his direct approach to scripture than were the orientalist philologists, Rammohun could still let go with some occasional speculation of the Jones variety of Guru English: "'Om' bears a striking similarity, both in sound and application, to the participle *wv* of the verb *Elul to be*, in Greek. . . . A reference to the Septuagint will shew that *wv* like 'Om' is applied to Jehova the ever existing God."[40] Rammohun is also credited with the innovation of the selective use of scriptures in prayer meetings later made famous by Debendranath Tagore and Mahatma Gandhi—indeed, a standard practice of Reform Christianity, but unknown even until the nineteenth century in the Indian context where scriptures were meant to be chanted whole.[41] Rammohun could, therefore, be described as a comparativist, in the vein of William Jones, with the addition of a practical and adaptive bent, but in retrospect, he was charting an alternative course for a brand new religion with secular and scientific overtones. One of the earliest published accounts of an encounter with him by an English traveler records that he "quotes Locke and Bacon on all occasions." He acted as the prototype of the liberal modernizer of India before liberalism was a full-fledged force in British society. Later, Max Müller would write a hagiographical appreciation, calling him "a great man in the highest sense of the word."[42]

Rammohun's trimming between Hindu and Christian doctrine and also tradition and secular modernization was indeed difficult to maintain rhetorically. To some extent, he had started off a Westernizer/modernizer and then swerved away toward a Unitarian-inspired but crypto-Hindu cosmopolitanism even while affiliated with many like-minded Unitarians in Britain and the United States. He was involved in the Calcutta Unitarian Committee from 1823; meanwhile formal Unitarianism was adopted in Britain and the United States by 1825. All the same, in 1828, he broke from the Bengali Unitarians and established the Brahmo Sabha, the beginnings of what would later become the Brahmo Samaj. According to Bruce Carlisle Robertson, the doctrinal change he effected was a shift "from hieratic authority to personal experience, from public ceremony to private worship not dictated by one's status in society."[43] While this resembles the post-Reformation European shift from communal to individual worship, it also contains within it the possibility of radical affiliation and assimilation with other like-minded deists, Unitarians, and cosmopolitans the world over. F.W.J. Schelling was interested in Rammohun (even if Arthur Schopenhauer was not), and to some extent Rammohun also contributed to the generalized European syncretism taking place, which began mistakenly to conflate Vedanta with Buddhism and some forms of atheism.

More intriguing for the purposes of evaluating Rammohun as a forbear of theolinguistics is his departure for England on November 17, 1830. Supposedly, every print shop in Liverpool displayed his image pending arrival, and even an eighty-year-old Jeremy Bentham, who referred to him as "Instructor of his Country," expressed a keenness to meet the man who had earned high praise as a "Bengalee Luther" and "Erasmus of India." Some of the work Rammohun hoped to do there was political, involving support of the Reform Bill—even while he had already been taken as a model by Swiss reformers such as Sismondi, by the Abbé Grégoire in the *Chronique religieuse*, and by others in Spain, Italy, Greece, Turkey, and Holland. Despite all the reform talk, Rammohun was officially in England as a representative of the Mughal puppet Akbar II, sent to beg the East India Company for an increase in the royal purse. Despite being politically powerless by that point, the nominal emperor gave Rammohun the title of Raja, and his family made substantial financial gains from his representations.[44]

However, there was also talk of Rammohun's eventual emigration to the United States, where he was the first major Asian religious influence, even while he was feted by aristocrat and Unitarian alike in Britain. In *The Newcomes,* William Thackeray's most popular novel during his lifetime, the character of Rummon Loll is some indication of how Rammohun also entered English literary representation, as are some impres sions gleaned from Harriet Martineau's *Autobiography.*[45] While his devotees perhaps make more of his American connections and the rumored multiple meetings with French Emperor Louis-Philippe in 1832 than is to be warranted, Rammohun's sudden death in Bristol in 1833 meant that a planned trip to visit various Unitarian associates in the United States did not take place, and his impact on potential American audiences remained forever untested. His skull, studied after his death by phrenologists, revealed "dignity of character."[46]

Although Rammohun's possible career as an American guru never played out, Brahmo literature nevertheless spread widely in the United States from 1850 to 1870. All indications are that an enthusiastic circle of admirers eagerly awaited his arrival, who spread his word even though he never set foot on American soil. The best North American hyperbole about Rammohun came from Jabez Sunderland, who calls him "India's immortal Moses, Mazzini, and Washington, all in one."[47] Such an assessment would have always gone down well in India, where colonialist ideas of native inferiority deemed that the emulative equivalents of Indian figures had to be measured against already established Western models for added value and reassurance. Ultimately, Rammohun was a hybrid of *philosophe,* guru, and baboo.

Rammohun's interest in Vedanta made him a deistic precursor of what was later to become a full-fledged revival. Hoping to establish an eclectic monotheism, he had nonetheless nudged the Brahmo covenant into positions resolutely against Hindu idolatry and toward pantheistic doctrines. Yet rather than taking to a hard-line iconoclasm, he argued that image-worship was a stopgap measure for those who hadn't yet managed to make the step toward pantheism.[48] David Kopf has succinctly summarized Rammohun's (and the Brahmo movement's) goals under the threefold headings of "liberal religion, social reform, and universal theistic progress."[49] While the first two goals were rooted in the problematic of South Asian society and culture, the third involved cosmopolitan outreach, which in Rammohun's case meant the worldwide Unitarian movement. Along with Dwarkanath Tagore (Rabindranath's grandfather) and William Adam (the Calcutta Baptist whom Rammohun converted to Brahmoism), Rammohun drafted a trust deed for the new Church he would have instituted, as an established form of general Universalist Unitarianism. There was talk of various Unitarian representatives from different countries (or at least from Boston, Bristol, and Calcutta) to meet and discuss common social, religious, and political goals, even though this much-anticipated confabulation never took place. But after Rammohun's death in 1833, there was a lull in Bengali Unitarianism at least until 1855.[50]

After the death of the "Bengalee Luther," Debendranath Tagore (Rabindranath's father) instituted the Brahmo Samaj as a Bengali-based organization according to dictates gleaned from Rammohun's teachings. What is perhaps even more significant is that by 1860, there were at least forty-five Brahmo Samajes in various parts of India. By 1867, Brahmo missionaries were using the newly created railway system to propagate their modern religion. Despite various schismatic breaks and personality clashes, the peak of the Brahmo Samaj occurred in 1912, when there were 232 branches throughout India. Rammohun Roy had been read enthusiastically outside South Asia, and the American Transcendentalists avidly followed Eastern religious literature. However, more time had to elapse before anglophone South Asian religious leaders could be showcased on a genuinely global scale. When it came to Rammohun's cosmopolitan universal legacy, the different outcomes generated by several of those who came after Rammohun and modified Brahmo doctrines to suit their purposes are worth pursuing.

NEW DISPENSATIONS

A fascinating successor case to Rammohun's Unitarianism was Keshub Chunder Sen's multistage universalist experiment culminating in the religion called Nava Vidhan or "New Dispensation," inaugurated in 1879.[51] Much like Jones and Rammohun, Keshub exercised himself considerably in creative theolinguistics. Joining Debendranath Tagore in a joint effort to revive the Brahmo Samaj in the late 1850s, Keshub initially ceded Bengali proselytization to Debendranath and himself systematically "held forth in English on the philosophical basis of Brahmaism and on the ethical aspects of the spiritual life." Keshub never learned Sanskrit and is reputed to have known the Bible better than he knew his Hindu scripture. From June 1860, he backed up his lectures with a monthly English publication entitled *Tracts for the Times*. In August 1861, he began another newspaper, *Indian Mirror*. Looking to form a universalist church with a cosmopolitan outreach, Keshub broke with Debendranath, who wished to stay within a national frame. Debendranath's Tattvabodhini Sabha held the line against Christian conversion.[52] Meanwhile, Keshub prospected for a cosmopolitan religion against factions such as Debendranath's who had turned toward Hindu nationalist influences. David Kopf has described Keshub as representing "philosophies of encounter and acculturation, best expressed in the ideologies of comparativism and universalism." Keshub used English as a written and spoken medium, and propagated a Westernized form of Brahmoism whenever he was outside Bengal. He made a conscious choice to use English, rather than Marathi, Tamil, or Hindustani in locales where those vernaculars were much more widely spoken. It especially helped his English-language proselytization that by 1839 Calcutta had twenty-six English-language newspapers including six dailies and nine Indian newspapers.[53] Furthermore, during his 1864 missionary tour of Madras, accompanied by Protap Chunder Mozoomdar, Keshub preached to Indian bureaucrats, teachers, and intellectuals entirely in English. Sometimes, there was literary entertainment in addition to religious instruction: for example, in Nainital, Keshub and Protap regaled audiences with readings from Shakespeare and Tennyson. English literature was often used to deliver moral education and Christian ethics to the working poor both in Britain and elsewhere since the early nineteenth century. Keshub and other Indian practitioners, likewise, used English literature in combination with varying cultural agendas for middle-class Indians.[54]

In his famous September 1866 lecture entitled, "Jesus Christ, Europe, and Asia," Keshub claimed Christ as a more natural spiritual leader for India than for Britain: "Shall I not rather say he [Christ] is more congenial and akin to my Oriental nature, more agreeable to my Oriental habits of thought and feeling? And is it not true that an Asiatic can read the imageries and allegories of the Gospel, and its description of natural sceneries, of customs and manners, with greater interest, and a fuller perception of their force and beauty, than Europeans?" Declaring Christianity "an altogether Oriental affair," Keshub started a New Brahmo Samaj in November 1866.[55] This organization evolved into a progressive and reformist religion within a Brahmo frame, along with a more populist turn to the faith-inspired Bhakti cult and its Vaishnava-related influences.

Keshub was well received on a trip to England in 1870, where he declared his new religious discoveries. He was accompanied by others, including Krishna Dhan Ghose, the father of Sri Aurobindo. In England, Keshub participated in thirty-six public meetings on social reform and temperance, and in addition, gave twenty-four religious speeches in fourteen towns over six months. He was heard by a total of about forty thousand people during his visit to the imperial heartland.[56] In the speech at his welcome soirée, which was attended by representatives of twelve different religious denominations, he would reiterate his orientalizing interpretation of Christ.[57] Queen Victoria gave him an audience, exchanging tokens of recognition with him and asking him for his portrait. He breakfasted with Prime Minister Gladstone, kept John Stuart Mill waiting to meet him while he finished his correspondence, and met a congratulatory Max Müller, who wrote later that Keshub was "a household name" in Britain. Most of the London newspapers covered his visit, and his daily routine was published in circulars that were distributed all over southern England.[58] Keshub's arrival was sufficiently newsworthy to merit an aggressive racist lampoon in *Punch*. The author of the doggerel verses cannot get beyond fetishizing the exotic rhythm of Keshub's name in English, a poetic refrain beating like a military tattoo on the anglophone ear. Ultimately, the lampoon creates a dialectic of domesticity, defamiliarization, and parody that indeed allows for the possibility of something like Guru English:

> This great Indian reformer is invited to a tea meeting by the British and Foreign Unitarian Society at the Hanover Square Rooms:
>
> Who on earth of living men,
> *Is* BABOO KESHUB CHUNDER SEN?
> I doubt if even one in ten
> Knows BABOO KESHUB CHUNDER SEN.
> Have *you* heard—if so where and when—
> Of BABOO KESHUB CHUNDER SEN?
> The name surpasses human ken—
> BABOO KESHUB CHUNDER SEN!
> To write it almost spoils my pen;
> Look BABOO—KESHUB CHUNDER—SEN!
> Or like "my ugly brother Ben"
> Swarth BABOO KESHUB CHUNDER SEN?
> From fair Cashmere's white-peopled glen
> Comes BABOO KESHUB CHUNDER SEN?
> Big as ox, or small as wren,
> Is BABOO KESHUB CHUNDER SEN?
> Let's beard this "lion" in his den—
> This BABOO KESHUB CHUNDER SEN.
> So come to tea and muffins, then,
> With BABOO KESHUB CHUNDER SEN.[59]

Meanwhile, the journalist for *Pall Mall Gazette* was impressed by a speech Keshub delivered, "with perfect fluency, with complete grammatical accuracy, and apparently without even the use of a note."[60] Perhaps somewhat quainter in its exoticist appreciation, if somewhat simpleminded, was Joseph Teenan's longer "Scotland's Welcome to Keshub Chunder Sen" that identifies the power of a "Hindoo Iconoclast" such as Keshub to take on the pastoral charge of reforming the "vicious an' confined . . . Oriental mind":

> Ye crack about the comin' man
> But here's a chap frae Hindostan,
> As rare as need tae be;
> I'd like the tawny hand tae grasp,
> O' this Hindoo Iconoclast
> Nae hypocrite is he.
>
> . . . .
>
> Some say the Oriental mind
> Is rather vicious an' confined
> Which pairtly true may be;
> But ye've a mind baith 'cute an' large
> An' abler for the pastoral charge
> Than mony that we see.
>
> . . . .
>
> Oor missionaries went tae you—
> They ca'ed you heathen then; but noo
> They'll hae tae change their tune
> Through the mire ye've trailed the robes
> O' Hindoo priests, an' made their gods
> Tae tremmle in their shoon.
>
> In your high mission persevere,
> Though men oppose you, never fear—
> Success yer work mann croon.
> The errors o' yer native land,
> The gods that in its temple stand
> Maun a' come tum'lin donn.[61]

More keen and cynical than Teenan's appreciation is the following send-up in *Saturday Review*, which both admired and satirized Keshub's performance as "Conundrum Baboo":

Nobody takes the posture you want like a Bengalee, and that distinguished reformer of Indian religion, Conundrum Baboo, answers every string his hostess pulls with a perfect adaptability. It is amazing to compare his performance with the clumsier gambols of his Western rivals. A flow of pietistic enthusiasm gilds the vagueness of his dogma; the Bible, instead of being vulgarly reduced to arithmetic, disappears in a cloud of Vedas; a gentle, pitiful shake of the head expresses the regret of the distinguished stranger over the blind antagonism of Western faiths; there is something irresistibly winning in his irritation to throw everything overboard, and exchange the convictions of Christendom for the dream of a handful of Hindoos. There is something exquisite in the perfect absurdity which expresses itself with such an air of prophetic persuasion, in the delicious way in which the shock is administered—not in the coarse, concrete fashion of Occidental heretics, but with a gentle titillation, which creeps through one's frames to the very fingertips. Unquestionably, if one is to try the *leo hereticus*, there is no lion like Conundrum Baboo.[62]

The subtle racism of this last piece gets us closer to grasping the stylistic and gestural architecture of Keshub's Guru English as it influences the satirist. The adaptability, erudition, and empathetic urbanity of the religious reformer of Hinduism are rendered as amusing aspects of a visiting colonial subject who has become the talk of the town. The "conundrum" of Keshub is the combination of gravitas and titillation in the effect he creates. Introduced into new surroundings where he sketches out reformist objectives, Keshub provides social entertainment along with religious incongruity. Dismissed as an absurd creature despite, or perhaps precisely because of, his cosmopolitan refinement, Keshub's status as colonial baboo nonetheless carries with it the status of incipient guru. The appreciation is orientalizing but ultimately not grudging: Keshub's religious patter is "irresistibly winning" when compared with the "clumsier gambols of his Western rivals." The implication is that if one desires to be seduced by heresy, one might as well surrender to the most exquisite titillation in the form of Keshub.

These popular literary and journalistic representations are notable for the fact that they explicitly recognize Keshub as a baboo even as they are also implicit acknowledgments that he is a self-styled guru (without quite using that word). The representations prove that there is relatively easy traffic between these two categories: if any native who is comfortable in English sociality at this point is rendered as a baboo, a guru is a special case, an especially difficult kind of baboo who poses brain-teasers and philosophical puzzles in theolinguistic idiom, or, a "conundrum baboo." Rather than recognizing that there might be religious beliefs at stake, the perception reduces these concerns to the level of idiom, style, and the aesthetics of conversational sociality. The same traffic between baboo and guru had been true of Rammohun, although in his case, the guru function was implicit in his posthumous legacy as well as his life. The equivocations, parabolic speech, and conundrum-talk that had been attributed to Baboo English are the stereotypical signs of linguistic incompetence or oriental slipperiness that the *Punch* and *Saturday Review* writers ridicule, except that here they are positively appraised as the high art of a confidence trickster. The same stereotype, when wheeled around and given a cosmopolitan future, becomes the metaphysical mastery and theolinguistic subtlety of Guru English as new orientalism.

The published British reactions to Keshub demonstrate the obsessions with form, language, and style that emerge—whether as hostility and derision, or as empathy and appreciation—from the public performances of an Indian native who can now be retroactively recognized as an early practitioner of Guru English. Even though he received many more invitations to lecture in England as well as in America, Keshub balked at the prospect of dying abroad as a missionary in the manner of Brahmos such as Rammohun or also Dwarkanath Tagore who had preceded him in the performance of reverse missionary endeavors. Keshub was torn between the prospects of establishing a national religion, a universal religion, and an apostolical religion.[63]

Inspiring doggerel as well as adulation in England, parody as well as congratulation, Keshub remained liberal in the early 1870s. However, after his decision to return to India, he slowly backtracked on the Brahmo social reform agenda later in the decade, becoming religiously conservative. This trend was exacerbated irreversibly after he lost face over the Cooch Behar marriage controversy in 1878. Pressured by the co-opting agenda of the British, Keshub agreed to marry his underage daughter to the Maharaja-designate of Cooch Behar. Loyalist till the end, and a proponent of a doctrine of the providential presence of the British in India, Keshub also began to lose support more generally, as nationalism was on the rise. Keshub's acquiescence to the British demand for a marital alliance despite his stated opposition to child marriage received wide coverage in the newspapers. Many of Keshub's progressive followers broke with him and formed the Sadharan (Ordinary) Brahmo Samaj. In the meantime, a hostile biography by a Bengali Christian contemporary accused him of "leading the life of a metropolitan magnate rather than that of a religious recluse."[64]

Keshub's search for a universal religion was to return in full force. In yet another dispensation based on harmony among all civilizations and justified by his theolinguistics, the future church would be based on the emulation and systematic study of great leaders the world over, including Moses, Socrates, Sakyamuni (the Buddha), the Rishis (Hindu sages), Christ, Muhammad, and Chaitanya (the mystic saint). In addition, imitating the Positivists who were wildly popular in Bengal, "scientific men" (Galileo, Newton, Kepler, Faraday, Sushruta), and "men of genius" (Emerson, Dean Stanley, Carlyle) would be separately considered as sources of inspiration. The Nava Vidhan, or New Dispensation of God, took some curious syncretic turns. In February 1880, Keshub's city procession during the annual Durga Puja festival took place by "fusing new Salvation Army techniques with Vaishnava appeal." Socrates,

Moses, and Muhammad were highlighted, even as a *nava śiśu*, or new child, was sacramentalized in a Christianized fashion, with Indianized ritual equivalents of rice and water substituted for bread and wine. Seeking theolinguistically to "combine types and symbols, ideas and principles," Keshub pronounced the following universalist dictum: "[L]et the embankment which each nation has raised be swept away by the flood of cosmopolitan truth."[65] Keshub calls "the new faith . . . absolutely synthetical." The New Dispensation "is the harmony of all scriptures and prophets and dispensations." The movement would immediately lead to the "transfiguration . . . [of] the educated modern Hindu cast in Vedic mould." Further, Keshub condemns "the grammar of modern theology" as an exclusionary "bad grammar" because "it [modern theology] makes no mention of the copulative conjunction. The disjunctive *Or* reigns supreme; the copulative *And* finds no place."[66] Perhaps this might be the closest example of a grammatical rule for Guru English, a theolinguistic prefiguration of E. M. Forster's liberal philosophy of "only connect," or even a foreshadowing of the Freudian idea of the expansive and inclusionary unconscious that knows no negation or exclusion. Keshub represents an exuberance felt upon the performance of religious mixture, an uncritical iconophilia in place of earlier iconoclasms.

Putting this copulative conjunction to work in his theolinguistics with a vengeance, Keshub mixed various religious symbols that became commonplace expressions of his universalism. The religion produced images of Buddha or Shiva on a cross or Christ as a yogi. Multiple religious symbols were present on the stage when Keshub spoke, including tridents, crosses, and crescents. These symbols were for popular worship, even as Keshub found several ways to argue for the cultural integration of Asia and Europe in a manner that would transcend the hierarchical realities of the colonial encounter that had brought them together as ruler and ruled. Yet, these attempts at syncretism—such as Keshub's imitation of the thirty-nine articles of Anglicanism with thirty-nine of his own—were dismissed by critics as "caricatures and burlesques, and their result is the universal derision in which the New Dispensation is held by our educated countrymen in general." Emulation from one standpoint became dangerously close to unwitting mimicry or blank parody from another. Now resonant as Guru English, Keshub's innovations were slavish Christian apologetics to his critical contemporaries.[67]

Keshub commissioned several disciples to work on different religions within his comparative framework—and therefore, Buddhism, Islam, and Christianity were all put into formal dialogue with Hindu universalism. Girish Chandra Sen translated the Qur'an into Bengali;

Gour Govinda Ray wrote a comparativist treatise on Krishna; and Aghori Nath Gupta, who was to investigate Buddhism, died before he could complete his treatise. Protap Chunder Mozoomdar, Keshub's most successful disciple, explored Unitarian Christianity.[68] In yet another publication, *India Asks—Who Is Christ?* (1879), Keshub highlights "the true Asiatic Christ, divested of all Western appendages . . . in his loose flowing garments, his dress and features altogether oriental, a perfect Asiatic in everything." Christ's doctrine "is essentially a Hindu doctrine," and furthermore, "Christ is a true Yogi, and he will surely help us to realize our national ideal of a Yogi."[69] Noting this indiscriminate eclecticism in Keshub's religion, evangelists such as J.F.B. Tinling would be dismayed, suggesting presciently that there would be "far more reason to expect Deism to reign in England than the Gospel to reign in India."[70] Meanwhile, the Unitarian minister Charles Dall had become "the first Christian and Caucasian to join a progressive, reforming and nationalist-oriented 'Hindu' movement."[71] Indeed, around the same time as Keshub was mining western techniques of proselytization for his new religion, the Salvation Army in Bombay was going native. Frederick Booth-Tucker, the founder of the Indian chapter of the Salvation Army, called himself Fakir Singh, his organization Mukti Fauj (Liberation Army), and dressed himself as a Hindu holy man with saffron-colored clothes and headgear, even as his wife wore a sari.[72]

In addition to all this Christian-Hindu syncretism, there was considerable exchange between neotraditional Hinduism and the Brahmos. Keshub had met Ramakrishna, then a relatively unknown but mystical priest in the Kali temple in Dakshineswar in 1875, and both holy men considerably influenced each other. Ramakrishna, even though of the Brahman caste, was an illiterate mystic from a humble social background, whereas Keshub, even as he admired Ramakrishna's inner realization of religious universalism (including Islam, Christianity, and Hinduism) gained the latter considerable social acceptance with the supercilious Bengali *bhadralok*. Ramakrishna's most important pupil, Narendranath Datta (later Swami Vivekananda) started off as a Sadharan Brahmo before he became the principal disciple of the sage of Dakshineswar. Like Ramakrishna, Keshub was also partial to maternal notions of deity. Their mutual intimacy (and to some degree, collusive credentialization) has led to schismatic recriminations subsequently. Max Müller suggested in his biography of Ramakrishna that the idea for the New Dispensation was taken by Keshub from the sage, a charge strenuously denied by the Keshubites. As Keshub's prominent disciple Protap Chunder Mozoomdar put it, "[W]hat is there in common between him [Ramakrishna] and me? I a Europeanized, civilized, self-centred, semi-sceptical, so-called educated reasoner, and he a poor, illiterate, shrunken, unpolished, diseased, half-dressed, half-idolatrous, friendless Hindu devotee?"[73]

However, just as Keshubite universalism was a tributary that took a different direction from the mainstream Brahmo nationalism that had developed after Rammohun's death, Keshub's death again resulted in a number of factional outcomes. Protap Chunder Mozoomdar remained especially taken with Christianity in an Asian frame, writing texts such as *The Oriental Christ* (1883) and *The World's Religious Debt to Asia* (1894), both indebted to Keshub's earlier forays in this area.[74] Mozoomdar had preached many times to anglophone Indians with Keshub when he was alive, and especially became known for his theolinguistic eloquence in the colonizer's language, impressing English Parliamentarians and also delivering the Lowell Lectures in Massachusetts. But in Mozoomdar's case, there were also fresh cosmopolitan winds blowing from the direction of Theosophy. Continuing in the vein of Hindu-Christian synthesis using techniques of comparative religion after Keshub's death, Mozoomdar would argue that, "the Old Testament corresponds to the Vedas, the Gospel to the Puranas, and the Epistles of St. Paul to the Upanishads. But Christianity in the Old and New Testaments has mainly the dispensation of the Father and the dispensation of the Son, scarcely anything that can be called the dispensation of the Spirit. When the last finds adequate record, the analogy between the Hindu and Christian schemes will become complete."[75] Very similar sentiments had been expressed a century earlier by John Zephaniah Holwell, except now a native pronounced these sentiments with due authority in the language of the colonial power.

This particular moment is also notable for the interesting fraud perpetrated by Nicolas Notovich, a Russian who generated considerable attention with his publication of *The Unknown Life of Jesus Christ*. The book argued that Christ had spent sixteen years (from the ages of thirteen to twenty-nine) in Kashmir, where Notovich claimed to have found a chronicle of this secret life, called "The Life of St. Issa," at a Tibetan Buddhist monastery.[76] Meanwhile, Mozoomdar took his syncretic teachings several times to the United States in order to argue that "Universal Wisdom is like unto itself everywhere," a trip that both Rammohun and Keshub anticipated taking but could not.[77] Received in Emerson's house, and having preached several times in Boston and at events such as the Social Science Congress at Saratoga Springs, Mozoomdar begins to appreciate the manner in which he was being treated as an Eastern guru for a Western audience. This entry from his diary, written in 1883, marks a significant early moment of self-recognition by a practitioner of Guru English:

How solitary, friendless and wretched when I arrived! I was a beggar of every man's freakful bounty, and felt fortunate if any one lifted up his countenance to me with an occasional smile. Today I am a celebrated man in America. This change in a little over one month. Every one pays his homage to me, courts my services, entreats me to speak that he might hear. The most prominent men, ex-governors, Presidents of universities, merchants, leading ministers give me an enthusiastic public reception. They are enchanted with my speech which I sincerely despise. Every newspaper praises "the Indian Teacher." They publish my books, apply to me for articles, it is lionizing run mad. And amidst this universal deluge of sugar plums, how feel you my friend Protap Chunder Mozoomdar? Are you convinced thou art a great man, indeed an unrecognized Sakya Muni [Buddha], a mute inglorious St. Paul? Poor, poor fellow![78]

Autobiographical self-dramatization, uncertainty, and a poignant and doubting self-reflexivity end Mozoomdar's rumination along with an opportunistic acceptance of the guru's social aggrandizement amidst an alien and gullible people. The synthesis of Hindu and Christian Unitarian impulses could undergo many generational permutations. Keshubite universalism was, nonetheless, to continue as a Brahmo quest all the way to Rabindranath Tagore, and his particular brand of romantic universalism was enshrined in the Viswabharati University in Santiniketan, which Tagore founded in response to the Brahmo ideals inherited from his family patriarchs. Rabindranath was a third-generation Brahmo founder (after grandfather Dwarkanath and father Debendranath), and he had to contend with a more polarized religious ethos. In the interim between Keshub's and Rabindranath's time, the *bhadralok* had been taken by storm by revivalists such as Bankim and Vivekananda. Rabindranath's resolute refusal to become a nationalist and his continued faith in cosmopolitanism kept one wing of the Brahmo religion alive, but times had also changed considerably.

VEDANTA AND YOGA

Held in Chicago in 1893 in commemoration of the quadricentennial anniversary of Columbus's voyage to America, the World Parliament of Religions was the first occasion when multiple Indian religious leaders were showcased simultaneously in a Euro-American location. The great attention gained by Ramakrishna Paramahansa's disciple Swami Vivekananda shot him into prominence both in India and elsewhere and resulted in the establishment of the Ramakrishna-Vedanta movement in the United States as well as in other countries. The story of

Vivekananda, who arrived at the Parliament uninvited and early, who was without resources and slept rough by the railway tracks for a month in anticipation of the congress, and who then took the assembled throng of six thousand by storm with his fiery oratory, became legendary. Speaking several times, Vivekananda also delivered a substantial paper on Hinduism in which he identified it, along with Judaism and Zoroastrianism as one of three prehistoric world religions that had survived in living practice. With pride, Vivekananda told the assembly that the Vedas were "the accumulated treasury of spiritual laws," and that "the discoverers of these laws are called Rishis." While Indians "honour [Rishis] as perfected beings," he was "glad to tell [his audience] that some of the very greatest of them were women." Succinctly explaining the mortality of the body, the eternal changeability of matter, the eternity of the soul, and the doctrines of transmigration and karma, Vivekananda propounded the "infinite universal individuality" of Advaita as the essence of Hinduism. Marshaling modern science in favor of Hindu religious doctrine as many practitioners would do later, Vivekananda declared, "[S]cience has proved to me that physical individuality is a delusion, that really my body is one little continuously changing body in an unbroken ocean of matter; and Advaita [nonduality] is the necessary conclusion with my other counterpart, soul."[79]

Other exponents of South Asian religion also presented papers, including Nara Sima Charyar (Narasimhachari), S. Parthasarathy Ayyangar, and Mani Lal Dwivedi, whom we can call "Hindus"; Virchand R. Gandhi, a Jain; Protap Chunder Mozoomdar, the Christianized Brahmo just discussed; Jeanne Sorabji, a Christian convert who nevertheless read a paper on Zoroastrianism; Alexander Russell "Mohammed" Webb, a Muslim and former Theosophist; and G. N. Chakravarti, a practicing Theosophist. Annie Besant attended the sessions but did not participate.[80]

Vivekananda's inception of "practical Vedanta" over two very long trips to the United States in the 1890s was most lastingly successful. He founded a Vedanta Society in San Francisco and a Shanti Ashrama (peace retreat). Returning home from his first trip only in 1897, he conducted a whirlwind speaking tour throughout India, and a number of English-language journals with an eye to foreign as well as domestic subscribers were launched. For instance, the *Brahmavadin*, calling itself "[A] Fortnightly Religious and Philosophical Journal started under the advice of Swami Vivekananda," publicized endorsements from Babu Pramada Dasa Mitra of Banaras as well as Max Müller. The *Prabuddha Bharata, or Awakened India* sounded an identical note of inspiration, with an endorsement from Annie Besant, just as its objective was "to present the truths of the Hindu Religion and the Vedanta in a simple and homely style, illustrating them by means of Puranic stories, philosophical tales and novels, and by the lives of great saints and sages." This periodical was a sophisticated theolinguistic organ, featuring stories of Vivekananda's missionary work, even as it retailed advertisements for photographs of spiritual leaders, "Hindu" timepieces, and books on Indian religion. In addition, advertisements in the journal hawked panaceas, special treatments, elixirs, and pomatums.

Vivekananda was subject to mass adulation in the subcontinent after newspapers reported his phenomenal success at Chicago. Upon his triumphal return to South Asia, his visit to Ceylon was greeted by tumultuous crowds. A typical admirer, A. Kulaveerasingham, praised him for having "proclaimed to the nations of Europe and America the Hindu ideal of a universal religion, harmonizing all creeds," and Vivekananda in response racialized religion as the Hindu's special contribution to the world. From Ramanathapuram in southern India, another admirer stated: "we have watched with feelings of genuine pride and pleasure the unprecedented success which has crowned your laudable efforts in bringing home to the master-minds of the West the intrinsic merits and excellence of our time-honored and noble religion. You have, with an eloquence that is unsurpassed and in language plain and unmistakable proclaimed to and convinced the cultured audiences in Europe and America that Hinduism fulfills all the requirements of the ideal of a universal religion and adapts itself to the temperament and needs of men and women of all races and creeds."[81] The following paragraph from Vivekananda's speech in Colombo demonstrates the close fit between cosmopolitan universalism and a racial essentialism of different cultures—each playing a designated role—at this late Victorian moment:

Each race, similarly, has a peculiar bent, each race has a peculiar *raison d'être*, each race has a peculiar mission to fulfill in the life of the world. . . . Political greatness or military power, is never the mission of our race; it never was, and, mark my words, never will be. But there has been the other mission given to us, to conserve, to preserve, to accumulate, as it were, into a dynamo, all the spiritual energy of the race, and that concentrated energy is to pour forth in a deluge on the world whenever circumstances are propitious. Let the Persian or the Greek, or the Roman, or the Arab, or the Englishman march his battalions, conquer the world, and link the different nations together, and the philosophy and spirituality of India is ready to flow along the new-made channels into the veins of the nations of the world. The calm Hindu's brain must pour out its own quota to give to the sum total of human progress. India's gift to the world is the light spiritual.[82]

To suggest that historical empires were only preparatory ditch-diggers for Indian spiritual currents to flow through these channels was a rhetorical masterstroke. While national revival was important for him, Vivekananda spoke often about India's reverse conquest of the world by the subtle message of Vedanta. Ecumenical and almost Unitarian during his sojourn in the United States, Vivekananda demonstrated chauvinist colors on his return to South Asia. In another speech he posits with scanty evidence that "before Buddhism, Vedanta had penetrated into China, into Persia, and Islands of the Eastern Archipelago," and that "Christianity, with all its boasted civilisation is but a collection of little bits of Indian thought. Ours is the religion of which Buddhism with all its greatness is a rebel child, and of which Christianity is a very patchy imitation."[83]

On home territory, he also began to attack Brahmos and Theosophists. As he continues to drive home in the same speech, "when the sledge-hammer blows of modern antiquarian researches are pulverizing like masses of porcelain all sorts of antiquated orthodoxies . . . here comes the philosophy of *India*, the highest religious aspirations of the Indian mind where the grandest philosophical facts have been the practical spirituality of the people."[84] The combination of organic and industrial imagery in Vivekananda's speeches posed no contradiction, but mirrored Romantic syntheses that proclaimed that India could have the fruits of scientific modernity and religious renaissance. Vivekananda would recommend abandoning the term "Hindu" for "Veidik" or "Vedantist." While great men in other countries took pride in being descendants of robber barons (a hit at the feudal lineages of Europe), according to Vivekananda, Hindus prided themselves as the descendants of religious sages, underscoring the moral superiority of Hindus to others. From this point of view, Christianity was spiritually emaciated, a sorry echo of a much greater and nobler Vedanta. At the same time, Vivekananda, a lover of beef, would advocate a muscular Hinduism that could combat its Christian counterpart only by carnivorous nourishment, which would mean giving up millennia-long vegetarian taboos among the upper castes and the religiously inclined for red-blooded self-assertion. Unlike many traditionalists who abandoned the spiritual status of those who converted to other religions as irreversible, Vivekananda openly advocated the reconversion of Hindus who had been converted to Christianity and Islam, including the descendants of earlier converts. Vivekananda was also attentive to new technologies of transmission, making a little speech into a phonograph, in which he emphasized the need for Shakti worship in India. In 1898, Vivekananda again left for missionary work in England and the United States, during which time he attended another Congress of

Religions in Paris in 1900. However, his health failed soon thereafter: he died in 1902, at the relatively young age of thirty-nine.

Even while these examples show the nationalist strain of Vivekananda's Vedantism within an Indian context, one should not forget that there was a parallel cosmopolitan strain that took on a different cast in the North American environment. As Carl T. Jackson suggests, the Ramakrishna-Vedanta movement was the first Hindu organization to establish itself lastingly on American soil. Its success results from religious flexibility revealed alongside organizational adeptness, whereby authority was negotiated and divided between local devotees and the headquarters at Belur, near Calcutta. Much oscillation took place on questions of message (for instance, whether to promote the abstract religious philosophy of Vedanta or the personal cult of Ramakrishna), and strategies for raising money were carefully developed. Jackson's scholarship confirms that the Ramakrishna Mission was one of the first neo-Advaitin movements based in the United States that used a number of newer techniques for garnering followers by combining personal instruction, newspaper advertisements, regular religious services, and the sale of devotional and religious literature to gain prominence.[85]

Romain Rolland had corresponded extensively with Sigmund Freud about the mystical "oceanic feeling" that he found remarkable about the psychic state of Ramakrishna, and Freud incorporated aspects of this exchange in his *Civilization and Its Discontents* even as he disputed whether such feeling was possible in modern times. In effect, the efforts of many practitioners of neo-Advaitin Guru English would be to argue that the mystical revelation of universal nonduality was entirely possible, even in modern times, to the dedicated spiritual seeker.[86] While this study does not provide a full reception history of Vedantic theolinguistics into the twentieth century, it is important to recognize that the Ramakrishna movement gained even greater prominence in the Hollywood era, when British writers such as Aldous Huxley, Gerald Heard, and Christopher Isherwood were associated with a monk of the Ramakrishna Order, Swami Prabhavananda. Living with the swami as a novitiate in his small religious commune for several years, Isherwood assisted him with translations of the Bhagavadgītā, Sankara's *Vivekachūdāmaṇi*, and some of the Upanishads, and even nearly became a monk of the order. According to a contemporary account about Isherwood in *Time* magazine,

three times each day Isherwood repairs to the temple, sits cross-legged between grey-green walls on which are hung pictures of Krishna, Jesus, Buddha, Confucius, other great religious teachers. The swami sits bareheaded, wearing a long, bright yellow robe that sweeps the floor. He too sits cross-legged, pulling a shawl around him, and for ten minutes meditates in silence. Then in a ringing bass he chants a Sanskrit invocation, repeats it in English, ending with the words, "Peace, Peace, Peace!" This dispassionate ceremony is the ritual of a mystical order of which slight, agreeable, cigaret-smoking Swami Prabhavananda is the Los Angeles leader.... Larry, the dissatisfied young hero of Somerset Maugham's current best-selling novel, *The Razor's Edge*, whose search for faith ended in Vedanta, is said to be modeled on Isherwood.

That Larry was based on Isherwood was a rumor subsequently denied by the author and the supposed model. However, the rumor began precisely because the relationship between the hero and Shri Ganesha, the holy man in the novel, seemed generally reminiscent of that between Isherwood and Prabhavananda. Isherwood, who wrote a fascinating memoir of his tutelage under Prabhavananda entitled, *My Guru and His Disciple*, also documents having given Maugham advice regarding the epigraph and the title to his novel, which was based on a translation of a verse from the Katha Upanishad that likened the difficult road to salvation to walking on a razor-sharp edge.[87]

While the Ramakrishna Mission showed the expansion of middle-class reform Hinduism in India and held considerable appeal for intellectuals and religious seekers abroad, it was but the first of several movements that formed the next phase of Guru English's global glut. Hindu "missions" in the West were sometimes experiments that adapted themselves very differently to their environment from their Christian evangelical equivalents in India. Proselytization was often subtler, as much of the emphasis was on communitarian living with the serious adherents mingling with the casually curious. As Isherwood relates, Prabhavananda's communal experiment was reined in subsequently by increasing interference from the headquarters in India.

At about the same time as Prabhavananda and other Ramakrishna monks were expanding the Vedanta Societies set up by Vivekananda, an independent guru named Paramhansa Yogananda achieved a phenomenal success in the United States with his pitch for a rejuvenating physiological technique named *kriya yoga*. The teachings of the creed, Yogoda, advised adherents to use mental concentration in order to resuscitate *prāṇa* or life-force ("life-trons") in the medulla oblongata, counseled "mental responsibility for chronic diseases," and proclaimed (perhaps very significantly so for the American context) that the technique "PUTS ON OR TAKES OFF FAT, JUST AS YOU DESIRE."[88] Yogoda, like many new creeds, sought to harmonize science and religion, and attempted to link a scientific meditation with a divine communion. Yogananda's message appears doctrinally ecumenical, with features that subordinate different aspects of Christianity as well as Sankhya, in the manner of many Brahmo universalists in the previous century. Kriya yoga was "a simple psychophysiological method by which human blood is decarbonized and charged with oxygen." Claiming that "Elijah, Jesus, Kabir and other prophets were past masters in the use of *Kriya*," Yogananda enthusiastically adds a variety of previous adepts to the list, from theologian Patanjali to Saint John and Saint Paul. A half-minute of kriya equaled one year of natural spiritual unfoldment. Therefore it was counseled that kriya was an opportunity worth seizing, in order to abandon the bullock cart vehicle of Western theological paths to God for the Hindu equivalent of the aeroplane—surely a fitting ironic reversal of the perception of India as a technologically backward and historically underdeveloped culture.[89]

Yogananda reached lasting popular fame with his best-selling *Autobiography of a Yogi*, first published in 1946. This personal memoir has probably done more than any single work to titillate postwar generations of Americans and Europeans with an account of the enduring spiritual mysteries of the East. Yogananda's personal history involves a colorful description of spiritual tutelage under an Indian teacher, Sri Yukteswar Giri, who was himself a disciple of another preceptor, Lahiri Mahasaya. Lahiri Mahasaya was the direct disciple of the living legend, Babaji, "a Yogi-Christ of Modern India" who appeared to inhabit a body of about the age twenty-five, but whose actual age was indeterminate (but probably over a thousand years), and who could materialize and dematerialize himself at will to his disciples. Babaji "is in constant communion with Christ; together they send out vibrations of redemption and have planned the spiritual technique of salvation for this age."[90] Yogananda was advised by his guru to attend college as he anticipated his disciple's mission to the West, whose people "will be more receptive to India's ancient wisdom if the strange Hindu teacher has a university degree." The West is praised for its progress, hygiene, and scientific advancement, even as India earned higher marks for its religious ideals and spiritual accomplishments.[91]

As autobiographies go, Yogananda's is eminently readable. Deftly putting aside literary expectations with the claim that "a discerning placement of the comma does not atone for a spiritual coma," Yogananda brings a refreshing degree of self-deprecation and lightness of tone to his command of Guru English as register.[92] This candor makes the spiritual mysteries being rendered along the way all that much more incredible. India being a country where "spiritual 'skyscrapers' may occasionally be encountered by the wayside," Yogananda took it upon himself to take accounts of these encounters to the land of actual skyscrapers.[93] Guru English's rhetorical adaptability in the phrases of

Vivekananda and Yogananda makes it shift gears from specific register to generalized discourse.

The single most memorable feature of Yogananda's autobiography is a repetitive insistence on collocating the miraculous and the quotidian. Yogananda assures his reader that anyone ought to understand, in the footsteps of Einstein, that "the law of miracles is operable by any man who has realized that the essence of creation is light."[94] The reader is entertained with an account of something like a miracle a page—involving telepathy, astral travel, levitation, wrestling successfully with tigers, drinking poison without harm, living underwater, materialization, and dematerialization. Other forms of miracle-work described in the book include psychic forms of telepathy, telephony, telegraphy, radio, and television. Not content with ordinary mind reading, the author includes anecdotes of making the blind see, the remote repulsion of mosquitoes, and the manipulation of others' actions through remote willpower. The reader also hears about the magical rejoining of severed limbs, perfumes being generated at demand, and seers who could maintain perpetual sleeplessness and also live perpetually without food. The book documents predictions by sages who accurately forecast their own death and that of others. Still other miracle-men cure the fatally ill and metaphysically transfer disease from one body to another. We are told about bodies that don't decay once they have died and bodies that are reported to appear in two different places at the same time, as well as the discovery of a reincarnated soul "through the microphone of the spiritual eye . . . using upraised hands and fingers as antennae."[95] The autobiography is actually an eclectic directory of sorts that might be dubbed a hitchhiker's guide to the paranormal galaxy. The reader is taken through brief encounters with a number of different gurus, with Yogananda efficiently cutting to the chase by discussing the most significant wonder-working occurrences that involved each of them. Taking these claims much further through aggressive marketing of kriya yoga by way of the organizing skills of individual chapters of the Yogoda Satsang and Self-Realization Fellowship, Yogananda worked the mass media and produced testimonials of miracle-work and magical healing. Yogoda, he claimed, would become the bombproof shelter for the human mind in the Atomic Age. A North American follower, Donald Walters (later Swami Kriyananda), also produced a well-written *Autobiography of a Western Yogi* in imitation of Yogananda.[96]

The guru would also attempt some literary criticism along the way, even if it almost always took the form of tendentious allegorical readings. The story of Adam and Eve and the serpent in the Garden of Eden could be understood in terms of the yogic concept of *kundalini*: "the 'serpent' represents the coiled-up spinal energy that stimulates the sex nerves. 'Adam' is reason, and 'Eve' is feeling. When the emotion or Eve-consciousness in any human being is overpowered by the sex impulse, his reason or Adam also succumbs."[97] At another point, Satan is interpreted according to the doctrine of *māyā*, and John the Baptist is deemed to be Christ's guru in a past life.[98] Yogananda also worked on a full-length reinterpretation of *The Rubaiyat of Omar Khayyam*, purporting to show the deeper religious meaning that was hidden behind the hedonistic surface of the Sufi poem. This approach is often heavy-handed in the extreme. Take, for instance, the first verse of Fitzgerald's famous translation:

> AWAKE! for Morning in the Bowl of Night
> Has flung the Stone that Puts the Stars to Flight:
> And lo! The Hunter of the East has caught
> The Sultan's Turret in a Noose of Light.

Yogananda's rendition takes the following structure:

Thus sang the inner Silence:

"Forsake your sleep of ignorance: Awake!

"For the dawn of wisdom has flung into the dark bowl of your unknown the stone of spiritual discipline—that weapon of divine power that can break the bowl and put to flight the paling stars of earthly desire.

"Behold, Wisdom—'the Hunter of the East'—has cast a noose of light to encircle the kingly minaret of your egoic pride: wisdom to free you at last from the long night of spiritual ignorance!"

And in like fashion, Yogananda produces a complete re-creation of Fitzgerald's poem as a tortuous prose allegory. Guru English is the register that allows the reader to make sense of what is otherwise an endless and uninspired shadow-commentary. Lovers of the Fitzgerald transcreation would find that Yogananda's arbitrary and tangential literalizations of allegory make a mockery of the delicate tracework of Sufi esotericism visible throughout the poem. Some might argue, however, that Fitzgerald's transcreation of the original was perhaps a more pleasing distortion of the Persian original, but no less a distortion than the botching of Fitzgerald by Yogananda.[99]

In retrospect, it is easier to see how these kinds of translation techniques—whether literary, religious, or philosophical—eventually led to the huge expansion of a number of cosmopolitan, comparative, and theolinguistic discourses in the twentieth century. There are at least two other Yoganandas who entered Guru English, unrelated to the founder of the Self-Realization Fellowship. There was Yogananda Saraswati, propounder of the doctrine of Adwaita Brahma Shidhi, who preceded him and preached that "one common religion of love and service based not on dogmas nor even on scriptures but on the universal spiritual experiences of the human race, will, ere long, be the meeting-ground of East and West." This Yogananda also argues that "from wireless telegraphy to thought communication is but a step."[100]

The last chapter in this book examines several post-1965 gurus who update older patterns of synthesis, propagation, and dissemination. Started by the orientalists, continued by Brahmos, and the first Western-oriented exponents of Vedanta and yoga, different techniques of direct marketing, word-of-mouth endorsement, and product testing made, and will continue to make Guru English into an especially persuasive form of rhetoric. While the Brahmos, Vedantists, and the Theosophists commenced Guru English on its course in the nineteenth century, the real guru glut and its saturation of global media can perhaps be related to the relaxation of U.S. immigration laws in 1965, and the parallel phenomena of increased international air travel, migration, and globalization. Several other factors would contribute, including the rise of late Romantic nationalism and the grand syncretism of Theosophy (as well as its skeptical debunking by others). Anglophone gurus would rise apace, even as new perceptions of technology and contemporary forms of media changed the objective, the message, and even the ontology of the discourse. Eventually culminating as the most recognizable form of South Asian cosmopolitanism, Guru English still has to be tracked through a number of noticeable transformations in the intermediary chapters before I can return to the banal levels of recognition it enjoys in the contemporary moment.

CHAPTER TWO

From Indian Romanticism to Guru Literature

> As a drop draws to water, so my Soul drew near to the Great
> Soul which is beyond all things. At that point, exalted in con-
> templation, I saw all Hind, from Ceylon in the sea to the Hills,
> and my own Painted Rocks at Such-zen; I saw every camp and
> village, to the least, where we have ever rested. I saw them at
> one time and in one place; for they were within the Soul. By
> this I knew the Soul had passed beyond the illusion of Time
> and Space and of Things. By this I knew that I was free.
>
> —Rudyard Kipling, *Kim*

INDIAN ROMANTICISM was the product of European intellectual diffusion, even as it also signaled prospective metaphysical futures. When
related to its European precursors, is this late Romantic strain in colonial India an echo? a copy? a supplement? a displacement? a fantasized
influence? a catachresis? If the late eighteenth century in Europe generated long-lived species of Romanticism that have subsequently billowed
outward into numerous afterlives, what remains outside this family of
Romanticisms? Dead classicisms? Liberal individualisms of various
sorts? Industrial capitalism anchored in a variety of alternative modernities? The anachronistic continuation of Romanticism beyond the so-
called Romantic Age is matched by its anatopian spread outside the
confines of a western European origin into eastern European, and also
tricontinental venues.[1]

Romanticism in a late-capitalist age has benefited from the retroactive
effect of a Freudian *Nachträglichkeit* or "deferred action," belatedly appearing as the representative of many other forms of organicism, local-
ism, and communitarianism. Through transcoding, Romanticism is the
trademark name for appeals to identity, community, and history. Its multiple versions result from an ex post facto positioning in cultural memory rather than as products of documentable influence. Romanticism as
lingua franca is therefore the outcome of a secret history of mergers and
acquisitions. By way of a translational hybridity, local historicisms resort
to the modular theory of Romanticism as a universal solvent. Grouping
all these variants under the universalizing umbrella of Romanticism
structures each of them as part of an open totality. Romanticism as an

explanation speaks to the vacuity and inexactness of the form as paradoxical evidence of the potency of the presumed "contents."[2]

Lacking a life of its own, Indian Romanticism was a graft onto the already hybrid trunk of British colonialism. It was obstructed by some
forces and enabled by others. The triumph of the anglicists and utilitarians such as Thomas Babington Macaulay and John Stuart Mill over
starry-eyed first-generation orientalists such as William Jones, Henry
Colebrooke, Thomas Charles Wilkins, and Nathaniel Brassy Halhed
was nonetheless countered by German Romantic representations of India
in a positive light that Ronald Inden has called "the loyal Opposition."[3]
German Romanticism took up the project of orientalism and deepened
it with enduring legacies such as the Aryan myth. The philological first
stages, discussed in the previous chapter, were followed by linguistic
research that established the idea of Indo-European origins that connected Europe and Asia. Johann Gottfried Herder, Friedrich Schlegel,
Friedrich Wilhelm Schelling, Arthur Schopenhauer, and Friedrich Max
Müller variously idealized what they recognized as the ancient fount
of Indo-European wisdom through their encounter with translations of
ancient Sanskrit texts (even if there was also debate generated among
German Romanticists by Hegel's downgrading of India). Abraham-
Hyacinthe Anquetil-Duperron, the translator of the quirky *Oupnek'hat*
(itself a translation of Dara Shukoh's partial translation of the Upanishads into Persian) would set the tone for many of the German idealists
by claiming that "anyone who carefully examines the lines of Immanuel
Kant's thought, its principles as well as its results, will recognize that it
does not deviate very far from the teachings of the Brahmins, which
lead man back to himself and comprise and focus him within himself."[4] Romantic interpretations of pantheistic monism and mysticism
would also help propel the abstract philosophy of Advaita Vedanta
into the position of prime representative of the construct called "Hinduism." The extended result of this operation was the prosthetic limb
of the Bengal Renaissance that would twitch in response to a long-
distance Romantically inspired language, generating the reformative
religious vocabularies that would later be variously named "neo-
Hinduism," "semitized Hinduism," "universal Hinduism," and "syndicated Hinduism."[5]

Therefore, anticolonial nationalism in India enacts a species of Romanticism that has been described by Partha Chatterjee as "a derivative
discourse" in the nationalist context, one that never altered the fundamental "thematic" of ascribing cultural essences to India and the West.
Arising within a "problematic" of Romantic orientalism that portrayed
the native as a stereotype, a residual essence, and a negative foil to

European domination, nationalist self-assertion took the form of a meticulous reversal of the orientalist-anglicist double hypothesis. Where the anglicist British colonizers saw native laziness and degeneration, the Indian nationalists saw the spiritual contemplativeness and renascent subjectivity seen by earlier orientalist forebears. The charge of native effeminacy was countered by the nationalists' embrace of androgyny and remasculinization. In addition, indigenous cultural resources were marshaled in favor of a recombinant neotraditionalism. First-wave positive orientalism was reclaimed and extended in a manner to refute dismissive judgments of Indian cultural competence and morality. But all this reassertion at the level of the problematic, as Chatterjee rightly points out, did not upset the belief in the underlying thematic of Romantic orientalism affirming the existence of cultural essences and civilizational norms and tendencies.[6] Simple reinterpretation of specific attributes—putting a plus sign where the colonialist had put a minus sign—did not unsettle the assumptions of the discourse, that there was a difference waiting to be elaborated, and that this difference is what testified to that central Romantic hypothesis that James Chandler has called, after Claude Lévi-Strauss, "the historiographical-ethnographic correlation."[7] The colonialist mapped a history onto a people, and the self-appointed representatives of the people responded by revising the values assigned to the interpretation without contesting the stability of the object of representation. One could call this species of Romanticism reactive, reassertive, or interpellational. A discursive "shifter," initiated by the colonial language, jogs a newly created subject into uttering a sentence that communicates more about the discourse of the precedent utterance than about local differences. That is the nature of a derivative discourse and exemplifies modular or mimetic Romanticism in a colonial strain. This does not mean that "religion" did not exist outside the colonial construction, but rather, that the framework of its apprehension altered its trajectory.

While some of the best-known lives—and afterlives—of Romanticism have incarnated in the guise of cultural nationalism, language essentialism, and the ideal of organic intimacy among the members of the chosen community, in this chapter I trace the manner in which Indian Romanticism does not just produce the expected form. In addition to transcoding universal Hinduism, Romanticism generates a religious cosmopolitanism in the outsider's language, one that would normally be rejected as a mere add-on and indeed attacked as illegitimate by various positions deemed Romantic and neo-Romantic. Constituting an anomaly, and therefore vulnerable to rejection, the cosmopolitan strain of Indian Romanticism comes alive through a series of transidiomatic practices, both hyper-Romantic and insufficiently Romantic, making it-self a type of language production identifiable as Guru English.

The colonial framework of Romanticism's application to India was imposed extraneously—saturated as the context was with the neces-sary ideology of English education as conceptualized by Macaulay's famous "filtration" theory. To this idea, the Schillerian project of aes-thetic education—that promises to make good on the Kantian impera-tive by democratic outreach—was simultaneously extended and also compromised by the inescapable bifurcation of the organic ensemble of Indianness. Unlike the folkloric or the ethnopopular that could be ap-pealed to by the middle class and then radicalized by popular support, as in the classic model of eastern European cultural nationalism, the multiple dimensionalities and fractures of the ethnoreligious identities in South Asia by religion, region, language, and caste—as well as the exteriority of the prestige culture of Englishness—made Romanticism a source of middle-class aspiration without the prospect of unmedi-ated popular identification.[8] Yet, if this situation was compromised by the fractured nature of the socio-intellectual field, the belief in organ-ism was more actualizable in practice than a theoretical understanding would allow. While others have examined the fuller profile of Indian Romanticism as a movement, this chapter focuses on one of the other accretions on that structure, as an artificial limb that could paradoxi-cally be said to have a more vibrant afterlife than the organism. Guru English is intimately linked to the afterlife of the colonial logic of late Romanticism. Not just perpetuating Romantic vacuity, Guru English rephrases the terms of nationalist discourse as a cosmopolitan supple-ment in excess of functionalist interpretations about its governmental-ity. This supplement will reveal itself to be commodifiable and ex-portable later in the century.[9]

From the beginning, English education acquires a life of its own, gener-ating alternative varieties of orientalism but also, this time, newer forms of subjectivity; Guru English, the offspring of English education and religious rediscovery, makes for new charlatanries and controversies but also newer syncretisms and continuities. While considerable de-bate continues between the primordialists and the constructionists re-garding the manner and moment of the communalization of modern India, Guru English arises precisely out of the ambivalence identified by this debate and correspondingly enjoys its multifaceted interpretive richness.

In the first section of the discussion that follows, I consider the Ben-gali novelist Bankimchandra Chatterjee's call for a renovated Indian subjectivity that endorses English as the language of objectivity. This crude separation of subject and object creates a nationalist subject who is expected to negotiate between two distinct spheres. But Bankim's innovation also recasts colonized religion within modernity. If Guru English had not existed already to some degree, it is launched fully armed as an indirect consequence of Bankim's belief in nationalist modernity. Rudyard Kipling's late-guard apologia for empire, chronologically after Bankim's, has often been interpreted as uninterested in the alterity of the native. However, there are peripheral recognitions of spiritual alterity and charlatanry in Kipling's work uncompromised by imperial commitments. Kipling can ventriloquize Hinduism and Buddhism and modernize their metaphysics effortlessly, even if his sympathies admittedly tend toward voicing familiar imperial themes. Sri Aurobindo, an inheritor of Bankim's vocabulary, subjects Guru English to further mystical transformations. As spiritual leader as well as literary aficionado, Aurobindo makes offbeat and futuristic contributions to Guru English. Aurobindo, as pre-independence India's premier anglophone guru, heralds many of the developments in the subsequent discourse. This futuristic angle will especially be on display throughout, in terms of the mixture of objective science and the religion of spirit in Bankim's rhetoric, the confusion between intelligence-gathering and metaphysical liberation in Kipling's fiction, and the fusion of "overhead" poetry and spiritual anticipation in Aurobindo's predictions of a coming age of supermen. Guru English emerges equally from Bankim's cryptic representations of heroic opposition, Kipling's renditions of imperial bureaucracy, and Aurobindo's plans for mystic fellowship. Like nationalism itself, Guru English is an ideology that implicates conservative, reactionary, and progressive, even as it takes into its sweep modernizers, imperialists, and revolutionaries.

BANKIM'S PROPHECY

In an essay, "The Confession of a Young Bengal," published in *Mookherjee's Magazine* in December 1872, Bankim observes in some detail how "English-educated Bengalis are rapidly getting Anglicized." "Our conversation is nine parts broken English, and one part pure Bengali. We have exchanged the cumbrous forms of Bengali epistolary correspondence for those of Cook's Universal Letter-Writer." This change in social appearance also registers a shift in mental attitude: "[O]ur Deism, our Theism, our Brahmoism, progressive or ultra-progressive, our Compteism [*sic*] . . . what are all these *isms* at bottom but merely so many different embodiments of a strong desire to exempt ourselves from the obligations of Hinduism?"[10] Bankim's concern about the religious deracination of his middle-class contemporaries is expressed elsewhere in terms of lively satire, and indeed self-parody, of the stereotype of the Bengali baboo. His flaying essay, entitled "Babu," describes the shallow and dissipated occupations of these representatives of the Bengali middle classes by parodic reference to the ten avatars of Vishnu:

> Like *Vishnu* they will be continually recumbent. Like *Vishnu* they too, will have ten incarnations—namely, clerk, tutor, Brahmo, commercial agent, doctor, lawyer, magistrate, zamindar, newspaper editor and idler. Like *Vishnu*, in all these incarnations they will slay powerful demons. The office-boy will be slain by the clerk, the students by the tutor, ticketless travellers by the station-master, the begging priest by the Brahmo, English traders by the agent, the sick by the doctor, the client by the lawyer, the plaintiff by the magistrate, the common man by the zamindar, the gentleman by the editor and the fish of the pond by the idler.[11]

Such ironizing of the baboo from the standpoint of Vishnu was indirectly generated by a colonial ideology that vilified the very class deliberately created by the colonizers. In keeping with Macaulay's dictum, imperial governance was enabled by an intermediary "class who may be interpreters between [the British] and the millions whom [they] govern; a class of persons, Indian in blood and colour, but English in taste, in opinions, in morals and in intellect."[12] However, the stereotypical effeteness and effeminacy of the Bengali baboo, whose languidness, according to Macaulay, came from living "in a constant vapour bath," while confirming orientalist disparagement of native degeneracy, was also a starting point for the incipient discourses of neo-Romantic nationalism. Bankim favored a code of self-cultivation, or *anuśīlan*, that would eventually lead in the direction of cultural, religious, and national regeneration.[13] The alienation of the elites was also occasion for their developing a new consciousness, and rediscovering traditions that they had abandoned in hedonistic pursuits and a slavish imitation of their colonial masters. One result was the consolidation of a religious identity deemed "Hindu," itself created out of a welter of overlapping but also noncongruent faiths and practices present in the territorial jurisdiction of the British Indian Empire. While Bankim had set his sights mainly on a rejuvenation of Bengali culture, the earlier preparation for Pan-Indian Hindu religious identity, created by European orientalist intervention and idealization, also played into the nationalist self-perceptions of his contemporaries. Furthermore, claiming to speak for Hinduism always had the possibility of generating a wider popular basis for nationalism, even if this national community had yet to be actualized.

Bankim as baboo, indeed "Bankim Babu," as he was called honorifically, fulfilled the expected tasks of a competent bureaucrat in the Bengal administrative hierarchy in a number of towns, where the job entailed inspection of facilities, adjudication of disputes, and the disbursement of state-sanctioned relief measures to the populace. In Khulna, he successfully tackled "the smallpox of piracy and the greater pox of Indigoism," according to Aurobindo, but ultimately fell afoul of two English superiors, who had him transferred to Jajpur in Orissa, from where he was recalled to Alipur and Hoogly.[14] Yet, as novelist and prose writer, he imaginatively defined Indian modernity, dueling his way through a number of religious controversies in order to suggest a doctrinal basis for a neo-Hindu nationalism. With the exception of a failed early novel written in English, *Rajmohan's Wife* (1864), Bankim wrote fourteen other novels in Bengali in addition to a range of pamphlets and other tracts in both Bengali and English. All the same, his highly crafted middle-class social romances had been translated into several major Indian languages (and English) by the late nineteenth century, with several works being subjected to multiple translations throughout the twentieth century. From regional novelist, Bankim rose to the status of Pan-Indian author.

Bankim's later political novel, *Anandamath* [Abbey of bliss] (1882) contributed significantly to the cultivation of nationalist sentiment after 1905. While the impact of *Anandamath* on the English-language novel has been deemed modest, this novel written in Bengali is an important progenitor of the nationalist version of Guru English. *Anandamath* is a peculiar political concoction, based on a willful reinterpretation of several episodes from colonial history. Known also as "Scott of Bengal" for his historical romances, Bankim clearly took something from *Old Mortality* for this implausible fantasy of martial monks engaging the government in military exchanges. *Anandamath* involves a group of renegade renunciates (self-styled *santhān*, or Children of the Motherland) battling British tax collectors and state militia with the goal of establishing self-rule in Bengal. Bankim's rendition of these politicized warrior-monks also owes something to the late-nineteenth-century European obsession with secret societies, ranging from the Freemasons to the French Jacobins to Mazzini's nationalist carbonaries who militated for the unification of Italy. This fascination with political secrecy had influenced late-nineteenth-century social organizations in Bengal as well.[15]

It is well known that in the novel Bankim transposed, conflated, and radically reimagined two different reactions to famine. The first involved the threat posed in 1768–70 by the "Sinassies, or wandering Fackeers" in Bengal to the Hastings government.[16] The other drew on a more recent trial involving Wasudeo Balwant Phadke—a militant rebel who dressed as a sannyasi and was known as Kashikar Baba—who had plotted to raise an army and loot the government treasury in

Khed. Phadke's aim was to relieve the populace in response to the 1876–77 famine in the provinces of western India, and his journal and autobiography were published in the *Bombay Gazette* during his highly publicized trial in 1879. And, of course, more than anything else, the novelistic revolt explored a counterfactual alternative to the history of the 1857 Sepoy Mutiny. What would it have felt like if the sepoys had overthrown British rule? A pre-Mutiny utopian novella in English by Koylash Chunder Dutt, entitled "A Journal of Forty-Eight Hours of the Year 1945," might have also influenced Bankim.[17]

The plot of *Anandamath* features the recruitment of a landowner, Mahendra Singha, for the nationalist cause. The self-styled Children [*santhān*] save him; his wife, Kalyani; and their daughter, Sukumari, from robbery in the midst of famine, and secrete the family away into safety even though Mahendra is misled into believing his wife and child are dead. The Children are under the command of Satyananda, a charismatic leader who disciplines his cohort by ironclad rules of personal comportment. All Children who join the cause are to renounce their family ties, abstain from sex and vice, and be willing to sacrifice their lives without notice. Satyananda's hypermasculine guerrilla army is penetrated by Shanti, the abandoned wife of one of his recruits in male disguise. Shanti demonstrates her martial prowess as a pure sublimation of her love for her husband, Jibananda, who is somewhat less successful in fighting his now-proscribed and therefore immoral passions for his wife. While Shanti, renamed Nabin, becomes one of Satyananda's most trusty lieutenants, Jibananda later loses his life in the final battle featured in the novel but is also miraculously revived at the close.

When *Anandamath* identifies the British as the enemy, it also singles out the feudal Muslim rulers of Bengal as collaborators of the British and, therefore, oppressors of the populace. Bankim's substitution of terms, edition by edition, partly to escape censorship by British colonial authorities has raised speculation (and there is evidence that his promotion was denied in response to one of the serialized episodes).[18] However, the fact that Muslims and British are substitutable for each other indicates the author's focalization on a militant Hindu nationalist subject. After the novel was first serialized in the monthly *Bangadarshan* in 1881–82, *rājā* in the first edition was replaced by *musalmān* in the fourth; *ingrez* (English) was replaced by *sepoy* in the second; and *sepoy* was replaced by *yaban* (a pejorative term for a Muslim as a foreigner) in the fourth. The first edition would also carry the ambivalent prefatory comment: "[R]evolutions are very generally processes of self-torture and rebels are suicides."[19] The novel's true nationalist impact did not occur immediately upon publication, but in 1905, when the

British proposed what turned out to be the highly unpopular partition of Bengal. At this point, nationalists seized upon the now famous song that one of the Children, Bhavananda, sings in *Anandamath*. Entitled "Bande Mataram," this composition subsequently became the famous musical correlative of Hindu/Indian nationalism and was also adopted (and later dropped in deference to Muslim objections) as the country's national anthem. The political controversy generated by this song continues, as it has been revived by some elements in the Hindu Right, even though the anthem was rerecorded in an updated and secularizing version for India's golden jubilee in 1997 by A. R. Rahman, an accomplished Bollywood composer who also happens to be of an Ismaili background.

One of the most evocative scenes in the novel takes place when Mahendra is taken to a hideout temple in the forest, a building architecturally reminiscent of religious periodization, according to one translation: "[A]rchaeologists could easily detect that it had first been a Buddhist *vihāra*, then a Hindu temple, and then a Mohammedan mosque."[20] Within this structure, Mahendra is shown several iconic images of India. After seeing an impressive tableau of Vishnu with his consort Lakshmi, the goddess Saraswati, and the decapitated heads of the demons Madhu and Kaitabha, Mahendra is puzzled at the marvelous form of a female figure lying on Vishnu's lap. He goes on to another room where he sees a richly ornamented image of *jagaddhātri*, or protectress of the world, also identified as mother of the Indian nation, as she was in the past. Following this vision, Mahendra is taken to a room housing the goddess of destruction, Kali, naked and garlanded with skulls, mother of the nation as she is then portrayed to be. The mother has assumed this malefic form given the ravaged nature of the country, which currently resembles a burial ground. After this frightening vision of the present, Mahendra visits a beautiful ten-armed golden goddess (Durga), placed in the middle of a marble temple. This is what the mother will become when the country is restored to its original grandeur.[21] Bankim's vision of the nation flirts with the shadow of a primordialist version favored by earlier orientalists but ultimately reveals this anteriority as an echo effect of its wholly modern form. According to Sudipta Kaviraj, "the elaborate form of the mother, the elaborate ritual, is simply a mediation of the collective self to itself" and ultimately reflects "a certain unprincipled use of Hinduism."[22] Of course, such "unprincipled" use was workaday neo-Romantic syncretism. There are other literary successors to this evocative scene denoting a site where the nation's essence can be discerned, or inversions, as for instance the Marabar Caves of E. M. Forster's *A Passage to India*, with their blank and atavistic echo. While refunctionalizations such as Forster's eventually displace the mythical origins of the Hindu nation into the realm of parody, Guru English shares the ambivalent origins suggested by Bankim. Atavistic rediscoveries of forgotten pasts jostle with modern reinventions of purportedly ancient wisdom.

As Kaviraj's supple reading of Bankim's historical novels suggests, "the fictional narrative is exactly the opposite of what [Georg] Lukács found in the European historical novel." Rather, "the point of these novels is precisely to 'falsify' history. They try deliberately to probe and use counterfactuals, to extend those lines in the tree of eventuation which were not actually followed up, [to] explore the peculiar terrain of history's nonactualized possibilities."[23] The orientalist affinity for conjectural history, discussed in the previous chapter, is continued through Bankim's Romantic speculations. However, Bankim's fiction of slain Englishmen is not pure fantasy, as a Captain Thomas and a Captain Edwardes were indeed killed in skirmishes of December 31, 1772, and March 1, 1773, respectively.[24] In his hands, however, the historical novel becomes utopian, and past and present facts of imperial subjection are gussied up into future imaginings of nationalist resurgence. High-nineteenth-century European realism does not seem to have affected Indian literary sensibilities: according to Meenakshi Mukherjee, the religious allegory of John Bunyan's *The Pilgrim's Progress*, as well as the moral philosophy represented by Samuel Johnson's *Rasselas* and Oliver Goldsmith's *The Vicar of Wakefield* were far more important in determining and satisfying aesthetic taste, as were popular romance writers such as G.M.W. Reynolds and Marie Corelli, who were less valued in Britain.[25]

Yet, what characterizes *Anandamath* is its immediate unsatisfactoriness even as wish fulfillment. At the culmination of the novel, after the Children have won the greatest battle and massacred the British-led opposition, Satyananda's dreams of political domination are shattered by the intervention of the mysterious *mahāpuruṣa* (or superman). Walking amongst the wounded and dying, the *mahāpuruṣa* performs the task of a physician on the battlefield. He magically resurrects the dead Jibananda. Holding Satyananda's hands, he suggests that the Children are better off conceding defeat in order to ensure that India has a still better future. Satyananda is therefore told to surrender and disband his holy army, and wait for the far greater Indian future that is to follow. On the brink of counterfactual instant realization, the nationalist fantasy collapses for the goal of delayed gratification.

The conclusion to the novel argues that the preferable outcome to the seizure of the state is general education, as there is no hope for revival if the English are not made rulers. Even if true Hinduism is based on knowledge rather than action, subjective knowledge cannot grow without first attending to objective growth. The last-minute guru intones, "[T]he English are great in objective sciences and they are apt teachers. Therefore, the English shall be made our sovereigns. Imbued with a knowledge of objective sciences by English education, our people will be able to comprehend subjective truths."[26] This concluding thought serves as a refrain for the entire Romantic genealogy of Guru English that is both nationalist and cosmopolitan, political and religious. Satyananda, who appeared to be the guru par excellence for most of the novel, is revealed to be a shortsighted chela aspiring prematurely to political subjecthood. This earlier guru-like figure is now himself rendered a chela to the *mahāpuruṣa*, the mysterious superman who is guru of all gurus. Satyananda's disappointed objections to surrender overruled, both figures disappear, hand in hand: "[I]t was as if, knowledge took the hand of Devotion, Faith of Action; Sacrifice, of active Duty." This refrain is repeated: "Sacrifice took away Active Duty."[27]

As *Anandamath* already features a subtle internal hierarchy of moral authority among the Children who defer to each other based on the moral intelligibility of their views, the advice of this superhuman guru—that English education rather than armed resistance is the facilitator to self-realization—makes that chosen category the purest means of achieving nationalist ends. This final thought of a guru who believes in English education at the culmination of the original Indian nationalist novel might be seen as a blatant contradiction, a complete sell-out, or at the very best, a remarkable paradox. After all, it was not untypical for contemporary critics, such as Rajnarayan Basu (or Bose), to have suggested that English education was "a machine for killing human beings."[28] It has been suggested that the scaling back of the military rebellion and the capitulation to English education is out of character in relation to the unfolding of the novel's plot, which was lurching inexorably toward the seizure of the state. Pro-British voices would later argue that the novel's creed of the fearlessness of the Englishman, and its finale suggesting the happy union of Britain and India, prove that Bankim could not be the nationalist icon he had been made into.[29] Other readings suggest that Bankim either lost his nerve or was worried about the colonial censor and therefore deliberately stated the inverse of what he wished to recommend.[30]

But as Partha Chatterjee has suggested through his acute analysis of Bankim as the generational precursor of Gandhi and Nehru, such a chiastic formulation characterizes accurately the predicament of Indian nationalist discourse. Nationalism lays claim to a simple reversal of the orientalist problematic that described Indians according to essentialized civilizational characteristics, even as it tries somewhat unsuccessfully to wrestle with the same normative thematic created by the orientalist expectations and mechanisms of the colonial state. While the nationalists overthrew imperial power and reasserted colonial subjectivity (the problematic), this desire was largely framed within the moral codes, social values, parameters, and ground rules set up by colonialist epistemologies (the thematic). Hence, Bankim's proposal for a moral rejuvenation and self-discipline—through the myth of a classical Krishna—reiterates values already imposed by a colonialist mindset. Chatterjee's argument proceeds in stages, from Bankim's elite program for self-discipline (a moment of departure) through to Gandhi's popular mobilization (a moment of Gramscian maneuver and an ostensible rejection of Western modernity) to Nehru's deployment of the post-independence state as the moment of nationalism's arrival, which glossed over all earlier contradictions by making the state the repository of cultural specificity and scientific progress. Chatterjee argues that the moment of departure was especially prone to the combination of Eastern spiritualism and Western science, and therefore, the novel's refrain regarding an objectivist-subjectivist combination acquires special relevance.[31]

While an evolutionary (sometimes dubbed "moderate") nationalist approach to the question of social progressivism and spiritual renewal might have married Western science with Indian philosophy, or Bengal's love of Auguste Comte along with Iswarchandra Vidyasagar's intelligent traditionalism, Bankim's solution even from early in his career was to seize the offensive against Christianity. Later, Islam increasingly comes under attack, although with some qualifications. Bankim's hard-hitting essay "Mill, Darwin, and Hinduism" (1875), defends Hinduism on an entirely rational basis, even as it charges that the Christian belief in a merciful God is scientifically flawed when compared with the Hindu doctrine regarding a divine trinity. With science designated as impersonal arbiter, Hinduism, while not purely scientific, is deemed closer to science than "the Christian religion supported by the scientific European people."[32] As Tanika Sarkar has pointed out, there is a turning point in Bankim's intellectual itinerary after the publication of the liberal-rationalist *Sāmya* [Equality] in 1879. Moving from a liberal-reformist and self-ironizing spirit to the revivalist politics of nationalism, Bankim's "self-critical, radical sensibility is transformed to an authoritarian, totalitarian and intolerant voice."[33] Bankim adopted an even more aggressive approach (perhaps a precursor of the "extremist" wing in the yet-to-be-formed Indian National Congress) after a controversy over the interpretation of Hindu idolatry with William Hastie in the *Statesman* newspaper in 1882. Especially as Christian missionaries were making inroads again in the late nineteenth century after the relative stalemate of earlier decades, advocates of a muscular Hinduism, including Bankim and Vivekananda, were reemphasizing what Milind Wakankar has called a "forcing-together of body-as-self and nation-as-ascesis."[34] A new ethics of individualist perfectibility obsesses this Romantic nationalist search for new theologies. Hence, we see Bankim's complete rewriting of Krishna's character in his late tract *Krishnacaritra*, undertaken again as a competitive exercise of one-upmanship against the comparative advantage the Christian religion was seen to have enjoyed because of the proven historicity of Christ's existence as compared with the legendary status of Krishna's. Kaviraj summarizes very well the changes Bankim wrought on Krishna, who was transformed almost unrecognizably from "a lovable popular figure of eroticism, excess, transgression, playfulness, a subject of both admiration and admonition, to a classic figure—calm, poised, rational, perfect, irreproachable." The consequences of this neo-Krishna "ought to be seen as a Sorelian myth, an ideal condensation of energies, a focus of national-popular mobilization."[35]

The conclusion to *Anandamath* could be seen as a bizarre result of Bankim's continuing fascination with updating and modernizing Hinduism, a process that eventually "transpose[s] discipline from an external religious-pedagogic authority to the self-monitoring ethical agent."[36] This effectively meant the direct transfer of energy from a character such as the *mahāpuruṣa* to the nationalist reader who continues the ethical battle as the novel closes. But this transfer is but one aspect of the concern with objective sciences and English education. Beneath the superficial contradiction between indigenous culture and modern science lies a more complex synthesis that could be a veritable "meeting-ground of incongruities."[37]

In his cultural history of modern India's obsession with science entitled *Another Reason*, Gyan Prakash has analyzed in great detail the search for an archaic Hindu science that anchored nationalist attempts to fabricate a Hindu universality. Various attempts were made to bolster the truth-claims of Hinduism through rationalist revision of its doctrines. Late-nineteenth-century movements from Dayananda's Arya Samaj to Blavatsky's Theosophical Society asserted that the Vedas were originally scientific texts with a materialist and experimental basis. Prakash suggests that the emphasis on science in the nationalist movement ought not to be read "too quickly as an expression of the organicity and atavism of nationalism." Instead, a cultural translation and repositioning of the Hindu past results, even as the universality of Hinduism is put forward not as an unbroken continuity but as the return of an estranged past that had been forgotten. This past miraculously renews a present in which, until recently, it had no share. Documenting the growth of local scientific societies and the inspired rediscovery of ancient Indian science and past knowledge of medicine, chemistry, and mathematics, Prakash suggests that these mechanisms, along with their encouragement by the colonial state, "materialized the imagination of India as a pre-political community" and established Indians as a "fictive ethnicity."[38]

Hence, even if it were primarily thought up as a dodge to keep the novel one step ahead of the censor, the conclusion to *Anandamath* presciently reflects the neo-Romantic nationalist desire to lay claim to a resolutely Indian science and spirituality. This was a change from the anglicist problematic that had juxtaposed a stark choice between a progressive Western science and a backward indigenous religion. The resulting synthesis of nationalism and modernity creates a modern India that never reaches back to the past in some simple act of retrieval and continuous tradition. Rather, there are displacements and undecidabilities that have come from the superman's precise collocation of objective sciences, English education, and subjective truths. A case in point is *Wisdom of the Rishis*, written by a promising young follower of Dayananda, Pandita Guru Datta Vidyarthi. The text distinguishes among "mythological, antiquarian, and contemporary methods of Vedic terminology" with a view to establishing the scientific nature of the Vedas.[39]

Understanding such troubled origins for modern Indian nationalist discourse might also lead us to realize that "English education" on Indian topics cannot be mere instruments that are discarded when the nationalist subject is made whole, even if that was the arguable intention behind the mysterious guru's comment (and even though, as is only to be expected, self-reliant wholeness never arrives at the height of crypto-nativist success). Even the infamous Macaulay Minute predicts that the intermediary class will be encouraged to "refine the vernacular dialects of the country, to enrich those dialects with terms of science borrowed from the Western nomenclature, and to render them by degrees fit vehicles for conveying knowledge to the great mass of the population."[40] Bankim's writings show that Guru English has a Hindu nationalist lineage as well as a secular cosmopolitan one. In *Anandamath*, Satyananda's *kṣātratejas* (military, or kshatriya intelligence) is counterposed by the *mahāpuruṣa*'s *brahmatejas* (priestlike, or brahminical intelligence). However, such an outcome might well be a recursive structure, as *brahmatejas* ultimately represents the sly return of the Bengali baboo, whose rationale favors a solution that gives greatest advantage to his already acquired cultural capital in English. This speculative suggestion injects a greater level of playfulness and self-critique into Bankim's *Anandamath* than has hitherto been proposed, but after all, his literary versatility was no stranger to satire, and especially self-satire of baboos. Perhaps the nationalist reception of *Anandamath* as the great political novel of modern India has hitherto precluded such a playful reading. If *Anandamath* was intended to get the male nationalist subject beyond the self-perceived eunuch-like status accorded him by Macaulay's curse, its final dicta return him to where he began, as a compromised creature created for the efficient and continuing saga of colonial governmentality, but who will nonetheless exceed that function in diasporic futures. As Mrinalini Sinha argues, "the self-perception of effeminacy was itself an expression of the hegemonic aspirations of the Bengali elite."[41] Underneath this wide cultural agenda of nationalism—political, cultural, and moral rejuvenation—also lurk the spiritual claims that led to Guru English. As nationalism attempts to turn away from Macaulay and go beyond him, it makes an ironic and inadvertent spiral, returning to the initial type. The elaboration of subjective truths, through Guru English, is the surprising supplement to the desire for scientific objectivity.

KIPLING'S PRESAGES

The objective need to learn English was originally phrased in Bengali by Bankim's superman. The Teshoo Lama in Kipling's *Kim* supposedly speaks Tibetan and Urdu—although this is the English representation of a different linguistic presentation. The lama does have knowledge of a few English words. Through the character of the lama, *Kim* provides a literary representation of the South Asian guru who opens up new traffic between religious and political vocabularies. Even though many prominent readings of the novel have seen a fatal weakness in the lama's subservience to imperialist explanation, Kipling signals the multidirectionality of the lama's pronouncements. Critics have patronized the lama as imperialist victim, but they often miss the implications of his newfangled platitudes as well as their gentle satire.[42]

Introducing himself to the children playing outside the Lahore wonder-house, or *Ajaib-Ghar*, the lama says,

> "I am no Khitai [Chinaman], but a Bhotiya [Tibetan], since you must know—a lama—or say, a *guru* in your tongue."
>
> "A *guru* from Tibet," said Kim. "I have not seen such a man. They be Hindus in Tibet, then?"[43]

While Kipling's silent translation converts "Bhotiya" to "[Tibetan]," "Bhotiya" at this point could possibly refer to a resident of another mountainous Buddhist kingdom, Bhutan, rather than a resident of *nishidh* (or forbidden) that would have been the term for Tibet.[44] The lama's translation of himself as "guru" presages, as it were, an interesting afterlife in the history of religious cosmopolitanism. Befriending Kim, who becomes his chela in the very first chapter, the lama becomes the boy's permanent companion, spiritual guide, and surrogate guardian. The lama pays for Kim's education at the Lucknow convent; in return, Kim performs his duty as the lama's principal disciple, protecting him from depredations on the road and during the denouement with the Russian spies at the end of the novel.

At the same time, readers have been uncomfortable with the lama's spiritual role and his guru-chela relationship with Kim. Edward Said, one of the novel's acute readers, raises the importance of the guru-chela relationship, only to dissolve it into the universal thematics of male bonding, adducing in the process American picaresque novels, Greek myth, Bunyan, Chaucer, and Cervantes. According to Said, "Kipling is less interested in religion for its own sake (although we never doubt the lama's piety) than he is in local colour, scrupulous attention to exotic detail, and the all-enclosing realities of the Great Game. It is the greatness of Kipling's achievement that quite without selling the old man short, or in any way diminishing the quaint sincerity of his Search, Kipling, nevertheless, firmly places him within the protective orbit of British rule in India."[45] There are a number of assumptions here that require interrogation: What does it mean to be interested in religion for its own sake? Why is the absence of that attitude seen as automatic indication of some deeper interpretive key? Why is local color and exotic detail deemed extraneous to an interest in religion? And why should the lama's Search be diminished in the narrative because it is "firmly place(d) . . . within the protective orbit of British rule"? As we saw in Bankim's conclusion to *Anandamath*, religion arises as remaindered or renascent subjectivity *in relation* to colonial English education: the guru affects English just as much as English affects the guru. In the rush to deem Kipling's vision imperial, many a critic following in Said's footsteps has tended to instrumentalize the religious representation as revealing the deeper presence of the Great Game. Consequently, we are treated to rich readings of the novel's Boy Scout ideology, its depiction of colonial aphasia, and its central involvement in intelligence gathering.[46] The intelligence chief Creighton's shadowy presence, and the surveillance aspects of the narrative have therefore been accorded greatest agency in relation to the lama's seeming obliviousness to the material machinations that take place around him. Of course, Kim; Mahbub Ali, the horse dealer; Hurree Babu (Kipling's contribution to baboo caricature based on Sarat Chandra Das of the Survey of India who met the Panchen Lama); and the omniscient narrator are often several steps ahead of the lama in anticipating potential dangers. But the lama anticipates metaphysically what the spies perform politically. Every key term of the Great Game is presaged by the lama's spiritual vocabulary: for all Kim's obsession with the Grand Trunk Road, there is the lama's reliance on the Wheel of Life, and his Search for the mystical River and the Four Holy Places; in relation to the secret maps that dominate Creighton's intelligence-gathering apparatus, there is the lama's torn cosmic chart guiding him on the religious quest; and all the discussion of imperial information is matched by an interfering discourse in the novel regarding religious doctrine. While the Great Game goes on around him, the lama remains unperturbed, in a different mental space. What he achieves is a symbolic vision of India that echoes aspects of the nationalist vision, and indeed can be compared with the map-as-icon temple scene in *Anandamath* already discussed, or Swami Vivekananda's nationalist-spiritual epiphany that had already taken place at the rock near Kanyakumari at the southernmost tip of the mainland. Paradoxically, this is a vision seen by a Tibetan, rather than by an Indian or a Briton:

> As a drop draws to water, so my Soul drew near to the Great Soul which is beyond all things. At that point, exalted in contemplation, I saw all Hind, from Ceylon in the sea to the Hills, and my own Painted Rocks at Such-zen; I saw every camp and village, to the least, where we have ever rested. I saw them at one time and in one place; for they were within the Soul. By this I knew the Soul had passed beyond the illusion of Time and Space and of Things. By this I knew that I was free.[47]

Empire is clearly central to the novel, and it would be foolish to argue otherwise. However, the hermeneutic operation of disclosing the imperial secrets represented by Creighton and the Great Game have dominated interpretive energies as being far more "real" than the lama's alternative, and equally intricate metaphysical discourse. The specific vocabulary of South Asian religious universalism, sometimes described as the lama's Buddhology, translates certain protonationalist expectations effectively into English, even as it makes visible indigenous self-perceptions regarding empire and religion. The lama's novelistic language is Guru English (even if his actual languages—Tibetan and Urdu—are silently translated by Kim or the narrator with a few native words and different rhythms thrown in for local color). In the broadest possible sense the lama's presentational language is a placeholder for a number of interspersed equivalences.

The framing chapters of *Kim* place the action within a resolutely spiritualist vocabulary. The hierarchy of the guru-chela relationship suggests, at the very least, a playful variant on the genre of the telemachiad, which educates novices for princely rule. Kim as an orphan runaway might structurally occupy the inverse social position to that of a prince. This inversion of the problematic takes place even as the Indian orphan turns out to be an Irish surrogate for British imperialism. By novel's end, Kim is a secular prince of sorts, ready to inherit the Indian empire in vicarious ways through Creighton's intelligence-gathering as well as the lama's Romanticism. While the lama as religious mendicant is the analog of a court-based political preceptor, the circumstances make his discourse resonate with nationalist sentiment. Given this context, the conclusion to the novel is hardly "chilling," as Sara Suleri suggests, unless the reader's position is so identified with Kim's adolescent subjectivity that it is unacceptable, as it is for any adolescent, for Kim not to have the last word.[48] Rather, in Partha Chatterjee's efficient formulation, the lama's Romanticism is yet another inversion of the problematic: it makes for an apprehension of an Indian reality through a neophyte discourse that perpetuates orientalist stereotypes. This is not a position extraneous to, or independent from empire, but one situated parallel to the colonial apparatuses and yet not reducible to empire as universal solvent.

The intelligence apparatus dominates the opening sequence through the specific cultural information gathering performed by the museum. Benedict Anderson has pointed out that museums, along with maps and censuses, create the modular recognition that literate nationalisms need, and *Kim* contains literary versions of all three of these devices, as well as a recognition of oral formulary, epic, and other mythopoetic narratives that Anderson ignores. While the cultural and the political are symbiotic modes of information retrieval for those who read empire as paramount in *Kim*, such readings can be further nuanced by the novel's inclusion of emergent strains of Guru English. The cultural information of the museum lends itself to neoreligious recuperations just as easily as to narratives of imperial suzerainty. An unrelenting focus on Creighton's shadowy agency only renders the lama's vocabulary as delusional in relation to empire as the higher and more realist translation. In retrospect, this approach needs modification.

The single-minded insistence on empire is the only fault with Thomas Richards's otherwise brilliant reading regarding Tibet as the fantasy site of the Victorian search for exhaustive knowledge. In what would appear as an uncanny echo of the conclusion to Bankim's novel, Richards reads Creighton as an "archival superman" and the apparatus of intelligence gathering deployed by his shadowy agents as a differentiated and deterritorialized "state nomadology." Alluding to Boltzmannian and Deleuzian "indeterminate determinacy," Richards sees the prophetic mission as indistinguishable from the state mission, as Kim's "social knowledge has become co-extensive with military intelligence."[49] The

British imperial system in India tapped into a sophisticated information order consisting of different professional functions, including those of itinerant spies, political secretaries, physicians, and astrologers, and the famous Grand Trunk Road incorporates the mechanisms of military espionage as well as the flow of religious pilgrims to important sites such as Allahabad, Benares, and Gaya that are en route. In like fashion, the Great Trigonometrical Survey of India penetrated Tibet by using peripatetic spies disguised as monks with walking staffs that hid surveying instruments, and who were armed with 100-bead rosaries to count their steps in readily computable increments (rather than the traditional rosaries that would have featured 108 beads). By such a reading, Creighton becomes Kipling's substitute for Captain Thomas Montgomerie, who organized the mapping of Tibet using surveyors in religious disguise, a venture that has been analyzed extensively by Derek Waller in *The Pundits*.[50]

The information society featured in the novel interanimates the religious turns of the Wheel with the political one-upmanship of the Great Game. However, despite the apparent dominance of the imperial order in *Kim*, the lama's self-reliance and childlike innocence suggest a native mastery of the metaphysical environment that is very different from the hybrid adaptability of his chela, Kim. For all their informational mastery, the British imperialists were unable to process "affective knowledge." This massive information failure contributed to the state's inability to foresee the Great Mutiny of 1857, as the British relied greatly on private and mediated information networks in India, at least when compared with the opportunistic use of patrimonial knowledge and mixed-blood populations in other locations such as South Africa.[51]

The absence of affective knowledge in imperial intelligence gathering recontextualizes the lama's Romantic metaphysics in Kipling's novel. The Great Game, with all its chesslike calculations concerning Russian designs, flows around the resolute reimaginings of the nation seen through the figure of the lama, who stands in for other neoreligious figures. The affective wisdom retailed through the lama's vocabulary frustrates imperial ambition just as much as it presages nationalist counterambition. The lama's religious discourse uncovers the hidden powers of corruption, transculturation, and universalism in neoreligious wisdom. Readers can bracket and misrecognize this vocabulary but never fully disempower it. Invulnerable to empire with his apolitical platitudes, the lama mouths the affective knowledge that the British are least capable of deciphering. His disarmed appearance in the context of the calculus of the Great Game is an indication of religion as a standing reserve that promises a deferred deployment of metaphysical politics from a "higher level." The lama suggests a hypertext of future possibilities that supplement the horizon of empire with a metaphysical beyond.[52]

A brilliant balance between objective intelligence and subjective reflection suffuses the novel's opening chapter in the museum or "Wonder House." First, Kim and then the Curator display religious and cultural artifacts, scholarly books, and photographs of religious sites to the lama (including pictures of his own monastery). Is the lama the only true believer, for whom these museological and decontextualized artifacts are being sacrally reintegrated? The Curator is capable of supplementing missing sculptural details with photographs, even as his role is "to gather knowledge" from informed visitors such as the lama (55). Yet, the lama cannot literally comprehend English, and therefore Samuel Beal's Buddhology and Stanislas Julien's translation of Hwen-Tsiang are inaccessible to him. The opening to the novel hence features what Philip Almond has described as *The British Discovery of Buddhism*, a synthesis that took place even later than the construction that Romila Thapar has described as "syndicated Hinduism." Others have characterized this moment of Buddhist synthesis with titles such as *The Awakening of the West* and *The Men Who Discovered India's Lost Religion*. Some of the key figures involved in this reappropriation of Buddhism include Francis Buchanan, George Turnour, Brian Hodgson, James Prinsep, James Fergusson, Colin Mackenzie, Alexander Csoma de Koros, Henry Steel Olcott, and T. W. Rhys Davids.[53] The term *Buddhism* entered English about 1829—at roughly the same time that the word *Hinduism* was first used by Rammohun. From early on, the Buddha's message was compared to Martin Luther's, framing a Romantic interpretation of the religion within an antiritualistic and reformist cast even though extant Buddhist practices often did not fit such criteria.[54]

By listening to the Curator render European orientalist information in Urdu, the lama informs himself of crucial details concerning his own religious quest. A painter of mandalas (or cosmic diagrams), the lama is made to understand a secular map of his religion for the first time:

> For the first time he heard of the labours of European scholars, who by the help of these and a hundred other documents have identified the Holy Places of Buddhism. Then he was shown a mighty map, spotted and traced with yellow. The brown finger followed the Curator's pencil from point to point. Here was Kapilavastu, here the Middle Kingdom, and here Mahabodhi, the Mecca of Buddhism; and here was Kusinagara, sad place of the Holy One's death. (56–57)

The narrator's rendition of the Curator's speech is a remarkable mediation of Buddhism for the non-Buddhist reader as well as for the learned lama, recognized by the Curator as "a scholar of parts." The lama's sense of his own religion undergoes an orientalist reeducation, even as the reader is informed of the religion's sacred geography. Loose analogy is deployed to render the religion substitutable for others, as in the casual phrase, "Mahabodhi, the Mecca of Buddhism." Especially as the Curator could not have explained things exactly in this way to the lama, one is struck by a sense of the novelistic language's elaborate translation and repackaging, whereby the lama relearns the full sacred parameters of his own "Search" only after a direct session with someone who is clearly not himself a believer, but possibly a surrogate for the Christian God, "a white-bearded Englishman" who has been identified as Kipling's father, John Lockwood Kipling (55). Yet, the Curator is shown to fall short, when confronted by the lama's naive insistence on asking him for the precise location of the River of the Arrow (58). The orientalist knowledge gathered by the Curator is inadequate to the desire of the believer to free himself from the Wheel of Things; and the Curator cannot go along for the metaphorical last mile that is the object of the lama's quest. At the end of the interview, the lama travels south by train with Kim, and the Curator smiles "at the mixture of old-world piety and modern progress that is the note of India today" (59).

What is witnessed here between the Curator and the lama cannot just be parsed with the reductive question of who holds the upper hand. The discovery of Buddhism by the West, just as the reorganization of Hinduism, led to a structure of "intercultural mimesis" between European-influenced scholar and native practitioner, as described by Charles Hallisey, relying on Homi Bhabha's theorization of imperial mimicry. The textualization of Buddhism and the stripping away of ritual practices as abuse also led to the structure of "Protestant Buddhism" discussed by Gananath Obeyesekere in the context of Sri Lanka. Kipling, always more sympathetic to Islam than to Hinduism, gives the devalued status of Buddhism an indirect boost in his representation of the lama's philosophy as a transidiomatic lingua franca. Buddhism, as a reformist movement that had failed to take proper hold in its country of origin, provides the alternative metaphysics of the order-producing law that Kipling found so attractive in Islam and the Old Testament of the Bible.[55] The lama's Buddhist philosophy is therefore stripped of its Tibetan particularities and rendered in terms of the larger picture of an "Indian" religion that was indigenous but also shorn of the ritual practices and polytheistic idolatry that so disturbed Kipling.[56] The lama's frequent references to "the Arrow," "the River," "the Wheel," and "the Way" correspond to the aniconic form of the representation of the Buddha favored by the Theravada school of Buddhism practiced in Ceylon—that reveres the footprint, the pipal tree, the regal parasol, or the empty throne—rather than the anthropomorphisms of Vajrayana Buddhism as practiced in Tibet, but which the lama rejects early on as *būt-parasti*, or "devildom, charms, and idolatry" (54, 57). Under these conditions, Buddhism is not at all a strange choice to represent India, especially when imaginarily re-created according to a belief in what J.M.S. Tompkins calls "Kipling's insistent and elusive concept of the Law," one that could partially analogize itself to the Buddhist *Dhamma* and partly, if somewhat contradictorily, to the military code of British imperial masculinity.[57] Keeping this double logic in mind, *Kim* demonstrates the doctrine of *pratītyasamutpāda* (interdependent origination) that serves Buddhism as much as it does empire; the lama's cultivation of an antiself rationalizes the *śramaṇa* tradition of renunciation and political quiescence; and the yoking of contemplation and action through the partnership between the lama and Kim synthesizes a vacuous remaindered subjectivism with imperial action.

The lama's doctrinal position is untypical when compared with contemporary accounts about so-called Tibetan lamaism by Austine Waddell and other Western observers. While Waddell will decry "primitive Lamaism" as retaining its character in Tibet, as "a priestly mixture of Sivaite mysticism, magic, and Indo-Tibetan demonolatry, overlaid by a thin varnish of Mahayana Buddhism," Kipling's holy man has to be a perennial philosopher and a religious dissident, derived as his philosophy is from the famous Victorian poem about the Buddha, *Light of Asia*, written by Edwin Arnold, the editor of the *Daily Telegraph*. According to the iconophobic lama, "it was in my mind that the Old Law was not well followed; being overlaid as thou knowest, with devildom, charms, and idolatry. . . . The books of my lamasserry I read, and they were dried pith; and the later ritual with which we of the Reformed Law have cumbered ourselves—that, too, had no worth to these old eyes. Even the followers of the Excellent One are at feud on feud with one another" (57).[58] The lama's quest for the true location of the River of the Arrow parallels the archaeological competition to discover the historical Kapilavastu that was taking place in the 1890s, and that culminated with the vindication of Austine Waddell and Vincent Smith and the exposé of the Austrian archaeologist, Dr. Alois Führer, who was caught red-handed salting his chosen site with fake Ashokan artifacts.[59]

In keeping with this idea of an imagined shift to a modern Buddhism under neo-Romantic auspices, the switch of the feather-light spectacles from the Curator to the lama, often interpreted as a sign of the lama's subordination to British patronage, is also very much the combination of piety and progress or objective science and subjective truth that can be traced to Bankim. Buddhism as estranged past—just as Hinduism was for Bankim—would rejuvenate the hybrid nature of the present even without having to resort to any simplistic myths of origination. This indecipherable and mixed origin cannot be rendered transparent to the narrative of British suzerainty. What has sometimes been forgotten is that the spectacles are not given where there are none—the lama's were scratched but had the same power—and the ophthalmological upgrade is further paid for by the lama's open-work iron pen-case, as "the collector's heart in the Curator's bosom had gone out to it from the first" (60). Along with the spectacles, the lama is given plain white paper and sharpened pencils to record his "Search." To that extent, the practical advantage the lama gained by the spectacles is exchanged for the collectible extracted from him, as instruments of vision and notation are exchanged for an antiquated receptacle for the implements of writing. If the exchange is one that infects the lama with an imperialist vision even as it grants him the power of (empirical as opposed to sacral) inscription, it could also be the oriental's renunciation of agency over the terms of objectivity that are granted to the colonizer alongside a mutually agreed upon repackaging of subjectivity in the interaction. And what to make of the transfer of the Chinese pencase from Tibetan to European, making the latter responsible for contextualizing the quotidian articles of the former as artifacts with a provenance, a material history, and an international exchange value made possible by the circuit of collectors, museums, and dealers in oriental antiquities? As Stanley K. Abe also suggests, the Chinese pen-case "makes the lama an ideal type of Asiatic religious man" and a stand-in for the Indian Buddhist, and to this can be added that the lama is being rendered substitutable not just for Buddhists but for other Indian gurus. However, if it looks as if the lama has irrevocably given up an item of museological value, the heavy iron pen-case reappears later as blunt instrument of battle reached for by the lama when attacked by the Russian spy; in fact, the lama also confesses to having fought with fellow-monks for religious commissions from the printing of prayers several times in his youth, using the long pen-cases as weapons (291, 309).[60] The lama has a seemingly endless supply of these pen-cases.

More than the practical gift of the spectacles or the extraction of the pen-case, the Curator's perspective transforms the lama's sense of himself; it is the effect of Guru English, not rendered to him in English (but supposedly in Urdu, to be sure) that makes the difference. According to the Jesuit Father Victor, the lama "hit the bull's eye" when he uses a letter-writer to translate his thoughts that "[E]ducation is greatest blessing if of best sorts. Otherwise no earthly use" (152). The formula followed here is reminiscent of Bankim's superman's injunction. The "best sort" of education that the lama wants for Kim is presumably the English education that gives access to objective sciences and technology, leading to significant earthly use. Only the best, or nothing at all; yet the value placed on earthly use leaves unexplained the uncharted area of metaphysical and religious education that the lama does not expect Kim to get at this school. The lama cannot capitalize in any ordinary fashion on the translation of his discourse as he is not anglophone, but his beginnings at the Ajaib-Ghar (the Lahore Museum) make him entirely angloprone, a political subject-in-process and an ideological work-in-progress, in the manner that Bankim's *Anandamath* had already presaged. The question of religious or metaphysical ontology and self-discovery would be deferred to a point of arrival after the acquisition of the objective scientific mind-set represented by that of English education. While Kim's self-rendition to objectivity was acquired, the deferral of the question of subjectivity to the future does not just make the lama a patsy to empire as is usually argued. Rather, the lama's Anglopron-eness allows a neoreligious and futuristic vocabulary to be formulated and pursued in his name, and its implications are unresolved without his ever succumbing to the Creighton agenda. Even if the lama is duped, his ethics are never compromised. Kim, in contrast, is an ideological contradiction, and his objectives diverge as a result of his dual agenda and his service to two masters, both Creighton and the lama. Even if the lama's commitment to his chela is misplaced, he sheds himself of the passions of retaliation that coincide with the agenda of imperialism. He looks more impressive at the conclusion than even the guru he claimed he was to Kim in the opening scene. Compared with Kipling's caricature of Hurree Babu, the lama-as-guru comes across with an impressive dignity. The metaphysical teacher maintains clear superiority over the imperial creature. We are, at the very least, brought to a point that has been defined well by David Bromwich as Kipling's "jest," according to which the question of the warrant of precedence between "the Great Game" and "the Search for the River" will always remain unanswered.[61] The enigmatic conclusion to the novel enunciates the lama's joyful epiphany in the limpid vocabulary of Guru English:

> "So thus the Search is ended. For the merit that I have acquired, the River of the Arrow is here. It broke forth at our feet, as I have said. I have found it. Son of my Soul, I have wrenched my Soul back from the Threshold of Freedom to free thee from all sin—as I am free, and sinless! Just is the Wheel! Certain is our deliverance! Come!"
> He crossed his hands on his lap and smiled, as a man may who has won salvation for himself and his beloved. (338)

The novel's finale leaves ambiguous whether the lama is ultimately deluded or genuinely enlightened, suggesting the epistemological unverifiability of all religious truth—caught between the lama's wisdom (is it senility?) and Kim's youth (is it insouciance?). Could it be that Kipling believes, at some level, in the lama's authenticity, even if his authenticity has to be rendered in English Romantic vocabulary through a range of neoreligious devices and a provisional Buddhology? While there are those who would like to know Kim's response to the lama in order to recenter the novel onto its eponymous protagonist, what if Kipling's deliberate intention is to reveal a displacement of empire toward metaphysics, just as much as the famous multiplication tables of intelligence-gathering in Kim's brain give way to the uncertain cadences of Guru English in the lama's represented diction? The incessant materialization and enumeration of empire teeters on the brink of a dematerializing metaphysical abyss when the novel ends with the joyousness of the lama in his qualitative and mythical identification with the story of *Ananda* [Joy], or that of the old elephant in the *Jataka* who helps liberate the fettered calf. Sliding from Urdu to Tibetan to Chinese when he tells the tale of the Lord Buddha to the captive audience in the railway carriage early in the novel, "the gentle, tolerant folk," who are his audience "looked on reverently. All India is full of holy men stammering gospels in strange tongues; shaken and consumed in the fires of their own zeal; dreamers, babblers, and visionaries: as it has been from the beginning and will continue to the end" (80). Some secularized gurus spearhead the nationalist counterpoint to empire: Parama Roy has recently argued that the lama is a feminized figure, who not only nurtures Kim and evokes Mother India, but who also anticipates another epicene figure at the heart of Indian nationalism: Mahatma Gandhi.[62]

The lama's deviation from the renunciatory objective of the Indian śramaṇa tradition represented by Buddhism, wrenching his soul back from the "Threshold of Freedom" to reclaim Kim for salvation, echoes Kipling's earlier exploration of this idea in his short story, "The Miracle of Purun Bhagat" in the *Second Jungle Book* (1895). Purun Dass, a prime minister of a native state and a recipient of the prestigious Knight Commander of the Order of the Indian Empire returns his honor the month after he received it: "[T]he priests knew what had happened and the people guessed; but India is the one place in the world where a man can do as he pleases and nobody asks why; and the fact that Dewan Sir Purun Dass, K.C.I.E. had resigned position, palace, and power, and taken up the begging-bowl and ochre-coloured dress of a Sunnyasi or holy man, was considered nothing extraordinary."[63] Now calling himself Purun Bhagat, the renunciate heads for the high Himalayas and encamps in a shrine near a mountainous village where he befriends wild animals. Recognized as a holy man and a miracle worker, the villagers give him succor. Purun Bhagat's religious quest of several years ends abruptly when he sacrifices his life saving the villagers from a landslide. The grateful villagers build a temple in honor of Purun's sacrifice, even as they do not have any inkling that "the saint of their worship is the late Sir Purun Dass, K.C.I.E., D.C.L., Ph.D., etc., once Prime Minister of the progressive and enlightened state of Mohiniwala, and honorary or corresponding member of more learned and scientific societies than will ever do any good in this world or the next." Local religion ironically trumps chains of imperial signifiers.[64]

At other moments in Kipling's vast Indian writings, local religion is experienced as transgressive surrogation and mysterious retribution when the monkey-god Hanuman is violated in "The Mark of the Beast" (1891), a disturbing story in which Hinduism is rendered as diabolism. In another short story, gullible natives make the comic mistake of conflating Irish working-class identity with divine visitation in "The Incarnation of Krishna Mulvaney" (1891).[65] Another fiction, "The Finest Story in the World," wrestles with the Indian doctrine of incarnation. While in these fictions native religion is rendered incomprehensible—as dangerous supernatural agency or as harmless self-delusion—in yet another, "The Sending of Dana Da" (1888), Kipling makes space for a satirical treatment of religious syncretism.[66] The beginning of the story criticizes an analog of Theosophy with acerbic wit:

> This Religion was too elastic for ordinary use. It stretched itself and embraced pieces of everything that the medicine-men of all ages have manufactured. It approved of and stole from Freemasonry; looted the Latter-day Rosicrucians of half their pet words; took any fragments of Egyptian philosophy that it found in the *Encyclopædia Britannica*; annexed as many of the Vedas as had been translated into French or English, and talked of all the rest; built in the German versions of what is left of the Zend Avesta; encouraged White, Grey, and Black Magic, including spiritualism, palmistry, fortune-telling by cards, hot chestnuts, double-kernelled nuts, and tallow droppings; would have adopted Voodoo and Obeah had it known anything about them, and showed itself, in every way, one of the most accommodating arrangements that had ever been invented since the birth of the Sea.[67]

The story features seemingly miraculous instances of telekinesis performed by a self-styled "Independent Experimenter" for monetary considerations (to fuel a whiskey and opium habit). Dana Da helps settle petty scores between an unnamed Englishman, a recalcitrant member of another mystical society, and the society's leader, Lone Sahib. Dana Da organizes a "sending" that persecutes the targeted ailurophobic Lone Sahib with a deluge of kittens on a daily basis. Kittens are found in different parts of his house, his closets, and his personal possessions. After initial resistance, when the members of the secret society send the Englishman a Round Robin challenge, his surrogate Dana Da arranges for yet another shower of kittens to arrive according to precise predictions. The secret society, which until then only experienced the materialization of letters and the mysterious playing of music, is humiliated by this spectacular evidence of greater occult powers from a rusticated member. However, at the end of the story, a dying Dana Da reveals his secret charlatanry to the unnamed Englishman for some more money. From the Bania caste and expelled from a mission school, the charlatan, with his self-taught "all mine English education," had taken up a number of itinerant occupations and "made up name Dana Da," and arranged for the kittens by paying "the Sahib's bearer two-eight a month for cats." As a result, there are "very few kittens now in the bazar. Ask Lone Sahib's sweeper's wife."[68] Dana Da dies as a result of his terminal addiction to opium and alcohol. Doing so, "he passed away into a land where, if all be true, there are no materialisations and the making of new creeds is discouraged." The name Dana Da suggests *giving* or *gift* in several Indian languages and the character's seeming supernatural adeptness. While Kipling's efforts are entirely satirical, in 1922 T. S. Eliot would adapt for *The Wasteland* the "Da" story from the Brihadaranyaka Upanishad. *Da*'s devolutionary offshoots are *datta* (gift), *dayadhvam* (compassion), and *damyatā* (order). From here it is perhaps a short step to Heidegger's *es gibt Sein*, but if so, Kipling's parody has presciently infected later metaphysics with the whiff of Guru English *avant la lettre*.[69]

Kipling's skepticism regarding Theosophy (when compared with his greater sympathy toward other neoreligious experiments) was echoed by Indian religious commentators and by some secular European compatriots. In an open letter written to the secretary of the World's Parliament of Religions in 1893, hoping "that in the fulness of time we will have one Catholic and universal religion," Swami Shivgan Chand identifies "another class of religious people generally known as the outcome of the British Rule and English Education and influence. This class, though yet in infancy, is divided into many divisions and subdivisions, the more important of which are the Brahmo Samaj, the Arya Samaj, the Theosophical Society, and the Sanatana Dharma Sabha."[70] Evaluating these syncretic religious vocabularies, the Swami says that Theosophy "wants the test of time before ready and general acceptance" because of "the prominence given to ghost phenomena and miracles."[71]

Kipling was peripherally aware of these incipient neoreligious discourses and seems to have agreed with this skepticism expressed toward Theosophy. Kipling was a reporter for the *Allahabad Pioneer* from 1887 to 1889, during which time the Theosophist A. P. Sinnett, author of *Esoteric Buddhism*, served as owner and founder of the newspaper. Kipling's father had met Madame Blavatsky earlier that decade and judged her an interesting and unscrupulous impostor. Bankim also distinguished between spiritual fraudulence in his satire *Muchiram Guru* and authentic renovation in his neo-Hindu tracts such as *Krishnacaritra*, and opposed the defense of Hinduism by pseudoscience when propagated by thinkers such as Sasadhar Tarakachuramani.[72] Such an ambivalent split between renovation and fraudulence characterizes the two opposing motions of Guru English. The next chapter will show how "theosophistries" make much productive use of this ambivalence. While Guru English oscillates between register and discourse in its early phases, Theosophy resituates its texts in order to fashion a transidiomatic environment.

The lama's lack of English paradoxically does not prevent us from appreciating his "Search," "Way," "Arrow," and "River" through Kipling's neo-orientalist translations. Dana Da's broken English, however, is rejected as charlatanry, and this schismatic, ambivalent approval of Guru English will always be a feature of its existence, in order to separate true believers from confidence tricksters, and religion from charlatanry. The message about religion that Kipling sends is that tradition could be renovated, perhaps even invented out of whole cloth, as witnessed by the lama's embodying a Romantic neo-Buddhism rather than its real Tibetan variant, but that the syncretic is fraudulent, especially when alluded to as Theosophy.

Rabindranath Tagore's *Gora* (1910) can be read not just as a native response to the imperial fiction in Kipling's *Kim*, but also as a deft transposition of the religious and nationalist dilemmas already posed, if somewhat abstrusely, by Kipling. As both Gayatri Spivak and Meenakshi Mukherjee have suggested, Tagore's experimental techniques in the original Bengali make it much more than just *Kim*'s echo-effect. *Gora*'s choice between Brahmanism and Brahmoism would be at one remove, a mirroring of the unbridgeable discrepancy between *Kim*'s professional services to Creighton alongside his affective identification with the lama. When, at the novel's conclusion, Gora discovers his adoption at birth, it reveals the unstated racial biology and body politics anchoring many of these metaphysical conundrums. Tagore's question is whether an Irishman can logically profess Brahmanism. We can remind ourselves of Charles Vallancey's Celtic-Indian speculations mentioned in the previous chapter and the Irishwoman Sister Nivedita's (formerly Margaret Noble) advocacy of Vedanta in her book, *Aggressive Hinduism*, as a background that might have helped assuage *Gora*'s metaphysical problem. It is suggestive that Gora is physically a product of the disorder during the Mutiny of 1857, when Indian nationalism, British imperialism, and cross-racial refuge come together. Gora's Irish birth mother is sheltered by Anandamoyi, his Bengali adoptive mother.

When the child of Irish parents is raised as the traditional Brahman and professes the indigenous primordialist's position, and when modernizing Indians, racially indigenous, equally turn to the Christianization represented by Brahmoism, the result is a representation of the denaturalization, and arguably, the deconstruction of religion from its racial constructions under the sign of empire. Reading *Gora* back into *Kim*, Kipling might be judged as taking the side of Gora before his disillusionment with Romantic Brahmanism, against the newfounded but dubious universalism of the Christianized Brahmo. Kipling's Buddhology participates in at least three styles of orientalism, the patronizing sort popularized by the early orientalists, the Romantic sort commenced by German Indologists and carried through by Bankim, and glimmerings of the preparatory aspects of the phase that the nationalist style under Swami Vivekananda or Sri Aurobindo would take over for a counterdiscursive turn.[73]

Pure roots are sometimes professed in relation to a background that is ironically hybridized. As Spivak suggests, Gora can usher in a regional Indian modernity precisely because of his illegitimacy, inaugurating a process of alienated residency and residential alienness, whereby it will not be possible in the future to make a distinction between imperialism and independence. Tagore's prescient allegory foreshadows the birth of right-wing Hindutva, not so much as the primordial traditional but as the fascist modern. However, what was a profound disillusionment for Gora becomes rich self-empowerment for other syncretists. Rather than oscillate between indigeneist self-affirmation or disillusioned depression at the discovery of denaturalization and fraudulence, syndicated Hinduism takes its alienated residency and residential alienness as a mark of freedom, going diasporically outward beyond national confines to Europe, America, and elsewhere.[74]

AUROBINDO'S LITERARY COSMOPOLITANISM

Sri Aurobindo's career as India's first fully modern guru developed in reaction to an earlier spell in revolutionary nationalist politics.[75] Guru English discourse advances from fictions imagined by Bankim and Kipling to Aurobindo's lived cosmopolitanism. Fictional precursors in novels are replaced by the speculative refrains of metaphysical poetry. Leaving behind a copious archive of high Romantic argument and so-called overhead poetry, Aurobindo straddles the doctrinal and poetical halves of Guru English as theolinguistics.

The young Aravinda Ghose was brought up almost entirely under European influence. He was the grandchild of Rajnarayan Bose (or Basu) mentioned earlier, who had initially favored and then opposed English education in "Then and Now" (1874). Born in 1872, and given the English middle name "Ackroyd," in 1879 the young boy and his two brothers were sent by their father to a clergyman in Manchester for schooling, "with strict instructions that they should not be allowed to make the acquaintance of any Indian or undergo any Indian influence."[76] Aurobindo studied English, French, Greek, and Latin literature and developed some familiarity with German and Italian as well. Continuing on to the elite St. Paul's School in London in 1884 and to Cambridge University in 1890, Aurobindo passed with a High First Class in the first part of the Tripos but did not graduate. Having passed all the written and oral requirements of the prestigious Indian Civil Service examination, Aurobindo failed by not appearing for the riding test—either because he lacked funds to take riding lessons or because he was indifferent to the prospect of joining imperial bureaucracy. While in Cambridge, he was active in a secret society called The Lotus and the Dagger, and participated in meetings of the mock-parliamentary Indian Majlis. After spending nearly fourteen formative years in England, Aurobindo returned to India in 1893. Employed by the Maharaja of Baroda to take an English teaching post in the Baroda State Service, he soon became active in the nationalist politics of the Indian Congress Party. Opposing the compromising tactics of "moderate" leaders such as Pherozeshah Mehta who wanted incremental reforms, Aurobindo allied himself with the "extremist" wing of Lokmanya Tilak, Lajpat Rai, and Bepin Pal, who preached full independence, to be achieved through a combination of passive resistance and violent actions. Extensive pamphleteering and political journalism for the nationalist cause launched Aurobindo into prominence as a young militant. His Romanticism was that of a Jacobin, whereas Bankim's had been restitutionist.[77]

When the highly unpopular partition of Bengal was proposed in 1905, Aurobindo and his younger brother Barindra were much influenced by Bankim's fantasy of a militant monastic brotherhood that could inspire national renewal and evict the British colonizers. Having translated *Anandamath* into English together, the two brothers collaborated on an idea to found a temple in the hills where a new monastic order could be trained. Aurobindo wrote a manifesto that delineates the mechanisms for physico-geographical rejuvenation in broad-brush strokes. Entitled *Bhawani Mandir*, the pamphlet echoes Vivekananda's epiphany about India while meditating on a rock at Kanyakumari, the southernmost tip of the continental landmass. It also reminds us of the fictional lama's geographical cognition at the end of Kipling's *Kim*. Bemoaning India's want of Shakti, or spiritual and physical power,

Aurobindo makes a bold attempt to give the Indian nation a mythological pedigree based on the origin of the goddess Bhawani or Durga:

> For what is a nation? What is our mother-country? It is not a piece of earth, nor a figure of speech, nor a fiction of the mind. It is a mighty Shakti, composed of the Shaktis of all the millions of units that make up the nation, just as Bhawani Mahisha Mardini sprang into being from the Shakti of all the millions of gods assembled in one mass of force and welded into unity. The Shakti we call India, Bhawani Bharati, is the living unity of the Shaktis of three hundred million people; but she is inactive, imprisoned in the magic circle of Tamas, the self-indulgent inertia and ignorance of her sons.

Drawing on the example of the resurgence of Japan through Westernization and religious nationalism, Aurobindo suggests that India follow this example. The pamphlet ends with the call for a new monastic order of celibate monks (a *dēva-sangha*) who will serve the mother country for four years. After this national service, the monks would be free to continue or return to family life. The main task of the organization would be the mass instruction of all sectors of society and also the education of some of the monks who "will be sent to foreign countries to study lucrative arts and manufactures," and who will, upon their return, "establish with the aid of the Order, factories and workshops, still living the life of Sannyasis and devoting all their profits to the sending of more and more such students to foreign countries." Much later, this Romantic nationalist idea was transformed into a spiritual utopianism. In a letter to Barindra in 1920, Aurobindo speculates that the new association would be "a free form that can spread itself out like the sea with its multitudinous waves—engulfing this, inundating that, absorbing all—and as this continues, a spiritual community will be established."[78]

Aurobindo also wrote a manifesto on nonviolent techniques. Entitled *The Doctrine of Passive Resistance*, it was serialized in *Bande Mataram* in 1907, leading to Aurobindo's first trial and acquittal for seditious activities. Even though it was for the most part theoretical, *Bhawani Mandir* again became the prosecution's evidence when Aurobindo and Barindra were put on trial by the British authorities for the Manicktolla Bomb Factory Case (otherwise known as the Alipur Conspiracy Case) in 1908–9. The manifesto was deemed by the authorities to be a "gigantic scheme for establishing a central religious Society, outwardly religious, but in spirit, energy and work political."[79] While Aurobindo was eventually acquitted for want of evidence in both the lower court and the Sessions court (in the meantime, one of the key witnesses was mysteriously murdered before he could testify), Barindra was sentenced to death (later commuted to transportation) as conspirator in an act of terrorism. Two British women had been killed when a crude bomb was lobbed into their closed carriage. The culprit was an associate of Barindra's. The bomb had been thrown with the intention to assassinate a British colonial official who was thought to be traveling in the carriage. Aurobindo was possibly a passive co-conspirator. However, by this time he was already obsessed with his newly developed yogic quest that had started parallel to his nationalist interest in 1904–5. Given these parallel political and spiritual interests, Aurobindo started *Karmayogin* after his acquittal in 1909. This was a weekly review intended to "unite [religion and politics] again into one mighty invincible and grandiose flood." During the year he was incarcerated awaiting trial, Aurobindo's nationalism took an irreversible turn toward the spiritual, first to be publicly revealed in his famous Uttarapara speech of May 30, 1909. Aurobindo had experienced a mystical vision in jail, when he saw the divine forms of Vishnu—Krishna, Vasudeva, or Narayana—everywhere. A few months before his arrest in 1908, he had been initiated into advanced yogic practices by a Maharashtrian guru, Vishnu Bhaskar Lele. In Aurobindo's own words, the new synthesis was "the religion which embraces Science and faith, Theism, Christianity, Mahomedanism and Buddhism and yet is none of these, [but] is that to which the World-spirit moves."[80]

According to the hyperbole of Aurobindo's biographer K. R. Srinivasa Iyengar, "the idea behind *Bhawani Mandir* was something akin to 'nuclear' action. It aimed at releasing infinite energy in every Indian and fusing these three hundred million such infinities into one gigantic, one irresistible, one illimitably stupendous dynamo of Bharat Shakti. . . . India was to be the Guru of the World . . . a new religion to the world, the true religion of humanity."[81] Aurobindo states it in terms only slightly less crude in his famous Uttarapara speech. He sees India as "rising to shed the eternal light entrusted to her over the world. India has always existed for humanity and not for herself and it is for humanity and not for herself that she must be great."[82] Using political nationalism as a stepping-stone to spiritual Romanticism, Aurobindo envisaged true Indian resurgence through religious innovation.

While the passage quoted earlier from *Bhawani Mandir* continues the theme identified by Bankim about the crucial necessity of English education for the objective improvement of the country, it had also silently moved from the seemingly inherent value of scientific truth to more economically viable "lucrative arts and manufactures," and from the domestic instruction of a baboo elite to the foreign instruction of an avant-garde of budding gurus. But the simple instrumentalization of education never stayed within clearly defined boundaries, and Aurobindo's feelings about English education, and those of many others, were therefore contradictory and ambivalent. He faulted British education as "disgusting[,] . . . tend[ing] to dull and impoverish and tie up the naturally quick and supple Indian intelligence, to teach it bad intellectual habits and spoil by narrow information and mechanical instruction its originality and productivity."[83] In parallel fashion, Aurobindo's admirer James Cousins deemed "the ideal condition of true education . . . [as] a community of interest worked out in co-operation, a revival of the ancient relationship of *guru* and *chela*." Aurobindo and many other gurus would attempt to achieve this ideal through their ashrams.[84] In his newspaper, *Bande Mataram*, Aurobindo adds that the newly proposed national education "has necessarily culminated in the production of a monstrous species whose object in acquiring knowledge cannot reach beyond the vision of mere luxurious animal life."[85] Yet it was a classic imperial irony that the Sessions court judge presiding over Aurobindo's Alipur Conspiracy trial, C. P. Beechcroft, had stood second to Aurobindo in the Greek paper of the Indian Civil Service exam, but had done better in Bengali.[86] Aurobindo admitted to having had no facility with vernaculars in his youth except for a smattering of Hindustani. However, he immersed himself in a deep study of native languages upon his return to India, when he mastered Sanskrit, Marathi, Gujarati, and Bengali literatures.

Aurobindo's mixture of desire and contempt for secular and economic progress is no special characteristic of Indian nationalist or religious discourse. Following Bankim's cues, Aurobindo's synthesis of nationalism with religion leads him to argue that, "nationalism is an *avatar* and cannot be slain. Nationalism is a divinely appointed s[h]akti of the Eternal and must do its God-given work before it returns to the bosom of the Universal Energy from which it came."[87] However, the dramatic shift made by the fiery and charismatic revolutionary after his acquittal in the Manicktolla case was a bombshell in its own right. Even as the extremists split from the moderates in 1907, spurred by Aurobindo's uncompromising political vision (he signed the decree mandating the split), Aurobindo himself quit nationalist politics in February 1910 on the basis of an inner spiritual command, or *ādesh*. Moving to Chandernagore and then almost immediately to the French sister colony, Pondicherry, partly to avoid rearrest by the British, Aurobindo eventually established himself as a highly cosmopolitan and modern guru with a large international following. Yet the neo-Romantic whiff of Bankim's superman was still in the air, as Aurobindo's renunciation of politics was in order to make preparations for the evolutionary emergence of a supermind that would transform the world. India would be the laboratory, sacred territory, and launching pad for this planetary rejuvenation. Aurobindo was influenced by the Bergsonian notion of orthogenesis, grafted onto a Hindu mysticism that promulgated the belief in the necessity for human spiritual liberation by the incarnation of the divine into human form. The ultimate and only goal for the divine was self-realization through the ascent of the spirit, rising back from human to divine consciousness. In *The Human Cycle*, Aurobindo would lean toward suggesting that soul factors and psychology were present behind economic and material causes. Using Karl Lamprecht's stagist categories, he would argue for a historical evolution in five stages. From symbolic forms such as the Vedas, to "typal" social ideas, Indian society had then collapsed into conventional conformism or orthodox inertia during the third stage (the first three stages having taken place in ancient India). The rise of reason and the individual constituted the fourth stage, enabled by the developments in the West, but the fifth "subjective" stage of the rediscovery of the spiritual was under way through a return to Indian mystical resources. Through a process of surrogation, a "gnostic individual" such as Aurobindo would accelerate the inevitable return of the subjective and pave the way for the rest of humanity's yogic salvation. Yet, even while caught up with this universal mission from the standpoint of India as a spiritual avant-garde, he would privately confess to his brother Barindra that he had "no confidence in guruhood of the usual type. . . . I do not want to be a guru."[88]

Ashis Nandy's provocative identification of Aurobindo as "India's first modern guru" contrasts him favorably with Kipling. According to Nandy, Kipling was "culturally an Indian child who grew up to become an ideologue of the moral and political superiority of the West," whereas Aurobindo was "culturally a European child who grew up to become a votary of the spiritual leadership of India." Nandy's chiastic contrast of the two figures is meant to make the point that Aurobindo's "search for a more universal model of emancipation, however sick or bizarre that search may seem" is superior to Kipling's disowning of his Indianness.[89] Such a psychologistic reading does not help define the transnationally mobile and yet culturally fractured patterns of Guru English.[90] Celebrating the "confused self-definition" of Indian culture while decrying the "professional debunkers" such as Nirad Chaudhuri and V. S. Naipaul, Nandy still adopts a defensive position.[91] Aurobindo's discourse, however, marks a literary turn in the fortunes of a Guru English that was always more free-floating than a merely pathological response to colonial humiliation by Indians with a spiritual bent. With this goal in mind, we might turn to Aurobindo's literary production for clues regarding Guru English's transnational futures.

In addition to definitive metaphysical treatises such as *The Life Divine*, Aurobindo wrote vast amounts of poetry throughout his life. He is especially known for his nearly twenty-four-thousand-line poem of Dantesque and Miltonic proportions, *Savitri: A Legend and a Symbol*, indeed the longest poetic epic written in English by an Indian. Earlier, he had also written a five-thousand-line unfinished poetic treatment on the Trojan War in quantitative hexameters, entitled *Ilion*, and published a vast corpus of dramatic and narrative poetry recreating classical Greek and Hindu myth. His verse dramas include *Rodogune* (1906), *Perseus the Deliverer* (1907), *Vikramorvasie, or, the Hero and the Nymph* (1911), *Eric* (1912–13), and *Vasavadatta* (1916). The poetic output includes *Songs to Myrtilla* (1895), *Urvasie* (1896), *Ahana and Other Poems* (1915), *Love and Death* (1921), *Baji Prabhou* (1922), *The Rishi* (n.d.), *Poems in New Metres* (1942), and *Metrical Experiments* (1934).[92] Deploying a vast knowledge of Greek and Sanskrit verse, Aurobindo was enough of a committed proponent of quantitative verse in English (especially the hexameter and the eight-syllable Sanskrit *anuṣṭup* meter) to write a technical treatise, *On Quantitative Metre*, justifying his prosodic innovations.[93] Always possessing considerable prosodic richness, Aurobindo's poems are often renditions of his spiritual experiences—which make them more metaphysical, abstract, and profound—or vacuous, impenetrable, and infuriating—depending on the individual reader's receptivity to his Romantic hierophany. While he later theorized his investment in the genre of "overhead" poetry, its effects can perhaps be best illustrated by a passage on the stilling of thought by meditation from an early poem, "Thought the Paraclete":

> Hungering, large-souled, to surprise the unconned
> Secrets white-fire-veiled of the last Beyond,
> Crossing power-swept silences rapture-stunned
> Climbing high far ethers eternal-sunned,
> Thought the great-winged wanderer paraclete
> Disappeared slow-singing a flame-word rune.
> Self was left, lone, limitless, nude, immune.[94]

When it came to the magnum opus *Savitri*, Aurobindo was anxious to remind his readers that it was not "a poem to be written and finished" but "a field of experimentation to see how far poetry could be written from one's yogic consciousness." He characterized his lifelong devotion to the production of this epic (barely finished when he died) as "an attempt to catch something of the Upanishadic and Kalidasian movement."[95] The end-stopped line gives the poem a subtle intensity despite its inordinate length. Giving up the weighty hexameter he loved earlier, and for the most part eschewing the run-on line, he composed *Savitri* as a blank-verse structure that displays many different aspects of "overhead" poetry. Mostly obsessed with psychic liberation, spiritual consciousness, and meditative epiphany, the poem provides a record of the poet's spiritual autobiography and with it, a theodicy and a cosmology. Based on the well-known episode from the *Mahābhārata* involving a devoted wife who cajoles the god of death into returning her husband from his foretold untimely demise, the poet introduces the allegorical method of the poem through this short note that is worth quoting in full:

> The tale of Satyavan and Savitri is recited in the Mahabharata as a story of conjugal love conquering death. But this legend is, as shown by many features of the tale, one of the many symbolic myths of the Vedic cycle. Satyavan is the soul carrying the divine truth of being within itself but descended into the grip of death and ignorance; Savitri is the Divine Word, daughter of the Sun, goddess of the supreme Truth who comes down and is born to save; Aswapati, the Lord of the Horse, her human father, is the Lord of Tapasya, the concentrated energy of spiritual endeavour that helps us to rise from the mortal to the immortal planes; Dyumatsena, Lord of the Shining Hosts, father of Satyavan, is the Divine Mind here fallen blind, losing its celestial kingdom of vision, and through that loss its kingdom of glory. Still this is not a mere allegory, the characters are not personified qualities, but incarnations or emanations of living and conscious Forces with whom we can enter into concrete touch and they take human bodies in order to help man and show him the way from his mortal state to a divine consciousness and immortal life.[96]

Aurobindo's final claim is of course the most arguable one, since the reader's position of belief and individual spiritual experience would radically alter the meaning of the poem from an aesthetic appreciation to spiritual revelation.

Originally planned in two parts—dividing Savitri's birth, quest, and marriage from her epic struggle with Death, the poem mushroomed into serial descriptions of a number of preparatory yogas and various steps on the ladder of spiritual evolution. To characterize it in its own words, the theme of the poem is about "the secret crawl of consciousness to light."[97] The epic grandeur is still maintained by the imposition of unities and double time (the entire action takes less than a single day). Dawn is the most potent symbol of the poem, symbolizing the incipient defeat of death, the advent of the supermind, and the moment of cosmological creation:

> It was the hour before the Gods awake.
> Across the path of the divine Event
> The huge foreboding mind of Night, alone
> In her unlit temple of eternity,

Lay stretched immobile upon Silence' marge.
Almost one felt, opaque, impenetrable,
In the sombre symbol of her eyeless muse
The abysm of the unbodied Infinite;
A fathomless zero occupied the world.[98]

After all the epic tribulations, including Aswapathy's astral time-travels on the world-stair, which take up fifteen cantos in book 2, the prediction of the appearance of the Divine Mother in book 3, yogic quests from book 4 to book 8, and Savitri's preparation and confrontation with death in book 9, the poem ends in book 12 just before the break of the "greater dawn." The triumphant couple returns to Earth unharmed by Death to fulfill a salvational mission.[99]

While the myth provides the poet with an objective correlative for his spiritual experiences, the anagogic overlay, however, is complicated in Aurobindo's case by more generalized allegorical hints that are never quite fully followed up.[100] The involved yogic quests by Aswapathy are thinly veiled spiritual autobiography, combined with intimations of divine incarnation: "His was a spirit that stooped from larger spheres / Into our province of ephemeral sight, / A colonist from immortality."[101] Aurobindo's organization and his personal life were run by Mirra Richard, a Frenchwoman he anointed as the spiritual co-leader even while the beginnings of the Ashram were taking shape in 1922 (the Ashram was not formally established until 1926). Richard first visited Aurobindo in 1914 with her husband and returned permanently in 1920. She was accepted as the living incarnation of Savitri, "the Divine Mother." Influences from Christian mariolatry, Bengali Shakti worship, Bankim's nationalist motherland worship, English Romantic epic, as well as the more generalized Hindu notion of incarnation are indicated in Aurobindo's theology and personal practice just as much as the specific contours of the ancient Savitri myth. The worship of the feminine principle in Aurobindo's case also had the contingent flavor of his earlier admiration of French (as opposed to English) values in his earlier political writings, as did his operation out of a French colony adjacent to British Indian territory for most of his life. Aurobindo died in 1950, shortly after Indian independence.[102]

Yet, while the promotion of a mystically chosen Frenchwoman into the top slot of the hierarchy contributed greatly to the organization's international appeal, this factor might have correspondingly diminished Aurobindo's appeal to many conventionally minded Indians. Entry into the organization was difficult, and hundreds of prospective disciples were turned away from Pondicherry. Access to

Aurobindo was next to impossible after the mid-1920s except to a closed circle of initiates. The Master, closely guarded by an inner coterie, appeared in public only three times (later four times) a year. A remarkable spiritual experience on November 24, 1926, led Aurobindo to the conclusion that Lord Krishna, "the consciousness of the Overmind," had descended upon his body and that this was eventually to make way for the descent of "the Supermind," which would culminate in the accelerated spiritual evolution of humanity. He was quick to remind the residents of the Ashram that their aim was not personal salvation as much as it was "the perfection of life" that would have a collective and cosmic impact. Given this aim, Aurobindo's renunciation of politics was never entire, as he claimed to follow world events and intervene on a spiritualist plane. Unlike many Indian nationalist leaders who were at best indifferent to Britain's war effort and who sometimes actively courted Britain's enemies (witness Subhas Chandra Bose's alliance of the outlawed Indian National Army with Japan), Aurobindo was convinced that Hitler and his followers represented "Asuric" (demonic) forces. Aurobindo and the Mother issued a joint declaration in favor of the Allies in September 1940. He made an especially intriguing claim that he foresaw the Allied victory and "inwardly, he put his spiritual force behind the Allies from the moment of Dunkirk." As such, this psychic intervention was acknowledged as hit-and-miss in its efficacy, because it was not from the highest and transcendental fifth-level "supramental" force but from its materially constrained inferior, the fourth-level "Overmind force." Aurobindo's claimed psychic intervention in the fortunes of world history also paralleled what he saw as "India's spirituality . . . entering Europe and America in an ever increasing measure."[103]

Despite Aurobindo's partiality for the Allies, there was of course no assurance that, putting aside the obvious Aryan genealogy of the swastika, Guru English could not be resorted to by Nazism as well. The strange and fascinating case of a French-Greek devotee of Hitler, Savitri Devi Mukherjee (née Maximiani Portas) has been highlighted in a recent biography. Savitri Devi argued that Hitler was a reincarnation of Vishnu as the tenth avatar, Kalki. Hitler represented for her a true Aryan paganism, as opposed to the Judeo-Christian "weakness" that had vitiated Western society with the "cancer" of humanism for two thousand years. Savitri Devi's bizarre genealogy of charismatic leaders included the Egyptian pharaoh Akhnaton and the Mongol Genghis Khan as Hitler's predecessors, who were also, like him, "Men Against Time." Several of Savitri Devi's tracts, especially *The Lightning and the Sun*, are popular with underground neo-Nazi movements currently synthesizing their pernicious philosophies with New Age religions.[104]

The odor of politics hovered around Aurobindo's religious pronouncements because of his Jacobin phase. However, it was ultimately his phenomenal productivity of political prose, narrative poetry, philosophical tracts, and especially literary criticism that more than confirmed the close coordination of his spiritual with his literary quest. The precision of his Guru English enabled a spiritual counterthrust against Western colonial masters. Writing about Aurobindo's extensive poetic output (well before the composition of *Savitri*) as "a meeting-place of Asiatic universalism and European classicism," the Irish Theosophist James Cousins predicts a new wave of spiritual poetry that follows neo-Romantic prophetic voices such as Walt Whitman, Æ, and Tagore in a kind of transcendental fellowship. Readers of the following movement of the "new writers of the West . . . catch the large accent, the forward vision of the self-realized and ecstatic soul."[105] Inspired by Cousins' essay, Aurobindo wrote a long justification of the spiritual and literary aims of his poetic endeavors, entitled *The Future Poetry*. The powers of English poetry and ancient Vedic incantation can be combined by "the discovery of a closer approximation to what we might call the mantra in poetry, that rhythmic speech which, as the Veda puts it, rises at once from the heart of the seer and from the distant home of the Truth."[106] In rhythmic movement, verbal form, and visionary insight, English poetry can match the mantric achievements of Vedic seers. Furthermore, "the Indian spirit could seize powerfully the spiritual motive in an age which lived a strenuous objective life and was strongly objective in its normal outward mentality."[107]

Aurobindo had celebrated Bankim's "Bande Mataram" as a powerful nationalist mantra, but as one that had eventually lost its efficacy. The greater mantra now had to come from a more rarefied transcendental plane.[108] This goes one step beyond Bankim's dictum regarding the objective instrumentality of English, as the spiritual initiative will be seized in the language of the objective, English, which will itself be subjectively deepened. It is perhaps unsurprising that Aurobindo strongly favored visionary Romanticism. His own poetry could be classified as extending a strain of Indian Romanticism, strongly influenced by orientalist and Victorianist classicism. Shelley's *The Revolt of Islam* was Aurobindo's favorite poem as a youth.[109] Shelley was clearly the favorite Romantic author for many who wished to combine politics with metaphysics. Many of Aurobindo's Indian Romantic precursors, including Henry Derozio and Michael Madhusudan Dutt had imagined a political future for India along the lines suggested by Shelley, even as they confused this future with an idealized Indian past that they wished to resuscitate. Bankim had done the same. Aurobindo's comparative assessment of Shelley's superiority to his Romantic contemporaries reveals other aspects of his poetic judgment. The following passage provides an economical sense of how Guru English can be a subject-position for metaphysical literary criticism, one that is, to date, strongly echoed in a section of South Asian literary criticism of English literature. Shelley, says Aurobindo the literary critic,

> is a seer of spiritual realities, much more radiantly near to them than Wordsworth, has, what Coleridge had not, a poetic grasp of metaphysical truths, can see the forms and hear the voices of higher elemental spirits and natural godheads than those seen and heard by Blake, while he has a knowledge too of some fields of the same middle realm, is the singer of a greater and deeper liberty and a purer and nobler revolt than Byron, has the constant feeling of a high spiritual and intellectual beauty, not sensuous in the manner of Keats, but with a hold on the subtler beauty of sensible things which gives us not their glow of vital warmth and close material texture, but their light and life and the rarer atmosphere that environs there on some meeting line between spirit and body. He is at once seer, poet, thinker, prophet, artist.[110]

Following Cousins, Aurobindo deems a vatic poet such as Whitman as the true successor to Shelley, because of Whitman's foresight that can include the cosmic, the universal, and the democratic within its vision. The future poetry, Aurobindo claims, will focus on "Truth," "Life," "Beauty," "Delight," and "Spirit," in equal measure.

The new poetry of the future is ushered in as a concrete reality, even as it is claimed that it will be more intuitive, less recondite, and better connected to the material life of man. While Aurobindo shies away from direct self-identification within this lineage, self-reference hovers in the background: "[T]he idea of the poet who is also the Rishi has made again its appearance."[111] Guru English does not mean only literature about the spirit; it means also the bonus, that of English poetry written by gurus, the foremost exponent being Aurobindo himself. Why would this not be true, especially when "the voice of poetry" is deemed to appear "from a region above us, [from] a supermind which sees things in their innermost and largest truth"? The "adequate" and "dynamic" degrees of poetic speech will correspondingly be raised to "intuitive and illuminative" powers, and this revitalized Guru English will be the distinctive feature of "nations of the coming dawn."[112] The guru, armed with the mantra of "overhead" poetry, will sing of the imminent arrival of the spiritual superman. Bankim's stirring song, "Bande Mataram," had been deemed by Aurobindo to function as potently as any mantra, and we might wonder whether, at this higher plane of "overhead" poetry, the verities of universalism, cosmopolitanism, and nationalism—and the desires for science, statehood, and spirituality—merge into one. From Bankim's physician to Kipling's lama to Aurobindo's poet, the guru eventually transitions to the higher Romantic universalist synthesis of object and subject that had been kept apart. Through the unification of man and superman, patient and healer, student and teacher, novice and artist, chela and guru, and nation and cosmos, the rifts of personality, society, history, culture, and religion are supposedly transcended. By either wonderful coincidence, or perhaps "overhead" poetic justice, an independent India would come into being on August 15, 1947, Aurobindo's seventy-fifth birthday.

So what have we learned about the colonial logic and postcolonial geography of late Romanticism and Guru English through the examples of Bankim, Kipling, and Aurobindo? These figures expose an unsurprising paradox, revelatory of universalizing Romanticism and its mergers-and-acquisitions process more generally. What seems most natural, organic, and authentic about Indian culture—whether in its national or its cosmopolitan version—is shown to be invented, prosthetic, and supplementary. This is perhaps no great discovery, even while Indian Romanticism can be allowed to take its rightful place alongside all the other products of modernity that ceaselessly invented a cultural tradition in the place of the multiple practices they erased. Despite their historical anteriority, German and English Romanticism did no better, and perhaps no worse. The history of the colonial detour of Romanticism is necessary—not just in order to fill out the picture—but to account for other transitions that have since occurred: nostalgia for the present, the logic of the simulacrum, and phenomena such as Guru English, all of which were incipient in early Romanticism. If early Romanticism indulged in premodern nostalgia and a lament for lost community, late Romanticism put forward revolutionary agendas while inventing both past and future. Scapegoated as they can be for their recognizable inauthenticity and less credible cultural vocabulary, such time-lagged Romanticisms are not housed easily in narratives of identity, whether high or low. Post-Romantic archivists might want to reject characters from Bankim to Aurobindo as pale shadows for their hybrid awkwardness. While imitation is the sincerest form of flattery, it becomes difficult for Indian Romantics to confess to it, especially when the continuation of Romantic values in official nationalisms and high aesthetics foreground originality, creativity, and individuality in great measure—even if derivation, forgery, and prosthesis, subtended by the anxiety of influence, are more accurate attributes of early Romantic energy. In Guru English is expressed the efficiencies of a cosmopolitanism, ceaselessly mopping up the various remaindered fractions that earlier Romantic particularisms and universalisms could not reach. Romanticism's afterlife is ensured in the flourishing of prosthetic devices and derivative discourses, such as Guru English.

CHAPTER THREE

Theosophistries

> Interrogated as to whether life there [in the astral beyond] re-
> sembled our experience in the flesh he stated that he had
> heard from more favoured beings now in the spirit that their
> abodes were equipped with every modern home comfort such
> as tālāfānā, ālāvātār, hātākāldā, wātāklāsāt and that the highest
> adepts were steeped in waves of volupcy of the very purest
> nature.
>
> —James Joyce, *Ulysses*

WHILE THE ECUMENICAL showcasing of Indian religious leaders in the
West took place in the context of the World Parliament of Religions in
Chicago in 1893 discussed in the first chapter, the Theosophical Society
was an important intermediary for the dissemination of modern Hinduism and Buddhism. The Theosophical Society was founded earlier,
in New York in 1875, by Helena Petrovna Blavatsky and Henry Steel
Olcott. Flirting with Dayananda's Arya Samaj and integrating itself into
the Buddhist and Hindu aspects of spiritual tradition, Theosophy was
a cosmopolitan alternative when compared with the parochial nature
of the Raj. Founded in the transidiomatic environment generated by
the British Empire, Theosophy explored the fungibility of occult practices drawn from plural religious and spiritual traditions. As Gauri
Viswanathan has recently argued, despite its creativity, Theosophy
aimed to decenter empire into commonwealth rather than seek its total
dissolution. British imperial race theory was transfigured and reapplied
in ways that could rationalize spiritual evolution without compromising the political structure that sustained such reflections.[1]

All the same, the cosmopolitanism enabled by the imperial situation
of Theosophy was versatile. Theosophy, of course, is much more than
the story of its reception in literature. By focusing on two important
novelistic responses to Theosophy, this chapter allows a measuring of
some of the literary consequences of the comparative philology begun
by the orientalists and their Indian imitators. Before getting to novels
by Joyce and Desani in the later sections, a discussion of the origins,
ideas, and potential outcome of the Theosophical movement is necessary in order to sketch the context of these literary interventions. It will

be my contention that *theosophistries*—extensions, satires, and parodies, as well as the comparative theolinguistics of Theosophy itself—are ultimately revelatory of hitherto unnoticed aspects of the movement's language. As pluralized spinoffs, theosophistries make open artistic use of fraudulence, license, and imposture, issues that were always present at the heart of the serious versions of Theosophy. The success of this modern religion is *perverformative*, as defined by Hent de Vries: "any religious utterance, act, or gesture, stands in the shadow of—more or less, but never totally avoidable—perversion, parody, and kitsch, of blasphemy and idolatry."[2]

Confronted by the successes of Theosophy, the notion of fraudulence appears to be hopelessly outmoded. Instead, it might be better to think of the movement's productivity through the help of previously debased alternatives to invention, such as prosthesis, simulation, and plagiarism. Theosophy, when exposed as a series of claims regarding miraculous special effects, also participated—wittingly or unwittingly—in its own perpetration and continuation, precisely in the way that the media-savvy argue that even bad publicity can be capitalized upon by intelligent marketing techniques. Remaining in the news meant creating a media image that invited denunciation, even as the resultant publicity led to the actual encouragement of further counterfeiting and special pleading regarding the phenomena. The publicity could also be treated as a reciprocal opportunity to question the ulterior motives of the accusers, who could in turn be exposed as the secular materialist scoffers that they often were.

Theosophistries—that aggrandize as well as deflate Theosophy—suggest that intercultural mimesis as well as inspired charlatanry characterize Guru English and theolinguistics. Through an account of Theosophy's trajectory from Helena Petrovna Blavatsky to Jiddu Krishnamurti, followed by readings of two well-known novels—Joyce's *Ulysses* and Desani's *All about H. Hatterr*—this chapter tracks the spectacular use and fictional interpretation of religious cosmopolitanism under the signs of skeptical debunking, secular scoffing, and performative anxiety.

TRACKING THEOSOPHY

Arising in the wake of several esoteric movements such as Freemasonry, mesmerism, and Swedenborgianism, Theosophy was a syncretic endeavor whose origins are ultimately inseparable from the colorful biography of Blavatsky herself.[3] A charismatic Russian medium (and likely a bigamist) with an astonishing capacity for the tall tale, Blavatsky (or HPB as referred to by her associates) claimed to have traveled to esoteric locations from Egypt to Tibet and conversed with spiritual masters belonging to a number of different traditions. Blavatsky suggested that non-European civilizations such as those of India, China, Egypt, and the Aztecs were far more spiritually evolved than their European equivalents. To back this claim up, she turned to occult lore and channeled (or invented) mystical wisdom. When the Society was started in New York in 1875, Blavatsky's interests focused on Jewish, Egyptian, and Hermetic traditions from Western sources, as can be seen in her first major publication *Isis Unveiled* (1877). This vast compendium refers to at least fourteen hundred occult works in many languages, but according to scholars of Blavatsky's creative plagiarism, these references were culled from about one hundred books on these arcana.[4]

However, the emphasis on Western Gnosticism and Egyptian Hermeticism was to shift when Blavatsky and Olcott decided to travel to India and meet Swami Dayananda who had founded the Arya Samaj, a Hindu revivalist movement. The two organizations merged for a short while but then parted after recriminations from Dayananda, who was considerably more xenophobic than the Theosophists had expected. The Theosophists had not bargained for Dayananda's wanting to occupy the position of paramount guru of the joint movement. Meanwhile, a considerable amount of Hindu and Buddhist doctrine and orientalist Indology was taken on board by Theosophy, and the direction of the movement radically changed toward a justification and synthesis of South Asian religious philosophies. With various Gnostic approaches now relegated to second place within a grand universal synthesis under preparation, HPB switched to describing herself as a Buddhist. *Isis Unveiled* had already begun a polemic against Christianity and modern science that would form the opposing prong to those religious cosmopolitanisms that were attempting to integrate these two Western-based challenges. By 1884, the Theosophical Society had more than a hundred branches (eventually growing to a presence in forty-five countries), and a vast tract of land had been purchased and developed for its world headquarters in a prime location at the mouth of the Adyar River in Madras (now Chennai). Blavatsky's rendition of wisdom from various "Adepts," "Masters," and a "Great White Brotherhood" intrigued and entertained journalists and seekers.[5]

Even though barely begun, the movement was embroiled in controversy over accounts of the supposed communication of *The Mahatma Letters to A. P. Sinnett* (published later in 1923). On a number of spectacular occasions from 1880 to 1884, these letters were "precipitated" through HPB's agency, involving a kind of spiritist human fax process, sometimes compared to photography. One of HPB's occult masters, Koot

Hoomi Lal Singh, describes the process of precipitation to Sinnett this way: "I have to *think* it over, to photograph every word and sentence carefully in my brain before it can be repeated by 'precipitation.' As the fixing on chemically prepared surfaces of the images formed by the camera requires a precise arrangement within the focus of the object to be represented, for otherwise as often found in bad photographs—the legs of the sitter might appear out of all proportion with the head, and so on, so we have to first arrange our sentences and impress every letter to appear on paper in our minds before it becomes fit to be read." The masters refused to give more spectacular proofs of their existence because "the world is yet in its first *stage* of disenthralment if not development, hence—unprepared"; "the world's prejudices have to be conquered step by step, not at a rush."[6]

These chatty letters from the gurus to Sinnett form the staple of early organizational history and engendered much speculation, especially as Sinnett's *The Occult World* provided a taste of what the letters were about.[7] However, the materializations had barely been publicized when Blavatsky's supposed shenanigans in the production of the letters—as they had precipitated into her study and other venues by the purported agency of her masters—were denounced to a Christian evangelical newspaper. The source of the scandalous testimonies was a French couple who had just left HPB's employment, Alexis and Emma Coulomb. The battle was joined: either the various precipitations were an elaborate hoax perpetrated by their employer on credulous followers, or they were elaborate proofs of the existence of a complex network of subtle spiritual teachers who had much to offer to the world. A full investigation by Richard Hodgson, who went to Madras on behalf of the London Society for Psychical Research and interviewed all participants, sided with the Coulombs and declared Blavatsky to be exceptionally fraudulent in that she was "neither the mouthpiece of hidden seers, nor a mere vulgar adventuress; [we think that] she has achieved a title to permanent remembrance as one of the most accomplished, ingenious, and interesting impostors of history."[8] Astonishingly, the widespread publicity of the Hodgson report across Europe and America did not seem to affect the extraordinary growth potential of the movement, even as angry Theosophists denounced the Coulombs and churned out pamphlets in defense of their beloved HPB.[9]

Of course, the Mahatmas had already declared that, "the charlatans and the jugglers are the natural shields of the 'adepts' from the wrath of an unready world when confronted with occult wisdom."[10] However, a more recent investigation into the Hodgson report by Vernon Harrison (also of the Society for Psychical Research) declares with deft handling of expert testimony that there were serious procedural errors in the Hodgson report, enough to render it null and void. Most of the allegedly damning evidence produced by the Coulombs (in the form of explicit directives from their employer, HPB) was never properly examined for forgery or preserved for future researchers. Meanwhile, another study has suggested that the exotic cosmic personalities of Master Koot Hoomi (or K. H.), Master Morya, and the Mahachohan were actually fronts for historical mentors such as Thakar Singh Sandhanwalia, Maharaja Ranbir Singh of Kashmir, and Jamal ad-din al-Afghani, who were advising Blavatsky, and perhaps conspiring with her to foment a revolt of indigenous royals against British rule in India.[11] The original dossier constituting *The Mahatma Letters*, now still housed in the manuscript collection of the British Library, continues to pose intriguing questions. The letters demonstrate a strange and compelling physical appearance in their use of a number of colored inks, papers, and handwriting styles.[12]

Theosophy's successes—even after two sets of controversies over *The Mahatma Letters* in the 1880s and again after their publication in the 1920s—were gained as a result of its collapsing the difference between the ancient notion of the miraculous and the thoroughly mediatized modern notion of the special effect. If the miracle could later be revealed as a special effect, such an exposure would not be lastingly deleterious to the belief-system. Rather than laying claim to the supernatural, the masters claimed to "but follow and *servilely copy nature* in her works," and their special effects were in fact manifestations "as reducible to law as the simplest phenomena of the physical universe." Later, writing in *The Secret Doctrine*, Blavatsky would insist that modern science was ancient thought distorted, and nothing more.[13] Blavatsky and her supporters blithely claimed to have counterfeited some of the events in order to put off the unserious followers from the real initiates. Such shifts suggest that the conceptualization of astral travel, telekinesis, and occult masters encouraged further interaction, investigation, and refictionalization of the interaction of technology and narrative, or miracle and doctrine. Theosophy could be repositioned as the original of all theosophistries, and its current decline might itself be a sign of its more lasting success through the generalized dissipation of the particular form of theolinguistics it brought into everyday life.[14]

Seemingly unfazed by all the negative publicity, Blavatsky departed from India for England and continued working on *The Secret Doctrine*, her massive treatise that recentered Hindu and Buddhist cosmology. Supposedly based on verses from an immaterial text called *The Book of Dzyan* (from Sanskrit *dhyāna*, or meditation, also the root of *ch'an* in Chinese and *zen* in Japanese) written in an unknown occult language called Senzar, most of the manuscript was an exposition of the occult history of the universe and the role of the current stage of human evolution within it. Putting aside the very interesting issues regarding the technical aspects of handwriting analysis, ink, paper, and the physical provenance of the origin of these doctrines, Theosophical revealed texts functioned as amazing works of doctrinal synthesis and sheer audacity. Exploring universal occult mysteries and a mystical history of the world and the human race, only two massive tomes out of a planned four—*Cosmogenesis* and *Anthropogenesis*—were issued in 1888. Perhaps the best literary exhibit of the creative powers of false etymology, the treatise inverts evolution to be one that proceeds from spirit to matter, and therefore also something that begins with the subtle East and then culminates with the grosser West. The soul was divided into several levels ranging down from the divine to the monadic, spiritual, intuitional, mental, emotional (astral), and finally to the physical level. Ultimately, the text was also, among other things, an indirect spiritual rejoinder to Darwinian thought. Much of the second volume, *Anthropogenesis*, describes the colonization of the earth by spiritual beings that arrived here from the moon and then slowly evolved into corporeal humans through a series of "root races."[15] While the imperialist appropriation of evolutionism in the form of social Darwinism belittled non-European cultures, Blavatsky's rejoinder writ social Darwinism large even as it turned it on its head by applying the notion of evolution to the sphere where European epistemologies were found wanting.

Given the limitations placed on the social aspirations of the native elite under imperial rule, to speak of heightened spiritual evolution, as Theosophy did, was potentially ironical. Anglophone Indian men, for instance, could mostly look forward to lower-level teaching or clerical posts in the vast imperial bureaucracy of the Raj, and to suggest that these individuals were spiritually superior to their imperial masters was a public relations masterstroke that hastened the recruitment of native elites to the movement. Where they were disparaged as baboos, these natives could see themselves as having a head start toward becoming eventually an adept, if not a guru. The promise of esoteric wisdom, combined with a flattering narrative of the superiority of Asian religions and doctrines, even when egregiously mischaracterized, was more than sufficient to garner a loyal following. Some of the first South Asians to proselytize in North America might well have been the itinerant Theosophists (and also Brahmos and Arya Samajists) Moolji Thackersey and Tulsidas.[16]

It should be noted that while Indians were favored as spiritually advanced, the speculative theory of root races dismisses Australian aborigines, Tasmanians, and Africans as Lemurians, belonging to the seventh subrace of the third type of the third root race. When compared with other dark-skinned races, Dravidians in southern India are deemed slightly advanced, being a combination of Lemurians and Atlanteans called Tlivatli. North American indigenes are the product of Toltecs (the third subrace of the fourth root race) and Mongolians (the seventh subrace of the fourth root race). Unsurprisingly, the most advanced civilizations were deemed to be Aryans of the more civilized fifth root race, that were divided into the five subraces of Indo-Aryans, Aryo-Semites, Iranians, Celts, and Teutons. Teutons, identified as the inhabitants of central Europe who now constituted the majority in North America, Australia, and New Zealand were "destined to build a world-empire and to sway the destinies of civilization." The sixth and seventh subraces of the fifth root race, and the sixth and seventh root races were to emerge in the future. Contradicting all this civilizational hierarchy was the organization's declaration of the "universal brotherhood of all human beings, irrespective of race, creed, or colour" to which "sex" was also added by 1888.[17]

After her death, Blavatsky's moral leadership was taken over by another versatile Victorian with a greater quotient of respectability, Annie Besant. Viswanathan characterizes Besant's "associative and coalescent form of thinking" as enabling syncretism more so than any "intellectual strategy."[18] This associationism, begun by Blavatsky through her successful integration of Western Gnosticism and Eastern esotericism, also indicates the transidiomatic comparativism at work in Guru English. Such a syntactic logic of combination—pursuing the copulative *and* rather than the disjunctive *or*, as Keshub had put it—allowed the discourse to brook a high degree of contradiction and perhaps even rival Freud's notion of the unconscious. Blavatsky's and Besant's great belief in universal brotherhood was very important, as was their flexible oscillation between the language of oriental mysticism and that of colonial uplift and education. Theosophy brought a new literary consciousness to bear on cultural communication, something that would generate profoundly comic and satirical effects in Joyce's and Desani's novels, just as much as it had serious followers from Yeats and Tagore to Cousins.[19]

Besant, who had been an atheist, a proponent of birth control, a temperance advocate, and a feminist, gave up her secular heterodoxy for the alternative neo-orthodoxy of invented tradition. She proceeded to reintegrate Christianity and Buddhism toward a messianic objective. Her lectures at the Sorbonne were attended by over four thousand curiosity-seekers. The worldwide organization began to focus on preparations for the coming of a World Teacher as an incarnation of Lord Maitreya, a combination of a Buddha and Christ figure. A number of young wards, including a young Brahman boy, Jiddu Krishnamurti, were chosen as suitable vehicles for this eventual manifestation. Fresh controversies resulted when the boy's father litigated for the return of two of his sons, who had been taken away for education in England, or kidnapped as their father alleged. The boys' preceptor, Charles Leadbeater, was alleged to have taught masturbation to several of his wards, an act of moral turpitude for the times. Besant lost the case in the lower courts but refused to hand over the boys for several years until the Privy Council ultimately threw out the ruling against her. In the meantime, another well-known Theosophist, Rudolf Steiner, had splintered off from the movement in 1909 to form his own creed of Anthroposophy.

While the messianic aspects of Theosophy crested under the aegis of a subordinate organization called the Order of the Star, the movement was dealt its heaviest blow in 1929 when its heir-apparent repudiated the stated objectives by declaring that "truth is a pathless land" and that no organization could help a seeker achieve spiritual goals. Krishnamurti (or K as he was sometimes referred to by his followers) subsequently became a versatile but untypical practitioner of Guru English. Repudiating all organized religion and conventional doctrines and traditions, he spoke, wrote, and lectured widely to large audiences as an anti-guru who publicly denounced all others and also openly challenged his interlocutors to question his own spiritual authority. Dozens of his books, dialogues, lectures, and journals were published over the years. K retained a loyal following of ex-Theosophists and religious skeptics, tailoring his teachings to a philosophy of confronting the conflicts of daily life as the twentieth-century substitute for ancient meditation techniques. His successful *Commentaries on Living* adopted the structure of brief reflections and evaluations following multiple interviews he had granted to religious seekers—who were often biographically and professionally described—as "the politician," "the spiritual leader," "the Utopian," "the housewife," "the doctor," or "the heavy-built man" but whose actual identities were tantalizingly suppressed. The specific encounter often leads to a meditation on the shallowness of some of the opinions expressed to him, the deep sorrow of his interlocutors, and meditations on the structure of thought as revealed through relationship. Comparisons and ideals were the biggest oppressors of the human beings who came to him presumably wanting to be free of their oppressions and conflicts, but who actually needed to free themselves of the expectations that trapped them into feelings of inferiority and dashed their hopes. The promises of gradualist self-betterment offered by other paths to self-knowledge were ultimately delusive.

K pronounced on the necessity for a radical psychological trans-formation of humanity—an inward Enlightenment—even as he cate-gorically rejected any possibility of spiritual evolution toward it. He suggested that any serious inquirer could achieve this radical transfor-mation only through a flash of insight. While K had himself beaten a somewhat anomalous path to "enlightenment" after having been groomed to be the World Teacher, he claimed others need not concern themselves with the invidious evolutionary discriminations made by the Theosophists. For him, radical transformation was timeless and had to be immediate, free of the cycles of spiritual, psychological, and temporal evolution (this assertion turned the Theosophical belief about civilizational advancement and evolutionary incarnation yet again on its head). This equalitarian "Eastern" religious approach to modern life was enunciated in the anglicized accents of a cosmopolitan world-traveler. Krishnamurti claimed to have forgotten the use of Indian lan-guages, spoke English, French, and Italian, and wore elegant clothes wherever he went. Yet, every year, reverential crowds listened to his discourses in India as well as in Europe and the United States until his death in 1986. Perhaps this self-transformation made K more ap-pealing to his interlocutors than many saffron-clad or mantra-spouting swamis. Shorn of most Eastern references, Krishnamurti's locutions are at the outer boundary of Guru English, where they merge with the transidiomatic sociolects of Anglo-American cosmopolitanism. In the United States, K was very popular with the Hollywood set in the 1930s and 1940s. Also a practitioner of meditative and mystical nature writ-ing, his appeal evolved into attracting the counterculture and the stu-dent movement of the 1960s and 1970s. He also conducted many dia-logues with intellectuals, scientists, artists, and politicians in search of an unconventional approach to religious and cosmic truth, whether in India, Europe, or the Americas. His many published dialogues with in-terlocutors included those with theoretical physicist David Bohm, cul-tural doyenne Pupul Jayakar, and practicing psychoanalyst David Shainberg. Sure enough, the self-styled anti-guru also had his share of detractors. A memoir by a former associate published after his death alleged hypocrisy and personal inconsistency.[20]

Krishnamurti's impact as a serious spiritual alternative to Theoso-phy came somewhat later than the literary challenges posed to the movement by the 1910s and 1920s. While K's nonfictional writings went beyond Blavatsky's theosophistry into a pared-down nature writing and Romanticism mostly shorn of orientalism, this was a somewhat later development. While K was the philosophical inheritor as well as repudiator of Theosophy, his occasional orientalism took the form of assertions such as "the tonality of Sanskrit words is very penetrating and powerful; it has a strange weight and depth." Or, indirectly acknowledging that he was discovered and prepared as the vehicle for the manifestation of the Bodhisattva, he would suggest that his religious upbringing was unrelated to his present teaching that maintained that these ladders of spiritual evolution were neither relevant nor necessary.[21]

However, earlier literary responses to Theosophical orientalism ran the gamut from emulative, imitative, satirical, critical, and parodic to reflective. Theosophical mysticism and the ensuing literature was, after all, an outcome of a particular orientalist interaction between Europe and India that derived meaningfulness from the maintenance of specific structural dissymmetries. Reading earlier writers such as Krishnamurti, Joyce, or Desani reacting to Theosophy's versions of Eastern religion in an European or commonwealth context can make visible the subterranean scenario of *transculturation*, defined by Fernando Ortíz as "the different phases in the transitive process from one culture to another." Ortíz describes these phases as quasi-evolutionary stages that include the agent's acquisition of culture (*acculturation*), the loss of the preceding culture (*disculturation*), and the generation of new cultural phenomena (*neoculturation*). Specific transcultural scenarios may, however, involve different "phase" dynamics. In some cases, phases may not follow an evolutionary sequence; in others, there may be an overlap involving the simultaneous coexistence of two or more phases; in yet others, the transcultural value of the scenario may depend heavily on the subject-position of the participant. In Krishnamurti's, Joyce's, or Desani's case, theosophistry would be the mechanism, and transculturation the effect. A genius at syncretism, Joyce makes visible acculturation, whereas Desani's mocking parodies display disculturation. Krishnamurti's meditative journals and observations about natural and human encounters could be seen as a form of Romantic neoculturation.[22]

These qualifications ought to be kept in mind when assessing the related antinomies of syncretism and iconoclasm concerning "Eastern" religions and Theosophy in meditative journals or postcolonial novels. Incorporating the culturally foreign, Joyce's Guru English succeeds in establishing the global phenomenon that is called aesthetic modernism. Even though Joyce parodies the spiritualist pretensions of the Theosophists and ridicules various Irish disciples of the movement, his iconoclastic gestures are wrapped up within a theosophistry that resembles Theosophy more than he may acknowledge. Transidiomaticity works very well for Joyce. In contrast, exposés of Eastern spiritualism as a sham—such as G. V. Desani's *All about H. Hatterr*—imply a generalized disculturation and incommensurability. Religious education, of the Eastern variety, is the target of Desani's novel as mumbo jumbo, or muddle, and the spiritual syncretism of Theosophy would just be a more attenuated variety. In his turn, Desani is more iconoclastic than Joyce. Given the unequal rhetoric of cultural exchange, it is unsurprising that Joyce is not charged with derivativeness, even though he freely borrows from a range of discourses such as Theosophy, whereas Desani's disculturated novel has frequently been introduced to literary audiences under the sign of a "Joycean" acculturation. In actual fact, Joyce is more of a Theosophical syncretist than a heterodox modernist. Likewise, Desani should be appreciated as a full-fledged modernist rather than just a Joycean imitator, and his exposé of gurus becomes a full participant of the discourse.

The combination of these specific references with a more generalized syncretism and iconoclasm in these novels, both published just after formal independence was granted to each respective country, Ireland and India, leads to different transcultural scenarios regarding the efficacy of religious satire. Joyce "passes" from self-exiled Irishman to transnational icon; his aesthetic success is certainly in contrast to Desani's farcical, mock-inauguration of the postcolonial Indian novel in English. Even if *Hatterr* achieved a certain underground status, it remains a minor curiosity at best. These postcolonial parallels, concerning the initial "failure" of Desani's theosophistry and the success of Joyce's when understood under the sign of transidiomaticity, demonstrate the differing status of each figure to the doyens of British, European, and Western culture. The asymmetrical power of English as a literary language for Irish national renewal is revealed when compared with its function in the Indian context.

Precipitating *Ulysses*

That Ireland and India were both British colonial possessions suggests how global anglophone literature simulates what Fredric Jameson has called an "internationalism of the national situations" when comparing literary traditions.[23] A comparison of Ireland's literary culture with India's relies on the reductive tool of a lingua franca that enables the comparison in the first place, and Guru English forms a greater component of that common language than has been acknowledged until now. At the same time, even as it creates the formal conditions for a dialogue between two countries that were British colonies, English cannot reconcile the myriad linguistic and cultural differences that separate these domains. Gaelic, Sanskrit, and the many vernacular Indian languages and literatures are subordinated if English is the common yardstick; when these linguistic cultures appear as grafts onto English-language representation, they do so as echoes or re-creations. Despite these limitations, the lingua franca features the ideologies of two distinct cultural nationalisms—Irish and Indian—in a manner that can allow mutual influence to be discerned. Annie Besant's participation in the politics of the Indian National Congress was remarkable, just as the importation of Indian religious mysticism by William Butler Yeats, George Russell (Æ), and W. K. Magee (John Eglinton) became a crucial component of the Irish cultural renaissance.

The incorporation of Indian cultural references as flotsam and jetsam is by way of Joyce's pillaging of Theosophical sources. As J. J. O'Molloy banters with Stephen in "Aeolus," "[W]hat do you think really of that hermetic crowd, the opal hush poets: A.E. the mastermystic? That Blavatsky woman started it. She was a nice old bag of tricks. A.E. has been telling some yankee interviewer that you came to him in the small hours of the morning to ask him about planes of consciousness. Magennis thinks you must have been pulling A.E.'s leg."[24]

This irreverent passage, one of several in *Ulysses*, ridicules Theosophy's popularity in Ireland that had resulted from the movement's transcolonial appeal. Ernest Boyd claims, in his *Ireland's Literary Renaissance*—published in 1922, as was *Ulysses*—that "the Dublin lodge of the Theosophical Society was as vital a factor in the evolution of Anglo-Irish literature as the publication of Standish O'Grady's *History of Ireland*, the two events being complementary to any complete understanding of the Revival. The Theosophical movement provided a literary, artistic, and intellectual centre from which radiated influences whose effect was felt even by those who did not belong to it."[25] O'Molloy ridicules literary figures such as Æ, who wrote that Irish writers ought to "disinter the long-neglected Gaelic heritage and simultaneously introduce some of the 'aged thought of the world' into Irish literature." *Ulysses* relies extensively on Theosophical syncretism notwithstanding the bantering tone of its attacks on Theosophy's adherents. Joyce's reading of Theosophical texts such as Blavatsky's *Isis Unveiled* and *The Secret Doctrine*, A. P. Sinnett's *Esoteric Buddhism*, Henry Steel Olcott's *A Buddhist Catechism*, and Annie Besant's *Key to Theosophy* and *Esoteric Christianity* have been well documented by scholars. These Theosophical references are extensively documented by one of Joyce's first explicators, Stuart Gilbert, who typically tends to gloss the content more than the context of their reworking. Joyce's recycling of this panreligious patchwork quilt of Victorian-Irish orientalism, after putting it through the shredder of parodic ridicule, is ultimately syncretic in orientation.[26]

While Joyce represents the syncretism that brought Irish nationalism and Eastern spiritualism together as ludicrous, he ultimately does not eschew the creative potential of a dialogue between this invented tradition of Fenianism and Guru English. The textual presence of Theosophy in *Ulysses* inscribes the phenomenon of transculturation, reabsorbing the initial parody to a higher symbolic reconciliation. Rather than assume that the allusions to Bruno, Boehme, Vico, and the Christian transsubstantiation are part of an eternally expanding harmonious syncretism—(Boehme had himself used the word "theosophy" to describe this process)—readers can expose rather than celebrate the overlay of bogus religious mysticism. Fixating on the relentless aesthetic correspondences in *Ulysses* that match their religious equivalents—as earlier critics did—reveals, if anything, the continuation of Theosophical gullibility as syncretic theosophistry. Readers who celebrate Joyce's aesthetic mastery in *Ulysses* are already anticipated as displaced and disculturated Theosophists. If marveling at her system-building ingenuity distracted Blavatsky's followers from interrogating her inspired charlatanry, the aesthetic complexity and encyclopedic allusiveness of *Ulysses* likewise distracts readers from posing searching questions about the underlying seriousness of Joyce's mock-epic. There is a religious theme at the heart of Joyce's aesthetic enterprise. Stephen Dedalus's ambition matches Joyce's novelistic endeavor to archive all possible worlds: Stephen's wish to document everything makes him think of Theosophical descriptions of an all-inclusive spiritual archive, "Akasic records of all that ever anywhere wherever was" (7.882–83). James McMichael suggests that *Ulysses* itself could be considered from the would-be writer Stephen's viewpoint as "a tiny fraction of the 'Akasic records.'" From such a perspective, the humanism of *Ulysses* is a tasteful realization of Theosophical universalism.[27]

Fashioning the word from Sanskrit *ākāśa* (space, sky, or ether), Blavatsky would describe the Akasic records as "the (to us) invisible tablets of the Astral Light, 'the great picture-gallery of eternity'—a faithful record of every act, and even thought of man, of all that was, is, or even will be, in the phenomenal Universe."[28] "Precipitation" from the Akasic records is also suggested indirectly through the enhanced role given to Theosophy from "Aeolus" to "Circe." Karen Lawrence, who like Hugh Kenner argues that a significant shift takes place in the narrator's voice from "Aeolus" onward, also describes this shift as if it were precipitation: "a language not its own, as if the pen received automatic writing [from] the text of received ideas."[29] In addition, the headline "FROM THE FATHERS" suggests the origin of this writing (7.841). It is no coincidence that this Joycean model of precipitated automatic writing leads back to Blavatsky's arcane output. The focus on the mechanism of writing emphasizes the occult interest in mediumship and trance states for further cultural dissemination.

"That Blavatsky woman," as O'Molloy refers to the founder of Theosophy, claimed to have studied with esoteric masters in Tibet for seven years. At odds with people like her were the efforts of organizations such as the Society for Psychical Research, the London Dialectical Society, and the National Secular Society, all of which set out to expose spiritualist charlatanry systematically.[30] In Blavatsky's case, the dubious claims of astral travel and the materialization of letters written in colored ink by the masters contributed to an ongoing production of what skeptics saw as a series of spectacular hoaxes. Blavatsky's spiritual master, Koot Hoomi (or K. H.), appears in the "Scylla and Charybdis" chapter of *Ulysses* along with a motley crew of Theosophical enthusiasts:

> Dunlop, Judge, the noblest Roman of them all, A.E., Arval, the Name Ineffable, in heaven hight: K. H., their master, whose identity is no secret to adepts. Brothers of the great white lodge always watching to see if they can help. The Christ with the bridesister, moisture of light, born of an ensouled virgin, repentant sophia, departed to the plane of buddhi. The life esoteric is not for ordinary person. O. P. must work off bad karma first. (9.65–70)

Slightly later in the chapter, Stephen will outline the Thursday meeting of the Hermetic Society that was actually disbanded later in the Bloomsday year:

> Yogibogeybox in Dawson chambers. *Isis Unveiled*. Their Pali book we tried to pawn. Crosslegged under an umbrel umbershoot he thrones an Aztec logos, functioning on astral levels, their oversoul, mahamahatma. The faithful hermetists await the light, ripe for chelaship, ringroundabout him. Louis H. Victory. T. Caulfield Irwin. Lotus ladies tend them i'the eyes, their pineal glands aglow. Filled with his god, he thrones, Buddh under plantain. (9.279–84)

Joyce's parodic excursus—through Stephen's favoring of the Akasic records—represents the neo-Platonist mysticism of Theosophy as a version of "Charybdis." This identification can help shed light on the Library episode. Concentrating on the exposition of Stephen's Shakespeare theory in relation to the allegorical "middle path" that Odysseus had to take between the rock and the whirlpool, critics have seen the middle path as allowing Shakespeare to negotiate the cosmopolitanism of London and the provincialism of Stratford, Socrates to escape the idealism of Plato and the realism of Aristotle, and Jesus to transcend the vagueness of mysticism and the entrapment of dogma.[31] However, there are some discrepancies in the episode that undermine the neatness of this symbolic reading. While Ulysses steered slightly closer to Scylla and lost six men in the process, his textual counterpart, Bloom, leaves the library walking between Mulligan and Stephen standing at the exit, in a manner that suggests greater proximity, indeed an erotic one, to Stephen: "The wandering jew, Buck Mulligan whispered with clown's awe. Did you see his eye? He looked upon you to lust after you. I fear thee, ancient mariner. O Kinch, thou art in peril. Get thee a breechpad" (9.1209–11). As Bloom is indeed drawn to Stephen, whose Theosophical speculativeness makes him much closer to the platonic idealism represented by Charybdis, this episode counterbalances the classical Ulysses' mild favoring of Scylla. Stephen in the manner of one of the "faithful hermetists" in Dawson chambers "await[s] the light, ripe for chelaship." As symbolic son, or as incipient chela, or disciple, to Bloom's guru, Stephen will seek the light in a father figure, a practice that replicates more directly the Indian religious seeker's practice of attaching himself to a charismatic teacher. Such a tradition, popularized in the West by Theosophy, along with the panoply of "adepts," "mahamahatmas," "planes of consciousness [buddhi]," "bad karma," "yogibogeybox," initiates, the "Buddh under plantain," and the Brotherhood of Man, explain Stephen's quest for paternity that structures Ulysses, just as much as more familiar oedipal and christomimetic narratives.

Even though Bloom is the representative of disculturated anomie and Stephen the idealist projector, readings of the novel's symbolic resolution often assimilate Stephen to an oedipal master-narrative routed through Bloom. While oedipalization-as-syncretism is the outcome of this particular routing, the reverse routing, through Stephen, may yield a different scenario of iconoclasm-as-disculturation. Stephen's convoluted discussion of the oedipal nature of Shakespeare's creativity suggests such a possibility, as it ironically signals that the oedipal master-narrative is a self-fulfilling tautology. If Shakespeare wrote Hamlet just after the death of his son Hamnet, and if Hamlet is also about the trauma of Hamlet Jr. at the death of Hamlet Sr., author and protagonist become functions of a cultural superpower: the overriding agency of oedipal myth. Analogy replaces syllogism for the (re)production of a psychoanalytical tautology. What is ignored here is the context of the reproduction. A different context can make the case for an "anti-oedipal" alternative of iconoclasm-as-disculturation, or still another replacement of Oedipus by the looming spiritual authority of Blavatsky and her epigones.

Filiation, whether figured as guru to chela, father to son, or gods to humans, requires the subordination of a multiplicity of affiliations. If readers forget that a particular filiation is a master-narrative, constructed as a pathway for ideological interpellation, they will naturalize certain forms of filiation and some quests for identity over others. Bloom's mourning of Rudy and Stephen's search for a guru are explicable by cultural affiliations other than the master-narrative of oedi-palization. For instance, what to make of Mulligan's suggestion in the above passage concerning Poldy's homosexual desire for Stephen ("He looked upon you to lust after you. . . . Get thee a breechpad")? While this desire could still be recontained within the oedipal master-narrative that enables a strong "European" reading of *Ulysses*, such assimilation threatens to shut out all competitors. For instance, Stephen's parodic dream of "chelaship," derived from a Theosophical appropriation of an "Indian" narrative of cultural filiation, takes the quest for paternity in a different direction. This symbolic crossing of Stephen's and Bloom's mutual desires, in an open-ended chiastic structure, does not cancel out desire with fulfillment. Rather, it demonstrates the multiple disculturated origins of competing desires for filiation and paternity.

Shakespeare is discussed, after all, in the Irish National Library. While Shakespeare is the poster boy of English culture gone global since the introduction of English literature to the colonies, in this episode Joyce simultaneously mimics the Irish cultural alternative in the figure of Æ, who is compared to Socrates. Æ juggles Indian mysticism with the nativist gestures of economic boycott familiar to students of Irish nationalism: "A tall figure in bearded homespun rose from shadow and unveiled its cooperative watch" (9.269–70). Not unsurprisingly, the successful politics of homespun cloth—cooperative economics and political noncooperation—was later imported to India under Mahatma Gandhi's leadership of the Indian National Congress's agitation for Home Rule. Ironically, agitators for Indian Home Rule such as Annie Besant, who was for a long time president of the Theosophical Society and was also briefly president of the Indian National Congress, opposed noncooperation as unconstitutional means that would lead to contempt of law. Besant, three-quarters Irish, was greatly sympathetic to both Irish and Indian independence even though she had never lived in Ireland. She employed the Irish nationalist poet, James Cousins, to be literary subeditor of *New India* in Madras. *New India* attacked the Raj and catered to the Home Rule constituency. Besant, closer to incrementalists or "moderates" such as Gopal Krishna Gokhale, and in opposition to self-rule "extremists" such as Bal Gangadhar Tilak, lost influence in the Indian nationalist movement after its radicalization at the end of World War I when populist politicians such as Gandhi gained the upper hand. As Besant was also a ceaseless antireligious pamphleteer from 1884 to 1887, her later conversion to Theosophy appears all that much more bizarre.[32] The mystical backgrounds of Irish cultural nationalism, which Joyce passingly refers to, can best be understood by reading Besant's and Blavatsky's copious Theosophical output. Both women expound the doctrine of metempsychosis extensively. For instance, Bloom's definition of the word that Molly asks Bloom about after her lively rendering of it as "met him pike hoses" is lifted straight out of Blavatsky's *Key to Theosophy* (4.339).[33] In fact, guru Blavatsky is known to have carried on a suggestive correspondence with her chela Besant addressing her as "My darling Penelope" and signing off as "Your . . . female Ulysses."[34]

The observed link here, between cultural nationalism and spiritual syncretism is already familiar from the Indian context. The spiritual sphere is reconfigured as an authentic source of cultural difference, while the area of the secular activity of the state is conceded to the colonizer as an inescapable function of modernity.[35] The attack on Theosophy in *Ulysses* is directly linked to Joyce's dislike of the Irish renaissance's reliance on mysticism, although his parody of its exemplars such as Æ and Eglinton is not as caustic as that of the anti-Semitic Fenian who appears in "Cyclops." Theosophical mumbo jumbo will reappear in "Cyclops," where a passage that involves "tantras," "jivic rays," "the path of pralaya," and astral travel suggests that what is at stake for Paddy Dignam here is nothing more than the quotidian banality of modern conveniences and creature comforts:

> Interrogated as to whether life there [in the astral beyond] resembled our experience in the flesh he stated that he had heard from more favoured beings now in the spirit that their abodes were equipped with every modern home comfort such as tālāfānā, ālāvātār, hātākāldā, wātāklāsāt and that the highest adepts were steeped in waves of volupcy of the very purest nature. (12:351–55)

Consumerist desire, of course, has to be ceaselessly incited in capitalist society. As an advertisement salesman, Bloom solicits the business of those who solicit desire. Bloom's parasitical subject-position in relation to the process of consumption structurally parodies the anti-Semitic rendition of the Jew—by the Citizen and others—as both culturally superfluous and financially necessary to the circulation of capital.[36] Additionally, the figure of the ubiquitous Ahasuerus, the "wandering jew" referred to in the Library episode, threatens Buck Mulligan with the archaic repressed of Western Christianity. At the other end of Christianity lies the messianic doctrines of Theosophy, articulated in a transidiomatic Guru English whose Western origins make it a neoculturation that cannot be apprehended as simply "Eastern" or "Western." Hence, the Theosophical presence in *Ulysses* forms another "parasitical" structure like the overdetermined choice of the Jew in a narrative that symbolically features the Christian transsubstantiation: extraneous, yet essential; cultural filler, yet interpretive key to the overall structure.

In this regard, Yeats's generous interpretation of Blavatsky's imposture is relevant. His complex defense of Blavatsky, in terms of a theory of "trance personalities," was as follows:

> I as yet refuse to decide between the following alternatives, having too few facts to go on, (1) They are probably living occultists, as Helena Petrovna Blavatsky says, (2) They are possibly unconscious dramatisations of Helena Petrovna Blavatsky's own trance nature, (3) They are also possibly, but not likely, as the mediums assert, spirits, (4) They may be the trance principle of nature expressing itself symbolically.[37]

This rationalization of the occult elements in *The Mahatma Letters* by Yeats (who also explores them in detail in his work, *A Vision*) has implications for questions of novelistic verisimilitude. Indeed, this brief rationale puts forth something like a Theosophical theory of the novel. What are characters in novels, if not imaginary forms created by suggestion? What is a reader's empathetic identification, if not the possibility that these forms could pass from Madame Blavatsky's [here substitute the novelist's] mind to the mind of others? And what is the celebration of Bloomsday but the proof of the fact that these novelistic forms, occasionally at least, acquire external reality? Yeats's appreciation of Blavatsky echoes the nationalist's desire for contemporary novels that provide thick descriptions of daily life, generate identificatory empathy, and unite the citizenry around narratives that celebrate nationhood. Despite Joyce's demurrals, *Ulysses* does for Dublin what Blavatsky did for the occult: the novelization and personalization expected in the move to nationalist modernity and diasporic cosmopolitanism.

Joyce's rendition of Theosophy is also a commentary on the changed status of religious practice. Theosophy is a perfect precursor to "New Age" religion, one that solicits its consumers with a plethora of rewards that deliberately obfuscates spiritual experience with the banalization represented by twentieth-century creature comforts. The craze around astral travel generated by Blavatsky—not unlike the marketing of levitation by followers of Transcendental Meditation—reinscribes spiritual power as status-consciousness amongst a bourgeoisie inclined toward meritocratic fantasies. Ultimately, this "debased" form of religion is not much more than a consumerist bauble or a lifestyle choice. It is perhaps not so incongruous, after all, that Blavatsky claimed to have first met her other spiritual teacher, Master Morya, during the time of that most cosmopolitan and commercial of events, London's Great Exhibition of July 1851. Yet as a sedimented form, religion has been reduced to its external trappings because of the inversion of use and exchange. If, in its precapitalist mode, religion was a set of beliefs and practices to attain the divine—through chanting, prayer, and ritual observance—modern religiosity inverts the process, seeking to harness the divine exclusively for materialistic and worldly ends. While religious simony has been the object of criticism since ancient times, the modern situation seems to reconcile Mammon and godhead genuinely, leading eventually, perhaps, to televangelism, religious direct marketing, and famous episodes documenting the material acquisitions of religious leaders, including Jim Bakker's air-conditioned doghouse and Bhagwan Rajneesh's Rolls-Royce collection. The ostentatiousness of modern religious practitioners is not necessarily new when compared with the sumptuous expenditures of theocratic states or the primitive accumulation exercised by the medieval popes and wealthy monastic orders. However, the adaptation of religion to materialism is a matter of different cultural and political adjustments in every era.

An increased responsiveness to consumerism and advertising characterizes contemporary religious innovation. Mystical forms, Theosophy's greatest obsession, reveal for Joyce the banal reality of commodified materialistic substances, as if they were an updated version of the display of the industrial products that took place at the Great Exhibition and its successor events: "tālāfānā, ālāvātār, hātākāldā, wātāklāsāt." Exercising his punning genius, Joyce transposes quotidian amenities into Sanskrit- or Pali-sounding gobbledygook. Evoking "avatars," "hathayoga," and also Buddhist theological vocabulary, these words represent exotic punning versions of domestic creature comforts: telephone, elevator, hot-and-cold (running water), and water closet.

The Citizen's crude Fenianism and Eglinton's complex spiritualism, therefore, meet at their lowest common denominator through this Joycean reduction. Both individuals rely on the intersection of economic and cultural motives to expose colonial oppression and fabricate a newer contestatory identity (with all its reactionary problems) of ethnic nationalism as a basis for political struggle. Cynical though it may be, this reductive insight of Joyce's deconstructs the invented cultural roots behind seemingly naturalized notions of difference. When compared with the brute basis of economic and social inequality, arguing on the plane of cultural equality and complementarity is itself an example of quixotism. Unmasking spiritualism and nationalism as different versions of consumerism, these episodes reveal the productive power of theosophistry even, or precisely at, the very moment of Theosophy's debunking.

Theosophy, while implicated in the early stages of late-nineteenth- and early-twentieth-century Indian and Irish nationalism, began to be an object of suspicion as a result of its mystical vagueness and organizational ineptitude. As already discussed, allegations of moral turpitude, spiritual charlatanry, and financial irregularity within the organization contributed to its decline but also its deliquescence into the programs of other gurus and organizations, even as separatist nationalists gained ground after discrediting Theosophy's brand of occult cosmopolitanism. Theosophy will reappear in the "Circe" chapter of *Ulysses*, predictably in a degenerate form. Mananaun MacLir will appear as an instance of a ludicrous Irish-Indian syncretism:

> (*In the cone of the searchlight behind the coalscuttle, ollave, holyeyed, the bearded figure of Mananaun MacLir broods, chin on knees. He rises slowly. A cold seawind blows from his druid mouth. About his head writhe eels and elvers. He is encrusted with weeds and shells. His right hand holds a bicycle pump. His left hand grasps a huge crayfish by its two talons.*)

> MANANAUN MACLIR

> (*with a voice of waves*) Aum! Hek! Wal! Ak! Lub! Mor! Ma! White yoghin of the gods. Occult pimander of Hermes Trismegistos. (*with a voice of whistling seawind*) Punarjanam patsypunjaub! I won't have my leg pulled. It has been said by one: beware the left, the cult of Shakti. (*with a cry of stormbirds*) Shakti Shiva, darkhidden Father! (*He smites with his bicycle pump the crayfish in his left hand. On its cooperative dial glow the twelve signs of the zodiac. He wails with the vehemence of the ocean.*) Aum! Baum! Pyjaum! I am the light of the homestead! I am the dreamery creamery butter! (15.2261–76)

Æ returns here as Mananaun, the Irish god of the sea. The Irish god utters Hindu mystical phrases and invokes the male and female principles of Shiva and Shakti. The admonition to beware of the left hand references the *vāmāchārya* cult of ritual sex in the Tantric tradition, enacting religious objectives elaborated in the *Pañcatattva* [Five elements]. Bloom's intercourse in the brothel with the prostitute Zoë (life) also mimicks its equivalent: the sexual union of Shiva ("White Yoghin of the Gods") with Shakti. One interpretation suggests that throughout *Ulysses* Bloom is in the business of performing *rajasik pūjā*, or the asexual worship of his wife as the embodiment of Shakti.[38]

Yet, replete with the symbols of the crayfish, the bicycle pump, and the cooperative dial watch with the signs of the zodiac (tradition, modernity, and economic and cultural independence), Mananaun MacLir is a composite product of Indian Brahmanical and Irish druidical lore: "punarjanam patsypunjaub" literally suggests that previous incarnation (*punarjanma* in Sanskrit) combines the Irish "Patsy" or "Paddy" with the well-known province of the confluence of five rivers with the Indus, the "Punjab." The reference to the creamery butter elegantly combines the dairy cooperativism of Irish boycotts with the Hindu practice of pouring oblations of clarified butter into the sacrificial fire. This comic confusion of authentic Celticness and archaic Indianness begins from the "Telemachus" chapter on, where Buck Mulligan turns and asks Stephen sarcastically, "Can you recall, brother, is mother Grogan's tea and water pot spoken of in the Mabinogion or is it in the Upanishads?" (1.370–71). This desired connection between Celtic and Indian mythology, whether "patsypunjaub" or Mother Grogan, goes back to Francis Wilford and Charles Vallancey's projections regarding ancient connections between the British Isles and India, discussed in the first chapter.

Joyce's parodies of Theosophists such as Blavatsky and Æ are funny but not as vicious as others written at this time. One homophobic burlesque of Theosophical credulity rendered Master Koot Hoomi as "Master Tooti Fruhti Fal Lal Lah," Colonel Olcott as "Colonel Occult," and A. P. Sinnett as "A. P. Linnet."[39] The composite Irish-Indian Æ is perhaps Joyce's parody of Blavatsky's prediction that an avatar, or Maitreya, would appear to free Ireland from British rule just as another would do the same for India. Richard Ellmann's biography, in fact, records the disillusionment of the youthful Joyce upon realizing that Æ was not the Irish savior.[40]

As "Circe" continues, the mock-Tantric sexual coupling is described by Virag in tones parodic of crude pornographic literature: "Woman . . . offers her allmoist yoni to man's lingam. . . . Man loves her yoni fiercely with big lingam, the stiff one" (15.2549–53). Virag parallels MacLir's mystical syllables with sexual gutturals: "Hik! Hek! Hak! Hok! Huk! Kok! Kuk!" (15.2603). While the Wagnerian *Nothung* of the *Walpurgis* night can be glossed according to its occult echoes to the *śūnya* of Buddhist negative theology, this symbolic climax of the Nighttown episode also foreshadows the vacuous irresolution of the echo of *ou-boum* in E. M. Forster's *A Passage to India* (15.4242). The *Nothung* is both "nothing" as well as "not hung." The desires for phallic plenitude and mystical godhead are answered at the climactic moment, by the sign of lack and impotence. The theory of androgyny explored above through tantric references to Shakti and Shiva, also echoes Stephen's ruminations on *Hamlet*: "in the economy of heaven, foretold by Hamlet, there are no more marriages, glorified man, and androgynous angel, being a wife unto himself" (9.1051–52). Stephen's "chelaship" to Bloom is parodically incorporated in Stephen's nonsensical mutterings that "Theosophos told me so." The transmission of spiritual wisdom from guru to chela, like that of oedipalization, is a crucial mechanism of cultural reproduction. Yet, the "resolution" of the symbolic trinitarianism of the novel in the culminating "Circe" and "Eumaeus" chapters is perhaps one more raid on the inarticulate, in this case the mystery of sexual union collapsing into the mystery of divine being according to Tantric insights.

In his analysis of *A Passage to India*, Homi Bhabha suggests that "cultural difference, as Adela experienced it, in the nonsense of the Marabar caves, is not the acquisition or accumulation of additional cultural knowledge; it is the momentous, if momentary, extinction of the recognizable object of culture in the disturbed artifice of its signification, at the edge of experience."[41] *Nothung* is a similar moment when the relentless cultural syncretism of *Ulysses* falls apart, although in a very different fashion than the symbolic disintegration of the colonial situation perceived by Adela in Forster's novel. Bella Cohen's brothel, like the Marabar Caves, is a place of hallucination and phantasmagoria. Suggesting both desire ("needful" in German) and lack ("nothing" "not hung") *Nothung* foreshadows the radical emptiness of a colonial lack, *ou-boum*, one that obscenely mimics the mystic plenitude of *Om* at the heart of a Hindu religious society. *Nothung* also thereby cancels the febrile imaginings of the midnight revelers, who are in search of their metaphysical origin, their *omphalos/om-phallus*.[42] The plenitude of "Circe" and the vacuousness of the caves lead to the same negative space of colonial unrepresentability, both suggested in nonrealist episodes that are structured parenthetically within the realist action of both novels. The standard narrative of the transmission of culture is always within crisis in a colonial context, whether the Irish one of *Ulysses* or the Indian one of *A Passage to India*. The continuity of tradition, in terms of the plenitude of *om/omphalos* is always threatened by the eruption of parodic echoes such as *ou-boum/Nothung*. To translate this insight in terms of Guru English, the perfect pun of *om/omphalos* is permanently threatened by the undermining effect of the signifier of iconoclasm-as-disculturation, *ou-boum/Nothung*. Theosophy, as we have seen, is often reduced to theosophistry. Writing from the other side of this opposition, Desani helps us understand this symbolic teetering of the parodic text into a discrepant modernism. His intervention makes visible the harder surface of a more uncompromising form of theosophistry.

Debunking Gurus

"All improbables are probable in India."[43] This clichéd maxim is one of the several excerpts, entitled "WARNING!" with which G. V. Desani's philosophical novel, *All about H. Hatterr* (1948) begins. On the face of it, this epigraph mouths the conventional "burra sahib" wisdom about oriental unpredictability, serendipity, and other-worldliness: India is that place where things happen to you, without warning; hence the need for issuing one. However, the structure of the novel, as a series of philosophico-linguistic investigations, reveals the existence of a subtler pun: "[A]ll improbables are probe-able in India." While the first possibility is that of India as a theater of fatalist occurrences, the second implies that India is a uniquely equipped laboratory, where the exceptional happenstance, or the extraordinary condition, can be investigated scientifically, as Richard Hodgson did when interviewing the participants in the affair of *The Mahatma Letters*. The quotidian nature of the miraculous and the ubiquity of religious wisdom are the central obsessions of this novel, as indeed they are of Yogananda's *Autobiography of a Yogi*. Yet the credibility of religious wisdom in *Hatterr*, like that of Theosophy in *Ulysses*, is progressively retracted in favor of iconoclasm. In true Joycean fashion, a self-reflexive philosophical inquiry into the nature of presumption and realism, the probe-able, is itself undercut by a plethora of linguistic and stylistic contingencies—those statistical probabilities and improbabilities generated by the coincidental countercurrents of literary language, whether theolinguistics or theosophistry. Yet another go at Desani's epigraph yields a different solution: "[A]ll improbables (and/or improbe-ables) are pro-babble in India." This triple reading of Desani's epigraph, concerning the existence of spiritual improbables, the activity of probing the improbable, and the resultant Joycean babble in the novel can explain Anthony Burgess's expressed enthusiasm for Desani's "Joyceanism" and its relationship to *Finnegans Wake*, Joyce's tribute to the ideal of Babel.

Hatterr is, in the words of its protagonist, an "autobiographical," "being also a mosaic-organon of *Life*" (23). "Hatterr" is a metonym of British colonial authority, alluding as it does to the idea of the *topīwāllā*, a disparaging reference to the hatted (and implicitly, suited and booted) attire of British administrators, incongruous in the tropical heat. At the same time, it is an obvious reference to the Mad Hatter in *Alice in Wonderland*. The novel's hero is the biological product of an improb(e)able interracial union. In his own words, "[B]iologically, I am fifty-fifty of the species. One of my parents was a European, Christian-by-faith merchant merman (seaman). From which part of the continent? Wish I could tell you. The other was an Oriental, a Malay Peninsula-resident lady, a steady non-voyaging non-Christian human (no mermaid). From which part of the Peninsula? Couldn't tell you either" (31). When the novel was reissued in 1970, Anthony Burgess used F. W. Bateson's concept of the *métèque* in order to characterize Desani's style in a laudatory introduction. The *métèque*, according to Bateson, can successfully attempt a stylistic effect on the English language because of his lack of a common linguistic, racial, or political background with the native English writer, who in turn respects the finer rules of the language but misses making the larger innovation. Burgess floats the idea that the best twentieth-century English writing has come from Poles and Irishmen (presumably, Conrad, Joyce, Yeats, and Beckett), but drops the concept of the *métèque* as unnecessarily pejorative. In Burgess's opinion, "[I]t is the language that makes the book, a sort of creative chaos that grumbles at the restraining banks. It is what may be termed Whole Language, in which philosophical terms, the colloquialisms of Calcutta and London, Shakespearean archaisms, bazaar whinings, quack spiels, references to the Hindu pantheon, the jargon of Indian litigation, and shrill babu irritability seethe together. It is not pure English; it is, like the English of Shakespeare, Joyce and Kipling, gloriously impure" (10). Burgess's "Whole Language" characterization of Desani repackages earlier forms of Baboo English and Guru English with sociological and transidiomatic supplements.

Desani's novel is a tissue of decontextualized snippets from Western and Indian classics, and *Hatterr* rehearses a variety of lexical jargons and regional idioms by way of colonial mimicry. The novel's episodes involve the exposition and corresponding exposé of one guru after another. Desani's demystification of religious pretensions overlaps Joyce's occasional treatment of this topic in *Ulysses*, and his systematic submission to the pun as a stylistic device echoes Joyce's spectacular reliance on that technique in *Finnegans Wake*. The predilection for the pun in a writer—whether Joyce before *Hatterr* or Derrida after it—has been attacked by cultural conservatives even as it has been defended as intellectually subversive. In Joyce's case, Richard Ellmann asserts that "[P]unning offers . . . counter-sense, through which disparates are joined and concordants differentiated.[44] Instantiating a modernist claim about the close relationship between linguistic and political disruption, punning subverts the institutional effects of the discourse of literature in a manner that questions the stability of origins. Beckett's sly speculation in *Murphy* that "in the beginning was the pun," is matched by Joyce's favorite anecdote that the existence of the Catholic Church rests on a pun, as Peter authorized himself as the rock (*petrus*) on which Christ chose to build the Church. More recently, Colin MacCabe says that "*Finnegans Wake*, with its sustained dismemberment of the English linguistic and literary heritage, is perhaps best understood in relation to the struggle against imperialism."[45] *Hatterr* harnesses the technical and the political effects of punning, echoing the Wakean refrain from the apotropaic British royal motto, "Honi soit qui mal y pense" through an irreverent wordplay, "Honey soot quay Malaypence" (105). Similarly Hatterr wants to rewrite imperial anecdote, by suggesting that Nelson could not have said, "Kiss me, Hardy!" but probably said, "Kismet, Hardy!" Of course, punning, dependent on contingent and arbitrary linguistic effects, can never exclusively serve a single political agenda. As a child of illicit love, Hatterr calls himself "a sinfant," remarks on the "parafunerallia" of a death, and again, as Joyce does in *Ulysses* and the *Wake*, runs a series of paronomastic variations on the Hindu mystic syllable, "Aum." Desani's punning resembles the synchronic etymologies of Blavatsky or the theolinguistic proposals of the earlier orientalists and their followers who stretch for Indo-Aryan analogies as already discussed in the case of Francis Wilford or P. N. Oak. However, in Desani's literary experimentation, punning has been pushed to its parodic extreme in a manner that highlights its playful, contingent, and artificial nature.[46]

While Desani's punning style has Wakean antecedents, the picaresque structure of his novel—replete with its own versions of sirens, lotus-eaters, and cyclopeans—is reminiscent of the mock-epic structure of *Ulysses*. The convoluted and interwoven structure of the plot alludes to both Indian and Western mythological and philosophical texts as well as folk and oral traditions. However, the broad bildungsroman structure and the generally humanist and comic vision are constantly burlesqued. At times, Desani seems more of a cynic, and a far more Juvenalian satirist than the Joycean epiphanist that at least mainstream Western culture has learned to celebrate. Joyce's high modernist epic, itself a mock-epic, is raised by Desani to the third degree: *Hatterr* is a mock-Joycean novel and hence a mock-mock-epic, indicative of the delirium of theosophistries once they get under way as language games.

Desani's novel consists of seven chapters that involve Hatterr's probing the mysteries of life, in the form of spiritual encounters with seven Indian gurus: from Calcutta, Rangoon, Madras, Bombay, Delhi, and Moghalsarai-Varanasi respectively, with the last chapter featuring "the Sage from All-India." Each chapter consists of a heading, called a "Digest," that summarizes the philosophical problem to be dealt with, mimicking many theological conundrums. For instance, the first chapter asks, "Has a man a chance in the world, or is it the fate of an icicle in Hades?" The second chapter would like to know, "Is woman worth it?" The Digest at the head of each chapter is followed by an "Instruction" that always takes the form of an obscure Sanskritic/Socratic dialogue with the specific guru in question. This section is followed by a "Presumption," or a generalization, sometimes erroneous, made by Hatterr on the basis of the received "Instruction," leading to a burlesque of the mistranslations that occur.

The chapters are longest in their respective fourth sections, entitled "Life-Encounter," always consisting of picaresque occurrences involving Hatterr. The Life-Encounters either elaborate or ironically refute the Instruction and/or the Presumption in a dialectical fashion that becomes increasingly complicated in relation to earlier chapters. For instance, in the first chapter's Instruction, the "Sage of Calcutta," by means of a parable concerning a potter, lets Hatterr know that "a wise man, therefore, must master the craft of dispelling illusions. He should be *suspicious*. The moral is, 'Be suspicious!' " (41). In his Presumption, Hatterr implicitly rejects the advice as "antithesis," "antithesis" being Hatterr's "parlance for the fellers who always oppose. They hate mankind" (41). In the Life-Encounter of the first chapter, Hatterr is ejected from the stuffy Englishmen's club that he belonged to after complaints from a washerwoman, reminiscent of the equivalent figure in *Finnegans Wake*. The scandal leads to the drying up of Hatterr's credit and the revelation of his Eurasian antecedents. Forced to seek a job, Hatterr signs up as a journalist for an Indian newspaper that sends him to interview a reclusive "Sage of the Wilderness" whose great scholarship "has been noticed in Europe and America" (49). Hatterr locates the man and is soon rendered the victim of a confidence trick by the guru and his chela that involves stripping Hatterr of his clothes. The guru is a mountebank, a secondhand clothes dealer masquerading as a spiritual leader with the help of his assistant. His reputation for scholarship was the result of publishing some erudite papers found in an estate sale through his regular professional activity as a used-goods dealer. Hatterr's world of debunked gurus, peopled with charlatans, quacks, mountebanks, and impostors, is that of Ben Jonson's comedy (but largely without the cruelty). More immediately, it represents the shady world of Theosophical mumbo jumbo, miraculous precipitations, financial scams, and internecine squabbles within religious organizations. The presumption that India is the land of mystic and spiritual knowledge is systematically and ruthlessly parodied, even as Hatterr concludes in Jonsonian fashion that the world can be divided into "Hitters and Crabs"—or rogues and dupes (60). There are two kinds of crabs—the victims and the retaliators, and Hatterr counts himself as a retaliator, however ineffectual his retaliations occasionally are.

The second chapter involves Hatterr's hilarious burlesque encounter with a Cockney couple called Bill Smythe and his wife Rosie, who are touring India as entertainment impresarios. Rosie is the bait with which the couple manages to hoodwink Hatterr into a surrealist performance, where a circus lion, Charlie, eats a huge piece of raw meat off Hatterr's bare chest. At this key moment, Hatterr passes out and has an out-of-body experience. Following this brush with the English working class, Hatterr's picaresque adventures continue in subsequent chapters with assorted gurus. Hatterr has another hair's breadth escape from Sadanand, or, "Always Happy XXth," a precocious boy-guru who implicates chela Hatterr in a violent preemptive strike on a spiritual rival who is encroaching on his religious territory.

Always Happy is planning to submit Hatterr to the final *sādhanā*, or the last renunciation. Hatterr escapes, and subsequently discovers that if he had stayed, the last renunciation he would have endured in that tradition would have been, Origen-like, his own castration. Another monkish guru, Ananda Giri-Giri (following Desani's lead, the literal translation of his pseudonymous identifiers would be "Happy Mountain-peak Mountain-peak") falls violently in love with Hatterr and attempts physical and spiritual union with him; Hatterr nonetheless escapes with another devotee's monetary offerings. A subsequent encounter with a *nāgā* ascetic, one of the celebrated Hindu gymnosophists, leads to a violent altercation in which Hatterr loses the same money in a windstorm. Hatterr is also frustrated in his ambition to be the first Eurasian to acquire a title in Indian music. Indian classical music is also handed down to its practitioners through the personalized pedagogic tradition of individual gurus. At the crucial moment during "this Indian Eistedfodd," Hatterr's wife, "the Kiss-Curl," appears with an Anglo-Indian lover on her arm and breaks up the competition with a six-gauge shotgun.

As Hatterr's personal, philosophical, and picaresque complications multiply, he is reduced to mouthing the pluralist dogma, stated in impeccable theolinguistic vagueness in the seventh Life-Encounter that, "all this shirtdom and skirtdom" merely demonstrates that "Life is contrast." Hatterr arrives at a deconstruction of the probe-able Eastern philosophy in favor of the creative confusion of language, or the pro-babble that we can designate as ultimately beyond merely religious vocabularies. This outcome is achieved through a delightful parody of Bertrand Russell and logical positivism. The deliberate focus on Anglo-American positivism is intended to demonstrate the surprising discovery of laughable incoherence at the heart of both occidental logic and oriental mystery:

A *Truth*-thing, or a *Truth*-idea, might be an *a*. By the time a feller has the notion of this *a*, a sensation of it, its nature changes. What a feller has is not an *a*, but an awareness of an *a*.

Below the belt! He hasn't the true *a*, but a *translation*!

Now, if a feller has to communicate his-own idea and awareness of this *a*—let's name it another *a*—to some feller, he has to use a word, a pointer, a shadowgraph, which might be a *b*. The message now is *a* (*Truth*), plus *a* (the notion of *Truth*), plus *b* (a word): *baa*. In other words, if a feller wants to tell another what *Truth-a* is like, he has to *aa* and *baa*!

All communicated and communicable knowledge is subject to this bashing-up: this Thus far, and no farther, you baskets! ruling.

Ball-bearings all the way: and never a dull moment! (274–75)

We are back to the bleating of the lamb and, indeed, a sly dig at the Lamb of God and *bābā*, or the guru as father. Spiritual syncretism, philosophical parody, as well as cultural nationalism suggest different (false) escapes from colonial mediocrity—whether through theosophistry or other means. Joyce's representation of Theosophy parodically echoes Irish Romantic nationalism's worship of the esoteric. The quotidian boredom of Bloom's job as an advertisement salesman is not merely the alienation that results from some general modern life. Rather, Bloom's double alienation as a member of a discriminated minority within an already oppressed Irish culture is a form of disculturation that occurs specifically in the context of colonial society (something like the Anglo-Indian heritage of Hatterr in the Indian context presented by Desani). Bloom's hyperactive dream-life is related, therefore, to a corresponding anticolonial megalomania. "Bloom" is, after all, the literary representation of the consciousness of a rare creature, an Irish Jew on June 16, 1904. Bloom generalized is, nonetheless, a British transcolonial subject, rather than some free-floating humanist individual. "Hatterr," likewise as an Anglo-Indian, a similarly rare creature, can aspire neither to the authentic position of native nor the powerful one of colonizer. He is as pusillanimous as Poldy and as mongrelized as Molly. He is also more deracinated and dislocated than Kim, the Irish-born intelligence agent who is contributing his mite to the winning of the Great Game by the British Empire. Hatterr's game is one of blundering and lurching forward from guru to guru and ultimately subjecting himself to the platitudinous conclusion that "Life is contrast." The structural parallels between Joyce's and Desani's "parasitical" representations of their protagonists resonate with a Jamesonian "internationalism of the national situations," within which theosophistry is the common language that allows them to relate to each other.

Krishnamurti, a quasi-guru himself when writing about gurus, would be acutely critical of gurus a few years after Desani published his novel:

Even in so-called spiritual movements the social divisions are maintained. How eagerly a titled person is welcomed and given the front seat! How the followers hang around the famous! How hungry we are for distinctions and labels! This craving for distinction becomes what we call spiritual growth: those who are near and those who are far, the hierarchical division as the Master and the initiate, the pupil and the novice. This craving is obvious and somewhat understandable in the everyday world; but when the same attitude is carried over into a world where these stupid distinctions have no meaning whatever, it reveals how deeply we are conditioned by our cravings and our appetites. . . . We choose our leaders, political or spiritual, out of our own confusion, and so they also are confused. . . . It is essentially for self-glorification that we create the teacher, the Master; and we feel lost, confused and anxious when the self is denied. If you have no direct physical teacher, you fabricate one who is far away, hidden and mysterious; the former is dependent on various physical and emotional influences, and the latter is self-projected, a home-made ideal; but both are the outcome of your choice, and choice is inevitably based on bias, prejudice.[47]

While Hatterr's literary genealogy goes forward to post-gurus such as Krishnamurti, it also goes backward to Guru English's closest cousin, Baboo English. Two of the most relevant texts are *Baboo Hurry Bungsho Jabberjee, B.A.*, by F. Anstey, published in 1897, and Colonel Henry Yule's lexicographical compilation of Indian English called *Hobson-Jobson*, published in 1903. Collections of spoof and genuine letters that make fun of colonial linguistic locutions, such as *Honoured Sir from Babujee* (1931) and *Babuji Writes Home* (1935) cater to the English interest in colonial deformations of the tongue. These precursors are rich sources for Desani's mining and reworking of the popular stereotype concerning Baboo English that crops up routinely in Victorian and Edwardian imperialist fictions. Here, Desani is looking toward England to find a distorted reflection of India, as if "in the cracked looking glass of a servant" according to Stephen Dedalus's famous words.

Often occupying or aspiring to a bureaucratic post or a teaching sinecure, the baboo is obsequious in the extreme to his superiors, while exhibiting petty tyranny toward inferiors. Baboos speak the Indian English of the Victorian era, replete with bureaucratic legalese. The Baboo's anglophilia is demonstrated most often by his incongruous literary allusions to canonical English authors such as Shakespeare and the Romantics, but this anglophilia is farcically undermined by the frequency of the baboo's unconscious lapses into vernacular locutions and native references (indeed reminiscent of Stephen's marginality despite his obsessive focus on Shakespeare in the Library episode). For example, Hatterr's brother-in-law Banerrji, who closely resembles Anstey's Jabberji, will say, "The Bard has rightly said, A horse! A horse! My kingdom for a horse! I am myself entirely devoted to the turf!" (67). While Bloom's social ineptness, hypererudition, and inability to rise above the glass ceiling imposed upon him in colonial Dublin is suggestive of his construction as an "Irish baboo," the Irish references in *Ulysses*, as some critics have argued, represent a resurrection of popular culture against the classical form within which this content nonetheless presents itself. Amplifying the relation of Guru English toward the empowering of its baboo variant, Theosophy emphasizes a felt need for a spiritual autoethnography of a denigrated culture. Even if this took the form of hypererudition and miniaturism, the cultural riches of Ireland—as depicted by the Irish literary revival—acquire a kind of overstated relevance when viewed against the nonchalant racist dismissals of Ireland at the height of imperial suzerainty.[48]

Unlike the self-effacing poltroonishness of baboos, gurus are authoritative, confident, and secure in their borrowings, translations, and pronunciamentos. Rather than apologizing for cultural bastardy and hybridity as baboos do, gurus perform their intercultural mimesis with impunity. Unfazed by the social and religious judgments of all except the targeted group of disciples, gurus mirror the imperious disregard of colonial masters toward their subordinates. Gurus' discourses are always coming into being and developing into something different from previous instantiations through their transidiomaticity. For this reason, Guru English often does not need to acknowledge itself, its historical roots, or its social positioning, instead orienting itself to a future synthesis of the sort that Aurobindo experimented with when he wrote "overhead" poetry. Guru English is a separate offshoot (with transcultural and diasporic implications) of the myriad forms that Indian nationalism took while developing a counterdiscourse to colonial ideology.

When David Lloyd describes the style of Joyce's *Ulysses* in the following way, it seems overstated for the institutionalized Joyce, but far more appropriate in relation to Blavatsky and Desani on either side of him: "its anti-representational mode of writing clashes with nationalist orders of verisimilitude precisely by allowing the writing out of the effects of colonialism that nationalism seeks to eradicate socially and psychically."[49] Desani's aesthetic project consists of a double negation of the two dominant strains in Indian English writing at that point: the bumptious nationalist realism of Mulk Raj Anand and the orientalist Romanticism of Henry Derozio, Toru Dutt, and Sarojini Naidu. The novel lambasts the imperialist figure of the pompous Englishman that is absent in *Ulysses*, even as it uncompromisingly repudiates the reverse nationalist myth of the oriental sage or master re-created by Theosophy and the neoreligious syncretisms that have followed.

Hatterr, conversely, will take the baboo-consciousness of Bloom and the desire for "planes of consciousness" that Joyce parodies through Æ, toward a different confrontation between theosophistry and secular debunking at a moment of postindependence transition. The baboo's colonial weakness for foreign credentials alongside a desire for spiritual evolution is an indication of the manner in which his subjectivity is shored up by supplementary, perpetually expansive, and increasingly meaningless honorifics. *Hatterr* contains an amusing instance of Hatterr's rosy vision of his own funeral, at which Leonardo da Vinci,

Goethe, Gauss, Beethoven, and Dante are pall-bearers (one is reminded of Keshub's predilection for a spiritual practice that would honor Great Men). The embossed Gothic micrography on the coffin reads as follows:

MAILED CASH ON DELIVERY TO WESTMINSTER ABBEY. H. HATTERR, ESQR. (ENGLAND), HON. TREASURER (U.S. OF INDIA), SENATOR (U.S.S.R. AND U.S.A.), M.A. (MISSISSIPPI), D. LITT. (OXON AND MOSKVÁ, ET LINCOLN, OXFORD, P.A.), MEMBER ACADEMY (FRANCE, TOKYO ROYAL), PRESIDENT (ROYAL STATISTICAL SOCIETY, FIRST HONS.), HON. M.D. (LONDON), DR (BULGARIAN GRAMATIKATA), DR (UNIWERSYTET POLSKI), DR THEOLOGICE (BAGDAD, SALERNO, MONTPELLIER, HIGHH'A SOPHIA, HEIDELBERG STADIUM), M.S. M.SC. (CANTAB.), HON. D.D. (CANTERBURY) . . . MEDECIN ORDINAIRE ET CONSEILLER DU MONDE, EX-SHERIFF, EX-IDEALIST, EX-HALL OF FAME, EX-SAHIB, EX-SPORTSMAN, EX-HUMAN, EX-PARTE, EX-POSTE FACTO. (91)

The baboo's consciousness is a complex racist testament. He apes the Englishman—his accent, demeanor, and dress—thus edifying the glory of English culture, even as his very aping is a performative parody that decenters, interrogates, and exposes the pretentiousness of the model. At the same time, the baboo is living proof of the impossibility, and hence the comedy, of his aspirations; the more the baboo imitates the Englishman, the more he is oblivious of his failure to "pass" even as it is comically obvious to others, that he is not English, and can never "pass." At this point, the resort to the guru, or the Theosophical option, transcends spiritually where social advancement was checked. But that leads to further ensnarement by a series of new confidence tricksters. The bluster of the guru is that of a fraudulent super-baboo.

The caricatures of the baboo are a small part of the racist characterizations of the black, brown, and yellow races that were circulated through the discourses of social Darwinism in the late-Victorian era; the spelling of *baboo* brought the term to be only a consonant away from the simian *baboon*. A curious anecdote brings these two words together as a punning concept. When in New York, Blavatsky kept a collection of stuffed animals in her study:

The star of the collection was undoubtedly a large bespectacled baboon, standing upright, dressed in wing-collar, morning-coat and tie, and carrying under its arm the manuscript of a lecture on *The Origin of Species*. . . . Labelled Professor Fiske after a prominent Darwinian academic, Madame Blavatsky's baboon signalled her own posture in this debate as an adamant anti-Darwinian.[50]

Joyce's riposte to the English literary tradition can itself be read as a baboo's response of cultural one-upmanship, utilizing but also parodying earlier attempts in the Irish national movement to use Guru English. To read Joyce, and Bloom, as Irish baboos, or to adapt yet another metaphor, as different kinds of "signifying monkeys" or indeed baboons, is to open up the most canonical text of European modernism to transcultural possibilities. A different light is shed on the simian parallel when we think of the amusing anecdote concerning the collapse of Yeats's Eastern spiritualist pursuits. As Declan Kiberd puts it, "the poet had hoped to visit India and to meditate there on a holy mountain, emptying himself of all earthly desire. However, the Steinach operation, which seems to have reactivated his sexual urge, put paid to that: literary Dublin, on hearing that monkey glands had been implanted, scoffed that this was like equipping a worn-out Ford with the engine of a Rolls Royce."[51] Obviously, Joyce's own disparagement of the cultural marginality of Ireland is nonetheless what makes available the differential economy of transculturation through theosophistry. As a result, Joyce and Desani, like Conrad or Beckett, provide a dangerous supplement to the narcissistic logic of arguments that propound the cultural self-sufficiency of mainstream Europe. If Theosophy was "raw material" for the high modernism of Joyce, such flows also produced the popular ripostes of theosophistry.

It becomes clearer from this discussion that Desani's parody of the baboo and the guru—the two kinds of Indian "professionals" that were for a long time the most visible in the West—makes visible these figures as submerged and displaced themes in *Ulysses*. Desani's transculturated novel provides different angles on the delusive search for symbolic paternity and thereby the cultural origins, that beset the Stephen-Bloom relationship in *Ulysses*. Attempting the syncretic assimilation of Eastern with Western, both baboo and guru express desires for *omphalos/omphallus*. Yet, they are both unworked by theosophistries, as well as by the larger dynamics of colonialist and racial inequality and dissymmetry, indeed the structural underpinnings of *ou-boum/Nothung*. As a result, *Hatterr* remains a ludicrous performance of a British colonial imaginary in debased modernist idiom. Desani's satirical rendition of a Joycean hypererudition that deliberately undercuts itself through the lens of baboo-consciousness points to the anomalous status of a postcolonial aesthetics. This problem can be seen best in the epilogue to the novel, which takes the form of a key to the obscurantism of the rest of it. It is written ostensibly as a defense of Hatterr by one of the minor characters, and entitled,

With Iron Hand, I Defend You,
Mr. H. Hatterr, Gentleman!
A CRITIQUE OF YOUR WORK

BY

YOUR COUNSEL

504 Sriman Vairagi, Parivrajaka, Vanaprasthi, Acharya

YATI RAMBELI

(*Formerly widely-known as Sri E Beliram. B. Com. Advocate,*
Original and Appellate, Civil and Criminal)
Om, Om, Om, Sri Sri Sri 1008 Gurubhyo namaha!
(Om, Om, Om, humblest obeisance to Sri Sri Sri 1008 Guruji!)
Shantihi! Shantihi! Shantihi!
(*Peace! Peace! Peace!*) (279)

Bolstered by his self-sanctification with Hindu benedictions that are intensified by auspicious numerological repetitions (504, 1008), Rambeli rambles on, attacking Hatterr's profanity and immorality even as he obsequiously displays his predilection for Guru English. His mock-erudition acknowledges Hatterr's and his own multiple critical sources. Rambeli is an ironical composite of guru, baboo, lawyer, and literary critic, and indeed a send-up of all those (including me and you, dear reader) who possess the bicultural equipment to decipher his banter. For this reason, Desani makes a literary critic think twice before earnestly glossing every religious reference in the manner of a signifying monkey or indeed baboo(n). Desani also switches genres, imitating an older literary spoof by an author of his own text, such as Alexander Pope's delightful *The Dunciad Variorum* on the heels of *The Dunciad*. The honorifics identify Rambeli as a sage detached from worldly affairs even as the other parts of the curriculum vitae emphasize total attachment to worldly hierarchies conferred by academic degrees and professional credentialization in general. This conclusion of Desani's is a prescient account of religious futures as they are poised today in relation to modernity and bourgeois-professional culture. The text of Desani's novel can be regarded as a spoof, not just of Theosophy, but of the colonized chattering classes. Additionally, the epilogue to his novel suggests a parody of the literary-critical exegesis of modernist literature that takes Guru English to the next level, perhaps à la Stuart Gilbert's explication of *Ulysses* or Eliot's self-authored notes to *The Wasteland* replete with Hindu and Buddhist references, and to that extent anticipates and mocks the writing of academic books describing the phenomena, including this one.[52]

In pseudoepigraphical material to the comical author's introduction to the novel, also listed as a "WARNING!" Desani quotes an unnamed Anglo-Indian writer as follows: "[M]elodramatic gestures against public security are a common form of self-expression in the East. For instance, an Indian peasant, whose house has been burgled, will lay a tree across a railway line, hoping to derail a goods train, just to show his opinion of life. And the Magistrates are far more understanding." A second epigraph asserts that the novel, as literary form, is also a gesture:

> INDIAN MIDDLE-MAN (to Author): Sir, if you do not identify your composition a novel, how then do we itemise it? Sir, the rank and file is entitled to know.
>
> AUTHOR (to Indian middle-man): Sir, I identify it a gesture. Sir, the rank and file is entitled to know.
>
> INDIAN MIDDLE-MAN (to Author): Sir, there is no immediate demand for gestures. There is immediate demand for novels. Sir, we are literary agents not free agents.
>
> AUTHOR (to Indian middle-man): Sir, I identify it a novel. Sir, itemise it accordingly. (12)

While these epigraphs reveal the straitjacketing of the novelist who has to dissimulate mastery, they also point to the melodramatic and provisional nature of all gestures of mastery, and especially those of the gurus that the novel ceaselessly features. The ontological status of mastery, the dominant colonial category, is reduced to the performative aspect of gesture, and perhaps Desani is indicating that the linguistic and cultural phenomena—of theolinguistics, theosophistries, or Guru English—are ultimately gestural. Desani's novel also gestures, therefore, toward the intersection between the political and historical heritage of colonialism on the one hand, and the aesthetic and philosophical posture of modernism, on the other, with theosophistry being the glue that brings history, language, and religion together under a critical lens. In both Joyce's and Desani's case, the legacy of colonialism formed one of the major contexts in relation to which the guru, as either modernist or revivalist agent, acted. It is only as a result of a deliberate forgetting that the textual result of this interaction, however brilliant and erudite, can be deemed to belong to "religion," "literature," or "art." Performance, or what Hent de Vries calls perverformance—involving perversion, blasphemy, parody, and kitsch—becomes the ontology of Desani's theosophistry. However, the colonial context just as often reduces the heroic stance of secular modernist aesthetics and Theosophy to the level of theosophistry; hypererudition, a major component of Joyce's literary genius, becomes just as easily in Desani's case what Burgess calls his "seething babu irritability," or in other words, his overactive Guru English, in search of a critical overthrow of the very conditions that created it. Never achieving the status of a full-fledged transcendental aesthetics, the gesticulation of mock-modernist postcolonialism and Theosophical religion revels in its own improbe-able probabilities, producing aesthetic and religious textuality in a postcolonial context laboring under the charge of economic (and therefore cultural) underdevelopment. Joyce barely escapes this fate himself. When it comes to Desani, there is less need to hesitate. Ontology is exposed as gesture, which in turn is disparaged as mimicry. Stephen Dedalus's emphasis on gesture as a language can take this in yet a different direction.

All the same, to call Desani an imitator because he gestures toward Joyce, or Blavatsky a plagiarist because she cannibalized Horace Hayman Wilson would be much like accusing Joyce of plagiarizing Homer. Blavatsky's incorporative theological voraciousness, often dismissed as inspired plagiarism, needs to be considered alongside what Christine Froula has called Joyce's aesthetic "phagiarism."[53] The decided cognitive excess produced by Blavatsky's, Joyce's, and Desani's literary works suggests an anti-oedipal economy based on excess rather than the more conventional psychic economy of oedipal lack. This kind of excessiveness, whether it is that of swallowing other discourses whole, or breaking the bounds of conventional psychoanalytical logics, indeed suggests attributes of other kinds of language games that we have been examining.[54]

Desani's legacy continues through an amusing Theosophical reference in Salman Rushdie's novel, *The Moor's Last Sigh*, where the half-Catholic half-Jewish narrator, Moraes Zogoiby, speaks of the embarrassment suffered by his great-grandfather Francisco da Gama when he privately published a paper entitled *Towards a Provisional Theory of the Transformational Fields of Conscience*. "The Moor" discusses his ancestor proposing "the existence all around us of invisible 'dynamic networks of spiritual energy similar to electromagnetic fields,' [and] arguing that these 'fields of conscience' were nothing less than repositories of the memory—both practical and moral—of the human species, that they were in fact what Joyce's Stephen had recently spoken (in the *Egoist* magazine) of wishing to forge in his soul's smithy: viz. the uncreated conscience of our race."[55]

The Moor goes on to tell his reader that the syncretic theory of the "Transformational Fields of Conscience" (TFC's, a term that mimicks the globalized web of TNC's or transnational corporations) was mercilessly ridiculed by a debunking press as "Gama radiation," turning Francisco from "emerging hero into national laughingstock."[56] In this way, the episode refers to the disculturating dynamic that discounted and undercut the religious vocabularies at work in discourses and practices of anti-imperialist cultural nationalism at that time. Francisco da Gama is said to have been active in the Home Rule movement alongside other Indian National Congress luminaries with Theosophical sympathies, such as Annie Besant and Jawaharlal Nehru's father,

Motilal Nehru. Rushdie's citation of Stephen's obsession with the Akasic records acknowledges Joyce's parodic-syncretic representations of Theosophy amongst the Irish revivalists, as well as Desani's debunking sensibility that enhanced theosophistry even as it deflated Theosophy.

Put in the position of speaking for a vast South Asian multicultural reality as diasporic writers, Desani and Rushdie often end up as postcolonial baboos, indeed signifying monkeys who demonstrate cultural richness and philosophical variegation. In this context, Rushdie's own characterization of *The Moor's Last Sigh* in newspaper interviews as investigating "the idea of the fundamentalist, totalized explanation of the world as opposed to the complex, relativist, hybrid vision of things" sounds like an updated Stephen, with one more shot at winning the syncretist merit badge reached for by other kinds of Guru English.[57]

Given that "filiation" is indeed the central theme of *Ulysses*, especially when it is read through the Oedipal lens through which we are invited to view the symbolic relation between Stephen Dedalus and Leopold Bloom, this chapter's reading of *Ulysses* alongside *Hatterr* under the sign of theosophistry—rather than investigating, as others have done, the extent to which Desani "inherits" from Joyce—suggests an alternative, transcultural outcome or affiliation. Desani's affiliation to Joyce (or K's to HPB) does not fit neatly into either of the generalized categories of "European" or "Indian." Desani's reworking of orientalist syncretism and iconoclasm—making use of an extensive network of Hindu and Buddhist references while subjecting this archive to ridicule at the same time—acknowledges cultural loss and a destabilizing satirical laughter. Is Desani making good on the promise of modernist iconoclasm made by an earlier Joyce-Stephen but which was not kept when *Ulysses*, after all the smirking, reinstated culture as religion under the sign of oedipal resolution?

While Theosophy has declined considerably at this moment and cannot be considered a principal influence on postcolonial literature despite occasional references, the orientalist/colonialist drift of current global multiculturalism continues largely unchecked, in the form of the developing archives of religious orientalism. The dialectic of cultural syncretism and iconoclasm that bedeviled Theosophy, and alternately, various cultural nationalisms, is still alive and well in the new heights scaled by Guru English's variant forms. The syncretic idealism of these new forms was exposed as vacuous early on—in fact at the very inception of Indian independence by a novelist such as Desani. It behooves scholars to maneuver these writers into different reading formations that do not just replicate the new orientalism that is postcolonial literature. Rather than performing information retrieval for the more efficient elaboration of neocolonial futures in response to religious orientalism, literary critics can document how various cynics, scoffers, and debunkers also created perverformance and theosophistry. This dialectic of dreamers and debunkers is what Guru English is ultimately about. Theosophistries debunk religious discourses, even as they reinstate an ambivalent relationship that is critical and yet comprehending, analogous to the way in which critics of popular culture have become its most avid followers. Such a process dissolves "Blavatsky," "Joyce," "Krishnamurti," "Desani," and "Rushdie" into an endless stream of interpenetrating voices, critiques, and more abstract restatements. Doing so, this strain of Guru English cuts the cord of one-way narratives of literary influence, originating from an *omphalos*, and instead replaces them with the crisscrossing of multiple threads. In this sense, the dialectic of postcolonial catachresis is one where the nation has to be simultaneously conjured and denied, created and disavowed. As postcolonial narrative and transidiomatic lingua franca, Guru English has enigmatically arrived, not just as a temporal phase, but as a retroactive perspective that dreams of filiation, even as these dreams are almost immediately debunked, thereby shattering what appeared to be a single complex into multiple fragments and frayed transnational affiliations.

CHAPTER FOUR

The Hindu Sublime, or Nuclearism Rendered Cultural

divi sūryasahasrasya bhavet yugapadutthitā;
yadi bhāḥ sadṛśī sā syāt bhāsastasya mahātmanaḥ.
ARJUNA: If the radiance of a thousand suns were to burst at
   once into the sky,
   That would be like the splendor of the Mighty One.
                                         —Bhagavadgītā, 11.12

kālo'smi lokakṣayakṛt pravṛddho
lokān samāhartum iha pravṛttaḥ;
Ṛte'pi tvām na bhaviṣyanti sarve
ye'vasthitāḥ pratyanīkeṣu yodhāḥ.
KRISHNA: I am Time grown old to destroy the world
   Embarked on the course of world annihilation.
   Except for yourself, none of these will survive,
   Of these warriors arrayed in opposite armies.
                                         —Bhagavadgītā, 11.32

As DEFINED BY Robert Jay Lifton and Richard Falk, nuclearism is a general deformation of attitudes toward weaponry created by a "psychological, political, and military dependence on nuclear weapons."[1] Ashis Nandy has subsequently argued that this deformation is well in place the world over, and therefore, "the culture of nuclearism is one of the true 'universals' of our time."[2] In this context, Guru English is a transidiomatic vehicle for state-sponsored rationalities to gain philosophical cover and cosmopolitan appeal. When the philosophy behind nuclear weaponry is associated with as well as interrogated by the premier religious text taken up by modern Hinduism, the Bhagavadgītā, as it already has been several times since the first nuclear explosion at Los Alamos, a profoundly ethical question is posed against the background of a metaphysical problem. This chapter explores the multiple factors that rationalize nuclear weaponry and state-sponsored genocide in terms of a "Hindu sublime" enabled by Guru English. A premier religious text such as the Bhagavadgītā has been exploited to defend as well as critique such rationalizations. The capacious ideological functions of religious texts are thereby rendered even more supple and unpredictable, and it will be the aim of this chapter to track these uses, whether they are by J. Robert Oppenheimer, the architect of the Manhattan Project who invented the nuclear bomb, or Mahatma Gandhi, the global apostle of nonviolence. There is a standard critical position that seems both necessary and inadequate at such moments, when the critic realizes that the analysis of religious pronouncements on scientific and military technologies is sometimes undertaken at the risk of implicitly granting performative power to tendentious arguments. Willfully ignoring dubious logics is no solution to the problem either. The ethics of detranscendentalization involves doing interpretive battle with sketchy and nebulous positions generated by the confusion of physics with metaphysics.

Critics of the hegemony of science within Indian modernity have argued that there is more than coincidence at stake in the nuclear scientist's pursuit of the marriage of religious doctrine with the fetishization of science. Ashis Nandy perceptively suggests that especially in the Indian context, "technology comes to represent an escape from the dirtyness of politics; it becomes an indicator of Brahminic purity." The idea of "an affectless pure science" and the search for it continues "somehow to endorse the Brahminic concepts of uncontaminated knowledge and purity of vocation."[3] The heroic, the transgressive, and the sublime come together in celebrations of atomic achievement— perceived as clean professionalism unsullied by moral qualms when located under the sign of Hindu religious hermeneutics—however unpersuasive such a construction might be when analyzed from outside that structure. Nuclear weaponry, with its exponential genocidal power and its capacity to destroy future generations by radioactive fallout, takes on cosmic significance.

As has already been discussed with respect to Bankim's refrain concerning objective and subjective truth, the novelty of Hindu nationalism was its attempt to lay claim to science *and* spirituality. Shoring up a base in religious discourses, neo-Hinduism sought to appropriate science and modernity to its camp, taking control of a state-centered nationalism in the process. Guru English has become increasingly useful and perhaps even crucially necessary for this process, especially as the ambivalent posture of the Indian state regarding nuclear weapons has been recently abandoned for an overt acceptance of their strategic necessity.

A lineage that incorporates and accounts for the different strains of Guru English (and its Pakistani equivalent of a "Mullah English," even if that is not the primary focus here) is neither desirable nor possible. Linked with nuclearism and a larger scientific rhetoric, Guru (or Mullah) English is not *essentially* responsible for all of the state-sponsored claims made by India and Pakistan concerning nuclear weapons. However, these theolinguistic discourses provide the hermeneutic or transidiomatic background against which the national recognition of various tendencies takes place. Both Indian and Pakistani nationalists aggressively use religious nukespeak only to the ultimate peril of their fragile polities. Within a phenomenon such as nuclearism, Guru English is an ancillary language that cannot sufficiently explain by itself the science, the military strategies, the global proliferation of weapons technology, and the increasing vulnerability of all populations to genocidal terror initiated by state and nonstate actors alike. Nuclear rhetoric makes its way through the religious sermons of modern gurus even as atomic physicists resort to Guru English, and rival state military establishments reenact orientalist language games when they name their weapons systems. When Guru English combines with nukespeak, we can witness the creative aggressions of satire, poetic license, and rhetorical positioning. For those who are still taken in by nuclearism, antinuclear critique exposes the manner in which religion, or the nationalist state apparatuses, can be subsequently debunked as a charlatanry that has forgotten its own dubious origins in convention and apocrypha. But is it possible, nonetheless, from this critical stance of antinuclearism neither to believe nor to dismiss the commitments made by innovators, practitioners, and believers, by scientists, generals, and politicians? The aim of this suspension of judgment is not to aspire to some Archimedean lever of neutrality, but to be able to analyze statements as counters within a larger discourse and discern a historical metanarrative whose identity can thereby be more satisfyingly revealed.

Critics of Guru English and nuclearism should seek to expose the hypocrisy and racism of discourses that use nuclear weapons and rhetoric to threaten and dominate others even as these dangerous resorts are denied to yet others who are patronized through a selective logic of nonproliferation. In *The Unfinished Twentieth Century*, Jonathan Schell has argued that the current Nonproliferation Treaty (NPT) regime of the nuclear big five is tacitly encouraging a new doctrine of "proliferance" in place of the Cold War doctrine of deterrence that has fallen apart because of the structural asymmetries between current nuclear weapons states.[4] Recent events have suggested otherwise, as the United States appears currently bent on a policy of aggressive, preemptive war on states that might currently possess weapons of mass destruction (WMDs) or even intentions to acquire them in the future. The unpersuasive doctrine of nuclear deterrence, crafted ex post facto during the Cold War, juggled the inherent instability of ideological and political enmity into a stable and controllable standoff between

NATO and the Warsaw Pact. While that logic of stability was never true except as a convenient appearance that simulated reality according to managerial claims of decision making, that perception no longer holds, opening up newer instabilities, asymmetries, and possibilities in a world of considerable military uncertainty and asymmetry, especially after the unleashing of U.S. military might in the aftermath of September 11, 2001. What is recognized less frequently than it ought to be is that the world of nuclearism, just like that of Guru English, was always, and continues to be, more "fictional" than "realist"—and not just in the sense of the infamous "sexed-up documents" used to justify the war against Iraq. Even if nuclearism is based on technical accomplishments and the credible support of hardware and scientific tests, it exists ultimately as a conceptualization of a language of exchange and threat, credible posture and discernible bluff. Nuclearism, therefore, creates a world in which materialist, rhetorical, and fabulist techniques could sustain the global citizenry by the utopian possibilities of resistance and criticism, just as much as by the dystopian (and now, alas, hegemonic) myths of apocalypse and genocide.

As Jacques Derrida has already suggested in paradoxical style, in our postnuclear era, "nuclear criticism" is both necessary and impossible. In nuclear logic, *doxa* and *epistēmē* become inseparable when "there is no longer any such thing as an absolutely legitimizable competence for a phenomenon which is no longer techno-scientific but techno-militaro-politico-diplomatic through and through." Nuclear gossip, opinions, and beliefs, or what could be collectively characterized as *doxa*, is all that remains at the end of the day, behind the realist and now neorealist bluster of nuclear strategy. In what follows, we will see that Guru English has formed an inevitable part of nuclear *doxa*, thereby adding a theolinguistic supplement to the techno-militaro-politico-diplomatic logic of this weaponry.[5] For these reasons, this chapter argues that if nuclearism can go cultural through mechanisms such as Guru English, the rational choice theories fostered by structuralist neorealism are complacent, inadequate, and dangerous. Nuclear weapons are never *merely* strategic or tactical weapons, but thoroughly a part of political gamesmanship even if they are not used on the battlefield. This chapter will attempt to read, understand, and expose the logic that integrates nuclearism with that of Guru English.

There is no choice for global humanity except that of postnuclear survival. It is my hope that the analysis in this chapter can ultimately help further the goals of multilateral nuclear disarmament, inspired by antinuclear movements that seek to denuclearize South Asia and the rest of the world in favor of futures without apocalypse.[6]

The Bhagavadgītā and the Bomb

According to "Newseum," an Internet archive of global journalism, the leading news story of the twentieth century was the bombing of Hiroshima and Nagasaki, well ahead of the mission to the moon, the bombing of Pearl Harbor, or John F. Kennedy's assassination.[7] The origin myth of the nuclear age billows out from a single incident in space and time. It was fifteen seconds shy of 5:30 a.m. when the first successful atomic explosion was conducted at the so-called Trinity site near Alamogordo, New Mexico, on July 16, 1945. Witnessing the blinding flash of light from the explosion, the architect of the top-secret Manhattan Project, J. Robert Oppenheimer, invoked the Bhagavadgītā to give this unprecedented event a vocabulary. Hanging on to the uprights in the control room, Oppenheimer characterized the blinding flash of light issuing from the blast as "if the radiance of a thousand suns were to burst at once into the sky" (*divi sūryasahasrasya bhavet yugapadutthitā*, 11.12), a reference to Arjuna's exclamation when Krishna's cosmic form was revealed to him. With this comparison, a different phrase wafted through Oppenheimer's consciousness a few seconds later as the mushroom cloud rose out over the surrounding desert. This was in the compelling voice of Krishna responding to Arjuna's adoration: "I am become Death, the shatterer of worlds" (*kālo'smi lokakṣayakṛt pravṛddho*, 11.32). James Hijiya characterizes this statement of Oppenheimer's as "one of the most-cited and least-interpreted quotations from the history of the atomic age."[8]

Oppenheimer was obsessed with Vedanta from his teenage years. While his quip at this epochal moment has been noted by many who were impressed by his knowledge of Sanskrit, which he had learned at Berkeley under the tutelage of Arthur Ryder in the 1930s, what are the deeper contingencies that link Hindu sacred text with the global nuclear event? Could any other quotation, sacred or secular, have carried the weight of an earth-shattering event (*lokakṣayakṛt*), through a cliché rendered literal and hugely symbolic at the same time? It had also been Oppenheimer's idea to name the test site Trinity, traced to a John Donne Holy Sonnet he was reading after he had heard of the suicide of his former lover, Jean Tatlock. The relevant lines were, "Batter my heart, three-person'd God; for, you / As yet but knocke, breathe, shine, and seeke to mend; / That I may rise, and stand, o'erthrow mee, and bend / Your force, to breake, blowe, burn and make me new."[9] At an altitude of seven thousand feet, the Trinity site was carved out of a Precambrian volcanic formation in New Mexico presciently named in Spanish as the Jornada del Muerto (day's journey of death). Even if the site for the bomb was already suggestively named in English and Spanish, the event itself evoked a different cultural text. If Oppenheimer had not actually thought of the words uttered by the Holy One (*śrībhagawān*) to his brother-in-law, Arjuna, before the commencement of the righteous battle (*dharmayuddha*), perhaps someone from the U.S. government might have fashioned an appropriate response from a Western classical source to put in Oppenheimer's mouth. William Laurence, the resident journalist with the Manhattan Project who later won the Pulitzer Prize came up with the obvious hyperbole: "it was like being witness to the Second Coming of Christ!" Indeed, another eyewitness compared the mushroom cloud to Matthias Grunewald's *The Ascension of Christ to Heaven* that features Christ rising with a blue halo around him.[10]

However, Oppenheimer's life was eminently well scripted, and this moment of creating and witnessing world history would not have limped along with any random phrase. It is probable that he turned to the eleventh chapter (*adhyāya*) of the Bhagavadgītā with great deliberation.[11] The doctrinal kernel of this grand metaphysical poem could be relied upon to provide the strong theolinguistic support that Oppenheimer needed to accompany his brainchild into the world with a memorable and resonant proverb. In this section, Krishna, Arjuna's noncombatant charioteer (*pārthasārathī*), reveals himself to his disciple in his cosmic form (*vishvarūpadarśana*). Many of his doubts about engaging in this great world war assuaged, Arjuna worships the revealed godhead. Krishna claims to be time himself (*kālosmi*, "I am time," alternatively translated by Oppenheimer as "Death the destroyer"). During the course of this vision, according to yet another translation, Arjuna perceives Krishna as "the supercosmic monster into whose gigantic gullet are sucked all *persons* existing from (or from before) the beginning of time."[12]

Oppenheimer's rendition of the nuclear explosion as a manifestation of the Hindu religious sublime has not been extensively studied. An exception is a dogged but literal-minded interpretation of the influence of the Bhagavadgītā on Oppenheimer's life by James Hijiya that interprets the scientist as living his life according to the principal tenets of "duty, fate, and faith" learned from textbook Hinduism. Through this psychobiographical approach, Hijiya speculates that, "Oppenheimer used philosophy as an anodyne for the pangs of conscience." Having been brought up as a Jewish child affiliated to Felix Adler's Society for Ethical Culture, Oppenheimer evolves into an adult who rejects the adaptative dictates of his childhood for an abstract philosophy of brutal detachment. Painstakingly tracing the details of Oppenheimer's life, Hijiya creates the picture of a tenet-driven actor whose actions, attitudes, and emotional states are explained clinically by the possibility that "Oppenheimer could derive an entire code for the conduct of life" from his study of this sacred text. Unfortunately Hijiya—who is not a scholar of Hinduism—understands the Bhagavadgītā somewhat rigidly, in the form of a moral science manual for solipsists.[13] The result is the inadvertent orientalism of conclusions about Hinduism meaning that "Oppenheimer achieved a kind of moral weightlessness as he drifted on the currents of other men's decisions." A blank commitment to duty—purportedly learned from Hinduism—makes Oppenheimer into a functional instrument of amoral efficiency within government. Oppenheimer was himself a melancholic, diagnosed with incurable dementia praecox (the old term for schizophrenia) as a youth.[14] While Hijiya's interpretation is nonetheless a welcome intervention that underscores the great relevance of the Bhagavadgītā for understanding the life of the director of the Manhattan Project, it is important that we move the interpretation beyond a painful restriction to Oppenheimer's lonely self-justification and private imperturbability.[15]

Putting aside Oppenheimer's personal melancholy, we can recognize the manner in which the Bhagavadgītā and the cataclysmic power of nuclear weapons both invite reflections on the unpresentability of genocidal situations to human reflection. Such unpresentability has been the focus of a branch of aesthetics and philosophical theorization, identified since the eighteenth century as the category of the sublime. Thomas Weiskel characterized the "prestige and attractiveness of the sublime" as "a direct function of the prevalence of or predisposition to melancholy."[16] Vijay Mishra has pointed out that, at least since Schopenhauer, Western understandings of the sublime have been rewritten through a principle of nirvana as an oceanic consciousness linked to Indian descriptions of this process.[17] The rhetoric of nuclear warfare has certainly proceeded in terminally melancholic fashion since (or despite) Oppenheimer, with its bland acronymic platitudes of ICBMs (icy beams, as well as intercontinental ballistic missiles), MAD (mutually assured destruction), and NUTS (nuclear utilization strategists).

In the case of Oppenheimer's transidiomatic application, military science, as a technology gone out of control, seeks a cosmology, and finds it in the metaphysical locutions of Hinduism. The diagram for public release after Los Alamos showed an inner cross-section of the bomb, stylized to look very much like a mandala.[18] Such uses of South Asian religion are cosmopolitan, proceeding from the scientific generality aspired to by a nuclear physics appropriating until-then hidden universals of metaphysical doctrines. Such a fusion of the "nuclear with the unclear" (to cite a typographical transposition and a critical accusation at the same time made by Derrida's essay on nuclear criticism) is just as much the confusion of physics with metaphysics, of politics with religion, and cosmopolitanism with nationalism.[19]

Arjuna's question to Krishna in the Bhagavadgītā is an ancient precursor of the nuclear impasse, as well as the Leninist one of "what is to be done?" Arjuna's quandary, as a *kṣatriya*, or warrior, is whether he should engage in a war that will destroy his own family and lineage (uncles, cousins, brothers, preceptors) and mongrelize the entire human race in a context where the purity of bloodlines is imagined as sacrosanct.[20] As is well known, Krishna's powerful response to the warrior's failure of nerve is supremely casuistical. Arjuna ought to fight, as it is his *dharma* as a *kṣatriya* to do so. It would be cowardly of him to flee the battlefield. A refusal to fight would also be a failure to acknowledge that the battle was inevitable and that its fate had been decided by the actions of the antagonists from many years ago. The divine Krishna had already foreordained the mass slaughter that was to follow in the next eighteen days of the battle, and his role as the ninth incarnation (*avatāra*) of Vishnu had been to root out the rampant unrighteousness (*adharma*) present in the Kaurava armies led by Arjuna's cousin Duryodhana. Krishna anticipates the reestablishment of the righteous path of *dharma* through the eventual victory of the Pandava (Arjuna and his brothers) and their allies. The fratricidal civil war that Arjuna attempts to escape is revalidated for him as an unavoidable *dharmayuddha*, or holy war. In the key stanza where Krishna acknowledges his role as universal destroyer, he also tells Arjuna that he will be spared as the sole survivor while all others perish (*lokān samāhartum iha pravṛttaḥ*, 11.32).

However, there is more to the Bhagavadgītā than the rationalization of warfare through religious justifications—whether ancient or postnuclear. The poem is allegorical, historical, and philosophical simultaneously. The teaching of Krishna is a metaphysical synthesis of philosophical and religious doctrines already extant within ancient India, especially those of *sāṅkhya*, *yoga*, and *uttara-mīmāṃsā* (*vedānta*), even as this teaching rejects and/or reintegrates some of the empiricisms, materialisms, and formalisms, such as *pūrva-mīmāṃsā*, *vaiśeṣika*, and *nyāya*. Krishna outlines the three yogas, or spiritual disciplines, by which the religious seeker can discover the eternal reality or self (*brahman* or *ātman*). There are at least three available paths, those of *jñānayoga*, *karmayoga*, and *bhaktiyoga*, or of knowledge, action, and devotion. Following this exposition, Arjuna is urged by Krishna to perform his functions while adopting the perspective of *niṣkāmakarma*, or disinterested action. Separating actions into their causes, their performance, and their future effects, Krishna tells Arjuna that as prior events have already determined the actions that are to ensue on the battlefield, it is Arjuna's *dharma* to ensure the performance of those actions.

However, what Arjuna ought to do as a *sthitaprajña*, or enlightened actor, is to separate his emotions and aspirations from the actions that ought to be performed without anticipation of their fruits (*karmaṇyevādhikāraste mā phaleṣu kadācana*, 2.47). The simultaneous conflict within the microcosm (Arjuna) and the macrocosm (the battlefield) is signaled through the powerful poetic pun of the *kṣetra*, a word that can be rendered as "field" but also as "body." The historic battlefield (*kurukṣetra*) refers to the ancestral heritage of Kuru (whose descendants are the Kaurava) but also suggests a field of action. The *kṣetra* (both microcosm and macrocosm, body and battlefield) is occupied by the eternal and enlightened reality/self (*brahman/ātman*). Indestructible, this reality/realization transcends the constraints of worldly actions. The seer is a *kṣetrajña*, literally the one who attains the wisdom of the principle (*ātman*) present in the field/body (*kṣetra*), thus learning the transcendence of the former in relation to the relative irrelevance of the latter. To act in relation to the field is justified only after fully understanding the hierarchical superposition of the principle/modality/reality of the contentless and formless Brahman that paradoxically evades conceptual categories (such as principle/modality/reality) attempting to grasp it.

The doctrinal disputations regarding the different paths to self-realization—while facing human and cosmic conflicts—has produced copious commentary on the text from well before its European phase, launched by Charles Wilkins in 1785. Sankara's *Advaitin* (or nondualistic) interpretation of the text rendered his preference for renunciation, the discipline of knowledge (*Jñānayoga*), and to some, his crypto-Buddhist biases. Ramanuja's *Viśiṣṭādvaitin* (or qualified nondualistic) interpretation demonstrates a preference for the discipline of devotion (*Bhaktiyoga*), and Madhva's *Dvaitin* (or dualistic) interpretation caters even more to a desire for worship. In addition, there were influential commentaries by Vallabha and Nimbarka. Therefore, for a very long time, the Bhagavadgītā had already been subject to hermeneutic pressure. Unsurprisingly, nationalists including Bankim, Tilak, Aurobindo, and Gandhi offered new interpretations of the sacred dialogue linked to their political beliefs and goals. To some degree, Sankara's illusionistic interpretation of the world (*māyāvāda*) was the hegemonic position for all nationalists to grapple with, as it allowed the dismissal of Indian philosophy as disengaged and aloof from worldly activity. Bankim had already produced a militant and stoic neo-Krishna in *Krishnacaritra*, an interpretation intended to enable political engagement by simplifying (and distorting) the ethically complicated renditions in the ancient texts. Both Tilak and Aurobindo fashion alternative uses of the text—for nationalist and cosmopolitan purposes respectively—uses that would have been alien to Sankara, even as Gandhi, meanwhile, attempted a synthesis of biblical and Hindu doctrine in terms of a desireless ideal of *anāsakti yoga* in a Gujarati (and coauthored English) interpretation.

Tilak, in the manner of Bankim and Vivekananda, put forward an unabashed interpretation of the secret doctrine (*rahasya*) of the Bhagavadgītā as that of works (*karma-yoga-śāstra*), a reading that flew in the face of the rejection of the synthesis of knowledge and action (*jñāna-karma samuccaya*) by commentators such as Sankara.[21] Written by Tilak in Marathi while in seclusion as a political prisoner in Mandalay, such an interpretation enabled a doctrine of active resistance to British colonial rule. The first edition of six thousand copies sold out in a week, and was compared by an admirer to the popularity of Burke's *Reflections on the Revolution in France* and Walter Scott's novels.[22] While the two-volume text was a work of considerable philological prowess (Tilak had earlier published erudite interventions on Aryan and Vedic astronomy in English, called *The Orion, or Researches into the Antiquity of the Vedas* and *The Arctic Home of the Vedas*), the *Gītā-Rahasya* was also a renovation of the Bhagavadgītā in response to Mill, Spencer, Kant, Hegel, Schopenhauer, Haeckel, and Nietzsche.[23] Tilak's characteristic motto, "*swarāj* is my birth-right," derived an additional political charge from the Bhagavadgītā's already having provided the disinterested actor a path to achieve philosophical autonomy. The political demand of *swarāj*, or self-rule, seemed a close correlative of an ascetic interest in self-control and abstinence. Tilak managed to attack Western utilitarianism as well as Vedantic monism, and locked horns with Sankara on an interpretive crux he had dismissed where the text appears to favor action over renunciation (*tayostu karmasaṃnyāsāt karmayogo viśiṣyate*, 5.2). Furthermore, he turned the tables on Christian apologia, such as Lorinser's 1859 German translation, which had argued for the influence of the Bible on the Bhagavadgītā, and insisted instead that there was more likely an influence of the latter on the former. Two kinds of *jñāna* could be separated from each other, and therefore worldly political actions and successes could be differentiated from transcendental religious wisdom; the disinterest cultivated by the text only meant eliminating the narrow considerations of self-interest. However, even though the English translation of the text was in preparation immediately after the Marathi text was published, it eventually appeared only in 1935, well after Tilak's death. As Vasant Kaiwar suggests, the essentials of a Hindu nationalist program were all anticipated in Tilak's thought: a racialized reading of history; the conflation of Hindu culture, religion, and the Indian nation; the unique position of India among the nations of the world; the mobilization of Brahmanical values in the creation of a right-wing version of the national-popular; this-worldly asceticism; the paradoxical commitment to an anti-modern modernity; not to mention virulent anti-Muslim and anti-secular polemics.[24]

Tilak's indirect endorsement of heroic violence was obviously not favored by Gandhi, the apostle of nonviolence, who claimed to have discovered a justification of nonviolence in the Bhagavadgītā—highly counterintuitive as that claim was. As discussed in the introduction to this book, Gandhi felt shamefaced upon learning about the Bhagavadgītā through Edwin Arnold's translation, entitled *The Song Celestial*, given to him by "two Theosophists brothers, both unmarried." Gandhi felt that Arnold's translation was the best and most faithful rendition even though it was not at all a conventional translation. Eventually, this religious text became for him "an infallible guide of conduct," and Gandhi kept dwelling on how he might adapt key concepts from that text to his political practice—including *aparigraha* (nonpossession) and *samabhava* (equability) toward the concept of trusteeship. Gandhi favored the first three chapters of the work that expounded "performance of one's duty with detachment" and rendered the whole to him as the "Gospel of Non-co-operation." Rather than a call to arms, the poem was about "a description of the duel that goes on in our hearts," an "allegory" about "self-less action."[25] In the clearest expression of Gandhi's dissenting view, he says, "I have the courage of saying that Krishna never taught violence in the *Gita*. . . . It does not deal with an earthly war but it deals with the ceaseless spiritual war going on in the human *Kurukshetra*. . . . It is a sermon of nonviolence. Fight, without anger and passion, can only be spiritual."[26] The move toward making the Bhagavadgītā the sole guide of ethics and politics might be interpreted as Gandhi's contribution to a "Protestant Hinduism," whereby spiritual mediation was displaced into direct access to a revealed text. As Gandhi puts it, "the *Shastras* [educational treatises] have enjoined the necessity of a *Guru*. But a *Guru* being rare in these days, a study of modern books inculcating *Bhakti* [devotion] has been suggested by the sages." Ultimately, religious experience is validated as a primary category of self-instruction in relation to the edicts of the designated Hindu equivalent of the Bible and the Qur'an. Gandhi would disavow charges that his version of Hinduism was crypto-Christian, even while these similarities were obvious to many observers.[27]

This syncretic approach was brought out by Gandhi's crucial intervention as the heir to Tilak's legacy, with new strategies that posed a body politics of moral victimization and martyrdom at the same time as making the demand for Home Rule. Aurobindo, on the other hand, despite his earlier affiliations with Tilak, opposed the interpretation of the Bhagavadgītā for the performance of politics through a disinterested perspective. For Aurobindo, the doctrine favored was a synthesis of the three paths into a *pūrṇayoga* (or integral yoga) that took the seer beyond the individualist first stage, and the communal (or political) second stage, into the "tertiary condition of our developing self-consciousness towards which the secondary is only a partial advance." The third and final stage, for Aurobindo, transcended politics and united with metaphysics. For Aurobindo, the Bhagavadgītā could not be reduced to a gospel of works.[28]

Aurobindo aside, it is odd that so many other nationalists turned so resolutely to a metaphysical poem for the justification of their action-oriented political philosophies, especially when ancient India had a range of political texts to choose from and accordingly modify. Kautilya's *Arthaśāstra*, for instance, has frequently been compared to Machiavelli's *The Prince* for its comprehensive exposition of political strategies and ethics. However, the enhanced status given to the Bhagavadgītā by its orientalist translators also played into nationalist desires. Why could not political, as well as religious and social morality, be derived from this single poem, when Muslims relied as much as they did on the Qur'an and Christians on the Bible? While there was no shortage of ancient texts invested with religious authority for the Hindus, their claims were multiple and regionally diverse. The Hindus had not until then fetishized religious authority on the basis of consensus around one book, but the Bhagavadgītā provided ample opportunity to do so. While for tradition the Bhagavadgītā was an important religious poem, it was elevated to extraordinary status by neo-Hindu modernity. For this to happen, the text had to be decontextualized from its precise location as one of the books of the epic *Mahābhārata* in order to be positioned as a primer of anticolonial revolution for those subject to Hindu idiom.

Unlike the universal and transhistorical truth embodied in *śruti* texts (or heard sacred texts such as the Vedas and the Upanishads, which are *apauruṣeya*, or authorless), *smṛti* texts (or recollected traditions, such as the *Mahabharata*, which are contextual examples of history or *itihāsa*) acquire greater situational relevance because they are authored narratives. History (or religiously inflected history) became much more relevant to the nationalists rather than religion in some pure fashion, which explains the greater prominence given to the Bhagavadgītā, itself contained within a discrete section of the *Mahabharata*. The fascination that the Bhagavadgītā holds for many of its modern readers derives from the balancing act it performs between a proto-Kantian, universalizing and decontextualized ethics that could be radical, and also a relativized situational ethics that was highly recuperative. From the *sthitaprajña's* point of view, all living things are equally endowed with *brahman*. However, the eighteenth and final chapter of the poem reiterates the validity of the caste system as *dharma*. The text can therefore accommodate Gandhian pacifists and right-wing fundamentalists; monists such as Sankara, emphasizing *jñānayoga*; and revolutionaries such as Tilak, finding license for militant resistance, through *karmayoga*. The Bhagavadgītā, then, is *smṛti* text that provides an interactive model of tradition modifying itself situationally in relation to *śruti*. Purushottam Billimoria puts this well in terms of a "metadialectical" interpretation: "Arrayed on either side were two disparate discourses, an unbending traditional heritage that virtually refused to acknowledge the passage of time since the medieval era, and an indiscriminate alien force determined in its self-interest to unseat the traditional roots of the society in the name of modernity."[29]

While nationalist refashionings (themselves in a kind of triage between the "unbending" native traditionalists and the "indiscriminate" British colonizers) were crucial for the modernization of the Bhagavadgītā, so were the full-length translations and interpretations in European languages by Wilkins, Schlegel (who translated the poem into Latin), Edwin Arnold, Christopher Isherwood, and Aldous Huxley.[30] Even the mystic poet and printer William Blake produced an etching of Wilkins translating the Bhagavadgītā and entitled it "the Bramins."[31]

Warren Hastings's preface anticipates the future reception history of the text for anglophone readers. Claiming to exclude European standards of assessment, the governor-general of the East India Company nonetheless expresses great excitement at the Christian fruits of Wilkins's labors. The text will reveal the "real character" and "natural rights" of the Indian natives that are destined to survive well beyond the British presence in India. For Hastings, the text's only blemish is its idolatrous conception of spirit. Overall, he says, the Bhagavadgītā is "a performance of great originality; of a sublimity of conception, reasoning, and diction, almost unequalled; and a single exception, among all the known religions of mankind, of a theology actually corresponding with that of the Christian dispensation, and most powerfully illustrating its fundamental doctrines." Hastings's literary comparisons make favorable connections between the translation and the French versions of Homer and also Milton's *Paradise Lost*. The original author of the text can "claim the merit of having first reduced the gross and scattered tenets of their former faith into a scientific and allegorical system."[32] Following Hastings's assessment, Wilkins's translator's preface speculates regarding the Unitarian goals of the text that have already been discussed in an earlier chapter. According to Wilkins, the most learned Brahmans were Unitarians, and he assumes that the author of the poem aimed to express "the unity of Godhead. . . . [H]is design was to bring about the downfall of Polytheism."[33]

Begun by Wilkins and Hastings, Western appropriations of the Bhagavadgītā for what Aldous Huxley would call "the perennial philosophy" gave it a global relevance that grew with each repetition. Witness the following lines quoted discontinuously from T. S. Eliot's "The Dry Salvages":

> I sometimes wonder if that is what Krishna meant—
>
> . . . .
> And do not think of the fruit of action.
> Fare forward.
>
> . . . . . .
> So Krishna, as when he admonished Arjuna
> On the field of battle.
>   Not fare well,
> But fare forward, voyagers.[34]

Through many such appropriations, Guru English fulfills the apodictic function of the wise man, prophet, or sage who has spoken and thereby made literary word into metaphysical Word. The Bhagavadgītā has demonstrably been subjected to many strong cosmopolitan as well as nationalist appropriations in the last two centuries, sometimes simultaneously.

At the same time, it would be a distortion to highlight the Bhagavadgītā's positive value for all those who read it. Hegel's savage attack on the text's metaphysical abstractions was influential and well known, even if reading it now, one is struck by the incapacity of a subtle metaphysician such as himself to understand other kinds of subtlety that, after all, ought to have been familiar rather than alien to his own mode of thought. Perhaps inaccurate translation is to blame for Hegel's incomprehension, but it needs repeating that the *advaitin* interpretation of the Bhagavadgītā is more Kantian, as a philosophy of spirit, than almost any other Western philosophical mode. The ideal of desireless action led Schlegel to remark that this "disposition of the soul . . . undeniably, on the philosophical plane, approaches the sublime."[35] More relevant regarding dismissals of the Bhagavadgītā, however, given the technological context highlighted here, is the strong rejection of the Krishna-Arjuna dialogue by Tagore, a vehement opponent of nationalism. Tagore, on a trip to Iran (then Persia) by plane in 1932, wrote the following sentences about his aerial experience, which throw some prescient light on what later became the Oppenheimer effect:

> The Earth which I knew for its variety and certainty through its many testimonies became tenuous and its three-dimensional reality gradually started reducing itself to what was a two-dimensional photograph. . . . The tenets and teachings of the Gita is such a kind of "aeroplane"—the mind of Arjuna tender with mercy was taken to such a height from where one could not discern who is the killer and who is the killed, who is your kith and kin and who is your stranger. Man has in his armory many such "aeroplanes" made of theories to cover up reality in his policies of aggrandisement in social and religious principles.[36]

Tagore is referring to the oft-quoted verses that emphasize the point that "he who thinks that he kills and he who thinks that he is being killed, both are ignorant, for he neither kills nor dies; even though the body is slain, the Atman is not" (*ya enam vetti hantāram yaścainam manyate hatam; ubhau tau na vijānīto nāyam hanti na hanyate; . . . na hanyate hanyamāne śarīre*, 2.19–20). These verses about immortality had already been a favorite of the American Transcendentalists, alluded to in poems such as "Brahma" (1856) by Ralph Waldo Emerson, who quotes the lines almost verbatim. Emerson had also deeply immersed himself in other translations of ancient Sanskrit texts including the *Vishnu Purana* and the *Bhagavata Purana*.[37] Equally impressed with ancient Sanskrit texts in translation was Henry David Thoreau, who would carefully read *The Laws of Manu*, and who also compared the waters of Walden Pond to the purifying properties attributed to the water of the Ganges, even as he famously admitted that, "in the morning I bathe my intellect in the stupendous and cosmogonal philosophy of the Bhagvat Geeta, since whose composition years of the gods have elapsed, and in comparison with which our modern world and its literature seem puny and trivial." Beside this "vast and cosmogonal philosophy . . . even our Shakespeare seems sometimes youthfully green and practical merely." His approval of the text would not prevent Thoreau from adding a nonviolent dissenting touch to his reading that would later hugely influence Gandhi. As Thoreau says, "no sufficient reason is given why Arjoon should fight. Arjoon may be convinced, but the reader is not, for his judgment is *not* 'formed upon the speculative doctrines of the *Sankhya Sastra*.' "[38] Such references were music to the ears of subsequent observers, one of whom would return the compliment by suggesting that Thoreau was "a Hindu philosopher of America . . . who lived in the forest like any Indian *rishi* of yore and devoted himself to prayer and contemplation."[39]

Gandhi would suggest that Arjuna had to continue with killing as advised by Krishna because he was not a conscientious objector (as Thoreau might have in part suggested) but a warrior. The tropology of warfare and violence in the sacred poem would be rationalized through an ingenious Gandhian metaphor that uncannily follows up on Tagore's "aeroplane" comparison with a railway analogy. Harboring considerable Luddite sympathies, Gandhi, no admirer of the railways that had spread the problems of urban to rural India as he alleged, explained Arjuna's situation in the following way: "[I]f a passenger going in a Scotch Express gets suddenly sick of travelling and jumps out of it, he is guilty of suicide. He has not learnt the futility of travelling or travelling by a railway train. Similar was the case with Arjuna."[40] It is interesting that in both Tagore's and Gandhi's cases, the machinery of modern travel is used as a metaphor for justifying the unjustifiable, in one case to criticize an ancient text's justification of violence through detachment as an aeroplane theory, and in another case to apologize for the text's seeming justification of violence underneath which purportedly lay a deeper justification of *ahimsa* or nonviolence. For Gandhi, the best solution for the conundrum of the traveler caught in the hurtling interior of the Scotch Express was for him to make a resolution not to travel by train in the future, even if he could not disembark instantaneously. Arjuna's last-minute qualms could not be resolved in any way except to continue in the war machine of his own making, whereas for Gandhi, Krishna's deeper message was that "*himsa* [violence] is impossible without anger, without attachment, without hatred."[41]

STATE WEAPONRY AND GENOCIDE

Much ink has been spilled discussing what makes nuclear weapons unprecedented in the history of warfare. The Second World War brought the perils of advanced technology, more specifically the "nuclear," together with the practice of genocidal extermination, or "holocaust," as one phrase signaling what a future world war might entail. The etymology of *holocaust*, from the Greek "to burn or sacrifice the whole," is problematic as the Shoah ought not to be even inadvertently exalted as a sacrifice. While the postnuclear age suffers from the perpetual anxiety of a mass incineration, the 1940s was a period when the "nuclear" and the "holocaustal" were defined, experienced, and instituted separately. The genocidal practices in the Nazi extermination camps were conducted even while the random targeting of civilian populations by both parties to the global conflict had already collapsed distinctions between combatant and noncombatant. Giorgio Agamben has suggested that the domestic victims of the Nazi concentration camps, whether Jews, gypsies, Slavs, or homosexuals, were targets of extermination as a form of nonsymbolic bare life that emphasized the sovereign power of the state of exception.[42] Bare life was already the target of policies of extermination in other parts of the globe since the introduction of settler colonialism and capitalist forms of slavery. Harsh labor, starvation, and disease were trumped by "a final solution" using industrial techniques involving poison gas and mass incineration. Nazi genocide was carried out on the basis of eradicating racialized others and sexual and criminal deviants. The news about the death camps trickled out slowly, only when the Soviets marched through Nazi-occupied territories and shocking photographs and testimonies were published globally, resulting in the further numbing of an already war-weary world.[43]

Even before the implications of the Nazi death camps were to emerge to the world at large, there was considerable outrage throughout the non-Western world about the Allied firebombing of Dresden and Tokyo, and even greater shock at Truman's decision to use nuclear weapons against Japan. Would the United States ever have used the technology of atomic weapons so readily if the target nation had not been as racially othered as Japan? Couldn't Japan have been warned with an ultimatum specifying the devastating potential of the bomb before actually deploying it? Given the complete chaos in the Japanese military leadership after Hiroshima, was the detonation of yet another nuclear weapon at Nagasaki necessary, when intelligence reports had already come in that the Japanese military regime was on the verge of surrender? Such questions worried discussions among Asian and African intellectuals even as their rational premises were ignored and denied in the United States through the single and oftentimes unconvincing utilitarian argument that the Pacific war would have cost many more lives if it had continued on a conventional footing. The allegations of racist premises behind the use of nuclear weapons were further strengthened when it was revealed that many of the civilian survivors of the aftermath in Hiroshima and Nagasaki were not given medical treatment by the Occupation forces but observed through clinical laboratory trials intended to study the effects of radiation sickness. The furtherance of military knowledge, it seemed, had overruled aid to the victims. The threat, danger, and experience of nuclear weaponry, often later exclusively associated with the Cold War between the First and Second Worlds, acquired a completely different degree of alienation and positional displacement when viewed from non-Western vantage points. The victimized position of Japanese civilians (*hibakusha*) was taken to be illustrative of the worst the West could do to its Asian others. The imaginative rendition of this identificatory position has been rendered copiously in postnuclear Japanese literature.[44]

A recent anglophone fictional response to this question is crafted through the character of the Sikh sapper, Kip, or Kirpal Singh, in Michael Ondaatje's novel, *The English Patient*. The novel ends with Kip's response to Hiroshima and return to India from Italy (a feature of the novel utterly ignored by its celebrated movie version directed by Anthony Minghella). When Kip hears about Hiroshima, his anger and alienation explodes. After such a bomb has been dropped, his job as defuser is useless:

> He feels all the winds of the world have been sucked into Asia. He steps away from the many small bombs of his career towards a bomb the size, it seems, of a city, so vast it lets the living witness the death of the population around them. He knows nothing about the weapon. Whether it was a sudden assault of metal and explosion or if boiling air scoured itself towards and through anything human. All he knows is, he feels he can no longer let anything approach him, cannot eat the food or even drink from a puddle on a stone bench on the terrace. He does not feel he can draw a match out of his bag and fire the lamp, for he believes the lamp will ignite everything.[45]

Ondaatje reminds his readers that the universalistic understanding of nuclear weaponry did not come easily to everyone. While Oppenheimer could make the giant leap from being observer to ventriloquizing the voice of the perpetrator as inventor, Ondaatje's Kip is incapable of comprehending the justification for the moment of first deployment. Kip, as a sapper, is a bomb disposal expert, meticulously dismantling unexploded ordnance without any room for error. Several of his colleagues, and his beloved English boss—who taught him almost everything he knew—had already lost their lives by misinterpreting the trigger mechanisms of unexploded bombs. Even though the bombs he dismantles are "conventional" ones, Kip's success is a classic instance of the coming together in warfare of physical projectiles and psychological projection, murderous intention and salvational counterintention. In order to understand the trigger mechanism of an unexploded bomb, the sapper has to imagine the psychology of the bombmaker, who each time creatively alters the circuitry, or puts in dud fuses in order to confuse the dismantlers and maintain the bomb's destructive capabilities and secrets even if it had not managed to explode upon impact. By the powers of concentration and visualization, Kip succeeds where many others before him had failed. However, he deserts once he feels that Hiroshima was an ultimate colonial betrayal of Asia by the English, even if the Americans had actually dropped the bomb: "American,

French, I don't care. When you start bombing the brown races of the world, you're an Englishman. You had King Leopold of Belgium and now you have fucking Harry Truman of the USA. You all learned it from the English."[46]

This transference of guilt is enabled by the fact that Hana (the nurse) and Caravaggio (the thief) perceive Kip in relation to his colonial precursor, Kim. Hana reads out lengthy passages from Kipling's *Kim* to the other characters in the novel. But while Kip, like Kim, is also an agent of the colonial system, he is an undoer of weaponry, and while not overtly political, he acts ethically in a manner that bespeaks a desire for the undoing of empire. Rendering Italy inhabitable again, and saving the booby-trapped art and architecture left behind by the retreating Nazis, Kip's desertion implies that with the bombing of Hiroshima, the world crossed a threshold that made conventional enmities devoid of meaning. Ever the dismantler par excellence, Kip is at a loss when he considers the racial injustice of the bomb, being dropped by the powers who until then had moral right on their side. Returning to India, Kip gives up on defusing a global imperial system that can no longer be deconstructed by way of bomb disposal techniques or by the visualization of enemy intentions.

The irrationality of Kip's response—confusing Nazis, British, and Americans from the point of view of a visceral racial logic—might be better contextualized in relation to Georges Bataille's suggestive reflections on Hiroshima, where he distinguishes the "animal experience" of the catastrophe as distinct from the "human representation" of it. To grasp the use of the bomb within the framework of some kind of instrumental rationality such as President Truman's, various alternatives and outcomes have to be argued and relative evils have to be weighed and justified. This realm of military strategy is one within which civilian deaths, even in the hundreds of thousands, are expendable as forms of collateral damage along the way to the realization of strategic objectives. While Kip is not himself in the Pacific theater, his reaction and desertion is a second-order act of refusal based on a sympathetic identification with dead Japanese civilians. It is his failure to adequately represent what has happened that leads to the emotional crisis and his desertion, precisely in the manner that genocides are often perceived to be unrepresentable from any standpoint, except perhaps from that of the killers. To think of collateral damage is to think from the military utilitarian standpoint, which is already to validate and normalize a "sadistic" epistemological position.[47]

Thomas Pynchon's *Gravity's Rainbow* (1973) thematizes Hiroshima in relation to orientalist interpretations of Buddhism, including many references to Kipling and Theosophy. After the bomb is dropped, the closing pages of the novel include "the face of the Buddha, looking down from the sky," and the ushering in of the "Order of the Golden Dawn." From Oppenheimer to Pynchon to Ondaatje, the bomb demands an Asian cultural subtext. The initial use of the bomb in the Pacific theater emphasized its genocidal function outside Western geography, much as the concentration camp emphasized the same function internally (and as Aimé Césaire would have it, the concentration camp was itself the "coming home" to the West of genocidal techniques experimentally perfected in the colonies).[48] From a South Asian point of view, nuclear weaponry, while experienced as the culmination of a global war that killed about forty-five million people, was also a technology applied against an Asian power whom some Indian nationalists wanted to emulate. Japan was a potential ally in the fight for independence, as the militant wing of the Congress Party with Subhas Chandra Bose at its helm had found. Powerful feelings regarding Japan's victimization by the West persisted. Radhabinod Pal, one of the Indian judges appointed as a member of the International Military Tribunal of the Far East, exonerated the Japanese military from having committed war crimes. According to a recent biography by Dietmar Rothermund, even Mahatma Gandhi, the famed apostle of nonviolence, kept his opposition to nuclear weaponry secret by a self-imposed silence on the topic until the British had announced the plans for Indian independence. Gandhi might have been concerned that nuclear weapons could be used in a manner to deny India's quest for self-rule, and therefore he was possibly allowing his ethics of conviction (which were antinuclear) to be momentarily silenced by a more prudent ethics of responsible action (which ensured that he not jeopardize Indian independence by speaking out against the Allied use of nuclear weapons).[49]

Even more important as historical coincidence was that the South Asian genocidal holocaust of partition followed closely on the heels of the death camps to the west and the mushroom clouds to the east, making the 1940s one of the most horrific decades in the history of human warfare and genocide. While Hiroshima and Nagasaki occupy the only "real" experiential vantage points on the nuclear (so far), the entire globe lurches toward comprehending it through a symbolic approximation in terms of the greatest genocidal civil disruption and carnage it could suggest to the imagination. The partition of British India into the states of India and Pakistan meant at least a million dead and seventy-five thousand women raped or abducted in the short space of two months in late 1947. South Asia's experience of genocide was also interpreted in India through the metaphysical lens of the Hindu sublime. A preference linked to Hindu nationalist reflexes, the aesthetics of the sublime suggested ancient spirituality as well as modern science.

The Indian state's desire for nuclear power proceeded from independence, despite the disavowals made through the official doctrines of nonviolence and nonalignment inherited from Gandhi and furthered under Nehru's stewardship.

A couple of years after Hiroshima and Nagasaki, the genocidal aspects of partition were experienced by the most affected Hindu and Sikh participants as a kind of *dharmayuddha*, and as a *jihad* for Muslims.[50] The genital mutilation of the living and the dead, the rape of "other" women, and the massacre of "other" children were carried out indiscriminately upon a recently identified enemy. Religious affiliation was the shibboleth of life and death, even as many were protected or given safe passage by those who did not wish to participate in the cold-blooded murder of human beings who had been, for decades, friends, neighbors, fellows, citizens, and relatives, rather than enemies. The South Asian version of genocide, so deeply linked as it is to state-supported modern forms of violence and social identity, was not far from contemporary understandings and projections regarding the nuclear bomb as the ultimate state-sanctioned genocidal weapon. Utilized with no moral distinction between combatant and noncombatant, or military and civilian "collateral damage," the love of the nuclear bomb corresponds with a sense of total war where the annihilation of the enemy and the purification of the self are utterly and inextricably confused, becoming for all practical purposes one and the same thing. And again, the *Mahābhārata* could be said to have anticipated such an outcome, one that renders the entire world a battlefield. In the battle depicted in the *Mahābhārata*, the final weapon of annihilation is that of destroying the futurity of the survivors. The sole surviving representative on the Kaurava side is Dronacharya's son, Aswatthama, who deploys a magical weapon to kill the unborn Pandava heirs. Krishna, the divine protector of the Pandava line, shields Arjuna's unborn grandson (and his own grand-nephew) Parikshit, from the powerful nonlocal weapon (*astra*) that attacked the fetus in the womb. Nationalists could indeed marvel at how ancient history (*itihāsa*) presciently rendered the dreadful effects of nuclear radiation on the unborn. The notion of the sublime activated in such fears of biological annihilation is similar to the Kantian one, that ultimately does not ground itself in objects, but in the unthinkable. As Frances Ferguson analyzes this structure, "the notion of the sublime is continuous with the notion of nuclear holocaust: to think the sublime would be to think the unthinkable and to exist in one's own nonexistence." The aesthetics of the sublime is matched by the metaphysics of annihilation: one study of the symbolic meanings of nuclear weapons suggests that they work according to the logic of potlatch and sacrificial substitution of the victim for the perpetrator. In this vein, yet another critic talks of "an emerging nuclear death cult" as the civic religion of the United States.[51]

However, if this condition of existing in one's own nonexistence is indeed a universal operator of nuclear desire, it also acquires highly specific cultural associations and retroactive recognitions in the Indian context. How else does one explain the Hindu nationalist reaction in 1948, expressed by M. V. Kamath, in the Constituent Assembly Legislative Debates, upon the proposal for setting up an Indian Atomic Energy Commission? Kamath suggests that

> [India's] seers and sages, four thousand years ago, perhaps in 2000 B.C., said something about [atomic] energy, which scientists today are propounding in 2000 A.D. [Freely translating a Sanskrit verse, he goes on.] In the infinitesimal as well as the infinite, in the atom as well as the universe resides the one *shakti.* . . . The *shakti* of the atom and the *shakti* of the *atman* are same *shakti,* . . . [and, in sum,] the analytical methods of science will bring us to the same view as was arrived at by the synthetic processes of our sages and seers.[52]

Nehru, who sponsored the bill, adopted the opposing tack, arguing that the atomic age was about modernity, development, and scientific advancement, and that India had in the past been "backward" precisely because of its lack of scientific achievement. Yet, we might see how the radical modernizer and the cultural atavist came together politically in wanting to deploy, pursue, and vindicate the country's past and future by possessing the secrets of the atom, much though official doctrine was oriented toward the "peaceful" use of nuclear energy.

Indeed, as Itty Abraham has argued eloquently while mentioning Kamath's and Nehru's interventions in his book, *The Making of the Indian Atomic Bomb*, the postcolonial state pursued atomic energy under the sign of socioeconomic and technological "development" as also in relation to the felt needs of national "security." Yet, India managed to maintain a policy of nuclear ambiguity for several decades. Gandhianism and the philosophy of nonviolence was promoted in international venues, and several prominent leaders, including decolonized India's first governor-general, C. Rajagopalachari, ceaselessly campaigned against the nuclear bomb by evoking a continental basis for the doctrine of moral responsibility enunciated in Guru English. According to Rajagopalachari, "now that Japan has fallen, India has a very great responsibility in Asia." The consequences of the bomb showed "the law of Karma," according to which could be witnessed "the pain and anxiety now suffered by all the victorious allies." The onward march of nuclear weaponry in the 1950s suggested, however, that "the Destiny of the Kaliyuga [the fourth and final epoch of the cyclical universe when

unrighteousness prevails over righteousness according to Hindu cos-
mology] is implacably working out its programme." Rajaji, as he was
known, was vindicated when some of his antinuclearist views were
published by the *New York Times*, and when Lewis Strauss, head of the
United States Atomic Energy Commission, suggested a conference of
all "human mystic studies" to discuss prevention of nuclear war.[53] The
bomb was pushed further into the background when Nehru, Nasser,
and Tito became the charismatic leaders of nonalignment after the Bandung conference in 1955. However, Nehru's implicit refusal to seek nuclear weapons was discreetly altered when his daughter Indira Gandhi
became prime minister. After the superpower brinksmanship that
threatened global intervention in South Asia during the Bangladesh War
of 1971, it was more than likely that military research and development
by the Indian establishment would be highly favored. When India tested
its first device and became a threshold nuclear power in 1974, the coded
message regarding that explosion, sent to Indira Gandhi by the scientists
was a piece of cryptoreligious nonsense: "the Buddha is smiling" (the
1998 tests inadvertently parodied this message with the added one that
"the Buddha has smiled again"). The doctrine of nonalignment that
India pursued in international forums allowed it to maintain an ambiguity between "development" and "security." The explosion of 1974 was
declared "for peaceful purposes." India was deploying the rhetorical
equivalent of eating its nuclear cake and having it too.

Even in the early 1980s, such an important nuclear physicist as Freeman Dyson could refer to the Bhagavadgītā as a resource for attitudes
that could help prevent a nuclear holocaust in his book, *Weapons and
Hope*, first serialized with much fanfare in the *New Yorker*. Dyson refers
to the famous doctrine of *niṣkāmakarma* as a middle way between nuclear expansion and unilateral disarmament:

> Perhaps the best answer to the question of active defense and all the other
> ethical questions of nuclear policy is to be found not in the professional liter-
> ature of twentieth-century strategists, but in an Indian poem . . . *the
> Bhagavad-Gita*. [Here is quoted the full verse regarding acting without re-
> gard to the fruits, 2.47.] You have a right to defend, but you have no right to
> count the fruits of defense. You have the right to try to save lives, but you
> have no right to count the lives saved. This answer is not easy for Americans
> to digest. We are accustomed to making Indians think like Americans. It is
> more difficult to persuade Americans to think like Indians.[54]

Dyson's ideas were influential enough to result in an important colloquium being held at the premier institution for South Asia studies in
the United States, the University of Chicago, with illustrious scholars

discussing whether there was a uniquely "Indian" (Hindu? Vedantic?) approach to nuclear disarmament. Opinion varied widely. Least sympathetic to this new bout of Indian Romanticism was the Sanskritist Wendy Doniger's paper, which dismissed the Bhagavadgītā as unabashedly idealist with no reference to Indian realities, and as a casuistical cover that allowed killing to take place (as Krishna's repeated message to Arjuna is to kill clinically without regard for consequences that had been predetermined anyway). However, the poet-scholar A. K. Ramanujan suggested that Indian ethics was highly contextual and that attempts to universalize from it to the nuclear question would create a highly distorted result. James Gustafson argued that the Bhagavadgītā could serve a "critical illuminative function" rather than provide a full-fledged moral theory for the ethics of nuclear weaponry. The well-known physicist and Nobel laureate, S. Chandrashekhar, interpreted the killing counseled by Krishna as acquiring a different metaphysical value as Arjuna was told that the slaughter had been foreordained. As a result, Arjuna's role was limited, rather than that of an ethical free agent. Mahatma Gandhi, of course, had attempted to interpret the text as not about a real battle but an allegorical one. This could be argued by seizing on the *kṣetra* trope, of the body itself being the battlefield, within which microcosm ethical action had to arise when conducted by mental discipline.

While Dyson's book distinguishes the rhetoric around nuclear weapons as consisting of two incommensurable languages, that of the warriors and of the victims, it could be argued quite easily, contra Gandhi, that the Bhagavadgītā favors the ultimate reassertion of the warrior's language over its momentary eclipse by victim psychology when Arjuna was in doubt.[55] Furthermore, Doniger's point that the doctrine of disinterested action could create clinical separation between the agent and the action—and therefore lead to the "banality of evil" syndrome that regards all killing as illusory, as the divine principle within all living things cannot be killed—was a powerful challenge to the more Romantic assumptions behind Dyson's and other Western appreciations of the Bhagavadgītā, undoubtedly influenced by the Gandhian philosophy of nonviolence. Doniger's treatment of disinterested action as radical evil echoes Hannah Arendt's earlier analysis of Nazi genocide. Faced with the sure prospect of genocide, Arendt says that radical evil dispossesses the observer of any agency over events, and because these acts "transcend the realm of human affairs," "we can neither punish nor forgive such offenses."[56] Nuclearist thinking makes its calculus by weighing the sustainability of comparative genocides. The notion of separate and specialized duty—one that authorizes professionals to do their job without bothering about the uses to which that job is put, and that has been criticized as the banality of evil by Arendt and others—is just as much a principle of modernized scientific bureaucracies as it is derivative from the special notion of *dharma* from the Bhagavadgītā.[57] This point harks back to Tagore's criticism of the disinterested action doctrine of the Bhagavadgītā as an "aeroplane theory." The famous split between Gandhi and Tagore occurred over the interpretation of an earthquake in Bihar that Gandhi had suggested was divine retribution for the social regressiveness of Hindu caste society's ostracism of untouchables. Tagore vehemently disagreed with this theory that gave divine power the capacity for radical evil, whereby the death of innocent victims was meant to send a message to the much more privileged and unharmed observers at a distance. Ultimately, the question is whether the juxtaposed integration of the sacred and the secular is fundamentally suspect in ways that cannot be rationalized through attempts to sanitize those juxtapositions according to a "correct" philosophical attitude.

Georges Bataille also attempts this integration in his reflection on Hiroshima, which considers the nuclear sublime as creating a distinction between "the man of equivocal sensibility," who is in denial of weapons of mass destruction and therefore a weak servant of "civilization" versus "the man of sovereign sensibility" who is willing to look the moment of present human misfortune in the face and find a radical ethics of survival in the face of ultimate powerlessness.[58] Interestingly, Bataille too has to commence at first with "the 'crucial' experience of sensibility found in the Christian meditation on the Cross and in the Buddhist meditation on the boneheap," only to ultimately turn away from these examples to the even more sublime "unequalled horror of Hiroshima" that disallows any easy transcendence. However, for Bataille, the Nietzsche-inspired solution to this unbearable immanence is the dream of an economy of expenditure rather than one of lack, whereby an utopian economic overproduction by the United States might turn into an immense gift to the rest of mankind through the mobilization of atomic energy. Unfortunately, such thoughts have not aged well.[59]

For all these reasons, we should return to Oppenheimer's seemingly throwaway citation as one that did not come from nowhere. There was at least a millennium and a half of Indian commentary and a century and a half of European absorption that supported Oppenheimer's successful linkage of the most earthshattering effects of physics with one of the subtlest products of Hindu metaphysics. Given the doctrinal differentiations that go back in time, it is tempting to speculate, in conclusion, about Oppenheimer's initial identification with Arjuna, which shifts, with the poem, to Krishna. Oppenheimer's profound ambivalence about the destructive potential of the atomic bomb, his initial opposition to the development of the hydrogen bomb (which he later dropped), his left-leaning sympathies, as well as his Communist and Jewish friends and relatives made him a victim of the celebrated witch hunts of Senator Joseph McCarthy's House Un-American Activities Committee. However, his internal self-justifications concerning participation in the Manhattan Project went along with the complex ethics of the doctrine of *niṣkāmakarma*, according to which one could participate disinterestedly without identifying with or desiring the results that followed on the successful fabrication of the bomb. From a battle-shy ditherer at the beginning of the poem to disinterested participant by the poem's end, the Arjuna-figure is clearly subjected to a powerful moral transformation. In the passage famously quoted by Oppenheimer, the revealed lord of the universe responds to Arjuna's laudatory appreciation of divine cosmic form. Arjuna sees the Holy One first as an effulgent light and an immense cosmic form (*vishvarūpa*). As his vision focuses on the divine face, the spectator Arjuna progresses toward the sublime experience of feeling engulfed, and witnessing the entire world devoured by the voracious cosmic mouth. The spectator, terrified and wonderstruck, prays to the divinity. All the warriors from the battlefield, says Arjuna addressing Krishna,

> Are hastening into your numerous mouths
> That are spiky with tusks and horrifying—
> There are some who are dangling between your teeth.
> Their heads already crushed to bits.

> As many a river in spate ever faster
> Streams oceanward in a headlong rush
> So yonder heroic rulers of earth
> Are streaming into your flame-licked mouths

> As moths on the wing ever faster will aim
> For a burning fire and perish in it,
> Just so do these men increasing their speed
> Make haste to your mouths to perish in them.

> You are greedily licking your lips to devour
> These worlds entire with your flickering mouths:

> Your dreadful flames are filling with fire,
> And burn to its ends this universe, Visnu![60]

> Vaktrāṇi te tvaramāṇā viśanti
> damṣṭrākarālāni bhayānakāni;

Kecidvilagnā daśanāntareṣu
samdṛśyante cūrṇitairuttamāṅgaiḥ.

Yathā nadīnām bahavo'mbuvegāḥ
samudram eva abhimukhā dravanti;
Tathā tavāmī nara loka vīrā
viśanti vaktrāṇyi abhivijvalanti.

Yathā pradīptam jvalanam pataṅgā
viśanti nāśāya samṛddha vegāḥ;
Tathaiva nāśāya viśanti lokāḥ
tavāpi vaktrāṇi samṛddha vegāḥ.

Lelihyase grasamānaḥ samantāt
lokān samagrān vadanairjvaladbhiḥ;
Tejobhirāpūrya jagat samagram
bhāsastavogrāḥ pratapanti viṣṇo.   (11.27–30)

It is, therefore, a moment of dramatic transformation, when this voice, so far that of the frightened observer of cosmic destruction, is dramatically replaced by the voice of the cosmic destroyer himself. The identities of the observer and the destroyer merge into each other in Oppenheimer's combination of a snatched phrase from Arjuna with one uttered by Krishna. The starting voice in Oppenheimer's quotation is that of Arjuna:

> If the radiance of a thousand suns
> Were to burst at once into the sky,
> That would be like the splendour of the Mighty One.

> Divi sūryasahasrasya bhavēt yugapadutthitā
> Yadi bhāḥ sadṛśī sā syāt bhāsastasya mahātmanaḥ.   (11.12)

Yet this voice, which emerges at the flash of light from ground zero, is replaced in Oppenheimer's consciousness by that of Krishna, the cosmic speaker, upon the sighting of the mushroom cloud several seconds later: "I am become Death, the destroyer of worlds." Or, in Van Buitenen's more poetic rendition,

> I am Time grown old to destroy the world
> Embarked on the course of world annihilation.
> Except for yourself, none of these will survive,
> Of these warriors arrayed in opposite armies.

> kālō'smi lokakṣayakṛt pravṛddho
> lokān samāhartum iha pravrttaḥ;

Ṛte'pi tvām na bhaviṣyanti sarve
ye'vasthitāḥ pratyanīkeṣu yodhāḥ. (11. 32)

If Oppenheimer was like Arjuna, the hero in need of instruction, he now speaks by citing the moment when the destroyer speaks in his own voice. The speaking voice is that of the preordained cosmic devourer, identifying the Holy One as global lord, and indeed, juggernaut (*jagannātha*). Now, was Oppenheimer himself the voice, or was he merely reporting on the emergence of apocalyptic newness to the world? Quoting from the Bhagavadgītā performs an ambivalent displacement. While such a quotation may initially appear atavistic, anachronistic, or even anatopian (geographically misplaced), it ultimately has the flavor of a catachronism, a voice from the future that is recuperating the present. The sublime meaning of nuclear weapons ultimately refers us to a futureless future that freezes the present in relation to that contemplation.[61]

The disposition suggested by Oppenheimer's focus on this exchange between Arjuna and Krishna also reflects the ecstatic position adopted in Donne's Holy Sonnet linked earlier with the naming of the Trinity site, where the speaker says, "I, like an usurpt towne, t'another due, / Labour t'admit you, but Oh, to no end, / Take me to you, imprison me, for I / Except you enthrall, never shall be free, / Nor ever chast, except you ravish me." The prospect of his own obliteration makes the rapt observer identify even more faithfully with the transcendental power of the divine. The aesthetics of the sublime combines with the metaphysics of rapture and a whiff of religious eroticism. A homoerotic master-narrative of obedient oedipalization is hinted at here, whereby the narrativity of the nuclear involves the hypermasculinity of the sublime and the appropriation of birthing metaphors alongside the effacement of gendered difference. The telegram to the president from Los Alamos upon the successful completion of the test said, "It's a boy," and the prearranged code if the test had failed would have been "It's a girl."[62]

Oppenheimer could identify with the role of detached but triumphal victor in 1945, getting the National Medal of Merit and even being declared, "Father of the Year" by the National Baby Institution.[63] Of course, later he was the scapegoated victim of the very security apparatuses he had helped propel to world dominance. The state, wishing to protect the secrets of the nuclear juggernaut he had helped unleash, turned on the orchestrator of the technology as himself a security risk. Oppenheimer and many of his fellow-scientists were, at the end of the day, more victims than victors. Shiv Visvanathan has persuasively argued that the nuclear scientist's career reflects the aspect of "a humanist Hamlet struggling against a scientific Prometheus" and that Oppenheimer thereby becomes the most Dostoyevskian figure of modern science, later punished for reasons political as well as powerfully symbolic.[64]

However, Oppenheimer's initial juxtaposition has made the sacred poem fittingly relevant to the situation of scientists struggling with their consciences while fabricating weapons of mass destruction. The staging of ethical questions regarding the cosmopolitical legitimacy of any form of globally annihilating warfare, when posed against a metaphysical background, could lead in very different directions—either to a philosophical interrogation that undercuts war aims (as did happen when Oppenheimer refused to work on the hydrogen bomb), or to the cynical sanctification of the worst military impulses (as one reading of the Bhagavadgītā can imply). Oppenheimer's tearful performance of the key moment from the Bhagavadgītā in relation to the moment at Los Alamos was repeated in his news conference and can also be heard in Edward R. Murrow's interview of him a decade later for CBS, and two decades later for the NBC White Paper television documentary, *The Decision to Drop the Bomb*. This performance has subsequently been taken up for further dissemination in Nitin Sawhney's hit music album, *Beyond Skin*.[65] However, Oppenheimer's contrite performance jars when compared with his reported exultation upon announcing the destruction of Hiroshima to the government employees at Los Alamos. The juxtaposition of sacred text and secular event continues apace, where each supports the other in making meaning of an event whose repercussions for world events are perhaps still waiting in the wings.

THEOLINGUISTIC NUKESPEAK

The doctrine of nonalignment that postcolonial India pursued in international affairs allowed it to maintain the ambiguity between "development" and "security." India's nationalist leaders balanced a revulsion for weapons of mass destruction against their ambition to be taken seriously as a world power. In a comprehensive historical study of the development of India's nuclear bomb, George Perkovich argues that India's acquisition of nuclear weapons over the last half-century features within an uniquely Indian political narrative rather than according to the "security-first" narrative of U.S. policymakers. The interpretive framework of the acquisition of nuclear weapons has to take into account the postcolonial nation-state's insecurity in relation to the great powers, the national pride in technological accomplishment, and the desire for recognition by former colonial masters as equals. The impact of Gandhian morality in Indian politics meant that the desire for nuclear weapons had to be masked by self-deceptive contortions. Within this context, the "essential duality and ambiguity" of India's nuclear program is indicated frequently by problematic generalizations about the "Indian"—often conflated with the upper-caste Hindu—mind. As an unnamed defense official confesses to Perkovich regarding India's nuclear ambiguity, "the Hindu mind does not accept the 'either/or,' 'black or white,' 'yes or no' template of the West. We prefer 'grays and browns' and 'yes and no.' "[66] Keshub's syncretic affirmation of the conjunctive *and* over the disjunctive *or* is echoed here, except there has been a transidiomatic switch from a context of religious inclusiveness to one of military incoherence. For decades, India was having it both ways: denouncing superpower nuclear rivalry, and building its own bomb. The peculiarity of India's political establishment kept the nuclear scientists autonomous from the military. Since independence, the Atomic Energy Commission and its dual-use policies came strictly under the purview of the prime minister rather than the Ministry of Defence. This decision kept the military on the sidelines of nuclear policy and considerably enhanced political decisions about testing and deployment that were made by the prime minister (who, despite the British parliamentary structure followed in India, seldom consulted the Cabinet on major nuclear policy decisions).

Rhetoric about development and security aside, the nuclear question brought on an extreme case of nationalist and religious-atavistic taunting on both sides especially after the Indo-Pakistan wars of 1965 and 1971. Pakistan felt that it had to respond in kind after being thoroughly instigated following India's "peaceful nuclear explosion" of 1974, and a nuclear competition between the two countries was under way from then until 1998. These ambivalences regarding an "Indian" way to own and yet disown nuclear weapons were blown aside when a Hindu nationalist government headed by the Bharatiya Janata Party tested five nuclear weapons on May 11 and 13, 1998. The governments in both countries could come clean by publicly acknowledging the presence of a nuclear arsenal, conduct atomic tests to garner world attention, and put each other on notice (even while India flirted with the idea that China was also a potential adversary). The code name for the Indian tests explained their rationale in a single word we have already encountered: *Shakti*. In a manner reminiscent of Bankim and Aurobindo, religious zealots suggested building a temple to the goddess Shakti in commemoration of the explosions. Incredulous as this may sound, some also suggested distributing dust from the Pokharan test site as a form of sacred ash, a proposal quickly put to rest when fears concerning the spread of radioactivity were aired.

The hawkish rhetoric of various hard-liners in the Indian government, including Lal Krishna Advani and George Fernandes, meant that Pakistan had to respond despite the threat of U.S. sanctions against both parties. Pakistan went ahead and claimed to have conducted six of its own nuclear tests on May 28 and 30, 1998, in the Chagai Hills of Baluchistan. Nuclear testing was indistinguishable from copycat posturing. Such had already been the case from the 1960s, when Zulfikar Ali Bhutto perhaps single-handedly gave the world an interpretation of nuclear weaponry with a religious coloring. From 1965 onward, his nationalistic comment that "if India built the bomb, we will eat grass to get one of our own," cleverly taunted nationalist Hindus into recognizing their deepest fears of being regarded as weakling vegetarians and considering cows holy, even as the statement also emphasized that a Muslim Pakistan would do anything Hindus would, even if it meant altering Pakistani identities and parodically resembling Hindus in order to do so. Bhutto's later claim in his autobiography, *If I Am Assassinated*, published just after he was executed in 1979, did enough to confuse Western nuclear strategists for decades by creating the specter of an "Islamic" bomb, an idea that remains anchored only in the realm of fantasy. According to Bhutto, "the Christian, Jewish, Hindu civilizations have this capability [of using nuclear weapons]. The Communist powers also possess it. Only the Islamic civilization was without it, but that position was about to change. What difference does my life make now when I can imagine eighty million of my countrymen standing under the nuclear cloud of a defenceless sky?"[67] Democratic politicians on both sides enhanced the likelihood that nuclear weapons were political footballs rather than the strategic insurance they were characterized as being in several Western countries, in a manner that allowed them to bypass democratic debate there. The Indian state, in the meantime, maintained a language of secular statecraft—given India's large Muslim minority population—always claiming that its nuclear deterrent was not just about Pakistan, but in response to China, and about its aspirations to a permanent seat on the United Nations Security Council. In both India and Pakistan, nuclear weapons were deeply caught up in domestic politics and competitive pride, even as the huge expenditures involved kept politicians searching for compelling security considerations to justify the outlay. There was always considerable incoherence in articulating Indian nuclear ambitions. The goal was to assert security considerations beyond that of the Pakistani threat while baiting China, who possessed overwhelming superiority in that area. More worrisome for Indian strategists was the possibility that Pakistan had bypassed any need to reach parity in conventional armaments by having acquired nuclear weapons, and that it could be tempted to use them preemptively because of its conventional disadvantage. (By some accounts, both countries had achieved this capability by the mid-1980s.) Nuclear weapons had acquired the position of being the great defensive leveler for countries at a conventional military disadvantage, and this indeed seems to be driving the arguments against nuclear nonproliferation.

After the blasts of 1998, the Indian state and media would especially capitalize on the fact that the architect of their nuclear tests, and hence the equivalent of India's Oppenheimer, was a Tamil Muslim. A.P.J. Abdul Kalam, the scientific adviser to the prime minister, was apparently aware of the legacies of the Oppenheimer effect, as he also happened to have a good knowledge of ancient Hindu scripture. A bachelor and a vegetarian, this "missile man" had led the Indian Integrated Guided Missile Development Program since 1983 and was the director-general of the Defence Research and Development Organization since 1992. Kalam was the perfect alibi for a long-standing attempt to disavow the bomb's Hindu coloring and instead celebrate the glory of secular Indian modernity. Kalam was not the only non-Hindu to be at the forefront of the Indian nuclear establishment. For its crucial first two decades, India's fledgling Atomic Energy Commission had been under the charismatic leadership of another bachelor from a prominent Parsi family, Homi Bhabha. However, with the exception of Bhabha and Kalam, it is also the case that in the last two decades many of the prominent Indian nuclear scientists have been of South Indian Brahman extraction: R. Chidambaram, V. S. Arunachalam, P. K. Iyengar, and Raja Ramanna, as well as a host of other midlevel functionaries and scientists. Kalam had already been given a Bharat Ratna, India's highest civilian award, for his role in missile development. But this celebration of Kalam's role was also a fragile pretense that could not be questioned too deeply, as much Muslim-bashing rhetoric came tumbling out in spontaneous right-wing Hindu public demonstrations. The Shiv Sena leader, Bal Thackeray, and the leader of the Vishwa Hindu Parishad, Ashok Singhal, responded from the deep well of emasculated Hindu masculinity when they said that the blasts were about proving that Indians were no longer eunuchs (*hijre*).

Kalam's autobiography, *Wings of Fire*, argues that India's search for military technology is a "story of national aspiration and cooperative endeavour." The message is a straightforward one of nationalist pride as the remedy for feelings of inferiority: "all these rockets and missiles are [God's] work through a small person called Kalam, in order to tell the several-million mass of India, to never feel small or helpless." Kalam's background is ecumenical. Overcoming discrimination by upper-caste Hindus in childhood, he tells a simple story of a lifelong obsession to build indigenous rockets (and then missiles) in order to create the military self-reliance that will free India from imperialism. His autobiography is scattered throughout with Guru English and inspired by religious syncretism, with quotations from the *Atharva Veda*, Milton's *Paradise Lost*, the Bible, the Qur'an, the *Ramayana*, Kahlil Gibran, and Ralph Waldo Emerson's "Brahma."

The political faith in "missile man" Abdul Kalam eventually led to his landslide victory in the indirect election for the highest office of the land. The elevation of Kalam, who has occupied the ceremonial position of president of India since 2002, suggests that nuclear weapons deliver the richest political reward of all. The nuclear scientist's desire to transcend quotidian politics is realized, even as the unquestioned importance given to his status indicates the bedrock of that politics.[68]

Does the South Asian nuclear tendency arise from an extreme form of sibling rivalry expressed toward the other party in the equation? While Praful Bidwai and Achin Vanaik question whether South Asian politicians are indulging in a false prestige derived from nuclear weapons rather than responding to the organic link of nuclear weapons with security, one might wonder whether these distinctions are themselves highly debatable and subjective.[69] The hatred that "nuclear feelings" express are a special, and indeed, perverted form of love. How, do these emotions traverse the individual and the group at the same time, or come together in a virulent form of mass hysteria? Opinion polls in India after the tests—even if conducted by very dubious sampling techniques—registered consistently above 90 percent approval ratings about acquiring the weapons as a matter of national pride. Yet, opinion polls taken two months later suggested the other side: 73 percent of Indians opposed their use.[70] Between their possession and their use lies the shadow? But with nuclear weapons, it could be said that possession is all. All the same, no equivalent to the popular antinuclear movements in Europe or the United States existed, despite India's open society and liberal media. Observers would also point out that Asia was the site of thirty out of forty-seven incidents since 1945 involving a significant threat regarding the deployment of nuclear weaponry. Even more troubling, direct or indirect nuclear threats were exchanged at least thirteen times during the Kargil border war between India and Pakistan that followed the 1998 tests. Meanwhile, Indian military analysts, confident from winning three wars with Pakistan since independence, were attempting to rationalize to themselves whether a Chinese threat existed. India had lost a war with China in 1962 and also had its moment of anxiety regarding superpower nuclear brinksmanship in 1971, when President Nixon sent the U.S. Seventh Fleet and the nuclear-armed aircraft carrier USS *Enterprise* to the Indian Ocean in support of Pakistan during the Bangladesh War.[71]

During the heyday of the antinuclear movement in western Europe, there was considerable attention paid to "nukespeak," or state manipulation of nuclear rhetoric that lulled citizens into a sense of complacency regarding the imminence of nuclear war. According to Paul Chilton, nukespeak consisted of a specialized vocabulary of habitual metaphors and preferred grammatical constructions that were ideologically loaded in favor of nuclear culture. Weapons were humanized as fathers, babies, and families; weapons grew old and retired, as human beings did, and were therefore frequently named as fetishized tools, gods, heroes, or animals. The interrogation of nukespeak by the citizenry was necessary as the language had powerful performative effects. Critics such as Robert Jungk and Elaine Scarry would demonstrate how "the sacred complex" of nuclear energy resulted in an atomic state (*atom staat*) fundamentally opposed to the democratic agency of its citizens.[72] While nukespeak in western Europe was deeply linked with hegemonizing the citizenry to put their trust in scientific experts and their rational oversight of both military and peaceful options, there was also a subsidiary desire to link the nuclear with traditional images. In postwar France, for instance, nuclear reactors were frequently compared to the Eiffel Tower, the Arc de Triomphe, and even Notre Dame cathedral.[73] Creating quasi-religious awe around nuclear power also helped diminish the sense of human responsibility and political agency over these real-world options.

Robert Jay Lifton has powerfully analyzed the illusions of foreknowledge, preparedness, protection, stoic behavior, recovery, and rationality, all of which surround the strategy of rendering nuclear technology credible as usable weaponry. The rise of world fundamentalism in the post-1970 period, he provocatively suggests, is linked to the rise of nuclearism and is a response to the threat of extinction, as well as the offer of a direct experience of the transcendental that religions provide. If nuclearism embraces the bomb as a source of salvation, fundamentalism also anchors global political uncertainties within religious imperatives that are unavailable for interrogation. While he does not refer to the Bhagavadgītā or Tagore's criticism of it, Lifton's perception of nuclear weapons as creating "the ultimate above the battle position" by now should sound familiar.[74]

While generations of ballistic weapons were humanized by advocates of nuclearism, those of the enemy were demonized. Although these developments help us recognize the crucial necessity felt by Western nuclear establishments to normalize public perceptions of weaponry that would otherwise seem unacceptable given their genocidal power, the South Asian media-rich context can be characterized as provocational rather than calming, and creating incredulity rather than confidence regarding rival claims. The combination of feelings of inferiority and superpower envy made these weapons popular in resource-strapped countries such as India and Pakistan, even while ignorance regarding nuclear radiation, fallout, damage to civilians, secure storage, or the possibility of political or military miscalculation was widespread except in a few urban centers with greater access to global information.[75] Two rhetorics—one more primitive, of a stylized imprecation and taunting of the enemy, and another more modern, of the efficient and rational deployment of credible force—come together in South Asian nukespeak. For these reasons, it might be worth turning in conclusion, from the sublime, to the ridiculous, or more precisely, from the analysis of sublime rationalizations such as the Bhagavadgītā to the ridiculing provocations of the state military establishments. Guru English provides the transidiomatic framework, revealing its fluid capacity to traffic between both the necessary and the contingent.

In response to the short-range Indian ballistic missiles with a range of 250 to 500 kilometers, called the *Prithvi* series (literally, "the earth" in Sanskrit and its cognates), the Pakistani army had already tested a series of rockets called *Hatf* (Arabic for "deadly," naming the lance of the Prophet Muhammad that never missed its target). This reference to Muhammad's lance mimicked Hindu nationalists who had previously located such weaponry in primordial magical weapons (such as the *brahmāstra*) presented in the *Rāmāyaṇa* and *Mahābhārata*. While *Hatf-II* was developed as a counterpart to *Prithvi*, the naming of the *Hatf* was unintentionally ironic, as rockets, not being true missiles, are much less accurate when fired. A few weeks before the Indian nuclear blasts, the Pakistani military came up with a public relations masterstroke that might have contributed its mite toward pushing India over the edge for the tests that took place in May. On April 6, 1998, Pakistan tested the *Hatf-V*, this time a true medium-range ballistic missile, with a claimed range of 1,700 kilometers and a payload of 700 kilograms, which was named *Ghauri*. As the Pakistanis had no known missile-building capability, Indian analysts speculated that this was a *Dong Feng-25* provided by China, or perhaps a North Korean *No-Dong-2*. Another standard accusation of technological theft by the Indian and Pakistani nuclear establishments is on display here, especially because truly indigenous creation is overvalued within a framework of postcolonial self-respect. Buying or stealing technology is considered "cheating," whereas homegrown scientific progress is interpreted as a sign of moral strength and national merit.

By naming the missile *Ghauri*, Abdul Qadeer Khan, the metallurgist who headed one wing of the Pakistani nuclear establishment, had tweaked a winning reference by underscoring the obsolescence of India's short-range *Prithvi* series. In addition to the earth motif in *Prithvi*, the name could also have alluded to Prithviraj Chauhan, the Rajput chieftain who was the last significant Hindu king of northern India before Muslim dynasties assumed control. Fragile northern Indian Hindu egos would have had to acknowledge that Prithviraj was defeated, captured, and finally executed by Muhammad Shahabuddin of Ghauri after the battle of Tarain in 1191. For the Hindu nationalist zealot, this event was the beginning of the long night of medieval Islamic rule. While Pakistan also gleefully emphasized that Prithviraj had lost to Ghauri in the battle of Tarain, his role in the Hindu imaginary derived from his being the sole Rajput chieftain who had successfully resisted Ghauri when he had overrun much of northwestern India earlier, from 1176 to 1182. Some medieval Rajput chroniclers claimed that Prithviraj chivalrically spared Ghauri's life in an earlier encounter, claims later seized for moral high ground.

Within this new nuclear logic, the idea was to test a weapon, name it provocatively, and thereby win a public relations battle. The second taunt was Abdul Qadeer Khan's boast that the *Ghauri* would be followed by another missile with a 2,000-kilometer range, the *Ghaznavi*. This next step in a not-so-complex rhetoric was to identify yet another renowned Afghan Muslim raider whom Hindu chieftains such as Prithviraj could not quell. Mahmud Ghaznavi (from the Afghan town of Ghazni) was an especially hated figure for Hindu nationalists, as he was reputed to have besieged and sacked the Hindu temple of Somanatha in Gujarat of its fabled treasures for eighteen successive years. In actual fact, Ghaznavi's identity telescoped a number of different warring twelfth-century chieftains, but it became the name that summoned the paranoid fantasy of the repeated humiliation of an effete Hindu polity at the hands of an emasculating Islamic enemy. That both sides could agree on this myth for exactly opposing reasons (even while the historical evidence for a repetitive annual depredation of Somanatha was scanty, as Romila Thapar has compellingly argued) reveals the collusive codependency between Indian and Pakistani dreams of nuclear dominance.[76] Much of this state-sponsored naming of weaponry suggests bluster rather than credibility, and so far, parody reigns over tragedy. While Pakistan had clearly won in April 1998, India responded by upping the ante with nuclear tests in May.

While it was widely acknowledged by the late 1980s that both India and Pakistan possessed nuclear weapons capability, rumor had to become established fact. India found that the noose of antiproliferation by the established nuclear five (not so coincidentally the same as the UN Security Council five) was tightening, with increasing pressure being applied to make all hitherto non-nuclear countries sign the Comprehensive Test Ban Treaty (CTBT). India made much of emphasizing the five nuclear tests it had conducted over two days, with two large tests (disputedly of 12 and 43 kilotons) and three smaller sub-kiloton tests. It was claimed that one of the tests involved a thermonuclear device (or hydrogen bomb), but reports by independent analysts suggested that the second step of this test had failed and that the sizes of the explosions might have been exaggerated. The United States had categorically threatened Pakistan with a cutoff of all military aid if it responded and also rewarded Pakistan by suspending all its nonmilitary aid to India. Despite the United States's further offer of a $15 billion economic package, the political pressure was such that Pakistan's then Prime Minister Nawaz Sharif had to respond at any cost. When Pakistan responded with its tests later in May, it was also pressured into claiming that five tests had been conducted on May 28. It did not help the Pakistani national ego when the U.S. government and the global media said that only one seismic wave was recorded. Pakistan then concluded its round of testing with another test on May 30 and thereby claimed it had tested six (or seven) weapons, when compared with the Indians' five. Within all this rhetorical maneuvering, analysts worried about the confusion of "strategic" and "tactical" nuclear weapons, or (defensive) deterrent and (aggressive) battlefield options. Meanwhile, India also announced with much fanfare its IRBM (intermediate-range ballistic missile) with a 2,500-kilometer range. Still, Russia and China are the only Asian powers with "true" intercontinental ballistic missiles. All the same, the naming of this Indian series as *Agni* has stayed with the elemental motif, except the naming has moved from "earth" to "fire," and perhaps the implication of a scorched earth counterresponse. Pakistan subsequently announced the *Shaheen* series with a range of 2,000 kilometers. All the one-upmanship appears to have led to a stalemate where both countries are now vulnerable to a nuclear weaponized attack by ballistic missile.

If one had to go into all the name games, it would be necessary to talk about the indigenous Indian tanks under development called *Arjun* after Krishna's interlocutor in the Bhagavadgītā, the antitank missiles, *Nag*, which referred to the fabled shape-shifting serpents of Hindu mythology, and *Parakash* (the Vedic sky), the multiple warhead system to shoot down Pakistani AWACS planes, even as another class of missiles were named *Trishul* (or trident), after Shiva's traditional weapon. Propaganda machines on both sides (and to some extent internationally) chose to minimize the indigenized aspects of weapons development by either side. Pakistan insisted that *Prithvi* missiles were fabricated through Soviet and French missile technology given to India, and India accused China of supplying their M-9 technology to Pakistan via North Korean surrogates. India says that Pakistan's nuclear bomb is a 1966 design of a Chinese bomb flown on a Chinese-supplied DF-2A missile. Neither side granted the other the scientific capacity to invent an indigenous weapon, even as the threat posed by the other's weaponry was always exaggerated for domestic political consumption and the support of retaliatory weapons development. Neutral observers and knowledgeable munitions experts also emphasized that many of these much-vaunted weapons posed no significant credible *strategic* threat, as their accuracy and range were exaggerated. What seemed less understood was the domestic political gamesmanship involved in these declarations. All the same, this insight only exacerbates the perception of destructibility alongside an utter lack of credibility regarding accuracy and intentionality. Critical strategists claim that these weapons need to be stockpiled in greater quantities in order to make them effective as battlefield weapons. Nevertheless, the weapons and the chaotic perceptions of their existence have set off a new arms race in South Asia and fomented much right-wing rhetoric on both sides of the India-Pakistan border.[77]

The logic of the naming of weaponry, while clearly provocative, also appears partly satirical, as it draws attention to ancient scores, even as the confusions multiply into comic-book caricatures of historical being. This South Asian nukespeak is a product of the historical trauma of partition, which intensified interreligious hatreds and desires for revenge that relocated themselves in taunting revisitations of historical disputes.[78] In this respect, the infamous destruction of the Babri Masjid in Ayodhya in 1992 by neo-Hindu zealots forms yet another powerful catalyst for these representations. The saturation-effects of television and the global media have exacerbated many of these forms of provocation in a manner that is clearly irreversible. It is arguable, however, whether these newer paradigms of media provocation and television diplomacy ultimately serve as a prophylaxis or actually instigate political decision makers into dangerous gambits.[79]

These observations bring us back to the question of whether documenting these dangerous forms of rhetoric—whether sublime through reference to the Bhagavadgītā and Qur'an or ridiculous by way of schoolyard-level taunting—can also lead to a critical discourse that would help both sides abandon their codependent relationship, even as they proceed on a mutually destructive path. While the official rhetoric of nuclearism claims guarantees of credibility in the capacity to use overwhelming genocidal force, the hyperbole of the South Asian claims threatens to push either side toward dangerous miscalculation. Is the satirical display of rhetorical pyrotechnics controllable? It is the creative, if unsavory aspects of this ersatz discourse that Arundhati Roy does not understand in her otherwise eloquent left-liberal plea against the nuclearization of South Asia, *The End of Imagination*.[80] As we will see in the next chapter, the question regarding the violence of rhetoric can never be categorically answered by merely taking the side of "innocuous" liberal free speech, or conversely by sympathizing with those who argue for strictures against offensive speech or blasphemy. Rather, these two positions are to be seen as structurally symmetrical in their binary enmity.[81]

For these reasons, the strategic analysis of nuclear weapons and the defense of their spread by Kenneth Waltz and the neorealist school is incapable of dealing with the rhetorical exaggeration and deliberate obfuscation of the supposedly rational linguistic intentional structures so highly valued by strategic analysts.[82] There are very clear implications that, subsequently, nuclear weapons are especially and even more symbolic in the South Asian context than they are elsewhere, as they are used to frighten, humiliate, and lower the self-esteem of adversaries before even the waging of any actual nuclear war. Or to turn doomsday scenarios of nuclear war on their heads, it might be asserted in postmodern fashion that the only nuclear war that can be waged as a comprehensive war is as a rhetorical war. Such a war is focused on symbolic status and potential (rather than actual) deployment. Whereas the neorealist international relations (IR) discourse would have us believe that the calculus of nuclear strategy works according to credible and rational notions of strike capability, deterrence, and mutually assured collateral damage, the danger and the pleasure of nuclear weapons lies in the melancholic imaginary, combined with dreams of the annihilation of the rival country, oneself, and all society in the process. To recognize this deep melancholic identification is not to apologize for it, or wax fatalistic, but to ensure that any opposition to nuclear weapons combines with an attack on the deeper causes of political disempowerment, cultural identification, and religious hostility. The game theory approach to the world endorsed by neorealists cannot take into account irrational aspects of processes that are hitherto unanticipated in the onset of violence, and to read weaponry only in terms of intentional and rational control processes makes a mockery of the history of human warfare that has often proceeded by accident and surprise despite the best-laid plans of mice and men. Given the history of aberrant leaders, extremist movements, and accident-prone militaries, it is astonishing that Kenneth Waltz and John Mearsheimer recommend a gradual spread of weapons of mass destruction as a means of ensuring greater international peace, but only do so by gambling on rationality as always being a last resort for hotheads.[83]

With the near completion of the military objectification of the world, the logic of nuclearist worlding veers subjectively inward toward virtualization, fantasy, and psychoanalytical conundrums.[84] Of course, even without a single nuclear weapon being detonated, the preparation for and investment in nuclear weaponry suggests massive economic devastation through arrested development for two countries that together contain several hundred million of the world's poorest, and some of the worst life-expectancy ratios for women. If scant resources in these countries are put toward their further nuclearization, nuclear weapons and the hypermasculine posturing these weapons encourage amidst general economic immiseration can only make gendered forms of oppression in South Asia worse than they already are.[85] Furthermore, as Bidwai and Vanaik rightly suggest, the Indian and Pakistani military establishments are among the most accident-prone and problem-ridden when it comes to their ability to ensure the integrity of hardware and the safety of their own personnel. The most chilling fact remains that the missile flight time from its launch to a population center—Bombay, Karachi, Delhi, or Islamabad—remains as little as three to four minutes, and at this point only the most rudimentary command and control centers exist on either side. The future of a nuclearized South Asia promises to be bleak, unless antinuclear movements can make some inroads.[86]

While the world has witnessed the unilateral deployment of nuclear weapons in Hiroshima and Nagasaki, it has yet to witness a nuclear exchange in neorealist terms. But in linguistic terms, we have witnessed nothing but a series of posturings, gestures, and rhetorical nuclear exchanges from 1945 onward. Nuclear rhetoric and counterrhetoric were crucial in the representations of the United States during the Korean War, the Cuban missile crisis, as well as the later Star Wars (and now the Son of Star Wars) scenarios currently under way. Rather than artificially separate the scientific and military content (nuclear weapons) from the political and cultural context (of South Asia) as physicists and military strategists are wont to do, it is important to recognize the thorough interpenetration of content and context, which makes both the language of weaponry, and the weaponry that is language, aggressive, dangerous, and performative. Nuclearism is not just about the potential threat of annihilation from the skies, but also about the actual transformation of collective perceptions on the ground. The transactional analysis of nuclear perceptions leads us in a very different direction from the war game scenarios favored by military analysts. The universals of nuclearism and Guru English come together in the aspirations of the Indian and Pakistani nationalists for global recognition and mutual one-upmanship, even as this union of science and spirituality particularizes South Asian nukespeak as a different discourse from nukespeak in general. Sublime effects pursue the cosmic aspects of these weapons. Pakistani nuclear ambitions, responding to Guru English, have Islamicized it to some degree, speaking not just of the Prophet's sword (*Hatf*), but also about the strike of a true believer (*zarba momin*) and a Qur'anic concept of war, whose principal aim is to strike terror in the heart of the enemy.[87]

Jacques Derrida's comment that the nuclear bomb is *"fabulously textual*, through and through," is a counterintuitive proposition that should by now have begun to make sense, especially as much of the previous discussion shows how it is even more relevant in the South Asian situation than in the global one that he was analyzing. The nuclear option, which appears to be the perfect form of blackmail, is one in which science and rhetoric, strategy and belief, *doxa* and *epistēmē* blur into each other. If the nuclear option appears at one level to be linked to the death drive, it is also linked to speculation and specularization. Nuclear proponents fantasize a scenario of survival, revenge, and witnessing, rather than just self-annihilation.[88] For instance, Piyush Mathur has discussed the manner in which the 1998 blasts generated a communicational frenzy during which "the mainstream Indian media, both regional and national, duped itself through nuke journalism by confusing populism with democracy, techno-machoism with diplomacy, and physics with politics." The event, generated by the media and the state, was a joint exercise that summoned "a people," hypermasculinized and bereft of women, seemingly willing to receive the event with joyous acclaim. A nuclear test—putting aside for the moment the dreadful possibility of a nuclear exchange of any sort—is the perfect pseudo-event to galvanize a discourse of religious nationalism and euphoria. Its relatively "peaceful" outcome until this point (putting aside the very real question of radioactive fallout, and the regressive episodes of domestic religious violence in India such as the Gujarat riots that are surely related to the outbreak of religious nationalism) nonetheless has significant political consequences, lurching the world toward greater brinksmanship and instability, and the increased likelihood of genocidal holocaust, set off by intention, accident, or even the ultimate aesthetic logic of the melancholic sublime. If such an event were to occur, it could be safely predicted that the resultant instigation of national and global hysteria would be fully aided and abetted by the linguistic (in)felicities of Guru English. That is, if there was a viable South Asian subcontinent, and indeed a world left, from which such a response could be crafted.[89]

CHAPTER FIVE

Blasphemy, Satire, and Secularism

> Being God's postman is no fun, yaar!
> —Gibreel Farishta in Salman Rushdie's *The Satanic Verses*

Is GURU ENGLISH a euphemization of Hindu English, itself standing in for other "Indic" religions? Are South Asian and diasporic Muslims also in dialogue with the multilayered phenomenon of Guru English, whether as register, discourse, environment, or cosmopolitanism? Putting aside the question of its antecedents, is Guru English to be regarded as a more generalized symptom of the crisis of Indian secularism?

In calling for an anthropology of secularism, Talal Asad has challenged the normative evaluation of particular societies according to the universalizing parameters of Western rationality. The epistemic category of the secular has to be differentiated from the political doctrine of secularism, leading to the appreciation of considerable historical variance. According to Asad, "the secular is neither singular in origin nor stable in its historical identity, although it works through a series of particular oppositions." The institutionalization of secularism does not merely separate religion from politics, but in the wake of that separation, leads to new concepts regarding religion, ethics, and politics. Asad's approach demonstrates that the concept of the secular cannot do without a concept of religion, and vice versa. Within the context of the circulation of global media, satellite television, and electronic communication, diasporic and immigrant sensibilities regarding religion are profoundly related to events in the geographically separated spheres of nationalism and state-informed public reason.[1]

The Rushdie affair, as it has now come to be known, features the clash between the secularity of literature as a modern epistemic category and the political doctrine of secularism as it was able (or unable) to guarantee the protection of the former with differential results in a number of locations. The diplomatic standoff between Khomeini's Iran and Thatcher's Britain also became a fault line separating the ambitions of secular bourgeois writers from those of revivalist religious clergy. Both these numerically small groups could command much larger followings by manufacturing outrage. The translocal nature of the disturbance created by the Rushdie affair has been cited repeatedly in relation to the global rise of "Islamic fundamentalism" and accompanying violence, but as several critics have argued, such accusations can only come from a singularization of Islam as a monolithic explanation of the religious sensibilities of almost a billion adherents.[2]

In this chapter, I seek to demonstrate the unique value of Salman Rushdie's *The Satanic Verses* as an exploration of the multiple discourses of blasphemy, commodification, cosmopolitanism and dispossession in novelistic narrative. Rushdie follows on the heels of the playfulness of earlier texts featuring Guru English, such as Joyce's and Desani's, but also presents potential apocalypticism in the manner of the global juxtaposition of the Bhagavadgītā and nuclear weapons just discussed. Rushdie's satire is ambivalent in its relationship to its religious theme. The parts that have been the most controversial and yet inadvertently effective are those where the author also singularizes Islam in the tradition of orientalist redaction and essentialist caricature. However, these parts are also rendered as pastiche in relation to a larger globalized South Asian diaspora in metropolitan London, wherein generalized interchange overcomes any definitive demarcations that delineate Hindu from Muslim or culture from religion. Guru English comes very close to defining several aspects of this production, especially the manner in which its mongrelized and commodifiable South Asian cosmopolitanism is ultimately indistinguishable from the fictional depiction of Gibreel Farishta acting in his various "theological" or "mythological" movies. The attacks on Islam in the novel resemble Western orientalist accusations since the medieval vilification of "Mahound," and also mimic the demonization of the religion by Hindu revivalists in India since the early twentieth century. Sometimes in the novel, Islamic and Hindu elements merge in a manner that would be anathema to purists but that feels entirely blasé to the cultural consumers of Bollywood spectaculars or postmodern immigrant literature. Whether in the novel itself or in the violence of its reception history, the transgression of symbolic hierarchies deprivatizes the differentiation of spheres supposedly instituted by secularism. The deprivatization of religion within the instantaneous flows of the global media and its perverformative effects is the ultimate legacy of the Rushdie affair. As defined by Hent de Vries, the perverformativeness of religion derives from the fact that "any religious utterance, act, or gesture, stands in the shadow of—more or less, but never totally avoidable— perversion, parody, and kitsch, of blasphemy and idolatry." While this has already been discussed in relation to the theosophistries of

Joyce and Desani, it acquires a greater amplitude and resonance when analyzing events with global multiplier effects such as the Rushdie affair.[3]

While Rushdie's novel has been defended from the standpoint of a Western liberal secularism, it undoes this very position, even if inadvertently. Rather than maintaining the presupposition that there is essentially one history of secularism and modernity with minor variations, the novel features an alternative modernities hypothesis. Rushdie also undermines self-congratulatory sanctimonies of all kinds. The novel demonstrates that secularism too, is a *faith* in the public exercise of reason, and that in the manner of many religious ideologies, it is somewhat impervious to deep critique—and perhaps rightly so. Would secularists really want to give up their belief that science and reason are on their side? The novel shows that any secularism is bound to smuggle in transcendental imperatives that are more than likely to exist in the precursor establishment of religious faith from which this secularism purportedly dissents. If the notion of "religion" as a separate sphere of *doxa* and praxis has irreducible Christian aspects to it, as scholars of religion suggest, Rushdie's satire hypertrophies religious sensibility in order to reveal a paradoxical desire to be free of religion altogether. In trying to smuggle in the perverformative as normative, the novelist is hoist by his own petard. If Rushdie became the cause célèbre of liberal defenders of literature and cosmopolitanism, in the aftermath of the controversy many of these supporters were themselves revealed as intolerant of cultural sensitivities and religious differences. Defending the presumed innocuousness of free speech against religious censorship and fanaticism is a dangerous exercise, especially when the author is deliberately seeking to deconstruct the artificial distinctions between free and hate speech by way of the offensive weapon of satire. Defending Rushdie by making analogies with the history of antireligious thought in Europe can only be partially effective, and calling him a Muslim version of Rabelais, Voltaire, Galileo, or Bruno could highlight competitive ironies between Islam and the West as much as it could assuage them.[4]

By decoupling literature from its anchoring within circuits of national responsibility and floating it onto the current of transnational Anglobalization, *The Satanic Verses* also reconfigures the chimerical presence of a global Islamic religious community in the place of the nation. The novel received an overwhelming reaction from a secondary audience more interested in condemning (and indeed burning) than reading the product from the standpoint of the offended religious community. Rather than functioning like the nation, such an imagined community of the *ummatu-l-muslimin*, is "ideologically not 'a society' onto which *state, economy,* and *religion* can be mapped."[5] Indeed, the community's non-place does not mitigate the severity of the critical fulminations of demonstrators from Bradford to Bombay. When Khomeini's Iran arrogated to itself the task of punishing Rushdie, the state's actions demonstrated the breakdown of the jurisprudential mechanisms of the four schools of Islamic religious law (*fiqh*) and exacerbated the rivalries among Sunni, Ahmaddiya, and Shī'ī sects. The self-aggrandizing Khomeini made a play for the larger stakes of Twelver Islam. As Mehdi Mozaffari has painstakingly demonstrated, Khomeini's death threat was not a *fatwa* at all, but was misunderstood as such almost from the beginning because of distorted interpretations by the European media—especially the *Times,* the *Guardian,* and *Le Monde.* Iranian media almost never used the term *fatwa,* instead opting for the Farsi term *payâm,* meaning "message." As Sadik J. Al-'Azm argues very convincingly, "it would have been in Rushdie's favor had the 'fatwa' been really a fatwa for two reasons: (a) because such a fatwa may be counteracted by an opposing fatwa from another doctor of law, Imam or Mufti (such as the Grand Sheik of Al-Azhar), and (b) because the procedural rules and conventions for issuing and dealing with fatwas are all well-known, well-established and well-observed by all the parties concerned."[6]

Global Islam, along with its various sects and subdivisions, is no stranger to dissent, schism, and internal debate, despite the seeming inflexibility and extremism of the singularized religion created by the television news cycle of response and counterresponse. Language and location are also very significant. Many modern Muslim authors have suffered and survived strictures through fatwas in Islamic countries for perceived transgressions even as they run afoul of the ambitions of clerics willing to issue these technical theological opinions that could be ignored, acted upon, or countered by yet other ones, depending on the circumstances. However, Rushdie's position, as arguably the most visible global author of Muslim heritage after Naguib Mahfouz, gave the perceived insult translocal and indeed global significance. His anglophone status and British citizenship gave the imbroglio an additional charge. Unfortunately for the author, the book became a contingent occasion that galvanized Muslims in many countries around a range of long-standing grievances regarding economic oppression and racial and religious discrimination. Rushdie's claim to "have tried to give a secular, humanist vision of the birth of a great world religion" came up a cropper when confronted by the novel's unintended effects.[7]

For these reasons, we can extrapolate further from Ashis Nandy's provocative position on how religious extremism within modernity can also couch itself in the language of secularism.[8] Something like the

Rushdie affair reveals the pathology of secularism just as much as it does the rise of fundamentalism, or indeed the exchangeability of one kind of state logic for another. While religionists attack specific secularisms for their hypocrisy and differential treatment of various religions, the defense of secularism increasingly sounds tone-deaf and supercilious toward those who wish an acknowledgment of offense or hurt. Guru English, while not a direct accessory to this standoff, can, if introduced to the analysis of the situation, demonstrate the fungibility and interchangeability of the fundamentalist and the perverformative diatribe in *The Satanic Verses*, as well as illuminate the complexities of the secular and the orientalizing gesture. As with secularism in English, so with Guru English in Anglobalization: the articulation of a language has a role in creating a series of connectivities for Rushdie's novel from register to discourse and from transidiomatic environment to cosmopolitanism.

The ubiquitous telekinematics of the global media created predictably violent, material effects. Lives were lost in several countries as police fired on anti-Rushdie demonstrations; there were attempted assassinations of Rushdie translators and publishers; books were burned all around the world; discourse-machines, both religious-fanatical and racist-imperialist, were cranked up everywhere to spew their output into the global information loop. Western liberal democracies allow antireligious discourse but at the same time elevate the state and the all-encompassing fiction of "national security"—as we have seen since 9/11—to a condition of unlimited paranoia, favoring censorship of secrets above and beyond any attempts at free speech or disclosure. The more recent anxieties concerning immigration and multiculturalism (as the Red scares recede, if only momentarily, to be replaced by an Islamic one) have, in retrospect, played *The Satanic Verses* according to another agenda from the beginning.

Censorship is immensely productive of satire, and *The Satanic Verses* is a satire combating several disparate censors (British, Islamic, and Indian) at once. The withering-away of the official censorship of aesthetics in Western democracies (even as the issues of decency and pornography continue to be resurrected by the Right) has led to its gradual replacement by consensus-seeking mechanisms (regarding appropriateness, taste, offensiveness) in the mass media and publishing. The Althusserian distinction between the repressive and the ideological state apparatuses (RSAs and ISAs) helps us distinguish subtler from cruder forms of censorship: while the Ayatollah Khomeini's or Saddam Hussein's censor operated from an RSA, the penetrating network of censorship provided through the ISAs, which legislate normativity in Europe and the United States, often goes largely unnoticed, as it works through the fine and intangible methods of auto-censorship, ritual exclusion, nationalism, and tokenism.

Many of those who have risen to Rushdie's defense, since Khomeini's death threat of February 14, 1989, have done so in the name of essentialized versions of literature, free speech, criticism, democracy, the West, or even Islam; and often these appeals to critical universalism have pretended to a metasocial function. A careful reading of Rushdie's book precludes the defense of his satire within such terms; a secular defense-initiative, like the Strategic Defense Initiative, could just as easily be used as a tactical offensive weapon. Defending satire of a long-standing historical and cultural "other," such as Islam, can very easily, if the satire is appropriated as a decontextualized "critique," serve the apotropaic function of insulting, frightening, and singularizing adversaries into one monolithic enemy, ultimately doing the ideological work of cultural imperialism. Such a defense illegitimately asserts the superiority of a Eurocentric viewpoint over that which is attacked. Homi Bhabha defines the problem succinctly:

> we are embattled in the war between the cultural imperatives of Western liberalism, and the fundamentalist interpretations of Islam, both of which seem to claim an abstract and universal authority. . . . Our experiences in the classroom, in community work and the media, have made us aware of the problems of the liberal democratic state and its sense of cultural supremacy and historical sovereignty. . . . Where once we could believe in the comforts and continuities of Tradition, today we must face the responsibilities of cultural Translation.[9]

Attempting a different cultural translation, Pnina Werbner plumbs the controversy as that between two different aesthetic takes on the power of the religious imagination—rather than the frequently stated opposition between its reception by (European) high and (Muslim) popular culture. For the Muslim faithful, the prophet Muhammad is *al-insān al-kāmil*—the perfect man—and an attack on his person is to attack the very aesthetic sublime that anchors Muslim identity. Its equivalent in the Western context would *precisely* be that of an all-out attack on democracy or free speech, and in that sense these two sublimes—a religious and a secularist symbology, respectively—become direct transcodings of each other. Werbner constructs an ingenious reading of the novel that would potentially please the sophisticated Muslim reader and reveal a pro-Islamic deep structure of the novel, but with mixed success.[10]

The sociolegal construction of blasphemy and the archaic nature of some of the extant antiblasphemy laws in the statutes also come to the fore in this controversy. Muslim minorities in Britain rightly pointed to the double standards whereby blasphemy laws protecting Christianity remain on the books, whereas Islam and other religions do not get accorded equal protection. What this approach elides, however, is the dubious role assigned to the state with respect to religious protection. The task of religious protection names a very different strain of secularism reminiscent of British colonialist policy in South Asia, where cow protection, religious reform, and separate civil codes for Hindus and Muslims were legislated in order to pander to and (atemporally freeze) religious sensibilities as found (or imagined) by the colonizers. To British Muslims who asked for equivalent protection for Islam just as for Christianity, more full-fledged secularists would have responded that for consistency these blasphemy laws would have to be removed entirely—indeed a difficult proposition in a country where the temporal head of state is the monarch and also the spiritual leader of the Anglican Church. The treatment of majority and minority religion in a genuinely equal fashion by the state is a complicated affair, as the recent headscarf debates in republican France continue to show. Secularism in a particular polity is often successfully achieved by the ongoing detranscendentalization of majority religion into a supposedly neutral secular culture, even as minority religious groups are challenged to assimilate to this dominant culture that in actual fact still contains vestiges of anterior majoritarian religion, often so naturalized as to be invisible. At the same time, minority desires to hold on to different religious views and practices are in danger of being scapegoated as religious atavism. Even though the question of Islam in *The Satanic Verses* is divided between aspects of the migrant and the postcolonial (or neocolonized) subject, as Gayatri Spivak has suggested, the gender implications of the representational apparatus of religion become the property of different ideological antagonists, whereby masculinist colonial mentalities and Islamic neopatriarchal opinions wrestle over the real bodies of Muslim women in the arena of rational debate.[11]

While the explosive aspects of the Rushdie affair continue to multiply surreptitiously, even as its media prominence has receded after Iran "suspended" its death sentence and Rushdie moved to New York, I have chosen to focus this chapter on those factors crucial to a reading of the novel in terms of "cultural translation," ranging from the book's "global" to its peculiarly Indian, Islamic, and British determinations by way of Guru English. I begin with an exploration of the "420" motif, which situates the novel squarely within South Asian terms of reference that retranslate blasphemy in terms of fraudulence, and then move to a consideration of the satirical treatment of Islam. Both religious fraud and satire of religion should already be familiar to the reader from the previous discussion of theosophistries. Following these sections, I assess the role of the devil as a figure for the slippage, mutability, and unpredictability of religious outcomes. Another section assesses the role of female religious leadership in the novel. The final section sketches the ongoing aspects of this political melodrama by furthering the discussion of nuclearism already initiated in the previous chapter. All of these sections ultimately demonstrate that *The Satanic Verses* is a satire about Islam written in the cadences of Guru English. Transgressing the Islamic injunction against depictions of the Prophet, the novel actualizes the verbal presentation of a visual representation, using the nightmarish imagination of the schizophrenic Gibreel Farishta. Realizing this fact can help us understand at least one major dimension of Guru English, as in this case a contingent vehicle for a global fiction about Islam that juxtaposes imperial, postcolonial, and transnational connectivities, just as much as it depicts diasporic Hinduism or ecumenical syncretism on other occasions.[12]

THE 420 CONFIDENCE TRICK

As the two principal characters fall from the sky toward the English Channel in the opening episode of *The Satanic Verses*, we hear one of them singing a strange air: " 'O, my shoes are Japanese,' Gibreel sang, translating the old song into English in semiconscious deference to the uprushing host-nation, 'These trousers English, if you please. On my head, red Russian hat; my heart's Indian for all that.' "[13] Even at the novel's publication in 1988 and yet more so now, a reader might interpret the song as expressing the conjuncture of globalization, in which worldwide contradictions between aggressive nationalism ("my heart's Indian for all that") and the unified global market (with Japanese, English, and even Russian goods) render an individual's clothing into multiethnic postmodern pastiche. While such a reading could be provocative, those conversant with Indian cinema would recognize a quaint translation of lyrics from a Chaplinesque number in a Bollywood musical of 1955, *Shree 420* [Mr. 420], referred to later in the novel (407, 440). The proximate cause of Gibreel Farishta's and Saladin Chamcha's parachuteless and involuntary free flight from the height of 29,002 feet, was the explosion of a terrorist bomb on a hijacked jumbo jet, AI-420. The precise height of the fall—one of the disputed mensurations of the height of Mount Everest—could imply both the Edenic and the Greek fall: the lapsarian logic of descent from the Indian subcontinent to English insularity, or the plunge into the Aegean as punishment for Icarus's hubris (307). The ultimate metaphor is of course that of descent from the heavenly to the terrestrial sphere, whereby gods descend to consort with human beings in the manner they do in Greek or Hindu myths. The notion of divine embodiment or incarnation (the *avatar*), by contrast, is strikingly absent in Islam, in which the highest position is accorded to Muhammad, a perfect man who is Allah's chosen prophet, but not of the same substance. Any confusion regarding the separation between the divine and the human in Islam is subject to scrutiny as religious fraudulence. The number 420, an inside joke between Rushdie and his readership on the Indian subcontinent, is therefore much more consequential to the understanding of this book than several other frequently untranslated and untranslatable colloquialisms, allusions, and choice epithets.

It happens to be one among several ironies that *Shree 420* is actually one of the more successful attempts at socialist fable by actor-director-producer Raj Kapoor—even if the song's decontextualized content might very well be taken to indicate capitalist commodity circulation. The protagonist, Raju (played by Raj Kapoor), leaves home to seek his fortune in Bombay, which is situated appropriately at a distance of 420 miles. He is ready to work hard and falls in love with Vidya (her name means *learning*: the European equivalent would be "Sophia"), a humble schoolteacher (played by the radiant Nargis). However, Raju meets the seductive Maya Devi ("goddess of illusion," played by the vampy Nadira), who introduces him to the unsavory methods of making a fast buck through her capitalist swindler friend, Seth Dharmanand. Raju bails out in time, renouncing riches for the love of Vidya. The film portrays all riches as ill-gotten gains, obtained by hoodwinking and cheating a gullible public: the rich man who exploits Raju and others is a "Mr. 420."

The hold of 420 on the Indian imagination does not just result from the movie, which is its product. Its origin lies in the juridical apparatus installed by the British Raj to better govern the country, an effort launched with the help of the forensic skills of Lord Macaulay in 1833, submitted to the Privy Council in 1837, and culminating in the Indian Penal Code, finally promulgated in 1860. As in many postcolonial societies, the colonial apparatus forms the basis for current law: the numeral 420 in India is still readily understood as an abbreviated reference to the section of the Code of Criminal Procedure under that number: "whoever cheats and thereby dishonestly induces the person deceived to deliver any property to any person, or to make, alter or destroy the whole or any part of a valuable security, or anything which is signed or sealed, and which is capable of being converted into a valuable security, shall be punished with imprisonment."[14] Section 420, frequently the abbreviated explanation for an arrest in Indian newspapers, alludes to those who attempt small-scale fraud and confidence tricks; however, in the popular imagination, the scope of 420 extends to the more significant villainy of politicians and businessmen.

The state of emergency declared by Prime Minister Indira Gandhi between 1975 and 1977, a period when civil rights were suspended and opposition leaders thrown in jail, relied on a panoply of ambiguous statutes, including Section 420 among others, to crack down on smugglers, hoarders, and other "anti-national elements."[15] However, the emergency was more significant as a cynical political exercise of staying in power at any cost. Rushdie's second novel, *Midnight's Children*, which won the Booker Prize and catapulted him into literary fame, mounts a savage critique of the emergency and of Indira Gandhi's personality, and Gandhi reportedly considered several options—including defamation proceedings—against Rushdie (after Gandhi's return to power as prime minister in 1980, Margaret Thatcher committed a well-known faux pas when she invited Rushdie to an official banquet for her Indian counterpart). Ironically, one of the most potent slogans in the brief campaign leading to Indira Gandhi's stunning defeat in the 1977 general elections was itself a numerical equation composed of political shorthand: graffiti appeared all over northern India asserting that Indira's younger son Sanjay's four-point program (which included the highly unpopular methods of monetarily induced, and sometimes forced, sterilization of adult males to check population growth, ruthlessly satirized and a major plot element in *Midnight's Children*), added to his mother's twenty-point program for national growth, made for a huge confidence trick, a 420. The economy of a graffito proclaiming $4 + 20 = 420$ also brilliantly proved that the Orwellian regime in those years (which managed to produce the protofascist slogan "Indira is India") was precisely one in which two and two was not four. It would not be far-fetched to see a convoluted counterallusion, in Rushdie's aeroplane-conceit of miraculous falls, to the anticipated continuation of the Indian subcontinent and its ruling dynasties despite the unnatural death of Sanjay, in 1980, precisely by aerial accident, when he attempted a daredevil stunt in a twin-seater aircraft right over New Delhi; of Indira, in 1984, by political assassination, when she was gunned down by two fundamentalist Sikh bodyguards; and of Pakistan's President Zia ul-Haq, in 1988, in yet another mysterious plane crash. The bomb on Rushdie's AI-420 is detonated by Sikh hijackers; the metaphor of the aeroplane as "ship of state" is particularly relevant to India, where the prime minister at the time of the publication of *The Satanic Verses* was Indira's older son Rajiv Gandhi, previously a commercial pilot for Indian Airlines before being inducted into politics by his mother after the aeroplane-death of his politically ambitious younger brother, who had until then been groomed as heir-apparent.

Gibreel, therefore, as he descends from the skies singing the song from *Shree 420*, is revealing himself in code early on as a charlatan, a trickster, and a conman. Anything he says, including anything about Islam, has to be taken with the greatest degree of skepticism. Defending his decision to leave India, the other principal character, Saladin Chamcha, says: "the earth is full of Indians, you know that, we get everywhere, we become tinkers in Australia and our heads end up in Idi Amin's fridge. Columbus was right, maybe; the world's made up of Indies, East, West, North" (54). In some ways it seems logical that India was also the first in a series of countries (including Saudi Arabia) to ban the novel. Syed Shahabuddin, a member of Parliament and an Islamic fundamentalist, led the attack. Shahabuddin reveals no awareness of the ironies involved in throwing legal challenges at Rushdie. But, in his dogged literalism, Shahabuddin exposes the structure of the fictional imposition. Addressing Rushdie in an open letter published in the *Times of India*, Shahabuddin says:

> Here in India, our laws are very clear. Though ignorance of law is no excuse, let me instruct you so that you are more careful if you wish to sell in India. Article 295A of the Indian Penal Code says: Whoever, with deliberate and malicious intention of outraging the religious feelings of any class of citizens of India, by words either spoken or written or . . . otherwise, insults or attempts to insult the religion or the religious beliefs of that class, shall be punished with imprisonment . . . or with fine . . . or with both. I wish you were in India, Mr. Rushdie, to face the music. And then there are other sections like 153A, 153B, 292, 293, 295, and 298 of the same Code which may be cited against you.
>
> This is the legal system of a civilised society.[16]

To help Shahabuddin splutter along to his logical conclusion, we might have added that Rushdie's own novelistic confidence trick, inducing suspension of disbelief amidst considerable religious trickery, could very well be indicted under Section 416, which deals at length with the prosecution of impersonations, whether they be of real or imaginary persons, or Section 499, which deals with the complex area of defamation.[17] After all, *The Satanic Verses* performs the most audacious fictional impersonations and substitutions. Most prolific are those by the schizophrenic Gibreel Farishta, whose favorite fantasy is to impersonate the Islamic archangel Gibreel and to use that role as a stepping-stone to the medieval baby-frightener "Mahound," as well as to a panoply of other fictionalizations of historical individuals linked to the founding of Islam.

Ultimately, these allusions to fraudulence, impersonation, and trickery evoke accusations of religious charlatanry as well as antireligious blasphemy. As the colonialists had thought about the protection of religion, it was clear that incitation could happen in both directions—by those offending tender religious sensibilities, but also by others stoking religious passions and demonstrating the entrepreneurial religious culture of South Asia that can often blend antagonistic religious strains. These mixtures occur not only in the "Mahound" episodes but also, as we shall see, in the "Ayesha" ones that have elicited fewer responses in the criticism following the novel's publication. If both Gibreel and Ayesha are religious tricksters, Chamcha is the novel's most secular fraud, playing carefully within the lines of commercial opportunity given him. As it happens, it is the secular Chamcha who eventually suffers the devil's horns that sprout on his forehead.

The conceit of the initial Alice in Wonderland–like fall into a fantasy world functions as a satirical invocation of a multiplicity of cultural allusions: "Just before dawn one winter's morning, New Year's Day or thereabouts, two real, full-grown, living men fell from a great height, twenty-nine thousand and two feet, towards the English Channel, without benefit of parachutes or wings, out of a clear sky" (3). One of these men is Gibreel Farishta, a famous Indian film star traveling incognito, and the other, Saladin Chamcha, is an Indian émigré who works for a British recording studio. Farishta contributes to popular culture by specializing in the Indian movie genre of the "theological," which involves bombastic enactments of Indian religious mythology. The "theological" is an obvious "420-ing" of a credulous and illiterate public who worships the film star as a divine incarnation. Various "theological" and "mythological" blockbusters produced by Indian cinema, while not unlike Hollywood counterparts *The Bible* and *The Ten Commandments*, go much further, enabling the cult-worship of film stars as demigods.[18] The southern Indian state of Tamil Nadu elected Marudur Gopalamenon Ramachandran, a film star who modeled himself on Douglas Fairbanks, to head its government in 1977, almost four years before the United States elected Ronald Reagan; when he died in 1987, after being elected three times, and having been in a coma for several months before his death, several fans immolated themselves in grief. Over two million mourners accompanied the film star politician's body to his funeral, and a temple was subsequently built in his honor in Chennai with "MGR" himself as presiding deity. Another political demigod to whom Gibreel is explicitly compared is Nandamuri Taraka Rama Rao, who devoted his career to star roles in Telugu-language "theologicals," and headed the government of the even larger southern Indian state of Andhra Pradesh in the 1980s (28). "NTR" played Krishna in seventeen films, starting with *Maya Bazaar*, and received fans as devotees in the manner of a living god outside his house. He also began to play multiple roles in several of these mythological-devotional movies and was known to cross-dress for artistic as well as astrological reasons. Farishta's schizophrenic and flamboyant character is a composite of "NTR" and a famous Hindi film star, Amitabh Bachchan, veteran of "angry young man" roles and a strong supporter of the Gandhi family and also once member of Parliament for the Congress Party.

If Farishta's largely visual impact concerns the technological modernization and commercialization of ancient religion and myth, Chamcha's contribution is auditory, as the dubbed voice that produces a postindustrial culture, peopled with space-age mutants, combining bodies with machines and extraterrestrials with nonwhites, and hastening the inevitable "Coca-Colonization of the planet" (406). In a job that shows the overlap among modern anxieties about race, gender, and technology, Chamcha works for a television sound recording studio on *The Aliens Show*, dubbing the voice of the male lead in this pastiche of the first two *Alien* films. His work on many other projects that collapse entertainment with advertisement signals the onset of post-Disney spectacle, combining commercial megaprofits with cultural imperialism (63, 405–6). Miraculously, both men land unhurt on an English beach as latter-day avatars, transmogrifying into the two eternal Manichaean adversaries, Gibreel and Shaitan. Subsequently, the novel deals with the complex trials of these two heroes in contemporary London, even as it uses this pretext for a cross-cultural rumination on emigration, exile, and evil in Thatcherite Britain.

THE SATIRICAL VERSES

Rushdie calls his fictional version of seventh-century Mecca "Jahilia," a term used by Muslim chroniclers to indicate the period of darkness before Muhammad's divine mission. The literary activity of Jahilia involves "minstrels singing vicious satires, vitriolic odes commissioned by one chief against another, by one tribe against its neighbour" (97). In pre-Islamic Arabian culture, according to Robert C. Elliott's now classic study of satire,

> the poet's chief function was to compose satire (*hijā'*) against a private enemy. The satire was like a curse; it was thought always to be fatal, and it was as important an element of waging war as the actual fighting itself. . . . The poet-satirist led his warriors into battle, uttering his wild imprecations, shod with one sandal, his hair anointed on one side only, his mantle hanging loose. . . . Satire among the Arabs was preeminently a weapon of war, a public weapon.[19]

Elliott prefaces his ambitious readings of English satire with considerations of common anthropological roots in ancient Greek, Irish, and pre-Islamic Arabian magic. The Greek Archilochus invented iambic verse as a satirical weapon in the seventh century B.C.; and Irish law linked satire with murder, bodily assault, theft, or sexual attack against a man's wife. Rhymers in ancient Ireland were ascribed the power of death—over humans or animals—through satirical utterance. Elliott also emphasizes the vocabulary that consistently renders satire in terms of excruciating physical pain: "cutting, blistering, biting, killing, stinging, stabbing, scorching, burning, withering, flaying, annihilating, . . . sharp, barbed, poisonous, malignant, deadly, vitriolic."[20]

Rushdie portrays and defends a Jahilian poet-satirist's vocation as follows: " 'You like the taste of blood,' he says. The boy shrugs. 'A poet's work,' he answers. 'To name the unnamable, to point at frauds, to take sides, start arguments, shape the world and stop it from going to sleep.' And if rivers of blood flow from the cuts his verses inflict, then they will nourish him. He is the satirist, Baal" (97). Baal's attitude acknowledges that satire "cuts," and cuts close to the bone. He is a performative polemicist who writes assassination songs. The "rivers of blood" his verses let loose are testimony to the magical powers of language. Apparently, the effects of satire were recognized even by the prophet Muhammad, who reportedly said that "the satires of the three poets caused more damage . . . than whole flights of arrows" after a battle, and who is then reported "twice to have ordered the execution of female satirists."[21] As Baal shouts to Mahound as he is led off to his execution, " 'Whores and writers, Mahound. We are the people you can't forgive.' Mahound replied, 'Writers and whores. I see no difference here' " (392). Rushdie discusses this historical context in an interview:

> When Mohammed returned to Mecca in power, he was very, very tolerant. And I think, if I remember correctly, only five or six people were executed after the re-taking of Mecca. And of those five or six people, two were writers, and two were actresses who had performed in satirical texts. . . . At the very beginning of Islam you find a conflict between the sacred text and the profane text, between revealed literature and imagined literature.[22]

Rushdie's novel also fictionally renders the episode concerning the historical Muhammad's rage at the role played by the Meccan woman Hind in the battle of Uhud (17, 119–21, 360–61). The novel suggests that the character Mahound's death resulted from Hind's witchcraft (392–93).

Etymologically, the word *hijā'*, indicating the genre of versified lampoon, is the same as the word for "spear" or a similar weapon.[23] The image of the satirical "barb" comes close to this linguistic contingency in English: the shaft launched toward a target attacks a person's reputation, even as it deals a body blow. The discomfiture of satire's designated victims reflects a further trap: to claim justice leads victims to acknowledge themselves to be the target, confirming the success of the satirical shaft as a performative injury, while a refusal to respond often confirms the constative interpretation in the eyes of others, that the allegations are true.

The "objectionable" sections of the book, from the Muslim perspective, arise from the satirical projections of the schizophrenic angel, Gibreel. Rushdie's choice of "Mahound" as the name for Gibreel's fictional self-projection is especially ironical, because it has been cited as proof of his bad faith, of having used a derogatory epithet for Muhammad. But the novel carefully explains this choice: "to turn insults into strengths, whigs, tories, Blacks all chose to wear with pride the names they were given in scorn; likewise our mountain-climbing prophet-motivated solitary is to be the medieval baby-frightener, the Devil's synonym: Mahound" (93).

In addition to the ability of satire to instrumentalize the dissident element into an engine of aesthetic production, it also has the capacity, especially in its Menippean variant, to signal novelty and regeneration, or investigating how newness comes into the world. Attacking culturally fetishized objects or ridiculing sacred cows and holy prophets has always, in the South Asian context, been a part of religious discourse itself, whether in the functioning of traditional schismatic divisions or the invention of modern theosophistries. According to one literary historian, the discourse of ancient religious satire in India also contains its fair share of "goatish gurus, profligate yogis, wanton monks, [and] horny ascetics."[24] Rushdie's attack on religion can be contextualized in terms of a longer genealogy of South Asian parodies of religion rather than just transhistorical treatments of Islam. Gibreel's delirious and voyeuristic dream about Mahound reveals a cultural reflex favoring multiple and intersecting religious identities rather than a singularized sensibility around Islam. In addition to the prospects of malediction and cursing, there are the apotropaic aspects of jesting, charlatanry, and mockery involved in such representations, akin to Desani's Hatterr who is very much Gibreel's and Saladin's forebear. While centralized religious authority has always been quick to deem any criticism blasphemy, the South Asian emphasis on orthopraxy rather than orthodoxy in religiously decentralized contexts has allowed for greater tolerance of religious mockery and doctrinal competitiveness. It is therefore unsurprising when an American Muslim scholar lambasts "the Hindu trappings of Rushdie's half-learned Islam," or another observer suggests that the novel's treatment of "incarnation, reincarnation, and transmigration of souls" makes it a fitting vehicle for the exposition of Hinduism.[25] What is at stake, however, is not so much Hindu "trappings" or even Hinduism as such, but the larger cultural syncretism and iconoclasm referenced by Rushdie in the cultural and linguistic context that follows on the heels of Desani's depiction, and what we have been describing as Guru English. Writing his novel in Britain, Rushdie internalizes syncretism and transidiomaticity while unfortunately ignoring the graver dangers of circulation and incitation by transnational media from a metropolitan center.

As we are told early in the novel, "reincarnation was always a very big topic with Gibreel"; one Babasaheb Mhatre "started Farishta off on the whole reincarnation business"(11, 21). After faking his death to escape fans and producers, Gibreel decides to rehabilitate himself by converting large sections of his satirical dreams about Islamic history throughout the novel into yet another "theological" movie. Gibreel had "spent the greater part of his unique career incarnating, with absolute conviction, the countless deities of the subcontinent"—from the blue-skinned Krishna to the elephant-headed god Ganpati Baba and the monkey-king Hanuman (16, 24). Gibreel's religious range was ecumenical, not just acting Hindu roles in the movies but those of other religious initiators, including the Buddha, and the Mughal emperor Akbar. Gibreel became something like a multireligious specialist in metempsychosis, "an omnivorous autodidact, devouring the metamorphic myths of Greece and Rome, the avatars of Jupiter, the boy who became a flower, the spider-woman, Circe, everything; and the theosophy of Annie Besant, and unified field theory, and the incident of the Satanic verses in the early career of the Prophet" (16, 23–24). The story of the birth of Islam in Gibreel's consciousness is positioned as one among a series of religious metamorphoses in the South Asian context, even as Gibreel's Bollywood backers, Billy Batuta and S. S. Sisodia, hope that the birth of Islam will generate a "theological but of a new type . . . about how newness enters the world." This cinematic novelty will beat the lame Hollywood version of Muhammad's story, *The Message* (272). Therefore, Gibreel's dreams are a dry run for a prospective film script about Islam. The film itself flops by the end of the novel. The jovial references to the Indian tradition of the "mythological," "devotional," and "saint" film genres are nonetheless very important, as Gibreel's visual fantasies evoke the Hindu practice of *darśan* that is at odds with conventional Islamic iconophobia. Emphasizing the irreducible visuality of the sacred, the co-presence of divinity and devotee through *darśan* involves a direct visual interaction between the two. Gibreel's role as a Bollywood film star is therefore a dead giveaway, compromising the iconophobic traditions of pure Islamic doctrine. What better iconophilic genre is there for such religious desire than film, the aesthetic medium that renders the moving image? To the extent that Gibreel's interpretation of Islam can be understood at all, it would have to be within a South Asian context of syncretism, parody, interreligious citationality, and inexhaustible visuality. That visuality is not given to us directly, but indirectly evoked through the textual mediation of Rushdie's limpid Guru English.[26]

Meanwhile, Gibreel's girlfriend, Allie, had hilariously started imagining multiple sequels to his Islamic mythologicals: *Gibreel in Jahilia*, *Gibreel Meets the Imam*, and *Gibreel with the Butterfly Girl* (345). Allie herself is an object of milder ridicule, as a glacial and tolerant Jewish mountaineer with fallen arches, and as a collector of dozens of representations of Mount Everest (including one in ice in the freezer, her favorite). Allie goes by the professionally appropriate name of Alleluia Cone, dream-analog of the fictitious prophet Mahound's favorite retreat for angelic revelation, Mount Cone. Corresponding to Mount Hira, the designated site for Muhammad's encounter with the angel, Cone's nickname, Allie, plays on *ally* but is also a familiar diminutive for *Allah*. These are the fictitious and narrative contingencies that antireligious satire linguistically exploits through Guru English alongside the referential tease to Islam.

One of the highly publicized satirical episodes that has incensed devout Muslims is Gibreel's dream, concerning the impersonation—indeed, literal reincarnation—of the Prophet Muhammad and his twelve wives by the satirist Baal and twelve prostitutes in a Jahilian brothel. This section dealt with as "Return to Jahilia," is Gibreel's fantasy and is very much elaborated under the pressure of the genre of the distorted "theological" movie unfolding in Gibreel's mind. The brothel, known as "Hijab, or the Curtain," is a further naming provocation, as it alludes to the historical Muhammad's divinely inspired decree instigating the separation of his women from visitors by a curtain, or veil. The practice was subsequently extended to create gender segregation among Muslims (357–95). According to Rushdie's satirical distortion, this innovation was an immense turn-on for customers and prostitutes alike, all of whom were secretly disgruntled by the new Islamic code and Mahound's ability to produce different standards for his own behavior. When Baal is forced to acknowledge his blasphemies, the audience is seized with uncontrollable mirth, despite the threat of instant reprisal by the authorities (392). Rushdie's confidence trick, inducing laughter in place of reverence, and substituting the brothel as a place for devotional circumambulation that mimics the holy site of the Ka'ba—is as unnerving as the satirist Baal's (381). The secret collusion that the fictionally imagined blasphemy supposedly entailed among Islam's first adherents threatens to contaminate the present. The criminal practical joke is to subvert, in carnivalesque fashion, the legitimacy and originality of Islam's founding order. Gibreel's mythological *darśan* is indeed a novelistic "420."

As a representative of Twelver Shī'ī Islam, Khomeini as the novel's Imam is also a traditionally sworn enemy of the leader of the Sevener Shī'ī, led by the Westernized Aga Khan, who Rushdie parodies as having reversed Christ's miracle by rendering champagne into water—in order to be able to imbibe alcohol but still stay technically true to Islamic principles (209). Similarly, Rushdie parodies other Muslim ritual obsessions, including the dependence of Mahound's disciples on water for purification: "in the sand-city, their obsession with water makes them freakish. Ablutions, always ablutions, the legs up to the knees, the arms down to the elbows, the head down to the neck. Dry-torsoed, wet-limbed and damp-headed, what eccentrics they look! Splish, splosh, washing and praying. . . . Their water-loving is a treason of a sort; the people of Jahilia accept the omnipotence of sand" (104).

Successful satire interpellates its victim as target; conversely, the very nature of the satirical barb's glancing and allusive action renders it ready to deflect and ricochet unto unintended, albeit self-designated victims. *The Satanic Verses* closely follows this pattern, with its satire working through metonymy, where the control of the part—a disputed element from Islamic history—grants the satirist the power to attack the whole—Islam *tout court*. But even as the satirical victim can respond only in the name of the "whole," with the complaint that satire has defamed a proper name, whether it be personal, corporate, political, or religious, Rushdie's phenomenological universe works according to the principle that the whole it attacks is only an accretion of parts. Following the law of association, these parts can always be reconstituted and displaced by others. This law of substitution threatens the logic, propriety, and self-identity of the "proper" name, "Islam." However, as with Guru English, critics miss the point with Rushdie's depiction of Islam when they deal with the question of his mistranslations. The issue here is not about translation as thought about conventionally, but that of pretended translation through Guru English as we saw with Kipling's lama.

This logic continues in the most widely publicized of the book's scandals, that of Gibreel's heterodox account of the incident of the satanic verses that gives the book its title. In fictionalizing Muhammad's purported acceptance and subsequent repudiation of a revelation that admitted the three goddesses, *al-Lāt, al-'Uzzá*, and *Manāt* into his monotheistic project, Rushdie powerfully activates the weapon of metonymy. If one verse could be successfully repudiated as satanically inspired, why not another—indeed, why not all? (89–127). Linguistic flexibility and ideological atomization characterize this strategy. The disputed verse, accepted by some Islamic scholars and repudiated by others, says of the three goddesses, "these are the exalted females whose intercession is to be desired" (*tilka al-gharānīq al-'ulá wa inna shafā'ata-hunna la-turtajá*) (340). According to one of the first historians of Islam, Ibn Jarīr al-Ṭabarī, this fifty-third surah of the Qur'an, enti-tled *sūrah al-najm*, was revised in order to expunge the earlier inclusion of the goddesses. However, the highly disputed historicity of the inci-dent explains the threat of a metonymic delegitimation of the religious veracity of the rest of the sacred text felt by some. Whether this inci-dent is an orientalist fabrication or not, Rushdie's satire at its most vir-ulent attacks all proper names and capital letters, and it is not surpris-ing that some of his detractors, such as Khomeini, reacting from different cultural and historical contexts, treated his satirical barb as a capital offense.

The traditional satirist's defense when faced with the eruption of the literal—the threat of real physical revenge—is to invoke the literary. The letter was only a letter is the standard plea, which requests that stinging missives not be responded to with Stinger missiles. The liter-ary genre of satire has indeed often been appropriated by a conserva-tive politics, as has its equivalent cultural practice, carnival. However, the contextual principle of satire—its essential instability—is always implicated in the slippery slope logic of eternal substitution. The repre-sentational mode leads to the self-deconstruction of the authorial per-sona and his ultimate disappearance, as in Jonathan Swift's *A Tale of a Tub*. Satire has often involved the use of extremely sophisticated, rational arguments to subvert certain unexamined foundations of ra-tionalism as a category. Modern post-Enlightenment satire, including Desani's and Rushdie's, can be characterized as an offshoot of radical skepticism within a disculturated postcolonial framework.[27] Satire's persistent auto-criticism, along with a deliberate flouting of generic and discursive protocols, makes it akin to that radical critique of West-ern philosophical method, deconstruction. Paradoxically, the existence of the law (which includes a certain law of literary genre and also im-perial and religious authority) makes possible postcolonial satire and deconstruction; the law designates a limit that such satire always con-tests, disputes, extends, and threatens but never entirely repudiates. As a parasite, postcolonial satire corrupts and destroys its host's preten-sions of autonomy and self-sufficiency. But as an operation that is in-deed beside the point, antireligious satire generates a parasitical logic of supplementarity, hybridizing its origins beyond recognition. Satire undermines the host's immunity even as it colonizes parts of the host to look like itself. Could there be a polytheistic blasphemy hidden behind every resolute monotheism? Could there be an immense joke hiding behind every theological truth? Could the charlatan's number, 420, explain religious representations just as much as the monotheistic 1?

Allah is parodied as an "allgood allahgod" who is obliged to resort to totalitarian techniques: "Then how unconfident of Itself this Deity was, Who didn't want Its finest creations to know right from wrong; and Who reigned by terror, insisting upon the unqualified submission of even Its closest associates, packing off all dissidents to Its blazing Siberias, the gulag-infernos of Hell . . . he checked himself: These were satanic thoughts, put into his head by Iblis-Beelzebub-Shaitan" (332). However, as this quotation confirms, *The Satanic Verses* is as much about the devil as it is about God. Diabolical and divine are mutually constitutive but frequently indistinguishable. We turn to the devil when we are confused and in need of interpretation; theology's most difficult task is that of seeking to keep the devil at bay, even as it obsessively describes evil.

Gibreel's accident—that put him on the path to his near-death experience and miraculous rebirth—took place on that overdetermined geographical spot for Indian religious and secular sensibility, the southernmost tip of Kanyakumari. This location puts Gibreel in dialogue with Vivekananda and Kipling's lama: "[H]e was filming at Kanya Kumari, standing on the very tip of Asia, taking part in a fight scene at the point on Cape Comorin where it seems that three oceans are truly smashing into one another. Three sets of waves rolled in from the west east south and collided in a mighty clapping of watery hands just as Gibreel took a punch on the jaw, perfect timing, and he passed out on the spot, falling backwards into tri-oceanic spume. He did not get up" (27). Yet, after the hospital experience (which alludes to a similar real-life incident in which action hero Amitabh Bachchan was injured), Gibreel embarks on a course that explores the blasphemous metamorphoses that offend all stationary doctrinal positions.

THE DIABOLICAL ANGEL

The visual and cinematic realm of religious phantasmagoria inhabited by Gibreel contrasts with the auditory realm of commercial advertising in which Saladin plies his trade. In the quasi-allegorical roles assigned to them, Gibreel is the frontman, the film star who appears on the screen, and the erotic overachiever torn with inner angst, whereas Saladin is the backroom toiler, the plain Johnny who never quite makes it socially or romantically, and the romantic failure who is nonetheless more solid deep down. Gibreel, the original angel (*farishta*), is the one who, in the manner of Lucifer, has the most Satanic thoughts (including the "Mahound" episodes), whereas Saladin, the original toady (*chamcha*), is the derivative mimic who creates the value-added for the commercial popular culture that is often so readily decried.

While the angel Gibreel represents a delirious Islam under the spell of Guru English and Indian mythologicals, the devil-slot in the novel becomes a symbol for Western-style secularism and migrancy. Saladin, seemingly an entirely unobjectionable, harmless victim of mistaken identity, undergoes a sudden Kafkaesque metamorphosis into the devil, complete with horns, hooves, and halitosis. While "Gibreel Farishta" literally translates as "Gabriel Angel," the name Saladin Chamcha combines the romanticized enemy of Richard the Lionhearted in the Crusades with a shortened version of his family name, *Chamchawala*, literally, "seller of spoons." Just as "Saladin" was originally *Salahuddin*, Chamcha contracted his name from "spoon-seller" to "spoon," in order better to serve English palates. The etymology hints at an elaborate cross-cultural intellectual joke, because Chamcha has no long spoon to sup with the devil; he is both devil and spoon at once. As Rushdie once wrote in a newspaper article,

> a *chamcha* is a very humble, everyday object. It is in fact, a spoon. The word is Urdu; and it also has a second meaning. Colloquially, a *chamcha* is a person who sucks up to powerful people, a yes-man, a sycophant. The British Empire would not have lasted a week without such collaborators among its colonized peoples. You could say the Raj grew fat by being spoon-fed. Well, as we all know, the spoon-feeding ended, or at least ceased to be sufficiently nourishing, and the British left. But the effects of the Empire linger on.[28]

Gibreel's monomaniacal angelic innocence is contrasted with Chamcha's multicultural diabolical experience. *Chamcha* (often contracted in the novel to *chumch* or "spoono") is, like 420, another common subcontinental term of derision, as seen in the teasing comment made by Chamcha's girlfriend, Zeeny, "[Y]ou name yourself Mister Toady and you expect us not to laugh" (54).

By acting as the eternal toady to the glories of English culture and wishing to forget his Indianness, Chamcha represents one of the typical qualities of metropolitan Indians who have now evolved beyond the baboo phase and become new migrants. Morally untouched by his metamorphosis into the secularized image of the devil in Britain, Chamcha experiences the subjectivity of the unwanted immigrant. The figure of the devil demonstrates a classic case of repression: the more

Chamcha runs away from his Indianness, the more he is confronted with it on all sides—especially when he is forced, in his diabolical state, to take refuge under the roof of the Bangladeshi eatery called the Shaandaar Cafe, an establishment run by twentieth-century transpositions of a Meccan couple who defied the historical Muhammad, namely, Hind and Abu Sufyan. Chamcha is the inassimilable remainder of Gibreel's mythological discourse on Islam. He will suffer the penalty, pay the price, and endure the taunts of those with the continuing colonial mentality that imagines every Indian to be a baboo, a guru, or a snake charmer. The Shakespearean slots for colonial subjectivity are similarly cross-wired in this novel. While, for Prospero, Caliban was "a devil, a born devil on whose nature / Nurture could never stick," the twist of postcolonial reverse perspective makes the assimilationist Ariel figure into the devil, while the schizophrenic, violent, and libidinal Caliban of this theatrical novel is Gibreel, occupying the spot of angel.[29] The immigrant's arrival on English soil, a reverse colonialism, is treated analogically with William the Conqueror's legendary first taste of a mouthful of English sand. On the beach, Gibreel tastes a mouthful of snow and "would have planted (had he owned one) a flag, to claim in the name of whoknowswho this white country, his new-found land" (130–31). Chamcha had been married to an upper-class English woman, "Pamela Lovelace," a Richardsonian composite, combining the name of Clarissa's rapist with that of the victim-protagonist in Pamela. Chamcha's life contains several autobiographical echoes to Rushdie's. Rushdie was also married to an Englishwoman called Clarissa Luard, whose name echoes Richardson's other famous heroine. Like Chamcha, Rushdie too had emigrated to London from Bombay and made a living writing jingles and other advertising copy. Finally, the story of the young boy who was forced to eat a kipper whole at boarding school is a traumatic autobiographical incident from his youth that Rushdie has already discussed several times in the past. Unlike Caliban, Chamcha has realized his Miranda. However, after the ordeal following the crash, he finds out that his wife has taken his best friend, left-leaning activist and martial arts instructor, Jumpy Joshi, as a lover on the very night of his presumed decease. His recording studio has fired him, and Chamcha finds that his carefully crafted British life has fallen apart. Chamcha is initially tempted by the hopes of the immigrant culture that surrounds him. As young Mishal tells Chamcha about his diabolical appearance, "[I]t's an image white society has rejected for so long that we can really take it, you know, occupy it, inhabit it, reclaim it and make it our own" (287).

However, after miraculously returning to his original body from the diabolical one, Chamcha decides, in a fit of jealousy, to plot the downfall of his angelic counterpart and fellow crash-survivor. The aging film star meanwhile fails at the attempted mythological movie comeback in which he portrays Mahound. The book ends with the spectacular self-destruction of the angelic Gibreel, while Chamcha's final decision to remain in Bombay (where he had returned to be reconciled with his dying father) and revive his Indian roots features the sly civility of the devil's ironical last laugh. The devil has conquered by fading away into innocuous moral virtue and postcolonial secularism. This nagging doubt suggests itself through the book's closing lines, which playfully reemphasize the repression of the diabolical rather than its expulsion from Chamcha's personality. Chamcha turns away from his Bombay window's westward and external view of the Arabian Sea to a presumably reaffirmed Indian subjectivity and domestic bliss with Zeeny, his Indian girlfriend. "To the devil with it!" he says, and his words of anomie are uncannily echoed by Zeeny's equally throwaway, "[L]et's get the hell out of here" (547). Ariel-Chamcha can "go native," after putting to rest his inner demons concerning colonial and native paternalism, while Caliban-Gibreel would always remain monstrously inassimilable, in the periphery and in the metropolis. This alternative is posed very well at one point: "[M]ight we not agree that Gibreel, for all his stage-name and performances; and in spite of born-again slogans, new beginnings, metamorphoses;—has wished to remain, to a large degree, *continuous* . . . so that his is still a self which, for our present purposes, we may describe as 'true' . . . whereas Saladin Chamcha is a creature of *selected* discontinuities, a *willing* re-invention; his *preferred* revolt against history being what makes him, in our chosen idiom, 'false'?" (427). Chamcha's falsity of self—his secular postmodernity in fact—is what Rushdie suggests might be at bottom, the concept of "evil," whereas Gibreel "is to be considered "good" by virtue of *wishing to remain*, for all his vicissitudes, at bottom an untranslated man" (427). The diabolism of Chamcha's secular postmodernity is enabled by endless and discontinuous cultural translation, whereas Guru English's eternal verities, present in Gibreel's multiple incarnations, stem from a certain irreducible untranslatability (or already translatedness, which results in the same outcome).

While discourses about the devil are rendered in relation to the racism of modern Manichaean categories, the linguistic creativity of Guru English discourse—witnessed in the etymological punning of the orientalists discussed earlier—is brought to bear on Islamic theology, itself ridiculed as various confusions about numerology. What do monotheists mean by one god? As Gibreel states his indifference to this question in salty language, "Mahound comes to me for revelation, asking me to choose between monotheist and henotheist alternatives, and

I'm just some idiot actor having a bhaenchud [sister-fucking] night-mare" (109). Critics of resolute monotheisms often point to the gray area between monotheism and monolatry, for instance, in the Penta-teuch, where there is a clear recognition that there are other gods but that these are false gods in relation to the one true God. The first reve-lation received by Muhammad began with a command by the angel Gibreel, *iqra'*, rendered by orthodox Muslims as "recite" but by revi-sionists as "read." "Recite" perhaps suggests unquestioning adher-ence, whereas "read" might offer interpretative discretion. The status of the Qur'an as divinely revealed depends on traditional accounts of Muhammad's illiteracy, which would prove to orthodox opinion that he could never have invented the complex poetic meter of the verses. Muhammad's answer to the angel, *mā'aqra'*, is glossed as "I cannot read" by the orthodox; revisionists maintain that it is a contraction of *mādhā'aqra'*, meaning "what shall I recite?" In the subsequent organiz-ation of the Qur'an, the first revelation is classified as the ninety-sixth sura, or verse. Sura 96 asks Muhammad to accept one god, Allah. Rushdie plays with the "eternal" nature of the year 1961 (the year Rushdie himself, and the fictional Chamcha, left for England), as it is "96" with "1" on each side, a figure for Muhammad's uncompromising monotheism. The date 1961, "a year you could turn upside down and it would still, unlike your watch, tell the same time"—gnomically sug-gests the logic of reversibility and specular oppositionality early in the novel (42). However, while 96 upside down remains the same, it could be read backwards as 69, suggesting the polyvalent sexual perversions of the monomaniacal Imam's she-devil enemy, the hedonistic demon-queen Al-Lat/Ayesha. The counterimage of Mahound the prophet leads to the sexual antics of Baal in the Jahilian brothel: the angel's 96 leads to the devil's 69, or in fact his biblical 666—in this context, his secular Indian 420. The novel's considerable play on numbers includes the duration of the hijacking, 111 days (consisting of three ones, as well as being divisible by three). Mahound's reply to the temptation of polytheism is "One one one," hinting at the paradoxical space for poly-theism created by the repetition of a "one" which cannot be identical with itself, even as it alludes back to the three goddesses in question (77, 102).

In addition to Chamcha, there are several other novelistic analogs for the author, including Salman the Persian and Baal the satirist. The precise linguistic, indeed palindromic, opposite of *muhammad*, "the glorified" or "the praised" in Arabic, is *mudhammam*, meaning "repro-bate" or "apostate." According to the Qur'an, apostasy, along with adultery and murder, is one of three crimes punishable by death. The satirist Baal is always in mortal danger, as is his lesser counterpart, the

Persian scribe Salman, the novelistic figure for Rushdie's hybridization and satirization of Islam who miscopies Mahound's revelations and believes him a fake, but is later pardoned by him (363–68). As the apostate's choice of reading or reciting God's word begins with a devil's choice, an ambiguity between *kashf*, manifested or revealed knowledge, and *satr*, the veiling of the divine message that leads to *sharı'a*, or decipherment of codified law, Rushdie's novel begins with the devil, even as it ends with his innocuous survival in a rejuvenated Chamcha. The book's epigraph is from Daniel Defoe's *History of the Devil, as Well Ancient as Modern*: "Satan, being thus confined to a vagabond, wandering, unsettled condition, is without any certain abode; for though he has, in consequence of his angelic nature, a kind of empire in the liquid waste or air, yet this is certainly part of his punishment, that he is . . . without any fixed place, or space, allowed him to rest the sole of his foot upon."[30] Rushdie's epigraph concentrates on the errancy of the devil, his vagabond nature, and his flight from the stability of a unified terrestrial locale. If we wish to spot the ruses of the devil, we are in a catch-22, or a catch-420, situation. The devil-catcher has to proceed in a vein more diabolical than the devil himself.

Freudian analysis of the devil emphasizes the dreamlike complexity of the diabolical persona. As Luisa da Urtubey's full-length study points out, one line of Freud's associations links the devil with the unconscious, the repressed drives, and the death-drive; the other identifies the devil as a representation of the father.[31] We might say that the slipperiness of the devil is that of the signifier itself; Islam looks very different when subject to the diabolical transformations of Rushdie's Guru English. The very indeterminacy of the devil's actions makes him diabolical. The Derridean *destinerrance* of the devil's vagrancy, his lack of address, which summarizes his delinquency, and the nomadic refusal to recognize the law of settlement, are all attributes of an eternal escape from the transcendental signified of godhead. One of Gibreel's childhood jobs in the novel is the urban vocation of *dabbāwāllā*, deliverer of lunch-pails to office workers and students. On the average, each illiterate *dabbāwāllā* had to carry and deliver about thirty to forty lunch-pails with accuracy (18). Gibreel's diabolical prank was to mix compartments from Hindu lunch-pails with Muslim ones, risking communal riot (91). Called *Shaitan* (devil) by his foster mother when he does this, he cannot help vindicating his Indianized version of *destinerrance*: "if the dabba had the wrong markings and so went to incorrect recipient, was the dabbawalla to blame?" (331). In Rushdie's hands, Guru English ultimately collapses Hindu-Muslim distinctions, leading to a carnivalesque South Asian multireligious secularism rendered through the optic of a celebratory Menippean satire. Gibreel's echo, "being God's postman is no fun, yaar," foreshadows the message taught by the events of the Rushdie affair, because the postal system could very well be used by the malignant forces as well—"God knows whose postman I've been" (112).

Saladin wreaks his revenge on Gibreel, employing the voice-imitation techniques he has acquired producing commercial jingles to make anonymous, vaguely threatening, singing telephone calls (444–46). The telekinematics of Saladin's threats—their exaggerated reception and power—proves that the voice is indeed infinitely imitable and decontextualizable, prefiguring the nature of the threats broadcast by the Iranian leadership against Rushdie, along with their highly effective material rhetoric. It is no surprise that in Rushdie's book the devil wins, but by losing all signs of diabolism and melting away into secular anonymity. As the devil is implicated in the very possibility of writing and interpretation, it can come about that any piece of writing can be used as an unconscious satire, even as intended satire can be taken for serious critique. In Greek, the word *diabolos* also means "slanderer." The devil is finally in the details—as Rushdie would discover the hard way with his fugitive existence, escaping the long arm of the fundamentalist assassin.

The conditions of production of any signature, indeed any authorization from "proper" origins, always include the necessary possibility of forgery. In seeking to describe the specularity of diabolical projection, therefore, we also need to recognize the paramount importance of gendered positions in relation to religion. One of the chosen topoi of the novel is the vexed role of feminism in Islam, and how this question can engage many of the orientalist as well as internal critiques of Islamic patriarchalism. After an analysis of this theme through the Ayesha episodes in the novel, the rhetorics of nuclear criticism are taken up and extended from the previous chapter. Rushdie's novel also touches on aspects of nuclearism, and the themes of mimetic rivalry and eschatology, along with the analysis of the blind spots of a message system featuring Guru English.

A Woman's Islam

The Satanic Verses organizes its satire of Islam around three characters. While two of these are taken up with the Manichaean dichotomy between untranslatable multireligious fecundity (Gibreel) and translatable secular postmodernity (Chamcha), these are masculine alternatives. The third religious figure in the novel pertains to the question of female leadership in Islam and to the larger implications concerning the gendered occupation of public space. Rushdie represents one woman's quirky engagement with Islam through the narrative of a spontaneous Haj led by a charismatic rural *kahin*, Ayesha.

The depiction of Ayesha propounds what might almost be an alternative feminist revision of Islam—if it were not so utterly compromised by spectacular and tragic failure. Also imagined by Gibreel as one of his more surrealist fantasies, Ayesha's quest takes up two of the novel's nine chapters and alludes to the bloody and unsuccessful military campaign conducted after Muhammad's death by his favorite wife, Ayesha, against the fourth Khalifa, Ali, the Prophet's son-in-law— a historical reference often cited by fundamentalists (both Sunni and Shī'ī) as proof that women should not enter public life. This incident of female futility is transposed into a twentieth-century odyssey of a young Indian Muslim *pir* who leads a band of credulous villagers on the Haj to Mecca, the pilgrimage that all devout Muslims hope to make once in their lifetime. An illiterate epileptic who made small enamel animals for a local toy business called *Srinivas's Toy Univas*, Ayesha graduates from peasant orphan to miracle worker. Wearing a saffron sari reminiscent of a Hindu sannyasini, the adolescent Ayesha assumes the role of an exalted Muslim saint of the region called Bibiji, who was reputed to have lived to the age of 242. Although the local area had once been renowned for its butterflies, these creatures had disappeared with Bibiji but had recently returned in a spectacular fashion and had become associated with Ayesha, who eats them and is clothed by them (217–24). Ayesha convinces the villagers of Titlipur (Butterfly Town), as well as Mishal, the cancer-stricken wife of Mirza Saeed Akhtar, the village's wealthy landlord, that the Arabian Sea will part, allowing them to walk to Mecca. The odyssey ends in a catastrophic mass suicide off the coast of Bombay (although Rushdie toys with the idea that the pilgrims might have miraculously made it to the other side in some alternative reality).

The Ayesha episode is based in part on the "Hawkes Bay" incident that occurred in Pakistan in February 1983, when a woman called Naseem Fatima led thirty-eight of her followers to death by drowning. To add insult to injury in a manner that could only happen on the subcontinent, the Pakistani police arrested the survivors and charged them with attempting to leave the country without applying for proper exit visas. The cult leader claimed direct contact with the lost twelfth Imam of the Shī'ī. Rushdie's Ayesha is more generically Muslim (rather than just Shī'ī), and the entire episode takes place in the hinterland of Bombay rather than in Pakistan. In addition to being the modern echo of Muhammad's favorite wife, Ayesha of Titlipur is the ascetic contrast to another novelistic counterpart, who happens to be the most popular prostitute in Gibreel's fantasized Meccan brothel. The character of Ayesha also alludes to the frightful white queen of H. Rider Haggard's imperial novel, *She*. The twentieth-century Ayesha repeats blandishments reminiscent of the controversies created by her Meccan original. The historical Ayesha played a disputed role in turning the faithful against Ali after Muhammad's death, eventually leading to the schism between the Shī'ī and the Sunni. While the Red Sea parted to allow Moses to lead the Jews to the Promised Land, the modern Ayesha's charlatanry ends up being fatal to many of those who follow her, dying by numbers in a macabre fashion also reminiscent of the cult suicide in Jonestown, Guyana.

In a compelling reading of the novel that focuses on the Ayesha episodes, Sara Suleri has suggested that *The Satanic Verses* is "an act of archaic devotion to the cultural system [Islam] that it must both desecrate and renew." However, Suleri is ultimately wary of the way the novel traffics in the "uneasy intimacies that proliferate among subcontinental Muslim and Hindu epistemologies," and expresses a concern that "if a bewildered popular opinion seeks to magnify the text into the sensational proportions of a 'theological,' it is the duty of the academy to ensure that such closure be arrested."[32] However, it has been the argument of this chapter that with the inception of Guru English, the theological horses have already fled the proverbial academic barn. As critics, we need to reassess if the genies can ever be commanded to go back into the bottle. Which academy is powerful enough to exercise a police function in relation to the dissemination of popular genres that are reproduced globally? As has been amply demonstrated, the sensationalism of the theological is at the heart of Rushdie's enterprise. At its most powerful, Rushdie's is a radical but open-ended satire that celebrates vagrant indeterminacy rather than aesthetic closure. Its parallel resonances make for a number of ways of appreciating the novel within the context of a theolinguistic hybridity and richness that participates and also interrogates the larger structure of Guru English through Islamic and Sufi syncretism—Rushdie's Ayesha eats only butterflies and wears a saffron sari—and embodies a syncretic mixture that resembles many aspects of South Asian religiosity without being doctrinally identifiable. The genre of the theological does not have to mean aesthetic closure. Ultimately, the leakage between Muslim and Hindu epistemologies cannot be stopped.

In fact, the Ayesha episode evokes many saint films made in several Indian languages about the medieval Bhakti poet, Meerabai, a Rajput princess persecuted by her in-laws when she abandoned her husband and became an itinerant devotee of Krishna. The hundreds of poems written by Meera are steeped in a popular idiom of bridal mysticism. A famous Bengali and Hindi version, *Meerabai/Rajrani Meera* (1933), featured Bollywood greats including Prithviraj Kapoor (Raj Kapoor's father), Durga Khote, and K. L. Saigal. An even more celebrated classic for its lyrical success was *Meera* (1945), directed by Ellis Duncan in Hindi and Tamil. This film about the itinerant female saint featured musical renditions by a number of singers (including renowned Carnatic vocal artiste M. S. Subbalakshmi, who rendered the songs both to Tamil and Hindi lyrics) in various regional musical styles.[33] Unlike the medieval Meera who sang of her devotion to Krishna, Ayesha claims to be a more modern Meera, who admits that in their mystical trysts Gibreel sings to her "in the tunes of popular hit songs" (497). At the same time, Ayesha's movement is attacked by Hindu zealots jealous of her appropriation of the tradition of pilgrimage by foot: "leaflets were being distributed . . . in which it was claimed that 'Padyatra, or foot-pilgrimage, is an ancient, pre-Islamic tradition of national culture, not imported property of Mughal immigrants.'" Ayesha's Haj turns into a recognizable subcontinental "communal" incident when her group is confronted by a rival religious mob calling itself "No Islamic Padyatra" (488, 490). Ayesha's foot-pilgrimage to the sea is also an echo of Mahatma Gandhi's secularization of a religious practice, when in 1933 he led a march to the sea protesting against the salt tax—prompting the roughing up and arrest of the demonstrators by the colonial authorities that became a political watershed for the nationalist movement. Whether religious or nationalist, these various foot-pilgrimages represent the stakes of symbolic actions. Some of these actions turn out to be political triumphs, and others end up as Pyrrhic victories.

The place of woman in Islam is nonetheless relentlessly pursued in satirical fashion by *The Satanic Verses*. If the episodes of the goddesses and the Meccan brothel show Islam as antifeminist, the characters of Ayesha, both the Jahilian and the London Hinds, Zeeny Vakil (Chamcha's Indian girlfriend), and Mishal Sufyan, the young daughter of the London Hind, indicate that there is no dearth of Muslim women portrayed as more resilient than their male contemporaries. Gayatri Spivak has suggested that Rushdie's "anxiety to write woman into the narrative of history" ultimately "record[s] an honorable failure." The media frenzy around the Rushdie affair ought to be contrasted with the furor around the Shahbano case in the late 1980s, when a Muslim woman was granted alimony in a divorce suit that went all the way to the Indian Supreme Court. Shahbano ended up being manipulated in a tussle between Islamic neopatriarchalists wishing to maintain a separate Muslim civil code and Hindu fundamentalists who wanted to use her case to attack the regressiveness of Islam. In contrast to the ritualized standoff between Khomeini and Rushdie, Spivak suggests that Shah-bano ought to be remembered as "the face that does not come together on the screen."[34] To apply this idea to the novel we should similarly not forget the lesson taught about the multivalent aspects of Islam by the Ayesha episode, rather than exclusively focus on the standoff between Gibreel and Chamcha. Likewise, the fictional Ayesha and the real-life Shahbano should not ghettoize understandings of Muslim women's lives in the subcontinent. January 25, 1987, marked the inception of a newer medium for the Indian theological: the beginning of the religious serial on Indian television. As Purnima Mankekar points out, with the runaway success of the televisualization of Hindu religious epics such as the *Rāmāyaṇa* and the *Mahābhārata*, culture became not just the site of the struggle for political supremacy but the very object. Presentations of traumatic episodes featuring women from epic— whether Sita's fire test or Draupadi's humiliation and attempted rape—resulted in renewed questioning by a variety of groups regarding the roles played by women in society.[35]

Rushdie's book also flirts with the generalized cultural anthropology of Islam's imposition of what was formerly local Meccan patriarchy and polygyny onto the rest of the Arabian tribes, which tended to exhibit matrilineal and polyandrous practices. Gibreel continues to fantasize gendered polarizations through numerous cameo-satires, including a particularly uproarious episode describing the paranoid Imam (a send-up of Khomeini himself) being guarded in London, even as he has sworn eternal enmity against his specular counterpart, a witchlike Ayesha who drinks blood or wine while the Imam drinks water. As Shī'ī Muslims are followers of Ali, whose caliphate was greatly undermined by civil war with Muhammad's favorite wife, Ayesha, it is entirely credible for the Khomeini figure to choose Ayesha as his devil. Gibreel's dream has the Imam triumph over a demoniac al-Lāt/Ayesha, turning into a people-devouring monster as he commences a new era of the exile's return, "the Untime of the Imam" which is something like the end of history (210, 215). The Imam associates the feminine wiles of Ayesha with time, while he sees himself as defending eternity: "[A]fter the revolution there will be no clocks; we'll smash the lot. The word clock will be expunged from our dictionaries. After the revolution there will be no birthdays. We shall all be born again, all of us the same unchanging age in the eye of Almighty God" (214). Satire, highly dependent on temporality and ambiguity, will not be possible after such a revolution, which will freeze history into a seemingly unchanging specular confrontation between the divine and the malevolent, patriarchal order and female evil.

Other misogynistic satires in the novel include that of the British prime minister, who appears as "Mrs. Torture" and is held culpable for the neofascist tactics of the British police force, descriptions of which ensue. Amusingly, Mrs. Thatcher was obliged to defend Rushdie publicly and grant him police protection after the death threats, in spite of her stated dislike of his book's politics. The description of populist satanic rites also involves burning wax images of Mrs. Torture as Maggie the Bitch (139–40, 157–58, 163–64, 449–56). The novel's generalized attack on religious totalization is matched by its symbolic violence toward female heads of state just as much as male ones. The satires of Thatcher are no less violent than those of Indira Gandhi in *Midnight's Children* or Benazir Bhutto in *Shame*. In the final analysis, the scope of a woman's Islam cannot be understood without a fuller grasp of gender and power in society as a whole.

Nuclear Rhetoric

In his article on "nuclear criticism," Derrida paradoxically questions whether there is indeed any room for such criticism, principally because *doxa* and *epistēmē* become inseparable when "there is no longer any such thing as an absolutely legitimizable competence for a phenomenon which is no longer techno-scientific but techno-militaro-politico-diplomatic through and through." Nuclear gossip, opinions, and beliefs, *doxa*, Derrida says, are all that remain, and, for their analysis, "newspapers have to be considered as the best corpus of study."[36]

In the Rushdie affair, the media took it upon themselves to perform God's task, adjudicating between two radically different frames of reference and coming to a predetermined conclusion. The satirist's arrow, once it is identified as literal as well as performative (through the workings of defamation or blasphemy), is often matched with a countershaft designed to damage the originator of the verbal attack accordingly. But the respondent in this war game can choose to raise the stakes, adopting more violently persuasive means: the machinery of international law, the threat of economic loss or social ostracism, judicial proceedings (according to whichever system of jurisprudence) leading to a sentence, perhaps even that of physical extermination, or, at the most extreme, extrajudicial assassination.

However, we might look at satire differently. A political analog of the satirical principle could be that of Georges Sorel's notion of the general strike: working from within the body politic, the general strike demonstrates the fundamental illegitimacy of bourgeois law even as it exploits a right given by that very law, the right to strike, just as satire exploits the right to expression. We might extend Walter Benjamin's perceptive analysis of the more radical kind of general strike as a suspension and displacement, rather than a direct attack on the violence of the law, to the "strike" conducted by satire, which suspends and displaces the symbolic violence of the cultural text.[37] The two activities, satire and strike, obviously mount tremendous symbolic violence by laying bare the status quo, even as they try their best to eschew the ethical illegitimacy of actual physical violence. Conversely, carnival transgresses by displacing social antagonisms through physical violence onto scapegoats who are external to the conditions of oppression that the operation is protesting against. Metonymy is at issue in the three examples of satire, carnival, and the general strike. The beginnings of small strikes spread contiguously from one part of the workforce to another, generating sympathetic copycat strikes, leading eventually to a general strike that contests powers other than those directly at issue when the disturbance began. By revealing the violence at the heart of the law, the satirist demystifies social fictions with repetitive familiarity. A satirist's favorite ploy is to reverse the performance of the fiction of the law, and its auto-foundationalism of *fiat lux*, best exemplified by Pope's famous gesture in the conclusion to *The Dunciad*: "Thy hand, great Anarch! lets the curtain fall; / And Universal Darkness buries All!"[38] This crucial self-deconstructive tendency implies that satire can never be successfully defended in terms of a weak pluralism that denies its potent activity as a material intervention in ideology. By treating satire as metaphor, liberalism both mystifies and contains the power and the danger involved in the creation of satire. Satire demystifies liberal democracy's limits as not qualitatively different from those of the positions it attacks, even if these are situationally external to liberalism. This is indeed the metonymic operation already at work, rather than any metaphorical message to be drawn from Rushdie's novel.

The uniqueness of the *payâm* publicized by the Iranian leadership is that it bypasses all these possibilities in going straight for the call to "execute" Rushdie instantly; rather than merely activating the temporal machinery of international or Islamic law, it pursues all possible means, including inciting its followers to murder, even as it mobilizes the international media to broadcast its cause. Then Iranian President Mohammed Ali Khamenei explained Ayatollah Khomeini's counterbarb as follows: "an arrow has been aimed at the heart of Salman Rushdie, the blasphemous bastard"; or, in another statement, "the long black arrow has been slung, and is now traveling towards its target. There is nothing more that can be done." The chilling phrase for "apostate" that was used was *mahdur al-dam*, the very formula utilized to murder and execute members of dissident religious groups such as the Baha'i.[39]

An arrow of such extreme precision, launched by the Iranian theocracy in counterattack, should also be seen as an arrow of recognition, perhaps even an arrow of love. The Ayatollah chose, by uncanny coincidence, February 14, St. Valentine's Day, a Christian feast (even if with pagan antecedents)—the very day secret lovers look forward to all year, so that they can send discreet, anonymous tokens of affection to loved ones. (Valentine's Day is indeed now under attack by the Hindu Right in India). Using this day to send the most directly signed, public example of a declaration of war against a single person, ostentatiously trumpeted and relayed throughout the international media, is a symmetrical reversal of the inflated bombast of a love letter. "I love you more than the whole world" undergoes satirical conceptual reversal: "I call upon the whole world to destroy you." St. Valentine's Day, as some of us might have been quick to note, also commemorates a massacre. Not just a false symmetry: otherwise, why the insistence by President Ali Khamenei on the arrow heading (apparently unchecked, gathering speed, creating a vortex around itself, and a veritable international storm, buffeting institutions, breaking diplomatic ties, and claiming dozens of incidental victims) for Rushdie's heart? Not just the kitsch of Valentine's Day greeting cards—plastered with hearts pierced by Cupid's darts—is at issue here. Even as the "offensive" weapon of satire sent the antireligious missile that suddenly turned into a missive, a story, a fiction, and a dead letter, the "defensive" outrage of the interpellated "victims"—those who speak in the name of different Islams—began as angry letters, impassioned appeals, demonstrations, book burnings, and condemnations, culminating in a globally publicized threat of the performative: that a designated party, namely Salman Rushdie, deemed to be the source of the injury, should be done to death, by the proverbial divine arrow, a thunderbolt, or indeed a nuclear missile, if its services were available. As thousands chanted "Death to Rushdie" and burned books in daily demonstrations of religious and political grievance around the world, the special nature of this death wish was its adversarial intensity. Khomeini's own artificial recourse to an older bogeyman, perhaps the oldest scapegoat of them all—"the Great Satan"—was replaced by a more immediate scapegoat—the diabolical Rushdie. Specularity, rather than legitimacy, was at work, perhaps in a linguistic manner as well: the palindromic Qur'anic opposition between *muhammad* and *mudhammam*.

The "artificiality" of this international storm, leading to deaths and inflamed passions, can obviously be blamed on nationalism, fundamentalism, the West, Islam, the machinery of the modern state, and even that ready-to-hand scapegoat, the international media themselves. As I have shown, all of these entities had no small role to play in this story, but the conjuncture of these forces depends on a more "nuclear" principle of exchange between the rhetorical and the political. While the traditional "free-speech" argument has to base itself on a pretended suspension, radically marking a line between language (only language) and the world (language's object), the Rushdie scenario depends on a certain collapse between *doxa* and *epistēmē*: "[W]hat can Khomeini do?" becomes entirely inseparable from "[W]hat does Khomeini say?"

Let us illustrate the uncannily "nuclear" aspect of the Rushdie episode with a motif from the cultural unconscious of the atomic age, taken from the newspaper corpus, as indeed Derrida recommends. Sir Philip Goodhart, a Tory British member of Parliament, writes a letter to the staid *Sunday Telegraph* recommending a solution to the state-incurred security expenses for Rushdie:

> It will be more expensive to protect him if he chooses to live in London, or Birmingham, or Bradford, or any other centre where there is a large Moslem [sic] population. It would be much simpler and cheaper if he would agree to live in Benbecula, the site of the NATO missile firing range in the Outer Hebrides, where it would be easy to provide accommodation within a secure perimeter, and potential assassins would be easy to spot.[40]

Goodhart finds it possible to associate with nuclear missiles the satirist's power to unleash apocalypse, even as the myth of deterrence, founded on mutually assured destruction and the pretended "unusability" of nuclear weapons, ensures their fetishization and presence. Yet could nuclear missiles withstand the presence of a satirist on the premises? Would the weapons still be taken seriously? Nuclear logic, implicated in the contingencies of "use it or lose it," could curiously extend to the guarding of a satirist, even as it might develop a scenario of use-as-last-resort; however, the poor satirist has now arrived at a function opposite to that of the pre-Islamic frontline figure: dubious "peacekeeper" rather than instigator of battle. The rules of geographical sanitation demand that the satirist be guarded, with the missile, on the very outskirts of British civilization—the Outer Hebrides. Indeed, the logic of contamination deems it so; with the population centers already unsafe with the "virus" of immigration, common sense demands such things as safe outer perimeters, where a blinding light is cast on the terrible phallic power of the missile (even if this light that guards the missile is but a weaker version of the explosion of energy it produces as apocalyptic threat). "Potential assassins," an ambiguous term, could also refer to those interlopers who might want to "assassinate" or disarm the missiles, not just those who would wish to rid the satirist of his teeth. Such an interloper would want to castrate the castrator and deprive him of his phallic threat. Given the political history of the antinuclear movement in Britain, these interlopers would most likely be women, latter-day Medusas daring to confront the missile.

Ironically, the confined satirist is an interloper par excellence, and by trespassing over the magic line decreed by the law and defiling hallowed ground, s/he slashes the fiction of identity. Also as iconoclastic interloper, the satirist lops, beheading the upright, uptight posture of the missile and the law, opting for the contiguous and horizontal dismantling of the partial objects that go into a missile and the edifice of the law. The logic of the nuclear impasse is precisely that of Rushdie's Imam, who will smash all clocks, permanently keeping alive the flame of eternity and truth as the potential for apocalypse. The saboteur, who dares stray within the perimeter and threaten eternal suspension with temporality, is satirist par excellence; otherwise, what would be the object of such a dangerous exercise, if one knows the vigilance of the militia, the peripheral police force that protects the idea of apocalypse, even as it is ensured, round-the-clock? The object of the satirical exercise of the interloper is to repeat parodically the justification for the missile, even while dismantling, deconstructing it, "to make sure it will never happen."

Yet the rationale of the Tory MP might show that he is himself the butt of the satirical joke. The banal reason that moves him to write this letter is to suggest ways of reducing the government's mounting security bills for Rushdie. In other words, Goodhart (in keeping with his name) wishes to keep an eye on that bottom line—economy. The "conventional" aspect of the nuclear missile, with its logic of mimetic rivalry, also underscores a certain unconventionality of the older weapons, which now acquire both anterior value and supplementary status in a different "weapon time" than that of the missile. Economy is, after all, the engine that drives the system that produces the weapons in the first place. One could credit the Rt. Hon. Goodhart with old-style ideological demystification, as well as intellectual perspicacity. His jocular wish to contain both satirists and nuclear missiles within safe areas, on the grounds of their being socially disruptive, is indeed typical British understatement. The very understatement of the missile as eternal peacekeeper, contrasted with the threat of an incredibly exaggerated response, confuses the founding law's reaction to the satirical missive. Missiles and missives get confused, because they are dependent on a rhetoric that has to articulate them in terms of response, threat, and status quo—expectation, projection, and conditionality, situated in a potential future that is projected as a future anterior to the temporal moment of "present decision." This mischievous implication in Goodhart's common sense goes further; nuclear logic is ultimately at odds with the demystifications of satirical logic. The logistics of nuclear trajectories, along with the "rational" calculations of response and counterresponse, is harnessed to an obviously irrational process. Satirical logic, on the other hand, deconstructs and also endlessly constitutes rationality, shamelessly trafficking back and forth over the perimeters and the dividing lines that set rationality apart. A satirist or interloper creates substitution and deferral where there was a zero-sum game of losses and gains.

Given the stakes of various linguistic mechanisms including Guru English involved in Rushdie's intervention, we ought not to reduce his novel "to the dull inoffensiveness that some would naively attribute to books," as Derrida suggests. Instead, we might consider that "it recalls (exposes, explodes) that which, in writing, always includes the power of a death machine."[41]

CHAPTER SIX

New Age Enchantments

> The Hollywood Hindus are Hindus who live in or near Holly-
> wood. They are holy, cultivated men who issue frequent bul-
> letins about the state of their soul, the complexities and varia-
> tions of which are endless and always worth description.
> —V. S. Naipaul, *The Mystic Masseur*

GURU ENGLISH HAS BEEN the name for something like a theory of excess. Such a theory does not disprove the functional role of orientalism
in colonial rule or displace the serious outcomes of the ongoing politics
of religion in postcolonial South Asia and elsewhere. What might seem
on occasion to be a frivolous counterculture of free-floating migrancy
and diasporic delight can also, at other moments, integrate itself seam-
lessly with new forms of capitalist exploitation and still elsewhere associate itself with alternative explorations of critical agency and social
transformation. A focus on the productivity of Guru English in a number of spheres leads us to the terrain of contemporary religious cosmopolitanism and a fuller account of its commodifiable as well as critical aspects, its literary framings as well as economic efficiency. Literary
and religious representations of gurus feature a nonteleological trajectory of intellectual goods that cannot be easily repatriated to rightful
cultural owners or saved from self-serving distorters. By looking at
some instances of gurus in fiction alongside intriguing episodes from
the sociology of gurus, this chapter forces an interdisciplinary confrontation of literary and historical epistemologies. What does fiction
teach us about contemporary religious imaginings? How do historical
gurus and their religious followings reveal new truths when subjected
to literary and discursive frameworks?

With the history of "Indic" religions in South Asia as background,
this chapter explores some of the facets of religious cosmopolitanism
as cultural exchange as well as literary currency. Gurus suggest particular forms of knowledge that mark a cosmopolitan presence the world
over. At the same time, it should be pointed out that this chapter is not
principally concerned with conventional religious nationalism of the
sort practiced by the BJP (Bharatiya Janata Party) and the VHP (Vishwa

Hindu Parishad), or that by Islamic- or Sikh-oriented minority parties in India; nor does it discuss (except fleetingly) the overseas offshoots of these religious-political organizations that may indeed work according to Benedict Anderson's analysis of long-distance nationalism, Chetan Bhatt's critique of new religious movements, or even more recent warnings regarding the right-wing agendas of organizations such as the Vishwa Hindu Parishad of America (VHPA) and the Hindu Students Council (HSC).[1]

To be sure, the apparatuses of colonialism vastly reconstituted and objectified religion, and made colonial, postcolonial, and even diasporic subjects identify themselves according to exclusive criteria— whereby religious identity became a political category and a language of association. Wilfred Cantwell Smith, Talal Asad, and Peter van der Veer have demonstrated in different ways that modern religion is a heavily constructed category rather than preformed and continuous from precolonial times. Anthropology, orientalism, and colonial policy worked together to demarcate the differences between religious texts, social practices, and doctrinal beliefs. Secularization was never any simple one-way decline of religious belief, but rather the repositioning and privatizing of religion alongside its discursive objectification. It is often forgotten that even if it could be granted that secularization was doing various things to religion and putting it on the defensive, religion was also recreating itself in a manner to seize the offensive after readapting to secular conditions.[2]

A few specific instances of re-creation through literature and practice— and representation and performance—are the focus of this chapter. What would it mean to construct a longer genealogy of contemporary neo-orientalist religiosity from literary as well as sociological criteria? When considering phenomena such as the movements generated by Maharishi Mahesh Yogi, Bhagwan Rajneesh (alias Osho), and Deepak Chopra, we could learn a great deal from simultaneously reading about their imagined literary cousins in novels such as V. S. Naipaul's *The Mystic Masseur*, John Updike's *S.*, and Hanif Kureishi's *The Buddha of Suburbia*. If today's gurus were anticipated by orientalist, Theosophist, and Vedantist precursors, their fictional surrogates were also heralded by the brownface renditions of Zaarmilla in Elizabeth Hamilton's *Translation of the Letters of a Hindoo Rajah*, Rummon Loll in William Makepeace Thackeray's *The Newcomes*, and Professor Godbole in E. M. Forster's *A Passage to India*. Consequently, self-orientalization is a relatively easy strategy for postcolonial anglophone writing. For instance, the volatile mixture of politics and religion involved in Mahatma Gandhi's presentation of himself as both revolutionary and sage is mimicked in Raja Rao's *Kanthapura* and R. K. Narayan's *The Guide*. Reading fiction and history together leads to interruptive as well as mimetic outcomes. Sometimes history and fiction reinforce each other, while on other occasions they pull in completely different directions. The empirical reaffirmation of the various ideological symptoms of orientalism and its reverse—nationalism in secular as well as religious versions—can therefore be subjected to detailed critical interrogation.

A Taxonomy of Gurus

Before reading the fictional record and the contemporary moment against each other, it is important to distinguish between the secularized esotericism of New Age movements featuring fragmentary aspects of many religious traditions, and new religious movements (NRM's) that testify to renaissances within almost all major global religions. The specific interaction among orientalist discourses, New Age practices, and new religious movements reveals interesting paradoxes with respect to neo-Hinduism and neo-Buddhism (and their multiple variants) outside South Asia. Under the sign of globalization and Americanization, neo-Hinduism and neo-Buddhism eventually allowed the flexibility of religious choice rendered by consumerist lifestyles for multiple practitioners. The new gurus proselytizing in the United States and Europe take for granted New Age rejections of materialism and Euro-American desires for a nondualist universalism. However, rather than promoting old-fashioned universalisms relying on the metaculture produced by the global religions, the synthesis of New Age desires and new religious movements is one that negotiates particularist identities and therapeutic outcomes within the framework of universalism.[3] Paul Heelas suggests that religious innovators such as Helena Petrovna Blavatsky, Carl Jung, George Gurdjieff, and Wilhelm Reich detraditionalized religion and heralded the New Age movements with modern theories drawn from anthropology, mythology, and psychoanalysis.[4] While skeptics are justified in identifying the self-spirituality, individualism, and experience-orientation of New Age religions as fundamentally different from old religious universalisms and their current renewals, the new sages of South Asia skillfully balance ancient theologies with new (theo)sophistries. If New Age discourses skilfully blend Western occult traditions with Hindu, Buddhist, and Native American ones, they also tend to exclude Islamic and African spiritualities (even if these are marginally included as Sufi practices and Egyptian cosmologies).[5]

While the relaxation of immigration policy brought many Indian spiritual practitioners to the United States after 1965, a text such as Wendell Thomas's *Hinduism Invades America* (1930) demonstrates that "a national brotherhood of Indianism" anticipated features of full-blown New Age religions.[6] The United States had wide and deep exposure to Hindu ideas through a host of figures already discussed, such as Vivekananda and Yogananda, as well as others, including Baba Bharati, Yogi Hari Rama, Swami Bhagwan Bissessar, Srimath Swami Omkar, Yogi Ramacharaka (William Walker Atkinson), and Kedar Nath Das Gupta of the Three Fold Movement. Religious journals such as the Vedantic *Message of the East* disseminated quotations, hymns, and myths, while the innovative Yogoda journal *East-West* married science with religion and featured spiritual journalism about the occult and the bizarre. Texts such as Yogananda's *The Science of Religion* discuss "Pranic current" or "Life-Electricity," and collaborated with movements such as Theosophy, Christian Science, and New Thought— all of which began in the United States and then spread around the world.[7] Yogoda adopted the structure of an American church and appealed to liberal Christianity even as it replicated the trappings of popular religion through Christmas cards, ornamental pins, and emblems. Organizations such as the International School of Vedic and Allied Research included distinguished American intellectuals such as John Dewey, the philosopher of pragmatism, and Charles Rockwell Lanman, the Sanskritist who founded Harvard's Oriental Series publications. At this time, Mazdaznan was introduced to the United States as a syncretic religion that amalgamated Zoroastrianism and Tibetan Buddhism under the inspiration of the Rev. Dr. Otoman Zar-Adusht Ha'nish. Along with the influx of missionaries from the East, there was a burgeoning supplement of colorful charlatans such as Joveddah de Raja, a mind-reading performance artiste. This early presentation of messages in Guru English was already effecting a transition from doctrines that counseled world-renunciation to techniques for relieving stress. Alleviating anxiety competed with the goal of finding exit strategies from modernity.

The multiplicity of religious institutions—with various schisms, offshoots, and personality cults—makes for a bewildering array of global possibilities. There is considerable overlap between the local appeal and international outreach of some gurus, and almost none with others. At the same time, the centrifugal fragmentation of the field amidst intense discursive productivity is countered by the occasional centripetal forces of doctrinal overlaps, ecumenical conclaves, religious recycling, and cross-affiliation. There are of course several sectarian monastic traditions internal to traditional Hinduism, such as the religious orders set up many centuries ago by Sankara, Madhva, or Ramanuja. Despite these structures, it has often been suggested that Hinduism lacks strong mainstream religious institutions (at least when compared with Catholicism, Islam, or Buddhism in some polities). However, a durable, if more flexible form of institutionality in neo-Hindu diasporic contexts exists through dispositions, practices, sodalities, and modalities, such as the guru-chela relation, yoga techniques, communal living in ashrams and monasteries in lieu of the family, and received philosophical attitudes. These conventions—or cultural traits—enable the unfolding of institutionality as a neotraditional performance on multiple occasions for new adherents and casual followers, rather than rely on worldly institutions to lay down rules, guidelines, and procedures. Institutionality as performance makes tradition atomizable, portable, adaptable, and deterritorialized. New religious formations make a linguistic and cultural combinatorium available to the consumer, especially when disseminated to other spaces where the question of linkage to extant cultural practices does not easily arise. The excessive fertility of discursive institutionality is paradoxically the reason for the existence of multiple traditions, sects, liturgies, and orders, even with respect to conventional Hinduism. While no powerful hierarchies have yet garnered centralized social power in Hinduism in the manner the Catholic Church did in medieval Europe, the rise of political Hinduism (or "Hindutva") in recent decades is altering the religious landscape within India and with respect to the Hindu diaspora—although its outcome with respect to the vaster panoply of New Age borrowings from India is still to be measured.

Social anthropologists seeking to define communities and identities as they are formed in minority contexts have undertaken some substantial studies of diasporic Hinduism. According to one such study that collates a number of sources, there are roughly over twelve million Hindus outside South Asia (and about nine million if Indonesia is excluded). Hindus of subcontinental origin have registered their presence in several parts of the world, from Britain, Canada, and the United States to the Caribbean, Fiji, and East Africa. Diasporic communities conduct their religious practices in novel ways, sometimes resorting to neotraditionalism and by reference to the sacred geography of the South Asian imaginary homeland, while at other moments aggressively syncretizing with local cultural forms and practices, as has happened in the Caribbean. Diasporic identities are subject to regional, linguistic, and generational constraints as well as new cultural opportunities.[8]

While diasporic studies help to outline cultural stability as well as hybridity, social structures, and political agency, they are not directly concerned with generalized diffusion. While neo-Hinduism reterritori-alizes itself in relation to some diasporic communities, a phenomenon such as Guru English is not primarily concerned with identity, ethnic-ity, or community, even though these categories are always relevant for secondary analysis. Discourse generated by practitioners of Guru En-glish forms an excess that can be consumed or deployed as a cultural and linguistic form without users necessarily having to claim identity or bear responsibility for the outcomes of their uses. One does not have to be a Hindu to read the Bhagavadgītā or a Christian to study the Bible, and one could even be a self-declared atheist consciously or un-consciously participating in neoreligious discourses and vocabularies. Such fleeting encounters with religious discourse cannot be studied so well by social anthropology, which tends to seek a reified and stable object of analysis. In certain cosmopolitan contexts, the lines between the cognitive and the conative, or knowledge and belief, increasingly become blurred. In this context, Guru English is made visible through the existence of a shadowy "literary" system that runs the gamut from conventional literature and feature film to mass-market self-help gen-res, New Age bookstores, targeted journalism, product advertising, and Internet communications.[9]

However, even if uses are subtle, the individuals involved—whether teacher or follower—can be analyzed. With gurus, individual charisma has always trumped the frequent lack of adequate institutional sup-port. Unlike religious institutions that produce abbots, bishops, and ecclesiastic authority, personal revelation creates a following that sub-sequently goes in search of mechanisms of organization, dissemina-tion, and social reproduction. This constant reinvention of the wheel makes almost every case of a newfound guru sui generis, and yet all too recognizable as a repetitive form of religious free enterprise. The growth potential of gurus suggests that the market for them is not a zero-sum game. Gurus have always been repositioning the religious through their personal aura and authority. If some religions are per-sonality cults with centuries of institutional history, gurus are living in-stances of religions-in-the-making (even if they often never get fully made). A living guru especially makes visible the function of the aura in religious ventures. The role of the darśan—or visual communion with the guru and his following—establishes the crossing of religious emotion within the form of the gaze. Visual communion presents a gamut of responses, from the believer's importunity, faith, or desire, to the guru's benediction, compassion, or wrath.

This function of the aura, as a living face-to-face interaction, is changing with the proliferation of the new media. As famously dis-cussed by Walter Benjamin in his essay, "The Work of Art in the Age of

Mechanical Reproduction," the power of the new media through technologies such as photography, cinema, and mass-market publishing devalues the special aura of the artwork but also holds out the potential for popular and democratic overturning of the older hierarchies created by aura.[10] We can carry over this argument about the artwork to the question of the role played by personal charisma in religious faith. Unlike the aura of a dead artwork, the unfolding charisma possessed by a living guru intersects with the historical time of devotees and their subjectivities. The proliferation of photographs, videotapes, books, and television programs leads to supplementary auras around the guru as icon, along with greater personal fetishism, rather than just a straightforward decline of aura as Benjamin argued. Similarly, Max Weber's prognosis of the failure of charisma along with the routinization of bureaucracy in modernity needs to be challenged. A communion with the guru's photograph becomes a functional substitute for *darśan*, and the photograph begins to acquire magical properties, generate sacred ash, and come alive to the believer. The photograph becomes the material support for spiritual experiences and visual communion with the guru.

The prime example of this work performed by the aura would be in the case of the cult around Sathya Sai Baba. A logic of substitution becomes a standard feature of devotional interactivity with the guru, as has often been claimed by Sai Baba's devotees. The photographic supplement anchors and even propagates the greater divine presence of Sai Baba's reputed miracle work. At the other extreme from the personality cult would be the suggestion that the guru is nothing more than a catalyst: "guru . . . does not refer so much to a human person as to the object of a shift in attention which takes place from the human person who imparts the teaching to the teaching itself." The guru in this pared-down version would take on the role of *kalyāṇamitra*, or "spiritual friend."[11]

The media generate newer kinds of religious aura even as they seem to have prompted its decline in the traditional mode as Benjamin perceived. As Jacques Derrida has suggested, the modern media are subjecting the world to an enormous wave of globalatinization (*mondialatinisation*), which for him is complicit with—but not reducible in any simple sense—to Christianization. Through globalatinization, iconophobic religions such as Judaism and Islam—that rely on commentary rather than the presence-making of communion—are placed at a disadvantage.[12] Faced with this Christian onslaught, the vocabularies of Guru English, just as much as those of various Islams, are under pressure to discover new approaches to the metaphysical aspects of presence and aura. However, iconophilic polytheism (such as the many practiced forms of Hinduism) is also proliferating alongside Christianity because of the televisual capacity for image-rich productions and replications. The media should never be understood as functioning only at the level of mimetic reproduction, within which certain preconceptions of the relationship between representation and society are stabilized. Media are also generating newer perceptions and realities through representational prospecting and presentational excess. Digital and interactive technologies are in the process of reconfiguring religion, and the newest innovations bypass the aging print technologies. Gurus have learned to combine techniques of commentary and the presence-making of themselves. Traditional forms of Hinduism have already taken very well to televisual presentation of religious rites and ceremonies, including the installation of television cameras in significant temples with cult followings, although many temples still maintain the deity's aura by disallowing direct shots of the principal icon in the *sanctum sanctorum*.

But when it comes to the idea of living and incarnated divine teachers, who are these personalities—living and dead—that possess global aura? To emphasize how widely South Asian–styled religious figures are (and have become) a worldwide phenomenon, consider the following list of names: Rammohun Roy, Keshub Chunder Sen, Dayananda Saraswati, Madame Blavatsky, Ramakrishna Paramahamsa, Swami Vivekananda, Sister Nivedita, Yogi Ramacharaka, Ramana Maharishi, Paramahamsa Yogananda, Baba Premanand Bharati, Sri Aurobindo, Annie Besant, Mahatma Gandhi, Swami Sivananda, Swami Chinmayananda, Swami Satchinanda, Swami Muktananda, Swami Paramananda, Jiddu Krishnamurti, Vimala Thakkar, Maharishi Mahesh Yogi, Guru Maharaj Ji (alias Balyogeshwar), Shirdi Sai Baba, Sathya Sai Baba, Meher Baba, Nisargadatta Maharaj, A. C. Bhaktivedanta Prabhupada, Baba Ram Dass, Acharya Rajneesh (then Bhagwan Rajneesh, then Osho), Deepak Chopra, Srimayee, Sri Sri Ravi Shankar, B.K.S. Ayyangar, Sayagyi S. N. Goenka, Yogi Bhajan, the Dalai Lama, Chogyam Trungpa, the Aga Khan, Nusrat Fateh Ali Khan, Mother Teresa. Even the Ayatollah Khomeini, long regarded by SAVAK, the shah of Iran's secret police, as a Kashmiri-born agitator, was inextricably associated with religion in India after his consequential intervention in the affair of a writer of Kashmiri heritage, Salman Rushdie.

What do all these "gurus" have in common? Would it be possible to consider them as a matrix of religious export potential? All these charismatic religious figures were born, bred, or are somehow associated with South Asia writ large, and their names are revered—or reviled—the world over. Indeed, many more names could be added to this list. However, there is no common religious or doctrinal position that can be imputed to the names; and it would be impossible to characterize reductively the religious "identity" of these figures. Using very generalized criteria in his early paean to Ramakrishna and Vivekananda, Romain Rolland discusses the fifth-century c.e. Pseudo-Dionysius (Denis the Areopagite) as a prophet of crypto-Vedanta philosophy; Plotinus also often comes up in the literature as another figure of this type.[13] While Mother Teresa could be called an Albanian-born Catholic nun, and the Dalai Lama a Tibetan-born dispossessed Buddhist theocrat, that does not adequately explain the religious context that anchors and indeed implicates all these figures in a global religious cosmopolitanism. The differences among those who may be vaguely characterized as participating in a Hindu religious milieu are sometimes just as great as their differences from those who could be identified as separate from it—whether Buddhist, Muslim, Zoroastrian, Ismaili, or Christian. There is certainly no single "tradition" that explains this phenomenon, even though many of these figures speak in the name of a number of traditions and sects, whether long-standing or self-styled. Compared with this list, no other list of South Asian artists, intellectuals, politicians, or Booker Prize winners would exercise anything like a comparable degree of name recognition the world over (the singular name of Salman Rushdie is an obvious exception for reasons that transcend literary criteria). The celebrity or cult status of many of these A-list gurus (to some, charlatans of different degrees) is no proof of their *analytical* cosmopolitanism. Each and every one of these names elicits interest in many different parts of the world in ways yet to be fully studied. Often, the whiff of cosmopolitanism arises because of the inclusive reinterpretation of various followers. It would be futile to search for the exposition of one identifiable doctrine of global or transnational unity in the teachings of specific individuals, even though universalisms of various sorts are indeed to be recognized with respect to most of these figures. Other observers may likewise dismiss these leaders as propagating religious charlatanry and mystical mumbo jumbo, or alternatively believe that the religious treasures of the "mystic East" have some special bearing on the world situation. Indeed it is difficult not to concede something to both extremes of this question. However, it is the characteristically discrepant—and flexible—organization of export-friendly religion that encourages a globally efficacious cosmopolitanism of *appearance*. The above list—which is not at all comprehensive but a sprinkling of recognizable names—can be expanded and parsed according to structuralist methods of binary opposition and grammatical combination. There will be different opinions about which figures are "genuine" and which ones "fraudulent"; some figures will be (paradigmatic) substitutes for others, while other figures will be (syntagmatic) connectors to yet others; principles of contradiction and noncontradiction can be creatively deployed to separate and unify doctrinal overlaps, personality clashes, regional identifications, and other criteria.

Surely, with respect to the names in the list, religious "archetypes" may be discerned: the mystic discovered by others (Ramakrishna, Ramana, Meher, Nisargadatta); the autodidact or disciple who organizes a movement (Rammohun, Keshub, Dayananda, Vivekananda, Besant); the transnational religious entrepreneur (Mahesh Yogi, Bhaktivedanta); the missionary of charity (Mother Teresa); the popularizer of Satyagraha who made fasting a political act (Mahatma Gandhi); the smiling theocrat in exile (Dalai Lama); the frowning theocrat in power (the Ayatollah Khomeini); the Western women (Blavatsky, Besant, Nivedita, and the "Mother" of Aurobindo Ashram, Mirra Richard); the miracle-worker or magus (Sathya Sai Baba); the yogi (Yogananda, B.K.S. Ayyangar); the Tantric hedonist (Osho); the spiritual management guru and marketing phenomenon (Deepak Chopra); the anti-guru (Krishnamurti, Vimala Thakkar); the boy-guru (Balyogeshwar, alias Guru Maharaj Ji); the mother-guru (Sarada Devi; Mirra Richard, or "Mother" of the Aurobindo Ashram; and Amritanandamayee Ma, the guru who hugs hundreds of disciples a day); and the plutocratic godfather and religious head of the Ismailis (the Aga Khan).

These religious figures (both present and past) vary considerably in their active (and also apparent) cosmopolitanism. Some are heavily invested in the organizational management of their flocks and their international growth potential, while others remain blithely unconcerned about the sociological contours of their following; some travel extensively to spread their gospels and tend to their spiritual (and commercial) assets, while others expect the faithful to track them to their ashrams. The heterogeneity of the pastors is exponentially reflected in their flocks. Some of these names mentioned are religious trademarks for extensive religious corporations and monastic orders, while others designate "enlightened" thinkers (in a very different sense from the Kantian nomenclature), respected by their admirers the world over. Guru English speaks to the efficient fit between modernity and orientalism, whereby repackaging is just as—if not more—important than the purported religious message.

An uneasy symbiosis exists within this series of sometimes overlapping but often widely unrelated figures that has been wrested into the category of South Asian religious cosmopolitanism through a thought experiment in taxonomy. There are occasional turf battles that erupt among some of these gurus, cults, and organizations, even as others are nonexclusive, in that their variable followings overlap amicably and even concertedly. Likewise, these gurus and their movements are sometimes heavily critical of each other and are also the butt of antireligious satirists who are indeed the antithesis of the putative native informants (here the success or failure of novelists such as G. V. Desani, V. S. Naipaul, Gita Mehta, or Salman Rushdie acquires new meaning). As has already been discussed in previous chapters, Guru English, from its inception, existed alongside extensive parody, satire, and general criticism of the phenomenon by Indians as well as others. But such criticism, it must be noted, is often just as much internal to its elaboration, with guru savagely attacking guru. Secularism has been taken on board by gurus as an adequate tool for the criticism of the adversary, even as other criteria of verifiability or belief are employed for the propagation of faith. This makes for a coexistence of multiple epistemologies, skeptical methods, and occasional leaps of faith.

Furthermore, the connection between various exported religious cosmopolitanisms and New Age "Californian" religions and "cults" is a very rich one, although there is also much sociological prejudice against these particularly evanescent and socially disruptive forms of group affiliation. In an excellent article on the anticult literature, Diana L. Eck identifies the problematic image this literature creates of a New Age Hinduism that is authoritarian, world-negating, brainwashing, and anti–nuclear family, and one that aggrandizes the self into the divine. However, similar characteristics are also discerned in criticisms of other "fringe" religions such as the Moonies, Scientologists, or UFO cults, and it would appear that differing rationalities are decried from normative Judeo-Christian expectations.[14] Of course, this is not to say that these religions are innocuous. Multiple, mobile, and fractured, many New Age affiliations rarely coalesce into religious identities, but ought not to be dismissed as passing fads.

Late modern religious movements of South Asian origin represent to their worldwide adherents both cosmopolitanism and what Michel Foucault has called "heterotopia." Rather than standard utopianism, which represents a particular utopia as an addressless and unspecific "nowhere," or a fundamentally unreal space, Foucault has suggested that heterotopias could be said to exist in "other spaces" that are empirically experienced, such as prisons, schools, or hospitals—where social organization differs markedly from that in the world at large, and where subjects are positioned in accordingly novel ways that allow critical purchase on power structures.[15] To a degree, ashrams, missions, and religious retreats also provide this combination of a materially lived and real situation, and yet at the same time, psychologically, designate a highly unreal and virtual space, within which normality and perversion, power and resistance are recognized and negotiated. Old orientalisms meet the new xenotropisms, and the metropolis and the postcolonial crisscross each other into increasingly tangled lines of flight. These spaces created under the influence of Guru English, therefore, represent each in their own way, escape and homecoming, materialism and spiritualism, critique and creed. Religious cosmopolitanism in late modernity reorders and reordains the rhetoric of self-reflexivity. For this reason, Guru English is a language that has also spawned a literature, one that reaches a demonstrably different cosmopolitan audience. By contrast, there has perhaps been too much global outreach ascribed to the overworked category of South Asian anglophone fiction, which sometimes passes for a substantial part of the new construct of postcolonial literature. Far more practically efficacious than the productions of South Asia's admittedly talented anglophone authors, Guru English is the most globalized of cosmopolitanisms, delivering orientalizing wisdom in modernized idiom. It may be worth considering whether Guru English is a transcontinental amalgam, a contingent articulation and unpredicted consequence of the British Empire that far exceeds Britain toward an American, and progressively, a worldwide destination.

A sampling of contemporary anglophone gurus can illustrate the interaction of late capitalism with alternative modernities, and that of globalization with Guru English. The unconventional language games these gurus play enable their participation in translocal flows of information, desire, and culture. Even as they invent an alternative cosmopolitanism, anglophone gurus reveal the very real limits and also the dangers of their vocabularies. Although Guru English *could* and occasionally does speak the language of the global popular, its integration with hegemonic structures leads to the neutralization of progressive possibilities. Even though the ultranationalist Vivekananda had insisted in the nineteenth century that Vedanta went hand in hand with socialism, today Guru English is very well ensconced in, and even relies on, the consumption patterns of late capitalist consumer culture. Perhaps this investigation also speaks to the Foucauldian paradox at the heart of many other analyses of global cultural circulation. The dissent expressed by desire turns out to be a productive effect of power, and institutional recuperation ensures that utopia is more elusive than when previously thought as possible, by way of heterotopia.

By surveying the legacies of anglophone gurus and their implications for the future alongside a number of literary parallels that anticipate and also challenge their historical legacies, the rest of this chapter methodologically "interrupts" sociology with literature. It is not surprising that successful cosmopolitan gurus tend to rely on a Sanskritic Great Tradition rather than parochial little traditions to attract novices.

Ecumenical and broadband Hinduism or Buddhism, especially at the front end of the teaching, would be more likely to go over to multiple audiences because of its greater familiarity, translatability, and transidiomaticity, given the loose spirituality posited for these religions through orientalist imaginings. Cultish aspects could always be kept in the background and wheeled out later for more committed devotees. However, the differences exhibited in the cases discussed below demonstrate that there is no simple lesson to be learned. In some cases, Guru English is used to rewrite religious cosmopolitanism as a scientific script; in others it foments countercultural provocations; and in yet others, functions as a management and marketing device for alternative mind-sets. Rather than reiterate the tautology of top-down cosmopolitanism, which is largely analytical and deductive, Guru English makes for a bottom-up version that is inductive, provisional, incomplete, and constantly on the move, although what it might be moving toward is not always clear, except to the individual practitioner who performs in dulcet tones. Literary representations and sociological instances, when considered together, unsettle the sharp division that is otherwise maintained between the sociology of religion and literary criticism. Looking at these phenomena, the critic can address new forms of religious enchantment rather than just describe the one-way process of disenchantment and secularism theorized by some analysts of modernity.

From the Mahatma to the Maharishi

As a practitioner of Guru English who anticipated later New Age developments, Mohandas Karamchand Gandhi managed—perhaps more effectively than any modern politician—to maintain both universal and particular casts to his politico-religious language. Gandhi's sobriquet, "Mahatma" (mighty one; great soul), is often used to refer to him in the most secular contexts without comment. It is worth noting that the Theosophists helped familiarize the anglophone world with the meaning of this divine attribute well before it ended up serving in the place of Gandhi's given name. Krishna is referred to as *mahātma* in the Bhagavadgītā, and when referring to spiritual mentors the term often does the work of linking the human with the divine. While the hierarchy-friendly Theosophists expected mahatmas to serve guru-like functions, Gandhi's transcendentalism took a different (and some would say, crypto-Christian) route, seeking politicoreligious meaning in corporeal embodiment, lived practices, and symbolic acts.

Was Gandhi a guru, or just one more in a long line of politicians who used religious vocabularies to disseminate their messages? Gandhi's capacity to act maternally as well as paternally suggests something of the vicarious parental function that gurus provide their followers. The psychoanalyst Erik Erikson saw Gandhi as a "religious actualist." Gandhi's professional identity evolved from barrister to politician and eventually to guru. Gandhi's sublimated maternalism and his assumption of "mahatmaship" was eventually connected to his privileging of living actuality over factual reality. For the psychoanalyst, therefore, Gandhi was "a very special kind of guru who would make radical and total use of an age-old emotional (and once well institutionalized) necessity for finding a second, spiritual father." The guru could play the roles of parental proxy, political leader, and spiritual counselor for his followers. Gandhi's integration of religious with political goals confused even his closest followers.[16] As Akeel Bilgrami's perceptive analysis has noted, Gandhi replaced the Kantian concept of the universalizable moral principle with the universal personal exemplarity of the religiopolitical agent. Bypassing criticism as epistemic violence toward others, the philosophy of nonviolence foregrounded the political demonstrator's lived actuality as a salutary instance. Denying the universalizability of morals meant that truth became an experiential rather than a cognitive notion, replacing objective politics with the subjective experience of the conscientious objector in a religious cast. This truth could then have a contagious effect on those who saw it in action—including especially the practitioner's political adversaries—but such a truth could not be extrapolated as a cognitive principle that could lead to the symbolically violent criticism of others.[17]

Gandhi led prayer meetings at places of political conflict, adapted ritual fasting to the political goals of a hunger strike, and developed a doctrine of *satyāgraha* ("the path of truth," "truth-force," or "holding to truth in the face of the other" that might also be translated more whimsically as "the embodied practice of speaking truth to power"). *Satyāgraha*, learned and adapted from Thoreau's pamphlet "On Civil Disobedience," put the protester/practitioner's body on the front line in a manner that performed a militant, yet nonviolent protest. The success of this political strategy in the Indian context came from employing powerful religious symbolism to score points that were political, but never merely secular. Rather than define secular space in opposition to religion, Gandhi used religious idiom for political purposes in ways that detranscendentalized religious belief even as the performance made visible religion intertwined with laicism.[18] Yet another of Gandhi's sobriquets, as *bāpū* (father), interacted with his appellation of "Mahatma" to create a pedagogical and paternal role just as with the figure of the *mahāpuruṣa* (superman) who arose at the end of Bankim's *Anandamath*. Gandhi's status as mahatma was endorsed by Sri Aurobindo and Rabindranath Tagore, both of whom nonetheless broke with him on key aspects of the struggle for decolonization. Tagore received the honorific of *gurudev* (divine teacher) from Gandhi in return. While it would be interesting to explore the analogy of guru in either case, it is difficult to suggest that either figure was appreciated solely as a religious teacher. The cultural transfer of religious inspiration to political and artistic endeavors makes clear-cut judgments very complicated—Tagore, while principally a writer and an artist, was also still the nominal head of his wing of the Brahmo Samaj, a religious role he inherited from both father and grandfather.

The literary self-expression of Gandhi's status as guru was not always evident throughout Gandhi's voluminous writing that was largely nonliterary—lawyerly petitions, political pamphlets, and didactic exhortations dominate the collected works. However, occasional classics in dialogue form, such as the famous *Hind Swaraj* (1909; originally written in Gujarati but translated by Gandhi himself as *Indian Home Rule*) make use of the protocols of homiletic and political argumentation to criticize modern civilization and praise the virtues of an idealized village life that existed more in Gandhi's mind than in reality. Taking issue with historical reasoning that was teleological and Eurocentric, *Hind Swaraj* proposes an outcome for Indian autonomy based on cultural essences. Gandhi's skillful development of a personality cult took place readily through his bodily performance, fasting, newsworthy loquaciousness, and self-imposed silences regarding everything from the state of the world to his bowel movements. In the guru's body, microcosm and macrocosm became one, and what often dominated was the secondary literature, the gossip and adulation, and the journalistic effects. Keeping in mind this particular outcome, Gandhi's later literary contribution was a spiritual autobiography in the grand tradition of Augustine and Rousseau, and also Paramahamsa Yogananda. *The Story of My Experiments with Truth* (1927–29), first published in newspaper installments in Gujarati, cleverly finds the political in the personal, and speaks of historical aspirations through the language of the spiritual quest. The autobiographical genre is criticized as an inauthentic approach to Indian identity even as it is hollowed out and occupied as an experimental and performative medium. Adopting a supposedly "scientific" or empirical model of "experiment," Gandhi disingenuously describes his subjective development and experiences in a manner that suggests self-anointment as spiritual master. The experiments are designated as taking place in multiple fields. In the manner of holistic spiritual quests, experiments involve putting to test the body as well as the soul, family life as well as the social world. Various areas of Gandhi's life—from his sexual practice, diet, and temperance, to larger political and moral visions—are addressed with the empirical naïveté of a novice as well as the authoritarian tones of a guru who knew what was best for others even if there was a facade of self-abnegation overall.

Theosophy initially stimulated the religious quest of the young Mohandas Karamchand Gandhi, who began studying law in London in the late 1880s. Gandhi also heard Annie Besant's oratory on behalf of Theosophy. Personally introduced to Blavatsky and Besant in London, the Theosophical connection continued for Gandhi in South Africa with activities in the Johannesburg Lodge. Rejecting the elitism and the supernatural investments of Theosophy, Gandhi nonetheless took on board its evolutionary and pseudoscientific premises. He also attempted an open dialogue with other religious interlocutors, such as Edward Maitland of the Esoteric Christian Union. In the manner of many of his compatriots, Gandhi was attracted by an Eastern twist given to Unitarianism by Theosophy. Theosophy offered the alternative to the Brahmo route adopted by Rammohun and Keshub. While the Brahmos reformed Hinduism under the pressures of Christian criticisms, Theosophy made a stronger claim to the religious priority of East over West. If all religious wisdom could be characterized as springing from the East, Western religious mysticism could then be accommodated to this framework, as for instance when Blavatsky juxtaposed texts such as Isaac Meyer's *Qabbalah* and the Vedas in *The Secret Doctrine*. However, Gandhi resolutely rejected Theosophical occultism for daily practices and social reform involving considerable personal and social experimentation. Ultimately, he was a self-made guru without a single direct teacher, although Raychandbhai Mehta, Tolstoy, and Ruskin were acknowledged as most exalted.[19]

Despite, and perhaps because of, his religiosity, Gandhi was understood as an exceptional politician within the Indian context. His mass appeal made the Congress Party use Gandhi as its mascot, even though his mercurial unpredictability had resulted in organizational control devolving to more able conventional politicians such as Jawaharlal Nehru, Chakravarti Rajagopalachari, and Vallabhbhai Patel. While supporters were often nervous about his maverick about-turns, Gandhi's motives were impugned by a number of political actors—the British, the Muslim League, the Hindu Mahasabha, and Dalit leaders. At the end of the day, politically *mahatma* was not the same as *guru*.

The iconic status of Gandhi as global guru has a different trajectory for transnational reception history. Gandhi's iconic status has led to his evocation as a metaphorical guru in diverse political struggles. Classic national liberation struggles and political power movements associate Gandhi's image and nonviolent tactics with figures as different as Martin

Luther King, Jr., Nelson Mandela, Lech Walesa, Benigno Aquino, Khan Abdul Ghaffar Khan, or Aung San Suu Kyi. At the same time, Gandhi's famous antimodernity, his adoption of homespun cloth against Manchester industrial products, and his criticism of the railways and celebration of the bullock-cart inspired the radical ecology of Arne Naess and the microeconomics of E. F. Schumacher. Gandhi's looming presence in the international philosophy of peace studies explains why the Nobel Foundation still puts out a long apology about why Gandhi never got the Peace Prize, even though he was nominated for it four times and was invoked as a comparable politico-religious precursor by the Nobel Committee when it awarded the prize to a guru-in-exile (if also aspiring theocrat), the Dalai Lama. The proliferation of Gandhi as a perennial global reference has led Ashis Nandy to refer facetiously to four Weberian ideal types: the Gandhi of the Indian state, the Gandhi of the Gandhians, the Gandhi of eccentrics, and the Gandhi of myth.

While Gandhi's rural utopianism was rejected resolutely by the state-centered socialist policies of Nehru, the vestiges of his antimodernity continued to have reverberations when it came to assessing the impact of heavy industry and the emergence of the postcolonial state amidst the genocidal violence of the 1940s. Claiming to be the proponent of a unified India, he nonetheless discussed the restitutionist return to "Ramrajya"—a mythical Hindu golden era of communal harmony; speaking for the Dalits (Untouchables), who had been excluded by Brahmanical religious practices, he nonetheless dubbed these outcast groups Harijans (Vishnu's folk); and while genuinely wedded to the idea of Hindu-Muslim unity, was probably more directly responsible for the partition of India than any other Hindu politician.

Novelists have imaginatively explored Gandhi's special ability to link religion with politics that confounded conventional expectations. One of the most celebrated examples is Raja Rao's experimental novel *Kanthapura* (1938), in which caste society in a South Indian village is overturned upon the intervention of Moorthy, a Gandhian activist. Rao represents village life as relying on the repetition of oral formulary and superstitious rituals. Hence, the socially revolutionary implications of Gandhianism has to be introduced by way of the *Harikatha*-man Jayaramachar, for whom Shiva's legendary three eyes are matched by the Gandhian objective of Self-Rule: "Swaraj too is three-eyed: Self-purification, Hindu-Moslem unity, Khaddar [homespun]." The story of Gandhi's birth in Gujarat becomes the storyteller's analog for the myths about the feats of baby Krishna. Just as the infant god slew demons and serpents, "so too our Mohandas began to fight against the enemies of the country . . . [and] so he goes from village to village to slay the serpent of the foreign rule."[20] Grafting nationalism onto religious vocabularies, Gandhianism also functions as a technique of mesmerism, whereby conversion experiences regularly occur when an opponent, skeptic, or hidebound traditionalist suddenly become "a Gandhi's man" through direct contact with the Mahatma. Moorthy, the youngest child of Old Narsamma, becomes a Gandhian after being patted on the back by the Mahatma, "and through that touch was revealed to him as the day is revealed to the night the sheathless being of his soul."[21] The rural Gandhians under Moorthy's leadership eventually suffer excommunication, bereavement, arrest, and police brutality, but also become surrogates of the Mahatma, using techniques such as religious fasting to organize civil disobedience among the socially disenfranchised, including the pariahs in the potter's quarter and the coolies in the Skeffington coffee estate. While village rituals are shown through an orientalizing lens that alternately suggest exoticism and superstitious ignorance (see Rao's pedantic footnotes for later editions of the novel), Moorthy's epiphany, in the dulcet tones of Guru English, offers a syncretism of Christ, Kabir, Gandhi, and Shaivism in a few lines also reminiscent of Vivekananda and Kipling's lama:

> Moorthy loosens his limbs and, holding his breath, says to himself, "I shall love even my enemies. The Mahatma says he would love even our enemies," and closing his eyes, tighter, he slips back into the foldless sheath of the soul, and sends out rays of love to the east, rays of love to the west, rays of love to the north, rays of love to the south, and love to the earth below and to the sky above, and he feels such exaltation creeping into his limbs and head that his heart begins to beat out a song, and the song of Kabir comes into his mind:
>
> > The road to the City of Love is hard, brother,
> > It's hard,
> > Take care, take care, as you walk along it.
>
> Singing this his exaltation grows and grows, and tears come to his eyes. And when he opens them to look round, a great blue radiance seems to fill the whole earth, and dazzled, he rises up and falls prostrate before the god, chanting Sankara's "Sivoham, Sivoham. I am Siva. I am Siva. Siva am I."[22]

Bhatta, the village priest, is the predictable enemy of this dangerous syncretism—but reform is portrayed as the work of progressive Brahmans who have to defeat their reactionary brethren even while members of lower castes remain in the position of followers. Furthermore, Badè Khan, the Muslim policeman, is demonized in the novel as a British stooge. However, Moorthy's letter to his compatriots at the end of the novel suggests that Gandhi's saintliness is also likely to render him gullible to English trickery, to which Nehru's "equal-distributionist" message is a necessary supplement. As with Vivekananda, a nationalist Guru English often requires socialist inflection. Rao's agreement with Gandhian ideology regarding India's "unchanging village republics" has also been criticized by Rumina Sethi, who sees the ahistorical portrait of Kanthapura as eliding political struggle. Rao, the most relentlessly philosophical of Indian novelists writing in English, visited several gurus, including Mahatma Gandhi, Sri Aurobindo, Ramana Maharishi, Narayana Maharaj, Pandit Taranath, and Swami Atmananda. Rao's other novels continue spiritual quests in Guru English of a high philosophical register. Kirillov in *Comrade Kirillov* (1965, 1976), and Govindan Nair in *The Cat and Shakespeare* (1965) feature trickster-gurus in an austere manner, as does his later novel initiating a dialogue between Hinduism and Judaism that won the Neustadt International Prize, *The Chessmaster and His Moves* (1988).[23]

Compared with the seriousness of *Kanthapura*, which was written well before Indian independence, R. K. Narayan's *Waiting for the Mahatma* (1955) is much more laconic about the Gandhian phenomenon. While the linguistic experimentation of *Kanthapura* anchors the politico-religious within a distanciated ethnography, *Waiting for the Mahatma* uses Gandhi's historical personage alongside the unfolding of a private—and essentially secular and depoliticized—romantic bildungsroman. In the novel, Gandhi succinctly states that his system follows very simple goals: "*Ram Dhun* [devotional music]; spinning on the *charka* [wheel] and the practice of absolute Truth and nonviolence."[24] Sriram, the novel's struggling Everyman, instantly falls in love with Bharati, an intimate member of Gandhi's entourage. He adopts Gandhianism and homespun as a way of getting closer to his love interest, even while he has to abandon an aging grandmother at home in order to do so. The heroine Bharati allegorizes the country [*Bhārat*], and was indeed so named by the Mahatma himself in the fiction. The novel acquires the status of a romantic potboiler based on the unfolding of historical events. Sriram and Bharati have to earn their right to marry through long travails (inevitably involving political imprisonment and separation) while working for the Gandhian political cause. However, the lovers gain the Mahatma's explicit blessings moments before his actual assassination by Nathuram Godse in 1948. Several Indian scholars criticize as inappropriate Narayan's trivialization of Gandhianism through comic irony. However, his novel presents us with a subtle interrogation of political virtue and religious leadership by way of the transgressive nature of that most banal phenomenon: middle-class romantic love. Ultimately, Sriram and Bharati take the wind out of the sails of Gandhian Guru English, something that had been puffed up by novels such as Rao's *Kanthapura*, Mulk Raj Anand's *Untouchable*, and others.[25]

V. S. Naipaul's *The Mystic Masseur* (1957) presents us with yet another prescient parody of rudimentary Guru English when used by political opportunists, this time in the context of the Caribbean diaspora. The novel charts the rise of Ganesh Ramsumair, a humble Trinidadian schoolteacher who began his professional career by substitute teaching a class that was "a sort of rest-station for the mentally maimed."[26] Inspired by Mr. Stewart, an Englishman dressed as a Hindu mendicant who gives him twenty copies of *The Science of Thought Review*, Ganesh tricks his father-in-law Ramlogan into endowing an institute for "Hindu Culture and Science of Thought in Trinidad." Ganesh subsequently begins a publishing career by producing a thirty-page booklet entitled *101 Questions and Answers on the Hindu Religion* that caters to a barely literate audience. The vapid booklet, featuring simplistic and literal-minded information, paradoxically becomes a best-seller in Trinidadian publishing.[27] Ganesh proudly sends a copy to Mahatma Gandhi, who is described within the booklet as the world's greatest modern Hindu. The pamphlet is succeeded by other amusing titles, including *What God Told Me; Profitable Evacuation* (a book on how to avoid constipation); and *Sparks from a Brahmin's Log Fire*. Ganesh's literary career culminates in *Years of Guilt*, an autobiographical cross between "a spiritual thriller and a metaphysical whodunit."[28] Ganesh uses his lowbrow religious publications to jump-start a career as faith healer and mystic masseur. To attract his clientele, his walls are "covered with religious quotations in Hindi and English, and with Hindu religious pictures." Combining "Hindu philosophy," "practical psychology," and knowledge of the techniques practiced by "Hollywood Hindus," Ganesh launches a shrewd advertisement campaign, "Who is this Ganesh?" to attract Afro-Caribbean and white clients in addition to the diasporic Indians. The novel laconically pans the Hollywood Hindus who inspired Ganesh as "holy, cultivated men who issue frequent bulletins about the state of their soul, the complexities and variations of which are endless and always worth description."[29]

Ganesh's successful hucksterism earns him the enmity of Narayan, a columnist in the *Hindu* newspaper with political ambitions. Ganesh overcomes this obstacle by strong-arm tactics when he takes over Narayan's Hindu Association with his acolytes.[30] Naipaul's satire of Ganesh's success reveals the limitations of Guru English as much as its opportunities. Ganesh's career as mystic propels him into becoming a member of the Legislative Council during Trinidad's first elections in 1946. But at this point, Guru English has to be abandoned as a vehicle of personal advancement in the transition from feudalism to capitalism.

Another of Ganesh's friends, the Oxford-educated Indersingh (loosely based on Naipaul's relative Rudranath Capildeo) promotes a Gandhian philosophy of "socialinduism" in conversation with Ganesh.[31] However, the eventual outcome is imperial assimilation, as Ganesh shuts down his publishing company and disavows his Indian roots. Turning into a staunch anticommunist and Europeanizing his name to G. Ramsay Muir with a deft paronomastic reversal, Ganesh cashes in, for the title of Member of the Order of the British Empire. The incipient guru who had attracted Christians, Muslims, and Hindus alike turns into a grotesque caricature of an English toady, becoming the first in a long line of Naipaul's mimic men.

The character of Ganesh Pundit shows up in other early Naipaul fictions and develops a similar character drawn with trenchant satirical intent by Naipaul père in his *The Adventures of Gurudeva*.[32] Gurudeva, the village bully, stick-fighter, and "bad-John," waxes religious after undergoing incarceration for rioting during the Trinidadian Muslim festival of Hosay. He returns from jail as a crusader of *Sanatanism* (a reform Hinduism akin to Dayananda's), but what initially appears as a spectacular change of heart is actually revealed to be charlatanry. Gurudeva's new identity as pundit reveals the vagabond's small-mindedness and roguish personality in ensuing interactions with his family, followers, and religious rivals. Mr. Sohan, the Christian schoolmaster in the novel, is shown to be much more knowledgeable and broad-minded about the meaning of Hindu religious belief and practice than the uncomprehending Gurudeva, who remains, at the end of the day, a petty wife-beater, social enforcer, and sexual opportunist, whose actions are aided and abetted by a traditionalist Hindu joint family. V. S. Naipaul suggests that his father's novel intimates "the Hindu reverence for learning and the word, awakened by the beginnings of an English education and a Hindu religious training."[33] But it also shows how regressive these neotraditionalist moments can be. While the satirical force of the father's fiction is turned inward into exposing the need for religious reform within the closed confines of the Hindu diaspora, the son's first novel indicts professional self-advancement at a moment of greater communication between Hinduism and other religions through English. The mystic masseur's inescapable ambivalence toward his profession has already been set up through a sly allusion that the novel makes to "the two stone elephants star[ing] in opposite directions" on his house as he gives up his religious career. The description evokes William Jones's orientalist misidentification of the elephant-headed god Ganesha with the Roman Janus—Ganesh is also originally from a village named Fourways. Faced with opposing choices, doorways, and indeed faces, this particular guru's end point evokes a Hindu platitude he doled out to his followers earlier in the novel: " 'we never are what we want to be,' he wrote, 'but what we must be.' " Perhaps this is not just his fate but also that of the more generalized phenomenon of Guru English that he represents.[34]

Following on the heels of *The Mystic Masseur*, R. K. Narayan's *The Guide* (1957) shows us that guruness is also a condition that can be thrust upon someone without warning. The novel features Raju, a one-time tourist guide and dance manager who has just left prison after serving a sentence for forging the name of his lover, Rosie Marco, on a bank check. Once released, Raju is thought to be a swami by uncomprehending villagers. Experienced in the art of being a confidence trickster, Raju plays along initially out of amusement, inertia, and the easy lifestyle the impersonation brings. However, when there is a serious drought in the region, Raju undertakes a Gandhian-style fast for rain that starts off in bad faith but becomes a good faith effort by a sudden change in circumstances, just as in the manner of his life as a whole. Raju drops dead just as it is hinted that the hoped-for rain is on its way, although it is undecidable whether this has happened by coincidence or causation (as religious causation always is from the agnostic's perspective). Narayan's ironic fiction therefore provides a surprising redemption to its raffish hero. The holy man scam can "work" beyond the level of ascertaining the individual motivations and intentions of the particular trickster. Rather, it is the power of social beliefs and the collective narratives that get spun around those beliefs, so much so that a religious movement was created around Raju, and the government was intervening to make him break his fast at the moment that he died.[35]

If midcentury fictional echoes of gurus in works such as Rao's, Narayan's, and Naipaul's allude to politicians using religious languages in order to communicate with diverse audiences alongside the exposé of these leaders as fakes or charlatans, the later example of the Maharishi Mahesh Yogi represents a Hindu religious leader whose message regarding the technique of Transcendental Meditation (TM) thrives in the postpolitical era of the later twentieth century. Known widely just by his epithet, the Maharishi ("great sage") originally trained as an engineer, moved to the United States in 1958, and very quickly established an impressive network of meditation societies. After some initial attempts to recruit from the countercultural and student movements in the 1960s, by the early 1970s the movement had begun targeting businesses, governments, and universities.

In February 1968, the Maharishi received a much-publicized visit by The Beatles. The fabulous four came to India with the intention to take a three-month course in TM at the Maharishi's ashram in Rishikesh after having met him the previous year in Wales. The Maharishi claimed to be "not pushing them too hard at first . . . feeding them high-level philosophy in simple words."[36] The association ended badly but eventually helped propel the guru into a position of even greater international public recognition. The Maharishi was already suggested to George Harrison by his association with the sitar maestro Ravi Shankar. Harrison says he sought out the Maharishi because he knew he "needed a mantra—a password to get through into the other world." Paul McCartney had an initial impression of the sage as "the giggly little guy going round the globe seven times to heal the world (and this was his third spin)." John Lennon's breezy first impression was that TM "makes you happy, intelligent and [gives you] more energy. I mean, look how it started. I believe he [Maharishi] just landed in Hawaii in his nightshirt—all on his own, nobody with him—in 1958." Later, he would opine that what the Maharishi "says about life and the universe is the same message that Jesus, Buddha and Krishna and all the big boys were putting over." Lennon, the most poetically talented of the four, riffs in a manner reminiscent of earlier Desani-style theosophistries:

> Cut to Maharishi's health farm on the tip of the Himalayas. Eye-ing, eye-ing, eye-ing. He picked the right mantra for me. OK, he's a lot balder now than when I knew him. How come God always picks on these holi-men? Ulcers, etc. "He's taking on someone else's karma." I bet that's what all the little sheep are bleating. He's got a nice smile, though. This is turning into *Autobiography of a Yogurt*, but isn't everything? I ask myself. He made us live in separate huts from our wives. . . . Can't say it was too much of a strain.

If there was a mutually beneficial exchange of media celebrity for religious aura in that association, the social images of both parties benefited as they used each other to shift phases and audiences. The Beatles soon broke with the Maharishi when they saw through his tactic of using them to recruit a larger following, but at the same time, their easygoing attitude suggested to many others that the mantra used in TM was like a chemical formula, a medical prescription, or an electronic password into the spiritual world. Many of the songs in the famous *White Album* alluded to the communal experience with the other star participants in the ashram, including "Tomorrow Never Knows," "Dear Prudence" (written to Mia Farrow's sister who was apparently an obsessive meditator who would refuse to come out to play), "Instant Karma," "Mother Nature's Son," "Ob-La-Di, Ob-La-Da," "Child of Nature" (later Lennon's solo "Jealous Guy"), "The Continuing Story of Bungalow Bill," and most sensationally, "Sexy Sadie" (originally written to the words "Maharishi, What have you done? / You've made a fool of everyone"). The Beatles were also miffed by the Maharishi's opportunistic tour with the Beach Boys. Harrison and Lennon (who stayed a full eight weeks while Starr stayed only two; and McCartney, four) left in the context of controversial speculations that were taking place regarding a supposed pass the Maharishi had made at Mia Farrow.[37]

The Maharishi's new strategy, by the early 1970s, downplayed his training in Advaita Vedanta and emphasized instead the scientific verification of his teachings. As one observer puts it, this resulted in a number of interesting transformations: "*God* became cosmic creative intelligence; *atman* became the pure field of creative intelligence within; *karma* became the law of action and reaction; *brahman* became the ground state of physics."[38] Promoting the practice of TM—intriguingly the same abbreviation as that for trademark—the Maharishi brought a far-reaching scientific investigation of mental and physical states to the analysis of psychic and spiritual phenomena. Despite all the potential incommensurabilities, TM's practitioners espouse the rhetoric of cooperation between religion and science—in the manner that Yogananda pushed universal scientific propaganda while insisting that Yogodans could still keep their religion even as they participated in breathing and meditation techniques that recharged their bodies and minds. Rather than make indirect references to a culture that is hard for novitiates to access, TM has substituted modern scientific terminology for that esotericism, and to some extent can do so precisely because the interpretations of modern science are themselves incomprehensible to most lay persons. Speculative hard science, especially in the areas of mathematical set theory, "superstring" theoretical physics, and molecular genetics, is squared off against Vedic wisdom. Hiding his religious light beneath a bushel of scientific discussions, the Maharishi has renamed the creed with the euphemistic tag "Science of Creative Intelligence" (SCI). An invented and objectified ideology using modern terminology has been substituted very effectively for Hindu cultural vocabularies. Science, spirituality, modernity, and ancient doctrine meld through this particular deployment of Guru English as a commodified cosmopolitanism. What was begun resolutely by Blavatsky's scientific occultism and mysticism has now found a contemporary articulation.

While much of the argumentative energy behind the TM literature explores abstruse connections between "Maharishi's Vedic science" and "modern science," the teaching focuses on promoting physical and mental health through stress-relaxation techniques and evolves from there to promising higher spiritual levels, posited as the seven states of consciousness.[39] The advantages of TM's methods of spiritual self-improvement are subsequently displayed in the literature with graphs of brain waves, metabolic rates, oxygen levels in the blood, and much medical-sounding terminology. The packaging has worked, to the extent that SCI claims to have earned the allegiance of three million to four million meditators worldwide, a thousand college chapters of the Students International Meditation Society, and an international university with campuses in Iowa and Washington, D.C., which is the movement's most public, cosmopolitan, and secular face.

Most impressive of all is how SCI showcases various mainstream organizations and institutions that have adopted its techniques. One such feather in its cap is the U.S. Army, whose soldiers are clearly in need of stress-reduction upon their return from various killing fields. The rapid action Delta Force in the military has bought into the idea of unlocking human potential, leading to the suggestiveness of army recruitment campaigns that feature the well-known slogan, "Be All That You Can Be." While the Maharishi has done a reasonably good job of finessing the stranger aspects of his program from media attention, full-fledged TM practitioners spend a surprising amount of time trying to levitate. Levitation is a yogic *siddhi* (or advanced skill) that obsesses the movement. More consequential (if proven) than levitation, perhaps, is the movement's claim to have affected world consciousness (and lowered crime rates) by means of elaborately synchronized mass meditation sessions. However, SCI's rhetorical investment in scientific jargon, notions of evidence, levels of proof, and seemingly endless instrumental calibration and documentation of these techniques and their impact on bodily states, brain waves, stress levels, and the like makes it very different from traditional forms of miracle work and meditation.

SCI's success has come from being able to convince secular organizations of the practical results. While much skepticism is still leveled at the movement, the organization engages its critics rather than just dismissing or ignoring them, as smaller, more embattled religions often do. A critical analysis of the movement has suggested that "science" for SCI is a stand-in for the role "mythology" played within traditional religions. As SCI goes about finding its hierophany by translating itself into modern structures of apprehension, according to Mikael Rothstein, it has taken scientific interest in grand unification theories (or unified field theory) to be "the academic expression of the perennial truth." For all these reasons, the academic and disciplinary literacy of the venture makes it produce copious amounts of Guru English. Clearly, in this venture there are elements of attempts by earlier gurus, such as Swami Dayananda and the Arya Samaj's emphasis on the scientific origins of Hinduism, but efforts that are now wheeled toward diasporic uses rather than Dayananda's nationalistic and anti-British framework. Another precursor could be Shri Dev Guru Bhagwan or Sattyanand Agnihotri of the Dev Samaj, who was active in Lahore in the 1920s, preaching the need for a science-grounded rather than an imagination-grounded religion through his books and journals. Similarly, Yogananda's early North American success with kriya yoga must have been remembered when the decision was made to shift the later movement toward holding out promises of supernatural powers to adherents. However, in a few decades, the emphasis was no longer on Vedic mathematics and lost scientific wisdom as a support for wounded Indian pride in the nationalistic phase, as it was in the late nineteenth and early twentieth centuries. Rather, bringing science and religion together with an Eastern flavor held out the solution of holistic living and thinking, an especially appealing prospect to the alienated middle classes and those seeking a more meaningful life when confronted with stress-ridden jobs. To combine religious profoundity and stress-relaxation into one technique and philosophy was no doubt a master-stroke of efficiency and modernity, and productive of an alternative rationality. And all practitioners had the satisfaction of being given a customized mantra that would be a secret between the guru and the disciple. Of course, this practice of the secret given by the guru to the disciple is a long-standing one—Swami Prabhavananda gave one such mantra to Christopher Isherwood—but in the case of TM it becomes the sole focus of personal advancement and spiritual power, as there is much less overt religious ritual to attend to, unlike in the case of the Ramakrishna Mission and many other similar organizations.[40]

The Maharishi, who attracts doctors, scientists, and politicians to his venture, also heads a World Plan Executive Council, a kind of synod that harbors pretensions of global governance and thereby suggests yet another translation of religion into cosmopolitan outreach. This bold step into parapolitical activity is a sign of the growing confidence of the new movements amidst current Western conjunctures of declining social structures and the increased stress on state-sponsored networks of medicine and mental health. Apart from expressing utopian notions of world government, views on population control, and proposals for reducing global warming as well as crime rates, the organization pub-licizes much ambitiousness and also a great deal for skeptics to laugh about. The all-too-easy integration of TM within various corporate and nongovernmental organizational networks shows that the utopian aims of the movement have fallen victim to its conventional worldly success. But such a bold attempt at institutional consolidation, as groups such as the Moonies and the Scientologists have done, suggests that a new form of a religiously based political party is possible, one that does not appeal to established conventions but which explores forms of association that break the bounds of religion as privatization.

Witness the following 1977 testimonial by W. K. Coors, president of the Adolph Coors Company, in the preface to a book entitled *TM and Business: Personal and Corporate Benefits of Inner Development*: "[N]or do I as a dedicated practicing Christian sense any conflict between TM and Christianity. Rather, I find both to be wholly compatible. I regard TM as a pleasant mental exercise which cleanses and refreshes the mind in the same sense that physical exercise cleanses and refreshes the body—nothing more."[41] Similarly, the Web page of the World Plan Executive Council proclaims, "TM does not consider itself a religion, and hence is compatible with all religions and faiths. . . . The only instruction with regard to practice is to meditate for twenty minutes twice a day."[42] Capping the mainstreaming of TM was John Hagelin's third run for president of the United States in 2000 as the candidate of the Natural Law Party, created in 1992 according to the Maharishi's teachings. Hagelin's candidacy received particular media attention in 2000 because of the dispute between his and Pat Buchanan's supporters for the Reform Party nomination and the campaign purse of $12.6 million in federal matching funds that went with it. Attempts will be made in the future by such movements, as well as others, to capitalize on new ecological sensibilities and fresh religious syncretisms. The reentry of religion into politics in this case means greater indeterminacies regarding policies, value systems, and institutional durability. By trademarking a process, TM has established itself well beyond its origin as the Maharishi's teaching, or for that matter superseded the goals of "Vedic science."

Earlier, a traditional sage who had been accorded the "Maharishi" title and who influenced several Western writers was Venkatramanan, the sage of Tiruvannamalai in southern India. Known as Ramana Maharishi, he is likely the original of Shri Ganesha in Somerset Maugham's *The Razor's Edge*, a novel that preceded Naipaul's use of a similar name for his mystic masseur by a decade. Maugham's portrait is entirely serious with no hint of parody or criticism. Larry, the novel's heroic religious seeker, learns yogic techniques of hypnotism and the mind control of others, and passes along hearsay of miraculous occurrences including that of walking on water after his visit to India. The basic premise of many of these narratives that we have encountered is articulated by one of Larry's Indian interlocutors who tells him that, "the East has more to teach the West than the West conceives." While it first seems we are in the miracle-infested territory made familiar by Yogananda's *Autobiography of a Yogi*, the actual encounter with Shri Ganesha results in Larry's being given the simplest

of messages that "Brahman alone is the Guru." Larry becomes an exponent of Advaita upon returning to Europe. He enacts the equivalent
of Hindu-style renuciation, giving away all his money, leaving society,
and traveling on a tramp steamer back to the United States where he
plans to drive taxis. Maugham translates the tradition of the wandering religious mendicant into a modern-day professional equivalent.[43]

FROM THE BHAGWAN TO THE DOCTOR

The legacy of Rajneesh Chandra Mohan, later Bhagwan Shree Rajneesh
(a.k.a. Osho) presents a different side of Guru English, its real dangers,
and also the promise of heterotopia. The author of about four hundred
books of lectures comprising some thirty-three million words, Rajneesh was a very syncretic religious thinker who could integrate Sufism, Christian mysticism, Zen Buddhism, Tao, and Tantrism, along
with a strong philosophical grasp of Advaita Vedanta. He penned ten
volumes on Patanjali's *Yoga Sutras*, and five volumes on the *Vijñāna
Bhairava Tantra*, entitled *The Book of Secrets*. Having started his adult career as a professor of English, Rajneesh could also, with relatively little
effort, integrate modern Western thinkers such as Friedrich Nietzsche,
George Ivanovitch Gurdjieff, Wilhelm Reich, and D. H. Lawrence into
his lectures. Some of his biographers claim that he voraciously in-
gested ten to fifteen books on philosophy and religion daily.[44] Rajneesh
also liked to compare himself to Jiddu Krishnamurti, whom he credited as being "enlightened," but the favor was not returned. Rajneesh's
religious appeal came from his relentlessly anti-institutional and anti-
normative teachings, delivered through Zen koans, Mullah Nasruddin
stories, and bawdy jokes just as much as through doctrinal disquisi-
tions. His systematic attacks on Gandhian asceticism, Nehruvian socialism, and orthodox Hinduism were combined with an injunction to
discover the source of religious transcendence by unleashing sexual
energy. There were certainly elements of tantra and kundalini yoga
involved, just as much as an opportunism that exploited the sexual
unconventionality of the hippies, the student movement, and the
countercultural 1960s as best evidenced by a book of Rajneesh's that
enhanced his notoriety with the media: *From Sex to Superconsciousness*.
At the height of his following, meditation centers and communes
based on this "religionless religion" could be found on all five continents and in at least twenty-eight different countries. His followers
were self-styled *sannyasis* (or renunciates) who improved the repertoire
of traditionally ochre- and saffron-colored robes to include purple, red,

yellow, and green, wore the *rudrākṣa* necklaces, and grew out their hair and beards. But all this refashioning, as the Neo-Sannyas International Movement in search for the new man, was very short-lived. The Rajneesh "episode," even while it suggests aspects of the communal experiments of the sixties (and also the utopian experiments of nineteenth-century America in places such as Brook Farm), reflects the differing ways that late modernity accelerates a range of chaotic inter-actions among several countries, worldviews, and local power struc-tures. This event could perhaps be characterized as an "implosion" rather than an "explosion," according to Arjun Appadurai's terminol-ogy for the description of interreligious violence in South Asia. Vio-lence and breakdown were not inevitable in all contexts, as we shall see, but two different situations led to related but different outcomes for the same movement.[45]

Rajneesh is now perhaps best known as being, at the very least, indi-rectly culpable for the breakdown of his communal experiment near Antelope, Oregon, in 1985. If one can judge by the extensive news cov-erage and following condemnation, the events at Rajneeshpuram trig-gered a mild bout of national hysteria and anticult xenophobia in the United States, as did the Jim Jones disaster in Guyana a decade earlier, and Heaven's Gate, and Aum Shinrikyo, a few years later. In a fascinat-ing analysis of the sociology of the Rajneesh experiment, Lewis F. Carter suggests that the utopian program and social structure of the group had built into it a five-year, seven-stage, boom-and-bust cycle in which disillusioned followers would be replaced by a newer set of committed movement builders.[46] Carter's analysis, occasionally sym-pathetic and yet profoundly critical, demonstrates the cosmopolitan relevance of the movement as evinced by the followers of the group. The historical circumstances of the standoff between a newly arrived group of eclectic foreigners and an insular local community, delineated carefully in Carter's account, does much to contextualize the exposé of the final fiasco, which involved gun-running, a high-level conspiracy to poison the local water supply and critics in the local community, arson, attempted murder, and also strong-arm tactics of political gov-ernance. The botched plan for gerrymandering involved shipping in the urban homeless from sixty-one different U.S. cities to alter the de-mographic pattern in the vicinity. This cynical ploy was an indication of even more scandalous events that were to follow. Rajneesh was largely complicit with these criminal activities, even if they were con-spiracies hatched by his mercurial secretary Ma Anand Sheela, who ab-sconded to Germany just before multiple indictments were served.[47]

As a separatist experiment, Rajneeshpuram was perhaps bound to fail, but its manner of failure brought to the surface a volatile mixture of ethnic cross-perceptions, sexually transgressive behavior, and group affiliations that included adults and children but challenged normative nuclear family structures. After an initial phase of arrogant openness toward the local community, Rajneesh's settlement was thrown on the defensive when its presence was resisted by state and local officials and by Oregon's attorney general. The governance of the commune changed from anarchic to totalitarian. Visitors and inmates were kept under sophisticated forms of electronic surveillance, and access to the guru himself was strictly controlled by an inner coterie. The parochialism of local hatreds expressed toward the Rajneesh followers by the residents of Antelope was surpassed by the meticulous criminal conspiracy to assassinate opponents and poison the water supply.

The Rajneeshees had moved to Oregon after a previous implosion at Rajneesh's ashram in Poona, India. In the Indian context, local residents had been better insulated from the sexual activities within the ashram and had also been direct beneficiaries of the spending that resulted from the influx of foreigners. Sections of Aubrey Menen's *The New Mystics* (1974) and Gita Mehta's *Karma Cola* (1979) satirize the sexually licentious, drug-induced phantasmagoria of the *sannyasis* in the Poona ashram.[48] Rajneesh was tolerated for quite a while before the state moved against him in India. An economic crisis within the organization also precipitated matters. The Poona ashram was disbanded by the hierarchy in anticipation of a crackdown by the Indian state for tax evasion, political provocation, and other irregular activities. It would be interesting to ask whether greater leeway was given to Rajneesh's form of religious experimentation within the Indian as opposed to the U.S. context. However, in India there was less opportunity and motivation for the group to adopt violent methods than there was in Oregon. The move to Oregon was preceded by Nostradamus-inspired apocalyptic predictions that the group would survive using its presumed psychic enlightenment. The U.S. Northwest did not take kindly to this reverse colonization, albeit by different kinds of "Indians" than those who had originally been dispossessed. Sure enough, the dispossession and instant auction of the guru's collection of ninety-three Rolls-Royces (many of which had been driven less than a hundred miles) was lapped up by the global media, along with all the titillating tidbits about sexual orgies and drug abuse among the inner coterie. The guru himself had developed a substance dependency on nitrous oxide (or laughing gas).

The terrible events at Rajneeshpuram do not necessarily invalidate or vitiate the cosmopolitanism of Rajneesh's language or the breadth of the appeal that it made visible. In a long critical analysis of the Rajneeshees first serialized in the *New Yorker*, Frances FitzGerald had also found within the group much "love, lightness, and laughter."[49] Rather, it is the collocation of Rajneesh's cosmopolitan appeal alongside the eventual catastrophe of the Oregon commune that underscores the dangers as well as the desires spoken by Guru English's wide-reaching vocabularies. While the number of full-fledged Rajneeshees at the commune was perhaps twenty-five thousand at the very peak, the impact of the movement was felt widely through global media coverage of the finale, and of Rajneesh's repeated expulsions from the United States, Crete, Switzerland, Sweden, Britain, Ireland, Spain, Uruguay, and Pakistan, until his return to India. His eventual death there resulted from a mysterious illness, rumored by some to have been AIDS, or thallium poisoning from when he was in U.S. government custody, as he alleged before he died. In the post-Oregon phase, Rajneesh assumed yet newer names. The Japanese name, *Osho*, meaning a spiritual guide, also suggested William James's "oceaning feeling" according to his disciples (themselves now renamed as "friends") as well as "The Blessed One on Whom the Sky Showers Flowers."[50] More briefly, he was also "Gautama the Buddha." It would take an entire book to conduct a literary critical analysis of Rajneeshisms as a form of Guru English, but typical of the mode was the free back and forth from Sanskrit to English through deep punning in the inimitable style of the first orientalists:

> You will be surprised to learn that the English word *love* comes from a Sanskrit word *lobha*; lobha means greed. It may have just been a coincidence that the English word *love* grew out of a Sanskrit word that means greed, but my feeling is that it cannot be just coincidence. There must be something more mysterious behind it, there must be some alchemical reason behind it. In fact, greed digested becomes love. It is greed, *lobha*, digested well, which becomes love.
>
> Love is sharing; greed is hoarding. Greed only wants and never gives, and love knows only giving and never asks for anything in return; it is unconditional sharing. There may be some alchemical reason that lobha has become love in the English language. *Lobha* becomes *love* as far as inner alchemy is concerned.[51]

Rajneesh's cosmopolitanism imploded because it was inassimilable to global structures of social management and, at the same time, could not develop a relative autonomy from those structures. Rajneeshees actively opposed those structures through a belligerent courting of confrontation, especially as the guru's teachings justified techniques of social confrontation from very early on. Confrontation was justified as awakening or enlightening others, a kind of generalization of a Zen master's spiritual techniques—or a neo-Reichian acting out—into daily social situations. In this regard, political and social institutions and random non-Rajneeshee interlocutors were considered equally fair game, as the confrontation itself could be abandoned as a "joke" when the strategy did not pay dividends or elicited too negative a reaction. Despite these manifested problems, misdemeanors, and even proven felonies, there were certain aspects of the Rajneesh experiment that were profoundly innovative and risky. While the failures foreground the symptomatic behavior and social irresponsibility of the seekers and the organizational hierarchy, these failures do not negate the potentially utopian unconventionality of the group's desires and practices. Rajneeshees at their best were unsettling, creative, and fundamentally anarchic in their refusal to accept institutions and social norms of almost any kind. On the other hand, even if its adherents prided themselves on shedding socialization as superfluous conditioning, the movement operated through a shadowy web of corporations, foundations, charities, churches, small businesses, and educational trusts, all of which were constantly being manipulated to suit the core organization's needs. The core organization was centered on the bottomless appetite of the religious leader for material wealth—whether in the form of a huge private estate (the Big Muddy Ranch in Oregon), private aircraft (Learjets and helicopters), expensive cars (the legendary 93 Rolls Royces about which Rajneesh quipped that even 999 would not have been enough), or extravagant jewelry (including several diamond-encrusted watches, and a request from Rajneesh for one that cost $1.2 million at which even the unflappable Sheela balked). The core could summon up considerable sums of money even while sustaining major losses of assets. Carter hence accurately describes the movement as "a multilevel marketing device with central control in a charismatic core."[52] The Rajneeshees may therefore represent an aspect of the global popular that is partly utopian and critical of normativity, even though it seems that this critique was entirely comfortable within the complex financial and corporate shenanigans characteristic of capitalist organizational life in general. All this is to indicate that new and sophisticated levels of commodification achieved by the use of diasporic Guru English do not necessarily allow any comforting way of separating the matter from the manner, or the teachings propagated from the means of propagation. Media helped expand Rajneesh's movement. Media also hastened its downfall.

Rajneesh's countercultural cosmopolitanism has been taken up for literary inspiration in the context of the checkered history of American utopian experimentation. In the last installment of a trilogy of novels rewriting Hawthorne's *The Scarlet Letter*, John Updike reinvents Hester Prynne as Sarah P. Worth in *S.* (1988). Descended from the Prynnes, Sarah is a long-suffering, forty-two-year-old housewife from Boston's North End. She abandons her adulterous husband for an ashram run by Shri Arhat Mindadali in Arizona, quickly rising to the positions of the guru's private secretary, accountant, and lover. Sarah reveals a savvy streak, preempting the guru's financial scams by her own capacity to embezzle ashram cash flows, after already having decamped with a substantial share of the joint assets held by her and her husband. The guru's commune is a thinly disguised version of Rajneeshpuram, where the renunciates also wore sunset colors, worked long hours laboring on agricultural fields, and built a central fountain and community hall while being constantly subjected to sophisticated forms of electronic surveillance. This community is also a literary successor to Hawthorne's debunking account of Brook Farm that was featured in *The Blithedale Romance*. Updike's "Arhat" (Pali for "deserving one," normally used to describe accomplished Buddhist monks) is finally unmasked as Art Steinmetz, a Jewish Armenian from Watertown, Massachusetts, who had gone to India but returned in the garb of a "guru obscuru" to take advantage of the religious opportunities of proselytizing Hinduism and Buddhism to Westerners attracted by the post-60s craze for a cocktail of sex, drugs, psychotherapy, and spirituality. The novel repeats in fictional form the meltdown that occurred at Rajneeshpuram when the commune was hijacked by Rajneesh's female inner coterie. Updike suggests that one of the causes for the failure might have been the decision to switch from "hard-core psychotherapy to large-scale utopianism."[53]

The novel's fictional cult combines "encounter therapy with tantric yoga," as did Rajneesh, throwing in primal scream therapy, hydrotherapy, dynamic meditation, bioenergetics and other practices from the human potential movement. "Unlike a lot of gurus he [the Arhat] didn't demand quiescence, he invited dynamism, and instead of just being a slave word by word to what Patanjali wrote about yoga over two thousand years ago he had heard of Freud and modern psychotherapeutic techniques and in this cosmically good-humored way of his was willing to give anything a shot." The book's extensive parody of the resultant technical terminology—when you give anything a shot—makes it especially distinctive as a work featuring Guru English in its aspects of specialized register. Theolinguistic vocabulary can be used to describe almost any activity, including that of ennobling group sex in the ashram when described by Sarah:

What I find sweet, in all this, and not so chauvinistic as it sounds, is that purusha, motionless inactive spirit, is male, and prakriti—active nature, you could say—is female, so that in the ideal maithuna, that's what they call fucking in Sanskrit, the woman does all the work! The men always sit and she is always on top, the way Shiva and Shakti do it! I was shy at first but now I like it, its being up to me, so to speak, even when there's all these men in one of these groups. They sit in a circle called the shri chakra and what you do is called chakra puja, or purnabhisheka, the complete consecration. You have to see them all as motionless purusha and your yoni as a purifying fire.

Rajneesh was indeed sometimes referred to as "the guru of the vagina," as his teachings are eloquent about the virtues of the female orgasm. A supposed lecture on Mahayana Buddhism by the fictional Arhat turns out to be a delirious paean to woman as sexual fount, and "the living wonder of the world." This satirical passage from S. reveals the free-floating associationism of many such religious lectures by Rajneesh—and Arhat Mindadali his fictional double—that catered to the spiritualization of sex as the ultimate wish fulfillment of those desiring both hedonism and spiritualism:

> The mounds of her body are like temple-mounds; they symbolize nirvana. The lotus of her body is the lotus of Sahasrara, of final illumination. "Buddhatvam yoshidyonisamritam." That is a very important saying. Repeat, please. "Buddhatvam yoshidyonisamritam." [*Responsive mumble.*] It means, "Buddhahood is in the female organ." The yoni. The cunt. Buddhahood is in the cunt. OM mani padme HUM. The jewel is in the lotus. The jewel is the mind. The lotus is nirvana. The mind dissolves in nirvana. But also the jewel is the linga, the cock. The lotus is the cunt. The cock in the cunt. This is bliss, rasa. This is samarasa, the bliss of unity. This is Mahasukha, the Great Bliss. This is Mahabindu, the great point, the Transcendental Void. This is maithuna—fucking. This is Shiva and Shakti united, purusha and prakriti united to make bliss; this is sahaja. Sahaja is the state of non-conditioned existence, of the pure spontaneity. When Kundalini unites with Atman, this is also sahaja. That is why we learn our mantras, learn our mudras. That is why we learn pranayama. That is why we strive to cleanse ourselves inside and out. To be non-conditioned, to have the pure spontaneity. Ommmm!

As every Sanskrit word can reveal "a whole *lotus* of meanings," Updike revels in Sarah's and the Arhat's free use of theological arcana. With a wicked translinguistic pun, the rarefied final illumination of the thousand-petaled seventh chakra of "Sahasrara" turns the novel's protagonist into its personified tranposition: "Rare Sarah." The vast number of technical Sanskrit terms used throughout the novel is listed and explained in a glossary of thirteen pages that Updike declares to be "the novel's music, the poetic essence, mechanically extracted, of the preceding narrative." Updike explicitly acknowledges a heady mixture of mythology, tantra, and Rajneeshpuram narratives as his sources, especially mentioning Mircea Eliade, Joseph Campbell, Frances FitzGerald, and Ajit Mookerjee.[54]

These linguistic additions form part of an epistolary novel that moves from the letter to the spoken word. While *S.* features conventional letters by Sarah to friends and family that emphasize the immediacy of an uncensored present, it also explores the format of providing transcripts of tapes of the Arhat's lectures and secret recordings of intimate conversations between Sarah and the supposed Supreme Meditator. Given that these recordings of sexual encounters are also made by Sarah for their potential use to blackmail the Arhat later, the innovation suggests the move in Guru English's trajectory from the written to the spoken, from the theologically theoretical to the economically practical, from the literary to the discursive, and from the philosophical to the scandalous. Secrecy has now become commodified and also expendable, rather than remaining as the unremoveable taint of original sin for Puritan society as portrayed in *The Scarlet Letter.*

The novel's commune, just like Rajneesh's, concentrates marketing energy on "Kali Club discos in places like West Germany and Israel, and meditation-and-massage centers, and of course bookstores and video outlets in a lot of malls and downtowns now across the U.S." However, even more significantly, the mail-order business is located in the tax haven of the Bahamas. Renamed as "Kundalini" herself by the Arhat, Sarah is the S. of the novel's title, reworking the "A" worn by Hawthorne's Hester. But the sibilant letter also evokes a syncretism, combining the uncoiling of the serpents of feminine energy released from the base of the spine in kundalini with the biblical myth regarding the temptation of Eve by the serpent, and also with the almighty $, or U.S. dollar that ultimately motivates both Sarah and the Arhat. Puritanism can be united with capitalism as Max Weber asserted, but in this new synthesis, also with hedonism and Eastern spirituality. Selves are shed like so many snakeskins to be born anew into both enlightenment and capital. Rajneesh's name for this unity was "Zorba the Buddha"— one of the names he resorted to for himself that combined the materialism of the character in Kazantzakis's Greek novel with the religious attributes of the ancient Indian sage.[55] One of his most popular slogans was, "Moses Invests. Jesus Saves. Bhagwan Spends." As we saw with Joyce's parody of Theosophy, everyday institutions are renamed in ways that pretentiously suggest spiritual outcomes: the ashram's discotheque is the Kali Club, "where the sannyasins express their joy and gratitude to Shiva for the eternal cycle of creation and destruction," and the wild prices charged at the ashram mall are justified because "all the profits go into the Treasury of Enlightenment and represent the love we feel for the Arhat." As Hugh B. Urban argues concertedly, in Rajneesh's movement charisma can be united with bureaucracy and the personal aura with the aura of the commodity in a manner that Max Weber did not envisage. If these new forms of religious synthesis speak of the commercialization of religion, they also present us with the etherealization of capitalism. As a memoir by one of his disenchanted associates alleges, Rajneesh had anticipated his future religious stardom by having carefully lit studio photographs made of himself from an early age so that he could look charismatic.[56]

Integrating phenomena such as the success of TM and Rajneesh's sexual and social experiments within secular frameworks, Hanif Kureishi's *The Buddha of Suburbia* emphasizes the banalization of "Eastern" religion in the London of the 1960s and 1970s. The eponymous Buddha is "a renegade Muslim masquerading as a Buddhist." Haroon Amir (the father of the narrator Karim or "Creamy") is a yoga teacher who has acquired his oriental wisdom largely from "books on Buddhism, Sufism, Confucianism and Zen which he had bought at the Oriental bookshop in Cecil Court, off Charing Cross Road." Haroon leaves his English wife for his lover Eva, who manages her lover's exoticism and preaching on meditation with the eventual goal of social climbing in mind. While Haroon had "spent years trying to be more of an Englishman, to be less risibly conspicuous," his turn to self-orientalization leads to his "speaking slowly, in a deeper voice than usual . . . hissing his s's and exaggerating his Indian accent" (one of Rajneesh's biographers would also emphasize "the hypnotic sibilances of his lingering 's's").[57] This "future guru of Chislehurst" and "great sage, from whose lips instruction fell like rain in Seattle"—ironically referred to by his adolescent son as "God"—addresses his audiences in suburban living rooms, "probably the only man in southern England at that moment (apart, possibly, from George Harrison) wearing a red and gold waistcoat and Indian pyjamas." At Eva's insistence, Haroon eventually begins charging for his weekly "guru gigs" and develops a "regular and earnest young crowd of head-bowers—students, psychologists, nurses, musicians . . . and a waiting list" that gets him local journalistic coverage and ancillary fame.[58]

Karim's alcoholic aunt and uncle react to his father's pretensions with outright hostility. His uncle Ted "said 'Buddhist' as he would have said 'homosexual' had he cause to say 'homosexual' ever, which he didn't." However, the same skeptic falls under Haroon's spell and undergoes a "conversion to Ted-Buddhism." The idea of "Buddhism," as wielded in the novel by this thoroughly secularized and adulterous guru, is inseparable from self-help and psychotherapy, just as the ideas of renunciation and detachment paradoxically become an efficient way to achieve upward mobility for guru and disciple alike.[59] The opportunistic Eva summarizes her world-view and indebtedness to her lover in an interview to *Furnishings* magazine, which is doing a photo spread on her flat that she will then sell to move up in the housing market:

> "Before I met this man," she said. "I had no courage and little faith. I'd had cancer. One breast was removed. I rarely talk about it." The journalist nodded, respecting this confidence. "But I wanted to live. And now I have contracts in that drawer for several jobs. I am beginning to feel I can do anything—with the aid of techniques like meditation, self-awareness, and yoga. Perhaps a little chanting to slow the mind down. You see, I have come to believe in self-help, individual initiative, the love of what you do, and the full development of all individuals. I am constantly disappointed by how little we expect of ourselves and of the world."[60]

The interview turns into a thinly veiled diatribe against social welfare and heralds the onset of Thatcherism that is chronologically just around the corner.

While the bemused narrator watches the activities around his father and Eva as phony, his own parallel itinerary suggests the familiar attraction of sex, drugs, and rock-and-roll alongside eventual success in a theatrical career after undergoing the humiliation of early typecast roles. The narrator and his father have a relationship reminiscent of that between Kim and the lama within an overall context where ethnic and religious identity crisis is transcended by being adept at shape shifting and syncretic versatility under empire in Kipling's novel, and its metropolitan aftermath in Kureishi's. Apprehending this similarity, Berthold Schoene asserts that "it seems as if Kipling's Kim has become Kureishi's K(*are*)im, that is, an intrinsically polycultural subject who has internalized, and now exudes, a multitude of cultural differences, deconstructively proliferating identities beyond restrictive binary oppositions whilst remaining ultimately indeterminate himself." However, while Karim is too much of a cynic to fall for his father's orientalist platitudes—"he is an Englishman born and bred, almost" in the opening sentence of the novel and remains emphatically so by the novel's conclusion—he is enamored of his stepbrother Charlie's success as pop music phenomenon, and that comparison provides him his greatest motivation toward a different kind of self-fashioning from the standard orientalist one. The Beatles-inspired ("I Am the Walrus") Karim represents the other side, or the beyond of Guru English, the metropolitan minority or migrant who is, like Rushdie's "translated man," fully cognizant of the orientalist stereotype as an option that can be refused or chosen, and yet imposed without choice at other moments.[61]

Karim concludes that his father's "guru business" would flourish as long as London "was full of lonely, unhappy, unconfident people who required guidance, support and pity."[62] This novelistic insight anticipates an entire integration of religion and capitalism, message and medium, doctrine and market. Guru English could aspire to the achievements of Christian televangelism.

Gurus increasingly enact parodies that, far from being original, are deliriously imaginary and yet ruthlessly functional. Compared with the complexities of the Rajneesh phenomenon, contemporary Guru English features workaday charismatic-corporate entrepreneurship. To date, it is perhaps as fully integrated into mainstream business culture as any other cultural commodity. Deepak Chopra, for instance, is a medically trained, highly successful, media-savvy guru who has penetrated several genres of mass-market publishing, including the self-help, diet, alternative medicine, and management markets. Gurus can become one with marketing, not just in terms of a strategy but as an academic discipline and also an end in itself.

The telegenic and very youthful-looking Chopra has obvious New Age (and sex) appeal. His followers (sometimes called Chopriites—it is tempting to call them "Shoprights," as many of his clients are reportedly just as well-accessoried as well-heeled) are middle-aged baby boomers with considerable disposable income. Many of them, it seems, can afford to spend thousands of dollars for a weekend therapy session with the great man himself. Within the spectrum of available gurus, Chopra stands for TM Lite. Chopra gave up his medical practice for an even more lucrative career that blends naturopathy, Ayurvedic principles, large amounts of guidance counseling, and pep talk. Several of his best-sellers, including *Ageless Body, Timeless Mind* and *Seven Spiritual Laws of Success*, have been read by millions.[63] Chopra counts among his clients such Hollywood celebrities as Demi Moore, Liz Taylor, and (the now deceased) George Harrison. Translated into twenty-five different languages, his books have recorded sales figures of several million dollars. Chopra was featured on the cover of the journal *Sales and Marketing Management* and was profiled in *Far Eastern Economic Review*. According to *Forbes*, his income averages around $11 million a year; some of this income derives from the lecture circuit, where he can command $25,000 to $30,000 per talk, five to six times a month. There is always lots of money available through corporations for motivational speakers. However, Chopra has managed to cross the older Dale Carnegie genre with Yogananda- and Maharishi-style showmanship as well as Oprah-style armchair therapy.[64]

As much as it shows cosmopolitanism at work in the marketplace, Chopra's itinerary reveals savvy consumerist product differentiation. Giving up his earlier career as an endocrinologist in Boston, Chopra joined the Maharishi, setting up the Ayurveda Health Center for Stress Management and Behavioral Medicine in Massachusetts. At this point he wrote *Return of the Rishi*, a spiritual autobiography of sorts that makes the bridge between Chopra's medical career and his adoption of the Maharishi's philosophy. Chopra's book is also a testimonial to several of the scientifically unproven activities of the Maharishi's followers, including the eyebrow-raising (torso-hovering) techniques of levitation.[65] However, Chopra broke from the SCI organization in 1991 and established other institutions. One of these is the Chopra Center for Well Being in La Jolla, California, which advertises alternative therapies and spiritual renewal, as well as Ayurvedic creams and herbal essences at inflated prices. Chopra is a truly North American guru, on a first-name basis with all his disciples. Holding weekend seminars named "Seduction of the Spirit" that run at $1,595 per person, Chopra offers a message barely distinguishable from the marketing hype that surrounds him. Reassuring his followers that "poverty is a reflection of an impoverished spirit," Chopra sells everything he can, including authorized books, audio- and videotapes, teas, vitamins, massage oils, and even silver tongue cleaners to remove undigested toxic materials. He has even tried to set his message to rap music and is frequently on television talk shows promoting his latest book. According to one report, sales of his featured book jumped by 173,000 copies the day after Chopra was featured on Oprah Winfrey's show. Chopra's television special for the Public Broadcasting Service, *Body, Mind, and Soul: The Mystery and the Magic*, aired during a funding drive, garnered PBS $2.5 million in pledges of support. His son Gautam, who renamed himself Gotham, has also tried to spread the father's message to MTV audiences of teens and twenty-somethings through a customized Web site.[66]

The banalization of aura indicated here shows a different kind of departure from conventional religious outreach. Made for the newer form of television, Chopra can wear several caps and perform extemporaneously, as patient listener, Eastern sage, or entertaining salesman. The performance leads, as many contemporary lifestyle marketing philosophies do, to the experience rather than the outcome, and the knowledge gained rather than the price paid. Interviewed in *Psychology Today*, Chopra rationalizes his upbeat account of how everything, and especially age, is only in the mind. Cancer victims are responsible for their disease, and if they cannot be blamed, society should be held collectively responsible for it. If bad genes have led to individuals' susceptibility to certain diseases, this is because "what I inherit is genetically there because it is an end-product of how my ancestors metabolized their own experience." Slowly it begins to dawn on the reader that such a statement resembles a postgenetics rationalization of the doctrine of karma.[67] Reading through his work, one can see secularized and Western transcreations of universalizing themes and concepts contained within Hinduism. All societies, according to Chopra, are naturally composed of the intellectuals, the warriors, the business class, and the working people, and such divisions are natural and normal parts of the social body. Indeed, this is a gross simplification of the *varṇa/jāti* (or caste) system in India, but such a classification translates and substitutes universally for the more difficult task of social analysis.[68]

Another best seller of Chopra's, *Ageless Body, Timeless Mind: The Quantum Alternative to Growing Old* is an intelligent synthesis of the systems of Ayurvedic medicine, quantum physics, and Advaita Vedanta. It advances a detailed refutation of mind-body dualism and biochemical determinism, in place of which Chopra proposes an awareness-, intelligence- and perception-based model of the mind and the body whereby the individual can will bodily health and mental happiness by being in touch with an eternal seer within who is immune to all change. The text lurches between translated religious doctrine, scientific studies concerning the role of free radicals in aging the body, and a "quantum theory" alternative approach to the body that seems to apply (but in actual fact loosely metaphorizes) the theories of Einstein, Bohr, and other physicists to cell biology and human health. Building up the category of awareness in relation to aging, proposing ways of defeating entropy, and initiating a new science of longevity, Chopra's book is targeted to the growing geriatric population in the United States and elsewhere, who are in need of psychological counseling in an atomized society as well as being newly vulnerable to updated versions of the age-old promise regarding the fountain of eternal youth. Whatever the status of Chopra's slippery truth-claims about the interpenetration of Hindu philosophy, quantum physics, and the latest discoveries of biochemistry and medicine, he is an accomplished practitioner of nonfiction English prose. Always ready with an illustrative anecdote or a pithy poetic quotation or metaphor, Chopra is an example of the new literary horizons of Guru English.[69]

Chopra's "Wellness Program on Interactive CD-ROM," entitled *The Wisdom Within*, was released by Randomsoft (a division of the publisher Random House) in 2000. The software unveils a "three-level program, incorporating all of the best elements from Dr. Chopra's writings, seminars, audio and video tapes in an easy-to-use and highly customizable environment." The three sections are entitled "Living in Balance," an Ayurvedic guide for nutrition, exercise, meditation, and massage; "The Field of Infinite Possibilities," where users can journey through three layers of being: body, mind, and spirit (which correspond to TM's objective, subjective, and transcendental existence); and "The Sacred Space," in which four background environments—mountains, sea, desert, and forest—can be explored and where the user can keep a personal journal, reach the Pool of Affirmations, and go through a list of recommended daily activities. The CD-ROM lists for $29.95, with a companion book thrown in for the price. Chopra shows us that Guru English will not lag too far behind in telemarketing, televangelism, or being able to go virtual. Indeed, in a figure such as Chopra, religion and retail therapy, alternative medicine and psychobabble, motivational speaking and psychical healing have all merged into a seamless continuum. Chopra's name recognition is such that a phrase from a book of his, "all our worst fears have already happened to us!" becomes the means for human contact between a stalker played by Robin Williams and his victim in the Hollywood movie, *One Hour Photo*.

The improvisational capacity of Guru English's practitioners was very much on display after the terrorist attacks in New York City on September 11, 2001. Deepak Chopra's reflections on the events were featured in a full-page advertisement in the *New York Times* of September 23 entitled, "The Deeper Wound," sponsored by ABC Carpet & Home. After discussing his shock during the aftermath of his departure from New York for Detroit by airplane "45 minutes before the unthinkable happened," Chopra moves on in a few paragraphs to seeking for "the root cause of this evil . . . at the deepest level." While this "has been a horrible attack on America," it is observed that the deeper wound is "a rift in our collective soul." The platitude offered in the conclusion to these reflections is that, "in this moment of deep sorrow for the wounding of our collective soul, the only healing we can accomplish as individuals is to make sure that our every thought, word and deed nurtures humanity."[70]

Another full-page newspaper advertisement appeared on September 25, announcing a public meeting led that evening in the Riverside Church by the Vietnamese Buddhist monk and peace activist Thich Nhat Hanh, entitled "Embracing Anger," and featuring also an organist and percussionist. These words are Buddhist messages about compassion and nonviolence, and the imperative that "responding to violence with violence is injustice not only to the other person but also to oneself; it only escalates violence, and will only make hatred grow one thousand-fold." Having experienced the bombing and destruction of his own country during the Vietnam War, the pacifist monk shares a poem he wrote after having heard of the bombing of Ben Tre, a city of three hundred thousand people that was destroyed. The message informs the public that Thich Nhat Hanh and his associates are fasting from September 21 to September 30 "in order to support all who have died and all who are suffering terribly in this moment." The monk further suggests, "America possesses enough wisdom and courage to perform an act of forgiveness and compassion. And I know that such an act can bring great relief to America and the world." While the bombing of Afghanistan had not unfolded yet, political prognosticators would have rightly pointed out that such nonviolent outcomes were extremely unlikely. So, who is this statement really addressed to? Antimilitarists, religious seekers, alienated individuals traumatized by the current events, but all without recourse to their own cultural resources for trauma relief? Of course, it is a contingency of newspaper proselytization that Thich Nhat Hanh's statement is the first of three different full-page advertisements about the events. The following page is a message of solidarity to New York from the citizens of Hamburg and on a later page there is also a statement of compassion from the American Society for the Prevention of Cruelty to Animals.[71] Guru English has to contend with the global juxtapositions that make its search for consumers particularly postmodern.

A third example of another full-page advertisement by a guru entering the realm of crisis management can be found in the *New York Times* on the one-month anniversary, October 11, 2001, from "His Holiness Sri Sri Ravi Shankar, Founder, Art of Living Foundation." According to this message, the long-term remedy for terrorism is to value life and diversity. "Force is inevitable to suppress terrorism in the short term; spirituality alone can root out destructive tendencies." Sri Sri's foundation also offers workshops "at no cost to aid those in the New York area who are affected by anxiety, fear and loss." A Web site address is given to access the complete presentation of the long-term remedy, as well as a toll-free national telephone number for information on guided meditation and music programs. The foundation claims to be active in nonprofit educational and humanitarian work in 132 countries around the world. Sri Sri, as it turns out, was yet another breakaway success story who began his spiritual career as an acolyte of the Maharishi. Sri Sri's emphasis on social service volunteerism, meditation and yoga camps, and a simplified message of joy, peace, reconciliation, and solidarity has recently stolen a march even on the Maharishi and Deepak Chopra. Sri Sri's Art of Living Foundation (abbreviated as AOL in his literature) claims to be "the largest non-government volunteer based organization in the world" with a self-declared base of twenty million people active in scores of countries. The organization's Web site explains Sri Sri's technique of Sudarshan Kriya (a registered trademark), based on rhythmic breathing techniques and tireless charismatic prose-lytization with selected groups, who then inculcate others in a gigantic religious pyramid scheme that resembles in many respects the prac-tices of Paramahamsa Yogananda and the Yogoda organization dis-cussed earlier. As with many religious attempts that deal with the needs of modern practitioners, Sudarshan Kriya is credited with re-ducing stress, cholestrol, anxiety, and depression while enhancing an-tioxidant protection and brain function.[72]

The very same *New York Times* that decided to run these full-length advertisements of questionable taste then turned on some of the very people it advertised, in an article on October 21, 2001, in the "Sunday Styles" section. Entitled "Spiritual Balm, at Only $23.95," the article sneers at the rush to heal: "As Americans grieve, panic, lie awake at night and turn over the fundamental questions of life, the world of healers—pop gurus, yogis, New Age nutritionists, workers—has spawned the first wave of marketing that offers the promise of spiri-tual and physical peace, in exchange for cash and publicity." Particu-larly put on notice are profiteers and opportunists including Deepak Chopra (whose portrait is plastered on the front of the article). Chopra is roasted for an e-mail message that went out to twenty-two thou-sand fans about the importance of spiritual comfort, on September 25, 2001. The e-mail had ended with a pitch for his novel about love sur-viving death and suffering called *Soulmate* that was, to Chopra's mis-fortune, very unpresciently released to the U.S. public just one day be-fore the 9/11 catastrophe. Chopra's electronic marketing missive had hoped that the book "won't be overlooked in these difficult days" and had correspondingly directed readers to a Web link where the book could be purchased. Confronted with negative reactions, Chopra sub-sequently apologized for the inappropriateness of the e-mail when in-terviewed. The article also mentions siddha yoga instructor Guru-mayi, who is guru to Hollywood stars such as Don Johnson and Meg Ryan. Gurumayi's Web site offers prayers and blessings for the vic-tims of the tragedy even as it simultaneously hawks a $108 prayer shawl and cassettes of lectures and chants by the mother-guru.[73] As argued earlier, Theosophy can coexist with theosophistry under the conditions of modernity, and likewise, a national daily such as the *New York Times* can indirectly promote gurus by accepting full-page adver-tising, and also scoff at them at the same time along with all the other arcane treatments they sell, including mudbath detoxifications, crys-tallographic remedies, and psychic counseling. Religious intervention can be timely at some points and blatantly opportunistic at others, and the judgment concerning its appropriateness lies in the eyes of the beholder.

Despite this broad survey of New Age enchantments in history and fiction, there still remain many questions about the spread of Guru English through actual gurus that may always go unanswered. Why were both Sai Baba and Rajneesh very popular in Italy? The persistence of miracle work has something to do with the former's success, but it cannot be the only explanation. Why is Vedanta so much more popular with Jewish Americans than with any other U.S. ethnic or religious group? It would be too simple to suggest that the similarity of an abstract iconoclastic monotheism with a tradition of religious commentary on sacred text allows for the crossover appeal, but this possibility does still come to mind. Why did so many devout Hindu industrialists contribute generously to Mother Teresa's explicitly Catholic mission? That "saints" in India are often transreligious in their appeal goes some way toward providing an explanation, as much as does the age-old technique of businesspeople giving to charity to assuage their consciences, but it would be foolhardy to expect that all Catholic hospices such as the Missionaries of Charity would get similar support from non-Catholics. Why is Guru English so overwhelmingly (even if not exclusively) a religious language resorted to by masculine practitioners? Clearly, through Guru English, we find one more instance of the fashioning of neopatriarchal authority, even though at the same time it has to be acknowledged that many gurus attempt, even from the male position, to enact an epicene and androgynous parenting of their disciples, as did Gandhi. But there are always many more questions that can be asked about Guru English than answered. How does the charisma of the traveling guru operate in a number of disparate media-saturated contexts, as compared with the guru in a single location who attracts clientele from many locales?

While the sociology of gurus is incomplete, and a new traveling theory of the interactions of the local, translocal, the religiously regional, and the doctrinally contextual may well be needed to complete it, Guru English is clearly a phenomenon that merits analysis of a kind that literary criticism can do well, especially when combined with the new methodologies of interactive history, comparative anthropology, and cultural studies. It appears that Guru English is a site not just for desultory cosmopolitanism but also for engaged criticism, perhaps because of its evanescent nature and its capacity to morph through science and culture, lifestyle and sacred text. Publishing categories (and even university disciplines) such as management, marketing, self-help, and motivational psychology have differentiated themselves from their earlier unity, which was found in the field of rhetoric, a field that predated what is now the field of literary study and cultural analysis. While one part of the job of literary critic as rhetorician would be to play the role of a debunker, as did Desani, exposing the naive use of rhetoric as marketing tool and manipulation, a more lasting advantage may be that of understanding rhetoric at work beyond instrumentalizing accounts rather than ceding the field entirely to marketers, healers, and professional inspirers. It is worth noting that Desani the debunker also ended up teaching Buddhism as a professor of philosophy at the University of Texas, proving that debunking charlatanry and the academic study of religion could go together. This reintroduces the study of rhetoric, not just as technique of communication, but as subjective disposition and postmodern individuality. When Indian gurus turn into marketing versions of Dr. Feelgood, it is high time that postcolonial theory goes in search of material in the airport bookshops and the marketing chains. If gurus go global, speak English, and generate a new literature because that's where the money is, scholars of English can rediscover the literature in the fictional boom and religious cant.

Cosmopolitanism as a political and rhetorical position is not divorced from the phenomenon of its commodification. As Deepak Chopra declares, "Action generates memory, which generates the possibility of desire, which creates action again. This is the software of the soul."[74] Is it fanciful to suggest that this doctrine alludes to the registered trademark of one-click virtual shopping? Actually, the thought is a free translation of a verse from the Bhagavadgītā, rendered accessible to the computer-literate. Perhaps in the same vein, this guru needs to be told that some of his followers may soon want an upgrade. Online gurus and other forms of virtual therapy should certainly be expected to proliferate in the near future, just as much as postmodern forms of religious organizing, fantasy, and community supplement and sometimes even replace the traditional religious forms that also continue to renew themselves. The recasting of South Asian anglophone religion as new "cults," "personalities," media tools, and literary representations can lead to further investigations of aura, not so much as esoteric halo, but as material patina, and telekinetic image. A greater understanding of the cultural history of colonial encounter has been achieved since the rise of postcolonial studies, but what still remains elusive for investigation are the hybrid outcomes of neo- and postcolonial futures. The new formations that might be anticipated involve underground religiosity without full-fledged religion, self-orientalization without colonialist orientalism, and transidiomatic cosmopolitanism without the need for a foundational universalism.

Instant karma's gonna get you
Gonna knock you right on the head
You better get yourself together
Pretty soon you're gonna be dead.
                                      —John Lennon, "Instant Karma"

WHILE THIS STUDY SKETCHES some historical and literary instances of Guru English in multiple contexts and investigates a number of ancillary phenomena under the rubric, it is neither a full-fledged survey of the four aspects (register, discourse, environment, and cosmopolitanism) of Guru English nor an exhaustive monograph of particular movements or practitioners, or of the vast range of the literature that could be summoned up under this rubric. There is an immense range of scholarship available to track the impact of particular religious leaders and movements in South Asian and diasporic contexts, and likewise, there are many works of literary criticism that focus on the representation of religion within literature. Cultural criticism of the nexus between religion and nationalism abounds, especially since the global rise of the religious Right in the last two decades. Rather than replicate the existing scholarship or commence on a very long compendium of all the materials available, my approach has been to initiate multiple points of intervention into a literature, both in terms of chronology and genre. Situated on the cusp where literary criticism, linguistic anthropology, and sociology of religion meet, this work makes no claim to satisfying fully the disciplinary demands of each of these enterprises. The technique adopted here might be characterized as cultural studies, political commentary, and historically inflected reading in equal measure, with some attention to interanimating these knowledge projects in relation to each other. While there is no deliberate urge to give offense (this is an academic study and not a satirical novel such as *The Satanic Verses*), religion or religious studies is not treated with greater reverence than any other field of inquiry. A lighter tone of inquiry can be justified, as Guru English is linguistically very playful. As an emergent discourse that uses parody, self-deflation, and antireligious satire as some of the tools in its own armory, Guru English merits a critical interpretation that displays its subtle tonal variety and ideological suppleness. Tracking Guru English shows that religion does not always need to go hand in hand with gravitas, ineffability, and the accompanying sanctimony. At the same time, Guru English's flinty lightness should not lull the observer into complacency, as it can sometimes be deeply implicated in political crises, and indeed cataclysmic events.

So then, is Guru English merely a vehicle for the translation of religious doctrines with the patina of ancient wisdom? Or has it exceeded its instrumental function of identifying anglophone subjects for proselytization? I have argued that Guru English is caught between authenticity and modernity: its proponents would wish to emphasize their updated retailing of ancient wisdom, even as its critics are more likely to point to its neophyte status as proof of inauthenticity, if not outright fraudulence. The complex legacies of "English education" in India have occupied many scholarly lifetimes, and it has not been within the scope of this study to account for all that it achieved for the nation-form as well as what has been wrought through the production of linguistic elites and social inequities. Looking for a genealogy of Guru English nonetheless anchors, for good measure, what is otherwise all too readily perceived as the perversity, excessiveness, and errancy of the productive capacities of this new type of orientalism.[1]

If Guru English allows familiar figures to be appreciated in novel ways, it might nonetheless be charged with the elitism characteristic of much South Asian anglophone literature. Tabish Khair's comprehensive reading of twentieth-century novels in *Babu Fictions* has charged that the genre collapses "all differences into a solid-state hybridity and a privileging of this hybrid subject."[2] Is Guru English an epiphenomenon of this larger field of Indian English, or is it a new development altogether? Indeed, Indian English literature is overwhelmingly urban, cosmopolitan, Brahmanized, and anglicized; most definitely the native, rural, deprived, and marginal elements are barely visible; even more tellingly, it can be argued that Indian English is really a grapholect, staging and fictionalizing a written form that is infrequently experienced as such but hyperbolically consumed as a represented object. Despite all the overblown claims and the publishing bonanza currently under way on its behalf, Indian English is an elite language, when compared with say, the ample social sweep of American or Caribbean English.[3] Guru English, however, is a special case that overlaps not just with Indian English, but also with Irish, American, and New Age vocabularies, giving its register a greater transidiomatic reach and making it a discourse that orients itself toward a future cosmopolitanism. In any case, it would be reductive to evaluate metaphysical and theolinguistic vocabularies through the litmus test of sociological realism. Like many other cosmopolitan discourses, Guru English derives its paradoxical power precisely from its referential inadequacy. Unable to refer adequately, it can conjure excessively. Why else would William Butler Yeats and Rabindranath Tagore exchange ideas about the mystical union of Celtic and Indian spiritualism when no self-respecting traditional Hindu or Catholic would venture in that direction? This willed confraternity of Irish and Indian nationalisms is none the weaker despite the flimsy intellectual grounds of religious commonality. While the sociological imperative should be brought to bear on Guru English (especially to expose its bombast and bring it down to earth), such necessary preliminaries should not substitute for other forms of internal and contextual analysis. Guru English is especially potent because its language, while inflected with the past and the present, is at its most evocative when regarding metaphysical futures.

At early moments of deployment by orientalists and Theosophists, Guru English follows patterns of resemblance and analogy that link words and languages with their deeper universal signatures. In a different context, Michel Foucault has characterized this type of reasoning as characteristic of the *epistēmē* of the European Renaissance. By contrast, the (neo)classical and modern *epistēmēs* featuring representation and historicity as their thematic focuses, and identified by Foucault as relevant for later modernity, are weak presences in Guru English. Even when Guru English is involved with questions of apocalypse or genocide or nuclear holocaust, the failure of representation or the collapse of historicity become urgently at stake. In contrast, the postmodern regime of simulation, as familiarized to us by Jean Baudrillard, seems very receptive to the theolinguistic phenomenon. This flight from analogical reasoning to simulated outcomes while evading the intermediary stages of full-fledged representation and historicity is also a lesson in the acceleration of time and the contraction of space created by postcolonial belatedness. The interaction between these European stages and the phenomenon of Guru English (which is European and South Asian as well as beyond both) demonstrates the alternative modernity of Guru English as distinct and yet recognizable within global history, and within the convergent dynamics of multiple cosmopolitanisms in the era of globalization.

Guru English overtakes some new areas such as the cultural situation of science and technology, even as it underwrites older formations of religion, spirituality, and universalism. It banalizes itself when assisting with the mundane tasks of ordinary people and simultaneously transcendentalizes itself by evoking the destruction of the human race as sublime apocalypse. Guru English creates new forms, evacuates older ones, and traverses yet others, sometimes linking by allusion, sometimes deceiving through false analogy. Propagating one idea and debunking another, the consumers of Guru English breathe the same air of global capitalism and its postmodernities, dreaming of different worlds and doctrines, imagining themselves beyond complicity and resistance. Guru English participates in an era when value has resolutely shifted from mechanical to mental labor, and where consumer culture is meeting the challenge by rising to target levels of immaterial lifestyle, experience, and ethos that can bypass cruder measures of the material product. Where capitalism has nearly exhausted nature as resource, culture is put forward as the standing reserve most prone to renewed exploitation. As Martin Heidegger puts it in "The Question Concerning Technology," "whatever stands by in the sense of standing-reserve no longer stands over against us as object."[4] Religious matter is one of the vast areas of standing reserve ripe for commodification, precisely because of its not being a natural object. With that irreversible shift from nature to culture under way, spirituality is undergoing its biggest consumerist renaissance.

Given its status as immaterial commodity, Guru English, when closely examined, can collapse into a series of gestures or appear as "mere" style. Sometimes, indeed, style does not just make the complete man as Buffon argued, but suggests a format for the understanding of discursive ordering within postmodernity. If a world of depths is being replaced around us by a confusing proliferation of surfaces, style is the red thread that connects and also unravels these planes of spirituality, reality, community feeling, and individuality. Gurus are fashionable because they are selling previously marginalized postcolonialism as an exotic commodity, but in a world where almost everything is commodified to a lesser or greater degree, the commodity can never be understood in its purely reductive sense as a potential use-value and its delirious surplus. Rather, the commodity becomes a vehicle that carries contingent values along with commercial ones, and multiple valuing audiences derive different cultural and critical relationships in addition to participating in the commercial aspects made available or inaccessible depending on the price tag.

Disciples are increasingly prone to guru hopping, a practice that suggests market-oriented practices and the benefits of modularity and interchangeability. Despite very specific doctrines and particular circumstances that are unique to individual religious teachers, there seems to be a nebulous system of valuation and transcoding that interanimates many of them for the religious consumer. Commodity culture, indeed the bane and the thrill of cultural life in general, is neither being celebrated nor denounced here (because an ethical relation to the commodity is compromised when even the intellectual labor as represented by this project is not outside a system of valuation that has material consequences). Philosophical critique and cultural investigation is still preferable to uncritical celebration and moralistic denunciation. We should not assume that all religious seekers are motivated by the market (even if the market is by no means just an economic concept but a profound value-regulating mechanism). An interest in Guru English as style, it is hoped, is not an apology for "philistinism" as disparaged by the doyens of high culture, but the beginnings of an embedded philosophical critique that traverses literary criticism, linguistic anthropology, and sociology of religion. Comparative literature can meet area studies halfway, as Gayatri Chakravorty Spivak has recently suggested, and through an ethical form of engagement with the topic at hand, the differentialism of planetarity can at least occasionally interrupt the identitarian narratives of globalization.[5]

Perhaps that step would be akin to a radical antimetaphysical take on a text such as the Bhagavadgītā, to be appreciated not for its ultimate content, which favors the continuation of the religiously sanctioned battle, but for its staging of the necessary suspension of the battle for the discourse's elaboration. While Krishna prevails over Arjuna's skepticism and criticisms in the original and launches him into the battle, looking at the warriors hastening into Krishna's mouth might give us pause, from Arjuna's perspective. The hope for an endlessly deferred suspension of the battle also hollows out murderous religious metaphysics for the ethical task of critical destranscendentalization. Such a critique can have a performative effect through its example rather than through claims about universalization, in the manner that Gandhi's interventions did at their best. However, in order for this to happen, teleology has to be reversed. Arjuna's trajectory has to proceed precisely backward, from certainty to doubt. If we backtrack from religious doctrine to literary theory, and from cultural commodity to philosophical critique, we will find, in lieu of the performative power of orientalist epistemology, the stylistic and deconstructive effects of Guru English.

Notes

Introduction

1. The top twelve languages (in order of greatest number of speakers) are Chinese, English, Spanish, Russian, Hindi, German, Japanese, Arabic, Bengali, Portuguese, French, and Italian. See Walter D. Mignolo, "Globalization, Civilization Processes, and the Relocation of Languages and Cultures," in *The Cultures of Globalization*, ed. Fredric Jameson and Masao Miyoshi (Durham, NC: Duke University Press, 1998), 39.

2. "I will refer to this topmost dialect in the local sociolinguistic hierarchy as acrolect (from acro- 'apex' plus -lect as in dialect). In most cases what is meant by 'Standard' English is either acrolect or something close to it." See W. A. Stewart in *Social Dialects and Language Learning: Proceedings of the Bloomington, Indiana, Conference, 1964*, ed. Roger W. Shuy (Champaign, IL: National Council of Teachers of English, 1965), 15. For a range of discussions on the global politics of English, see Richard W. Bailery and Manfred Görlach, eds., *English as a World Language* (Ann Arbor: University of Michigan Press, 1982); Braj Kachru, *The Alchemy of English* (Oxford: Pergamon Press, 1986); Robert Philippson, *Linguistic Imperialism* (Oxford: Oxford University Press, 1992); Alastair Pennycook, *The Cultural Politics of English as an International Language* (London: Longman Press, 1994); and David Crystal, *English as a Global Language* (Cambridge: Cambridge University Press, 1997).

3. See Homi Bhabha, *The Location of Culture* (New York: Routledge, 1994), 102–22, and Gauri Viswanathan, *Outside the Fold: Conversion, Modernity, and Belief* (Princeton, NJ: Princeton University Press, 1998).

4. See Braj B. Kachru, "English in South Asia: An Overview," in *The Indianization of English: The English Language in India* (Delhi: Oxford University Press, 1983), 19–22.

5. The best lexical resource for all these variants remains Henry Yule and A. C. Burnell, *Hobson-Jobson; A Glossary of Colloquial Anglo-Indian Words and Phrases, and of Kindred Terms, Etymological, Historical, Geographical, and Discursive* (1886; new ed. by William Crooke, London: Routledge and Kegan Paul, 1968).

6. Cited in Tapan Raychaudhuri, *Europe Reconsidered: Perceptions of the West in Nineteenth-Century Bengal* (Oxford: Oxford University Press, 1988), 17, 21.

7. See Braj B. Kachru, "The Pragmatics of Non-Native Englishes," in *The Indianization of English: The English Language in India* (Delhi: Oxford University Press, 1983), 215.

8. See Tabish Khair, *Babu Fictions: Alienation in Contemporary Indian English Novels* (Delhi: Oxford University Press, 2001).

9. See Probal Dasgupta, *The Otherness of English: India's Auntie Tongue Syndrome* (New Delhi: Sage Publications, 1993), 48. With somewhat more technical

terminology than I have indicated above, Dasgupta explains that the tolerance for FESH (or Formal Elaboration of Social Hierarchy, as instantiated in structures such as the caste system) allows "Asian" areas to sustain long-term diglossic differentiations. Putting aside an obvious residual orientalism in this assessment (that makes the arguable assumption that Asia is more hierarchical than the presumably egalitarian Euro-America), it might be worth asking if FESH is also an index of continued neocolonialism (in which case, diglossic differentiation would be just as typical of Euro-American interaction with South Asians who are often formally their inferiors in social situations or professional organizations).

10. M.A.K. Halliday, *Language as Social Semiotic: The Social Interpretation and Language of Meaning* (London: Edward Arnold, 1978), 31–32.

11. Sudhir Kakar, *The Analyst and the Mystic: Psychoanalytic Reflections on Religion and Mysticism* (New Delhi: Viking Penguin, 1991), 55–56.

12. I pun here deliberately on the astrological/astronomical etymologies of *consider* and *influence*.

13. South Asian English includes the significant use of English in Pakistan, Bangladesh, and Sri Lanka just as much as in post-1947 India. While there might be legitimate objections to the conflation of Indian with South Asian English, it should be noted that Indian English is itself an amalgam of various regional variants, subject to multiple regional vernacular interferences and cultural references. While Guru English is a register within South Asian English, its (largely Hindu and some Buddhist) religious concerns make it more significantly, although not exclusively, Indian. I will discuss the capacity of Guru English to interpellate South Asian Islams in chapter 5.

14. For a salutary discussion of Bombay English and Ebonics, see Homi Bhabha, "Queen's English," *Artforum* 35, no. 7 (March 1997): 35.

15. Cited in Raychaudhuri, *Europe Reconsidered*, 147.

16. Bankim Chandra Chatterjee, *The Abbey of Bliss*, 5th ed., trans. Nares Chandra Sen-Gupta (Calcutta: Cherry Press, 1905), 199.

17. Marco Jacquemet, "Transidiomatic Practices: Language and the Global Situation," in Language and Cognition, University Seminar #681, Columbia University, January 31, 2002, 45–51, http://www.columbia.edu/~romez/langcog.html; and Jacquemet, "Ska Probl'em M/Don Uorri: Transidiomatic Practices in Albania," in *The Paradoxes of Progress: Globalization and Postsocialist Cultures*, ed. Rachael Stryker and Jennifer Patico, Kroeber Anthropological Society Papers, vol. 86 (Berkeley, CA: Kroeber Anthropological Society, 2001).

18. Naoki Sakai, *Translation and Subjectivity: On "Japan" and Cultural Nationalism* (Minneapolis: University of Minnesota Press, 1997), 3.

19. Kalidas Nag and Debajyoti Burman, eds., *The English Works of Raja Rammohun Roy Pt. IV* (Calcutta: Sadharan Brahmo Samaj, 1947), 127; also cited in Saumyendranath Tagore, *Rabindranath Tagore and Universal Humanism* (Bombay: M. Chatterji, 1961), 5.

20. Tzvetan Todorov, *The Morals of History*, trans. Alyson Waters (Minneapolis: University of Minnesota Press, 1995).

21. For the "older" kind of universalist cosmopolitanism in recent iterations, see Francis Fukuyama, *The End of History and the Last Man* (New York: Free Press, 1992); Julia Kristeva, *Nations without Nationalism*, trans. Leon S. Roudiez (New York: Columbia University Press, 1993); Martha C. Nussbaum, with respondents, *For Love of Country: Debating the Limits of Patriotism*, ed. Joshua Cohen (Boston: Beacon Press, 1996); Ross Posnock, *Color and Culture: Black Writers and the Making of the Modern Intellectual* (Cambridge, MA: Harvard University Press, 1998); Richard Rorty, *Achieving Our Country: Leftist Thought in Twentieth-Century America* (Cambridge, MA: Harvard University Press, 1998); and Amartya Sen, "East and West: The Reach of Reason," *New York Review of Books* 47, no. 12 (July 2000): 33–38.

22. For a representative sample of the "newer" cosmopolitanism from below, see Benedict Anderson, *The Spectre of Comparisons: Nationalism, Southeast Asia, and the World* (London: Verso, 1999); Arjun Appadurai, *Modernity at Large: Cultural Dimensions of Globalization* (Minneapolis: University of Minnesota Press, 1996); Tim Brennan, *At Home in the World: Cosmopolitanism Now* (Cambridge, MA: Harvard University Press, 1997); Homi Bhabha, "Unsatisfied: Notes on Vernacular Cosmopolitanism," in *Text and Nation: Cross-Disciplinary Essays on Cultural and National Identities*, ed. Laura García-Moreno and Peter C. Pfeiffer (Columbia, SC: Camden House, 1996), 191–207; and "Editor's Introduction: Minority Maneuvers and Unsettled Negotiations," *Critical Inquiry* 23, no. 3 (Spring 1997): 437; Pheng Cheah and Bruce Robbins, eds., *Cosmopolitics: Thinking and Feeling beyond the Nation* (Minneapolis: University of Minnesota Press, 1998); Pheng Cheah, *Spectral Nationality: Passages of Freedom from Kant to Postcolonial Literatures of Liberation* (New York: Columbia University Press, 2003); and James Clifford, *Routes: Travel and Translation in the Late Twentieth Century* (Cambridge, MA: Harvard University Press, 1997).

23. Étienne Balibar, "Ambiguous Universality," *Differences* 7 (Spring 1995): 55.

24. Rabindranath Tagore, "Nationalism in the West," in *Nationalism* (London: Macmillan, 1917), 15; see also Rabindranath Tagore, *Towards Universal Man* (London: Asia Publishing House, 1961); for an interesting discussion of Tagore's opposition to nationalism, see Ashis Nandy, *The Illegitimacy of Nationalism* (Delhi: Oxford University Press, 1994).

25. Tariq Ali, *The Clash of Fundamentalisms: Crusades, Jihads and Modernity* (London: Verso, 2002), 211.

26. See Bernard S. Cohn, "The Command of Language and the Language of Command," in *Colonialism and Its Forms of Knowledge: The British in India* (Princeton, NJ: Princeton University Press, 1996), 16–56, 26, 56.

27. See Nicholas B. Dirks, *Castes of Mind: Colonialism and the Making of Modern India* (Princeton, NJ: Princeton University Press, 2001), 88, 81–106. See also, Jennifer Howes, "Colin Mackenzie and the Stupa at Amaravati," *South Asian Studies*, no. 18 (2002): 53–65; and Maria Antonella Pelizzari, ed., *Traces of India: Photography, Architecture, and the Politics of Representation, 1850–1900* (Montreal: Canadian Centre for Architecture and Yale Center for British Art, 2003).

28. See Mildred Archer, *British Drawings in the India Office Library*, 2 vols. (London: Her Majesty's Stationery Office, 1969), 1:53.

29. "Biographical Sketch of the Literary Career of the Late Colin Mackenzie, Surveyor-General of India; comprising some particulars of his collection of manuscripts, plans, coins, drawings, sculptures, etc., illustrative of the antiquities, history, geography, laws, institutions, and manners of the ancient Hindus; contained in a letter addressed by him to the Right Hon. Sir Alexander Johnston, V.P.R.A.S., etc. etc.," *Madras Journal of Science and Literature*, no. 2 (1835): 265–66; cited in Dirks, *Castes of Mind*, 99–100.

30. A colonial official writing at the onset of World War I, J. N. Farquhar, provides a slightly different periodization of modern Indian religious movements until that point. Farquhar sees a first phase of orientalists and missionaries including the indigenous voice of Raja Rammohun Roy as occurring from 1800 to 1828, and a second phase of largely Brahmo Samaj activity from 1828 to 1870. A very fertile third phase, from 1870 to 1895, includes Max Müller's contributions, the Harvard Oriental Series, and the rise of several movements including the Arya Samaj and Deva Samaj, Theosophy, and the Ramakrishna Mission. The fourth phase, from 1895 to 1913, sees the rise of the Indian national movement that begins to occlude and/or partly integrate religious modernization. See J. N. Farquhar, *Modern Religious Movements in India* (New York: Macmillan, 1915), 14–28.

31. See Graham Huggan, *The Postcolonial Exotic: Marketing the Margins* (London: Routledge, 2001).

32. Mohandas Karamchand Gandhi, *The Essential Writings of Mahatma Gandhi*, ed. Raghavan Iyer (Delhi: Oxford University Press, 1993), 65–66; cited in Robert J. C. Young, *Postcolonialism: An Historical Introduction* (Oxford: Blackwell, 2001), 319.

33. See Talal Asad, *Formations of the Secular: Christianity, Islam, Modernity* (Stanford, CA: Stanford University Press, 2003).

34. Gayatri Chakravorty Spivak, "The Secular University Today," public lecture, annual convention of the Modern Language Association, San Diego, CA, December 27, 2003.

35. See Partha Chatterjee, *The Nation and Its Fragments* (Princeton, NJ: Princeton University Press, 1994); and Benedict Anderson, *Imagined Communities: Reflections on the Origin and Spread of Nationalism*, rev. ed. (London: Verso, 1992).

36. For two recent studies that demonstrate a competent coverage of these areas, see Chetan Bhatt, *Liberation and Purity: Race, New Religious Movements, and the Ethics of Postmodernity* (London: University College London Press, 1997); and Richard King, *Orientalism and Religion: Postcolonial Theory, India, and "the Mystic East"* (London: Routledge, 1999).

37. See Steven Vertovec, *The Hindu Diaspora: Comparative Patterns* (London: Routledge, 2000); Arjun Appadurai, "Disjuncture and Difference in the Global Cultural Economy," *Public Culture* 2, no. 2 (1990): 1–24; rpt. in Appadurai, *Modernity at Large: Cultural Dimensions of Globalization* (Minneapolis: University of Minnesota Press, 1996), 27–47.

CHAPTER ONE
THEOLINGUISTICS: ORIENTALISTS, BRAHMOS, VEDANTINS, AND YOGIS

1. Romila Thapar, "Syndicated Hinduism," in *Cultural Pasts: Essays in Early Indian History* (Delhi: Oxford University Press, 2000), 1047, 1025–54.

2. Garland Cannon, ed., *The Collected Works of Sir William Jones* (New York: New York University Press, 1993); Garland Cannon, *The Life and Mind of Oriental Jones: Sir William Jones, the Father of Modern Linguistics* (New York: Cambridge University Press, 1990); Charles Wilkins, *A Grammar of the Sanskrita Language* (New Delhi: Ajay Book Service, 1983); Charles Wilkins, trans. *The Bhagvat-Geeta; The Heetopades of Veeshnoo Sarma*, intro. by Michael Franklin (London: Ganesha Publishing, 2001); Nathaniel Brassy Halhed, *A Code of Gentoo Laws; or, Ordinations of the Pundits* (London, 1776); Halhed, *A Grammar of the Bengal Language* (London, 1778; rpt., Calcutta: Ananda, 1980); Rosane Rocher, *Orientalism, Poetry, and the Millennium: The Checkered Life of Nathaniel Brassey Halhed, 1751–1830* (Delhi: Motilal Banarsidass, 1983); John Rosselli, *Lord William Bentinck: The Making of a Liberal Imperialist, 1774–1839* (Berkeley: University of California Press, 1974); Humphrey Trevelyan, *The India We Left: Charles Trevelyan, 1826–65; Humphrey Trevelyan, 1929–47* (London: Macmillan, 1972); C. D. Dharker, ed., *Lord Macaulay's Legislative Minutes* (New York: Oxford University Press, 1946); James Mill, *The History of British India*, 3 vols., (London: Baldwin, Cradock, and Joy, 1817), vol. 1: xii, xv, xvi, xix.

3. Mircea Eliade, *The Myth of the Eternal Return*, trans. Willard R. Trask (New York: Pantheon Books, 1965); Eliade, *Yoga: Immortality and Freedom*, trans. Willard R. Trask (Princeton, NJ: Princeton University Press, 1970); Louis Dumont, *Homo Hierarchicus: The Caste System and Its Implications*, trans. Mark Sainsbury, Louis Dumont, and Basia Gulati (Chicago: University of Chicago Press, 1980).

4. David Kopf, *British Orientalism and the Bengal Renaissance: The Dynamics of Indian Modernization, 1773–1835* (Berkeley: University of California Press, 1969); Susobhan Sarkar, *Bengal Renaissance and Other Essays* (New Delhi: People's Publishing House, 1970); Javed Majeed, *Ungoverned Imaginings: James Mill's* The History of British India *and Orientalism* (New York: Oxford University Press, 1992); Sir Syed Ahmed Khan, *The Causes of the Indian Revolt* (Lahore: Book House, 1970); G.F.I. Graham, *The Life and Work of Sir Syed Ahmed Khan* (Karachi: Oxford University Press, 1974).

5. For a useful anthology that showcases several of the intra-subalternist disciplinary skirmishes, see the collected essays in Vinayak Chaturvedi, ed., *Mapping Subaltern Studies and the Postcolonial* (London: Verso, 2000). While Rosalind O'Hanlon, David Washbrook, and Sumit Sarkar still defend a hard-line Marxist approach from what they see as 1990s deviations toward post-modernist uncertainty, others, such as Ranajit Guha, Partha Chatterjee, Gyan Prakash, Dipesh Chakrabarty, and Gayatri Chakravorty Spivak, explore a number of different cross-fertilizations of the Gramscian theory of subalternity with partly Foucauldian, deconstructionist, comparativist, and feminist outcomes.

6. See Ashis Nandy, "Contending Stories in the Culture of Indian Politics: Traditions and the Future of Democracy," in *Time Warps: The Insistent Politics of Silent and Evasive Pasts* (New Delhi: Permanent Black, 2001), 13–35.

7. In analyzing the multiple global receptions of Hollywood action-attraction cinema, Simon During has suggested the *global popular* as a counterterm to *cultural globalization*: "The histories of these shows do not narrativize the past of any discrete community or valued cultural traditions; they present a particularly ambiguous, tangled mass of continuities, discontinuities, repetitions, and displacements." Simon During, "Popular Culture on a Global Scale: A Challenge for Cultural Studies," *Critical Inquiry* 23, no. 4 (Summer 1997): 824, 827.

8. See Graham Huggan, *The Postcolonial Exotic: Marketing the Margins* (London: Routledge, 2001).

9. However, an excellent start is provided by Richard King's recent study that locates the invention of neo-Hinduism and neo-Vedantism in the colonial period. See Richard King, *Orientalism and Religion: Postcolonial Theory, India, and "the Mystic East"* (New York: Routledge, 1999).

10. Bruno Latour, *We Have Never Been Modern*, trans. Catherine Porter (Cambridge, MA: Harvard University Press, 1993); Barbara Herrnstein Smith, *Contingencies of Value: Alternative Perspectives for Critical Theory* (Cambridge, MA: Harvard University Press, 1988); Gauri Viswanathan, *Outside the Fold: Modernity, Conversion, and Belief* (Princeton, NJ: Princeton University Press, 1998), 158.

11. Peter van der Veer, *Imperial Encounters: Religion and Modernity in India and Britain* (Princeton, NJ: Princeton University Press, 2001).

12. F. Max Müller, *Three Lectures on the Science of Language* (London: Longman, 1891), 44; Dugald Stewart, cited in F. Max Müller, *Lectures on the Science of Language* (London: Longman, Green, 1885), 2:391.

13. Amitav Ghosh, *In an Antique Land* (New Delhi: Ravi Dayal Publishers, 1992); and Amitav Ghosh, *The Calcutta Chromosome: A Novel of Fevers, Delirium, and Discovery* (New Delhi: Ravi Dayal Publishers, 1996).

14. For the best study of English educational policy in India during the colonial period, see Gauri Viswanathan, *Masks of Conquest: Literary Study and British Rule in Colonial India* (New York: Columbia University Press, 1989).

15. P. J. Marshall suggests that Wilkins's translation was the first of any major Indological work into a European language. See P. J. Marshall, *The British Discovery of Hinduism in the Eighteenth Century* (Cambridge: Cambridge University Press, 1970), 4. However, O. P. Kejariwal points to a 1651 Dutch translation of Bhartrihari by Abraham Roger, *De Open-Deure tot het Verborgen Heydendom* [The open door to hidden heathendom], and also other instances, such as Father Thomas Stevens's publication in Portuguese of a Konkani grammar in 1579. See O. P. Kejariwal, *The Asiatic Society of Bengal and the Discovery of India's Past, 1784–1838* (Delhi: Oxford University Press, 1988), 14.

16. Marshall, *The British Discovery of Hinduism*, 193.

17. Marshall, *The British Discovery of Hinduism*, 193–94.

18. Jones, cited in Marshall, *The British Discovery of Hinduism*, 245.

19. See Ludo Rocher, ed., *Ezourvedam: A French Veda of the Eighteenth Century* (Philadelphia: Benjamins, 1984); and for the first exposé of the Jesuit authorship, Pierre Sonnerat, *Voyage aux Indes Orientales* (Paris, 1782).

20. See Thomas R. Trautmann, *Aryans and British India* (Berkeley: University of California Press, 1997), 69, 70.

21. Trautmann, *Aryans*, 90, 95. See also Francis Wilford, "An Essay on the Sacred Isles in the West," *Asiatic Researches* 8–11 (1805–10); and Charles Vallancey, *The Ancient History of Ireland, Proved from the Sanscrit Books of the Bramins of India* (London, 1797); and Vallancey, *An Essay on the Primitive Inhabitants of Great Britain and Ireland* (Dublin: Graisberry and Campbell, 1807).

22. Joseph Priestley, *Comparison of the Institutions of Moses with Those of the Hindoos* (Northumberland, PA, 1799). In a similar vein, see also Thomas Maurice, *Dissertation on the Oriental Trinities* (London, 1800); and Maurice, *Indian Antiquities*, 7 vols., (London, 1794–1800).

23. Edward Pococke, *India in Greece, or, Truth in Mythology: Containing the Sources of the Hellenic Race, the Colonization of Egypt and Palestine, the Wars of the Grand Lama, and the Bud'histic Propaganda in Greece* (London, 1851; rpt., Delhi: Oriental Publishers, 1972); P[urushottam] N[agesh]Oak, *Christianity is Chrisn-niti* (New Delhi: Institute for Rewriting Indian History, 1978).

24. Monier Monier-Williams, *The Study of Sanskrit in Relation to Missionary Work in India* (London: Oxford University Press, 1861), 54; cited in Peter van der Veer, *Imperial Encounters*, 109.

25. See Trautmann, *Aryans*, 96. Trautmann also intriguingly suggests, contra Martin Bernal's assertion in *Black Athena*, that Egyptomania and Indomania went hand in hand until Champollion's decipherment of the hieroglyphs.

26. See P[urushottam] N[agesh] Oak, *World Vedic Heritage* (New Delhi: P. N. Oak, 1984); P. N. Oak, *Indian Kshatriyas Once Ruled from Bali to Baltic and Korea to Kaba* (New Delhi: P. N. Oak, 1966); P. N. Oak, *Great Britain Was Hindu Land: New Discovery* (Bangalore: Manasi S. Oak, 1976); P. N. Oak, *Some Blunders of Indian Historical Research* (New Delhi: P. N. Oak, 1966); *Some Missing Chapters of World History* (New Delhi: Itihas Shodh Sansthan, 1973); P. N. Oak, *The Taj Mahal Is a Hindu Palace* (Bombay: Pearl Books, 1968); and Stephen Knapp, *Proof of Vedic Culture's Global Existence* (Detroit: World Relief Network, 2000).

27. Nathaniel Brassy Halhed, *Testimony of the Authenticity of the Prophecies of Richard Brothers* (London: H. D. Symonds, 1795); Halhed, *Two Letters to the Right Honourable Lord Loughborough, Lord High Chancellor of England, on the Present Confinement of Richard Brothers, in a Private Mad-House* (London: B. Crosby, 1795).

28. Rocher, *Orientalism, Poetry, and the Millennium*, 184; see especially the chapter "Waiting for the Millennium: 1795," 156–91. For an important discussion of the Indian scholars often left out in discussions of Jones's intellectual genius, see Rocher, "Weaving Knowledge: Sir William Jones and Indian Pandits," in *Objects of Inquiry: The Life, Contributions, and Influences of Sir William Jones (1746–1794)*, ed. Garland Cannon and Kevin R. Brine (New York: New York University Press, 1995), 51–79.

29. Ranajit Guha, *Elementary Aspects of Peasant Insurgency in Colonial India* (Delhi: Oxford University Press, 1983); Charles J. Ryan, *H. P. Blavatsky and the Theosophical Movement* (Pasadena, CA: Theosophical University Press, 1975).

30. Rammohun Roy, *Translation of an Abridgment of the Vedant* (London, 1817), viii.

31. Rammohun Roy, *Translation of the Céna Upanishad* (London, 1816), v.

32. Rammohun Roy, *A Defence of Hindoo Theism in Reply to the Attack of an Advocate for Idolatry* (Calcutta, 1817), 1.

33. See Lynn Zastoupil, "Defining Christians, Making Britons: Rammohun Roy and the Unitarians," *Victorian Studies* 44, no. 2 (Winter 2002): 222.

34. There is an extensive literature on Rammohun Roy. For a brief sampling, see Bruce Carlisle Robertson, *Raja Rammohan Roy: The Father of Modern India* (Delhi: Oxford University Press, 1995), 26; and J. K. Majumdar, *Raja Rammohun Roy and the World* (Calcutta: Sadharan Brahmo Samaj, 1975). Not knowing Persian, I have read the translation. See K. C. Mitter, *Rammohun Roy and Tuhfatul Muwahhiddin, Tuhfat* trans. Obaidullah Obaide (Calcutta: K. P. Bagchi, 1975); and *The English Works of Raja Rammohun Roy with an English Translation of Tuhfatul Muwahhiddin*, ed. Jogendra Chunder Ghose (Calcutta: Cosmo, 1982).

35. Roy, *A Defence of Hindoo Theism*, 3. Sankara Sastri was later attacked by Alexipharmacus on January 13, 1817, in the *Madras Courier*, and Rammohun thanks the author of this pseudonymous intervention.

36. For some of this information on Rammohun in the missionary journals, I am indebted to J. K. Majumdar, *Raja Rammohun Roy*, 99–104.

37. Adrienne Moore, *Rammohun Roy and America* (Calcutta: Baptist Mission Press, 1942).

38. The Serampore Baptists were established in a Danish colony as early as 1799, because the East India Company still did not allow missionaries for fear of antagonizing the natives. After Parliament gave in to the missionary lobby in 1813 allowing evangelical activity, a Baptist mission was established in Calcutta in 1817. The rival factions united in 1837. See Zastoupil, "Defining Christians, Making Britons," 226.

39. Rammohun Roy, *A Letter on English Education: Brahmunical Magazine 4* in *The English Works of Raja Rammohun Roy*, Jogendra Chunder Ghose, ed. (Calcutta: Oriental Press, 1885), 471, 472.

40. Kalidas Nag and Debajyoti Burman, eds., *The English Works of Raja Rammohun Roy Pt. II* (Calcutta: Sadharan Brahmo Samaj, 1947), 78fn.

41. Arvind Sharma, *Modern Hindu Thought: The Essential Texts* (Delhi: Oxford University Press, 2002), 32.

42. Lt. Col. Fitzclarence [Earl of Munster], *Journal of a Route across India, through Egypt to England* (London, 1819), 106–7. Friedrich Max Müller, *From Rammohun to Ramakrishna* (Calcutta: S. Gupta, 1952), 18.

43. Robertson, *Raja Rammohun Roy*, 170.

44. Majumdar, *Raja Rammohun Roy*; Zastoupil, "Defining Christians," 216–17.

45. I thank Mandakini Dubey for suggesting to me that Thackeray's Rummon Loll could also be a reference to Rámon Lull, the medieval Spanish theologian, mathematician, and esotericist.

46. Van der Veer, *Imperial Encounters*, 146.

47. J. K. Majumdar, *Raja Rammohun Roy*, 113.

48. Rammohun Roy, *Translation of a Sungscrit Tract, on Different Modes of Worship* (Calcutta, 1825).

49. David Kopf, *The Brahmo Samaj and the Shaping of the Modern Indian Mind*

(Princeton, NJ: Princeton University Press, 1979), 3. See also, Niranjan Dhar, *Vedanta and the Bengal Renaissance* (Calcutta, 1977).

50. Kopf, *Brahmo Samaj*, 15.

51. Prashant Kumar Sen, *Keshub Chunder Sen* (Calcutta: Keshub Chunder Sen Birth Centenary Committee, 1938), 19. For other biographies, see Protap Chunder Mozoomdar, *The Life and Teachings of Keshub Chunder Sen* (Calcutta: Baptist Mission Press, 1887); Manilal C. Parekh, *Brahmarishi Keshub Chunder Sen* (Rajkot: Oriental Christ House, 1926); Kasinath Kayal, *Keshub Chunder Sen: A Study in Encounter and Response* (Calcutta: Minerva Associates, 1998); Gouri Prasad Mazoomdar, *Keshub Chunder Sen and the Schools of Protests and Non-Protests* (Calcutta: Art Press, 1928); and Meredith Borthwick, *Keshub Chunder Sen: A Search for Cultural Synthesis* (Calcutta: Minerva Associates, 1977).

52. See Satyendra Nath Tagore, "Introduction," in *Autobiography of Maharshi Debendra Nath Tagore*, ed. Satyendra Nath Tagore, trans. Satyendra Nath Tagore and Indira Devi (London: Macmillan, 1916), 14–17.

53. See R. C. Majumdar, ed., *The History and Culture of the People of India* (Bombay: Bharatiya Vidya Bhavan, 1965), vol. 10, pt. 2, 225; cited in Julius Lipner, "A Remaking of Hinduism?" in *Religion and Media*, ed. Hent de Vries and Samuel Weber (Stanford, CA: Stanford University Press, 2001), 326.

54. Kopf, *Brahmo Samaj*, 251; Spencer Lavan, *Unitarians and India: A Study in Encounter and Response* (Boston: Beacon Press, 1977), 131; Suresh Chunder Bose, *The Life of Protap Chunder Mozoomdar* (Calcutta: Nababidhan Trust, 1927), 63.

55. See Keshub Chunder Sen, *Jesus Christ: Europe and Asia* (London: John Snow, 1866), 24.

56. For instance, see *Report of a Special Meeting at the New Town Hall, Shoreditch, of the East Central Temperance Association on May 29, 1870 with the Speech in Full of the Baboo Keshub Chunder Sen* (London: Haywood, 1870). The figures are estimates given by Rev. R. Spears in the Farewell Soirée.

57. See British and Foreign Unitarian Association (London), *A Welcome Soirée to Baboo Keshub Chunder Sen in the Hanover Square Rooms London, April 12th 1870* (London, [1870]), 17.

58. Antoinette Burton, *At the Heart of Empire: Indians and the Colonial Encounter in Late-Victorian Britain* (Berkeley: University of California Press, 1998), 39.

59. *Punch* April 16, 1870, 155; cited in G. C. Banerji, ed., *Brahmananda Keshub Chunder Sen: Testimonies in Memoriam* (Allahabad: Keshub Centenary Series, 1938), 98–99.

60. *Pall Mall Gazette*, April 25, 1870, 24.

61. *The Scotsman*, August 19, 1870, cited in G. C. Banerji, *Testimonies in Memoriam*, 457–59.

62. *Saturday Review*, June 11, 1870, 763–64; cited in Borthwick, *Keshub Chunder Sen*, 115–16.

63. Protap Chunder Mozoomdar, *Life and Teachings of Keshub*, 210, 350.

64. Ram Chandra Bose, *Brahmoism; or, the History of Reformed Hinduism* (London: Funk and Wagnalls, 1884), 151.

65. Cited in Kopf, *Brahmo Samaj*, 269, 274–75.

66. The Brahmo Somaj [Keshub Chunder Sen], *We Apostles of the New Dispensation* (Calcutta: Bidhan Press, 1881), 9, 25.

67. Bose, *Brahmoism*, 137.

68. Kopf, *Brahmo Samaj*, 279.

69. Keshub Chunder Sen, *India Asks—Who Is Christ?* (Calcutta: M. M. Rukhit, 1879), 4, 14, 15.

70. J.F.B. Tinling, *An Evangelist's Tour Round India, with an Account of Keshub Chunder Sen and the Modern Hindu Reformers* (London: William Macintosh, 1870), 121.

71. Lavan, *Unitarians and India*, 122.

72. Van der Veer, *Imperial Encounters*, 154.

73. See B. Mozoomdar, *Professor F. Maxmüller on Ramakrishna and the World on Keshub Chunder Sen* (Calcutta: Lawrence Printing Works, 1900); and Protap Chunder Mozoomdar in *Theistic Quarterly Review* 3 (October 1879), cited in Borthwick, *Keshub Chunder Sen*, 221. See also F. Max Müller, *Ramakrishna: His Life and Sayings* (New York: Scribner, 1999).

74. Protap Chunder Mozoomdar, *The Oriental Christ* (Calcutta: Navavidhan, 1933); and Protap Chunder Mozoomdar, *The World's Religious Debt to Asia* (Lahore: Punjab Brahmo Samaj, 1894).

75. Protap Chunder Mozoomdar, *The Spirit of God* (London, 1893), 51.

76. Nicolas Notovitch, *La vie inconnue de Jésus-Christ* (Paris: Paul Ollendorff, 1894); English translations include *The Unknown Life of Jesus Christ*, trans. Alexine Loranger (Chicago: Rand, McNally, 1894); *The Unknown Life of Jesus Christ from Buddhistic Records*, trans. J. H. Connelly and L. Landsberg (New York: G. W. Dillingham, 1894); and *The Unknown Life of Christ*, trans. Violet Crispe (London: Hutchinson, 1895), which is the official translation and includes a note by Notovitch. Notovitch's claims were extensively rebutted by Max Müller.

77. Protap Chunder Mozoomdar, *Debt to Asia*, 7.

78. Diary, October 8, 1883, cited in Bose, *Life of Protap*, 93–94.

79. *The Complete Works of Swami Vivekananda* (Calcutta: Advaita Ashrama, 1970), 1:3–14.

80. See John Henry Barrows, ed., *The World's Parliament of Religions* 2 vols. (Chicago: Parliament Publishing, 1893); Richard Hughes Seager, ed., *The Dawn of Religious Pluralism: Voices from the World's Parliament of Religions, 1893* (LaSalle, IL: Open Court, 1993); Marie Louise Burke, *Swami Vivekananda in the West: New Discoveries* (Calcutta: Advaita Ashrama, 1973); R. K. Dasgupta, ed., *Swami Vivekananda: A Hundred Years since Chicago* (Calcutta: Ramakrishna Math, 1994) and William Radice, ed., *Swami Vivekananda and the Modernization of Hinduism* (Delhi: Oxford University Press, 1998).

81. See Vivekananda, *Lectures from Colombo to Almora* (Calcutta: Advaita Ashrama, 1963), 56.

82. Vivekananda, *Lectures from Colombo to Almora*, 10–11.

83. *The Complete Works of Swami Vivekananda* (Calcutta: Advaita Ashrama, 1970), 1:276.

84. Vivekananda, *Lectures from Colombo to Almora*, 12.

85. See Carl T. Jackson, *The Oriental Religions and American Thought: Nineteenth-Century Explorations* (Westport, CT: Greenwood Press, 1981), and

Vedanta for the West: The Ramakrishna Movement in the United States (Bloomington: Indiana University Press, 1994), 49.

86. See Jeffrey Moussaieff Masson, *The Oceanic Feeling: The Origins of Religious Sentiment in Ancient India* (Boston: D. Reidel, 1980).

87. See *Time*, February 12, 1945; Christopher Isherwood, *My Guru and His Disciple* (Minneapolis: University of Minnesota Press, 1980), 181–85; Christopher Isherwood, *An Approach to Vedanta* (Hollywood, CA: Vedanta Press, 1963); Christopher Isherwood, ed., *Vedanta for Modern Men* (London: George Allen and Unwin, 1952); and Christopher Isherwood, ed., *Vedanta for the Western World* (London, 1963).

88. Paramhansa Yogananda, *Scientific Healing Affirmations* (Los Angeles: Yogoda and Sat-Sanga Headquarters, 1925); Yogananda, *Yogoda or Tissue-Will System of Body and Mind Perfection* (Los Angeles: Yogoda and Sat-Sanga Headquarters, 1925), 21; Yogananda, *Psychological Chart* (Los Angeles: Yogoda and Sat-Sanga Headquarters, 1925).

89. Paramhansa Yogananda, *Autobiography of a Yogi* (Los Angeles: Self-Realization Fellowship, 1956), 243–49.

90. Yogananda, *Autobiography*, 307.

91. Yogananda, *Autobiography*, 107.

92. Yogananda, *Autobiography*, 135.

93. Yogananda, *Autobiography*, 34.

94. Yogananda, *Autobiography*, 279.

95. Yogananda, *Autobiography*, vi, 13, 47, 52, 65, 158, 264, 383.

96. Yogananda, *Autobiography*, 236; Swami Kriyananda (Donald Walters), *The Path: Autobiography of a Western Yogi* (Nevada City, CA: Ananda Publications, 1977).

97. Yogananda, *Autobiography*, 177.

98. Yogananda, *Autobiography*, 279, 327.

99. Paramhansa Yogananda, *The Rubaiyat of Omar Khayyam Explained*, ed. Donald J. Walters (Nevada City, CA: Crystal Clarity Press, 1994), 2–3.

100. Yoganda Saraswati, *A Message of Hope* 10, 2–3; see also Yogananda Saraswati, *The Living Knowledge, or Adwaita Brahma Shidhi* (Calcutta: Dasarathi Banerjee, 1926). For another Yogananda, see Sudhamoy Chatterji, *The Re-Born* (Calcutta: Saniranjan Press, 1976).

CHAPTER TWO
FROM INDIAN ROMANTICISM TO GURU LITERATURE

1. For an extended discussion of anachronism and anatopism in relation to the "pre-Romantic" thought of Giambattista Vico, see Srinivas Aravamudan, "The Return of Anachronism," in *Periodization: Cutting Up the Past*, a special issue of *Modern Language Quarterly* 62, no. 4 (December 2001): 331–53. For further discussion of anachronism and anatopism, see also James Chandler, *England in 1819: The Politics of Literary Culture and the Case of Romantic Historicism* (Chicago: University of Chicago Press, 1998), 107–9. For an exposition of Anouar Abdel-Malek's notion of tricontinentalism, see Robert J. C. Young,

Postcolonialism: An Historical Introduction (Oxford: Blackwell, 2001), 4–5, 170–74. For a deconstructive meditation on prosthesis and the (crypto-Romantic) myth of origins, see Jacques Derrida, *Monolingualism of the Other; or, The Prosthesis of Origins*, trans. Patrick Mensah (Stanford, CA: Stanford University Press, 1998). For a compelling account of the organicism of German Romanticism and its futures in terms of the anxieties of postcolonial nationalisms, see Pheng Cheah, *Spectral Nationality: Passages of Freedom from Kant to Postcolonial Literatures of Liberation* (New York: Columbia University Press, 2003).

2. For a fuller definition of Freudian *Nachträglichkeit*, see J. Laplanche and J. B. Pontalis, *The Language of Psycho-Analysis*, trans. Donald Nicholson (New York: Norton, 1973), 111–14. For an analogical application that interprets the backward creation of the "Enlightenment" by the French Revolution, see Roger Chartier, *Les origines culturelles de la Révolution française* (Paris: Seuil, 1990). For a postcolonial reading of eighteenth-century colonialist literature on similar lines, see Srinivas Aravamudan, *Tropicopolitans: Colonialism and Agency, 1688–1804* (Durham, NC: Duke University Press, 1999).

3. Ronald Inden, "Orientalist Constructions of India," *Modern Asian Studies* 20, no. 3 (1986): 401–46; Inden, *Imagining India* (Oxford: Blackwell, 1990).

4. Cited in Wilhelm Halbfass, *India and Europe: An Essay in Understanding* (Albany: State University of New York Press, 1988), 67; see also Vasant Kaiwar, "The Aryan Model of History and the Oriental Renaissance: The Politics of Identity in an Age of Revolutions, Colonialism, and Nationalism," in *Antinomies of Modernity: Essays on Race, Orient, Nation* Vasant Kaiwar and Sucheta Mazumdar, eds. (Durham, NC: Duke University Press, 2003), 13–61.

5. Romila Thapar, *Interpreting Early India* (Delhi: Oxford University Press, 1992), 60–88; Veena Das, *Critical Events: An Anthropological Perspective on Contemporary India* (Oxford: Oxford University Press, 1995); Chetan Bhatt, *Liberation and Purity: Race, New Religious Movements, and the Ethics of Postmodernity* (London: University College London Press, 1997); and Richard King, *Orientalism and Religion: Postcolonial Theory, India, and "the Mystic East"* (London: Routledge, 1999).

6. Partha Chatterjee, *Nationalist Thought and the Colonial World: A Derivative Discourse* (Minneapolis: University of Minnesota Press, 1986), especially chapter 2, "The Thematic and the Problematic," 36–53.

7. Chandler, *England in 1819*, xvi.

8. See E. J. Hobsbawm, *Nations and Nationalism since 1780: Programme, Myth, Reality* (Cambridge: Cambridge University Press, 1990).

9. In this respect, I am somewhat skeptical of the governmentality thesis in relation to the Bengal Renaissance as elaborated in Henry Schwarz, "Aesthetic Imperialism: Literature and the Conquest of India," *Modern Language Quarterly* 61, no. 4 (December 2000): 563–86.

10. Bankimchandra Chattopadhyay [Chatterjee], "The Confession of a Young Bengal," in *Bankim Rachanavali*, ed. Jogesh Chandra Bagal (Calcutta: Sahitya Samsad, 1969), 137, 138, 140.

11. "Lokrahasya," in Bankimchandra Chatterjee, *Sociological Essays: Utilitarianism and Positivism in Bengal*, trans. and ed. S. N. Mukherjee and Marian Maddern (Calcutta: Ṛddhi, 1986), 28. For a discussion, see Partha Chatterjee, *The*

Nation and Its Fragments: Colonial and Postcolonial Histories (Princeton, NJ: Princeton University Press, 1993), 68–71.

12. George Malcolm Young, ed., *Speeches by Lord Macaulay with His Minute on Indian Education*, intro. G. M. Young (London: Humphrey Milford for Oxford University Press, 1935), 359.

13. Thomas Babington Macaulay, "Warren Hastings," in *Critical and Historical Essays* (London: Longman, Brown, Green, and Longmans, 1843), 3:345; John Rosselli, "The Self-Image of Effeteness: Physical Education and Nationalism in Nineteenth-Century Bengal," *Past and Present* 86 (February 1980): 121–48; Milind Wakankar, "Body, Crowd, Identity: Genealogy of a Hindu Nationalist Ascetics," *Social Text* 45 (1995): 45–73; Mrinalini Sinha, *Colonial Masculinity: The "Manly Englishman" and the "Effeminate Bengali" in the Late Nineteenth Century* (Manchester, Eng.: Manchester University Press, 1995).

14. Sri Aurobindo, *Bankim Chandra Chatterjee* in *The Harmony of Virtue: Early Cultural Writings*, Birth Centenary Library (Pondicherry: Sri Aurobindo Ashram Trust, 1972), 3:83.

15. Sisir Kumar Das, *The Artist in Chains: The Life of Bankimchandra Chatterji* (New Delhi: New Statesman, 1984), 140.

16. George Robert Gleig, *Memoirs of the Life of the Rt. Hon. Warren Hastings*, 3d ed. (London: R. Bentley, 1841), 1:282.

17. Bimanbehari Majumdar, "The Ananda Math and Phadke," *Journal of Indian History* 44, pt. 1, no. 130 (April 1966): 93–108; William Wilson Hunter, *Annals of Rural Bengal* (London: Smith, Elder, 1897), 13–55. Bankim added an introduction to the second edition (1884) that quoted from Gleig (*Memoirs*) and Hunter (*Annals*), even though he still was uncomfortable about owning up to the novel as a political allegory or historical fiction regarding the current national situation. See also William R. Pinch, *Peasants and Monks in British India* (Berkeley: University of California Press, 1996) and Koylash Chunder Dutt, *A Journal of Forty-Eight Hours of the Year 1945* (Calcutta, 1835). Cited in Apurba Kumar Ray, "History and the Romantic Imagination," in *Bankimchandra Chatterjee: Essays in Perspective*, ed. Bhabatosh Chatterjee (New Delhi: Sahitya Akademi, 1994), 513. Dutt might have been himself influenced by Sebastien Merçier's Rousseauistic utopian novels such as *The Year 2440*.

18. Tapan Raychaudhuri, *Europe Reconsidered: Perceptions of the West in Nineteenth-Century Bengal* (New Delhi: Oxford University Press, 1988), 117–19.

19. Bankimchandra Chatterjee, *Abbey of Bliss*, 5th ed., trans. Nares Chandra Sen-Gupta (Calcutta: Cherry Press, 1905), xi. I refer to this translation unless otherwise indicated. Unfortunately, the only currently available English translation of *Anandamath*, trans. Basanta Coomar Roy (New Delhi: Vision Books, 1992), is clearly the least faithful, as it omits some key passages, including the encounter with the *mahāpuruṣa*. See also Das, *Artist in Chains*, 142.

20. This is an interesting twist quoted from the otherwise corrupt Basanta Coomar Roy translation.

21. For Aurobindo's evocative translations of the scene in the temple and of the "Bande Mataram" song, see *Translations from Sanskrit and Other Languages*, Birth Centenary Library (Pondicherry: Sri Aurobindo Ashram Trust, 1972), 8:307–14, 343–46. For a discussion of the gendered aspects of *Anandamath*, see

Sangeeta Ray, *En-Gendering India: Woman and Nation in Colonial and Postcolonial Narratives* (Durham, NC: Duke University Press, 2000), 39–48.

22. Sudipta Kaviraj, *The Unhappy Consciousness: Bankimchandra Chattopadhyay and the Formation of Nationalist Discourse in India* (Delhi: Oxford University Press, 1995), 140, 141.

23. Kaviraj, *The Unhappy Consciousness*, 133.

24. In the prefatory note to the third edition, Bankim adds, "the name of Major Wood has been used in the place of Captain Edward[e]s" (*Abbey of Bliss*, xi).

25. Meenakshi Mukherjee, *Realism and Reality: The Novel and Society in India* (Delhi: Oxford University Press, 1985), 10. See especially Priya Joshi, *In Another Country: Colonialism, Culture, and the English Novel in India* (New York: Columbia University Press, 2002), 74–87.

26. Bankim, *Abbey of Bliss*, 199. Aurobindo's brother Barindrakumar Ghose renders the key phrase as follows: "[T]he English are past masters in the knowledge pertaining to the material world. They are adepts in the art of teaching. So we shall make the British our rulers. Through English education, our people attaining knowledge of the material world will also be made capable of understanding inner knowledge." See Bankimchandra Chatterjee, *Anandamath*, trans. Aurobindo Ghose and Barindra Kumar Ghosh (Calcutta: Basumati Sahitya Mandir, 1909), 192.

27. Bankim, *Abbey of Bliss*, 200–201.

28. Rajnarayan Basu, "Then and Now" (1874), quoted in Roselli, "Self-Image of Effeteness," 124; Chatterjee, *Nationalist Thought*, 65.

29. J. N. Samaddar, *The Creed of Bankim Chandra* (Calcutta: Kuntaline Press, 1922).

30. For instance, Nirad Chaudhuri suggests that the contradiction arises from Bankim's confusion regarding the role of the British. Priya Joshi has ingeniously argued that Chaudhuri's reading is itself a subterfuge, as it is on page 420 of his text (420 being the section number of the Indian Penal Code drafted under the aegis of Lord Macaulay to deal with fraud). See Nirad C. Chaudhuri, *Autobiography of an Unknown Indian* (New York: Addison Wesley, 1989), 420; Joshi, *In Another Country*, 288n.41.

31. Chatterjee, *Nationalist Thought*, 36–53; and also his *Nation and Its Fragments*.

32. See Bankim Chandra Chatterji, *Sociological Essays: Utilitarianism and Positivism in Bengal* (Calcutta: Ṛddhi, 1986), 60–70, 70.

33. Tanika Sarkar, "Bankimchandra and the Impossibility of a Political Agenda," in *On India: Writing, History, Culture, Post-Coloniality*, ed. Suvir Kaul and Ania Loomba, special issue of *Oxford Literary Review* 16, nos. 1–2 (1994): 195.

34. Wakankar, "Body, Crowd, Identity," 46.

35. Kaviraj, *Unhappy Consciousness*, 91, 106.

36. Sarkar, "Bankimchandra," 195. Priya Joshi suggests that in genre terms, the use of the swami or mahatma figure in Bankim's later novels helps transform the indigenous novel form into "an encyclopedic compendium of narrative modes with epic, history, and fiction coexisting in powerful synergy." See Joshi, *In Another Country*, 168.

37. To quote one critic about the terrain covered by Bankim's neo-Hindu doctrinal synthesis: "In this meeting-ground of incongruities, here held up in perspective, one recognizes Pantheism and Agnosticism, Positivism and Asceticism, Renunciation and Ritualism, Gnosticism and Justification by Faith, the Gospels of Work and Prayer, Church Authority and Individual Judgment, Free Will and Fate, Progress and Order, Spiritual Worship and *Avatarism*, Historic Religion and Evolution, Hindu Nationalism and cosmic Propagandism, the Material Civilization of the West and the Spiritual Renunciation of the East." See Brajendranath Seal, "Neo-Hinduism," in *Bankimchandra Chatterjee: Essays in Perspective*, ed. Bhabatosh Chatterji (New Delhi: Sahitya Akademi, 1994), 86.

38. Gyan Prakash, *Another Reason: Science and the Imagination of Modern India* (Princeton, NJ: Princeton University Press, 1999), 89, 202.

39. Pandita Guru Datta Vidyarthi, *Wisdom of the Rishis* (Lahore: Arya Pusthakalaya, 1930), 6. The brilliant Vidyarthi died of consumption at the age of twenty-six in 1890.

40. Young, *Speeches by Lord Macaulay*, 359.

41. Sinha, *Colonial Masculinity*, 7.

42. A wonderful exception is Mandakini Dubey's dissertation, *Orientalism and Esotericism* (Ph.D. diss., Duke University, 2003).

43. Rudyard Kipling, *Kim* (New York: Penguin, 1987), 53. All further references to the novel will be to this edition, with page numbers parenthetically cited.

44. I thank Gayatri Chakravorty Spivak for alerting me to this ambiguity, especially in Bengali.

45. Edward Said, "Introduction," in Kipling, *Kim*, 15. In this regard, Mark Kinkead-Weekes's elegant reading of the lama as "an anti-self so powerful that it became a touchstone for everything else" is an earlier formulation that also runs the danger of dissolving the specificity of his Guru English back into a generalized aesthetic framework for the novel. Mark Kinkead-Weekes, "Vision in Kipling's Novels," *Kipling's Mind and Art*, ed. Andrew Rutherford (Stanford, CA: Stanford University Press, 1964). Cited in Said, 21–22.

46. S. P. Mohanty, "Kipling's Children and the Colour Line," *Race and Class* 31, no. 1 (July–September 1989); Sara Suleri, *The Rhetoric of English India* (Chicago: University of Chicago Press, 1992), 111–31; Thomas Richards, *The Imperial Archive: Knowledge and the Fantasy of Empire* (New York: Verso, 1993); see also the criticism collected in the recent Norton Critical Edition of *Kim*, ed. Zohreh T. Sullivan (New York: W. W. Norton, 2002).

47. Kipling, *Kim*, 337. Said says of this passage that it involves "some mumbo jumbo" but that "it shouldn't all be dismissed" (19). However, he also acknowledges that "the lama's encyclopedic vision of freedom strikingly resembles Colonel Creighton's Indian Survey" (19).

48. Suleri, *Rhetoric of English India*, 130. Suleri also overstates the case when she suggests that the novel depicts "the Anglicists clearly winning over the Orientalism that the lama represents" (128).

49. Richards, *Imperial Archive*, 12, 22, 26, 30.

50. See Derek Waller, *The Pundits: British Exploration of Tibet and Central Asia*

(Lexington: University Press of Kentucky, 1990); and for another reading of *Kim* along these lines, Ian Baucom, *Out of Place: Englishness, Empire and the Locations of Identity* (Princeton, NJ: Princeton University Press, 1999), 93–99.

51. For some of the assertions made in the previous sentences, I rely on the magisterial study by C. A. Bayly, *Empire and Information: Intelligence Gathering and Social Information in India, 1780–1870* (Cambridge: Cambridge University Press, 1996), ix, 7. See also Manuel Castells, *The Information Age: Economy, Society, Culture*, 3 vols., (Oxford: Blackwell Publishers, 1996–98).

52. This apparent lack of nationalism among the natives in *Kim* is also remarked upon by John A. McClure, *Kipling and Conrad: The Colonial Fiction* (Cambridge, MA: Harvard University Press, 1981), 79–80.

53. See Philip C. Almond, *The British Discovery of Buddhism* (Cambridge: Cambridge University Press, 1988); Stephen Batchelor, *The Awakening of the West: The Encounter of Buddhism and Western Culture* (Berkeley, CA: Parallax Press, 1994); and, for a heroic account of British derring-do in this regard, Charles Allen, *The Buddha and the Sahibs: The Men Who Discovered India's Lost Religion* (London: John Murray, 2002).

54. See King, *Orientalism and Religion*, chap. 7.

55. For the notion of intercultural mimesis in relation to the modernization of Theravada in Sri Lanka, see Charles Hallisey, "Roads Taken and Not Taken in the Study of Theravāda Buddhism," in *Curators of the Buddha: The Study of Buddhism under Colonialism*, ed. Donald S. Lopez, Jr. (Chicago: University of Chicago Press, 1995), 31–61; and Gananath Obeyesekere, "Religious Symbolism and Political Change in Ceylon," in Gananath Obeyesekere, Frank Reynolds, and Bardwell L. Smith, *Two Wheels of Dhamma: Essays on the Theravada Tradition in India and Ceylon* (Chambersburg, PA: American Academy of Religion, 1972), 58–78. For specific accounts concerning the "discovery" and textualization of Tibetan Buddhism, see Peter Bishop, *The Myth of Shangri-La: Tibet, Travel Writing and the Western Creation of Sacred Landscape* (Berkeley: University of California Press, 1989); Bishop, *Dreams of Power: Tibetan Buddhism and the Western Imagination* (London: Athlone Press, 1993); Donald S. Lopez, Jr., *Prisoners of Shangri-La: Tibetan Buddhism and the West* (Chicago: University of Chicago Press, 1998); and Charles S. Prebish and Martin Baumann, eds., *Westward Dharma: Buddhism beyond Asia* (Berkeley: University of California Press, 2002).

56. Of course, there is also the possibility that the lama was based on a historical individual who visited Kipling's father in Lahore. This monk was from Tso-chen, a Red Hat monastery 450 miles east of Simla and 200 miles north of Kathmandu (which Kipling renders as "Such-zen"). See Peter Hopkirk, *Quest for Kim: In Search of Kipling's Great Game* (London: John Murray, 1996), 41–42.

57. See J.M.S. Tompkins, "Foreword," in Shamsul Islam, *Kipling's "Law": A Study of His Philosophy of Life* (New York: St. Martin's Press, 1975). In a full-length reading of the trope of law in Kipling's oeuvre, Islam identifies three broad areas of Kipling's "law": moral (religious) values, the Imperial Idea, and the ethics of disinterested suffering and positive action.

58. L. Austine Waddell, *The Buddhism of Tibet or Lamaism: With Its Mystic Cults, Symbolism and Mythology, and in Its Relation to Indian Buddhism* (Cambridge: W. Heffer and Sons, 1958), 30.

59. See Allen, "The Search for Buddha's Birthplace," in *The Buddha and the Sahibs*, 256–79.

60. Stanley K. Abe suggests that the fact that the pen-case is Chinese is indication that the Curator is assessing the lama's value as greater than that of any other Tibetan monk. To my knowledge, Abe is the only scholar who has noted the crucial significance of the exchange of the pen-case for the spectacles. Abe's assertion that the "Curator's gifts, modern and utilitarian" are exchanged for "a barren artifact of the past, valuable only through the special training and mediation of the Curator," can be supplemented with the notion that a neoreligious metaphysical subjectivity is also being generated through this exchange. See Stanley K. Abe, "Inside the Wonder House: Buddhist Art and the West," in *Curators of the Buddha: The Study of Buddhism under Colonialism*, ed. Donald S. Lopez, Jr. (Chicago: University of Chicago Press, 1995), especially 64–69.

61. David Bromwich, "Kipling's Jest," *Grand Street* (Winter 1985): 175.

62. See Parama Roy, *Indian Traffic: Identities in Question in Colonial and Postcolonial India* (Berkeley: University of California Press, 1998), 90.

63. Rudyard Kipling, "The Miracle of Purun Bhagat," in *The Best Short Stories of Rudyard Kipling*, ed. Randall Jarrell (New York: Doubleday, 1961), 278.

64. Kipling, "Miracle of Purun Bhagat," 287.

65. Rudyard Kipling, "The Incarnation of Krishna Mulvaney," and "The Mark of the Beast," in *Life's Handicap: Being Stories of Mine Own People* (London: Macmillan, 1891), 1–32, 208–24.

66. Kipling, "The Sending of Dana Da," in *The Collected Works of Rudyard Kipling* (New York: Doubleday, Doran, 1941), 2:289–300.

67. Kipling, "The Sending of Dana Da," 2:289–90.

68. Kipling, "The Sending of Dana Da," 2:299–300.

69. Kipling, "The Sending of Dana Da," 2:300.

70. Swami Shivgan Chand, *The Divine Wisdom of the Indian Rishis* (Lahore: Oriental Press, 1894), 22, 7.

71. Chand, *Divine Wisdom*, 12.

72. Matilal Das, *Bankim Chandra, Prophet of the Indian Renaissance: His Life and Art* (Calcutta: D. M. Library, 1938), 56, 62–63.

73. I take this useful heuristic classification of orientalist styles from Peter Heehs, "Shades of Orientalism: Paradoxes and Problems in Indian Historiography," *History and Theory* 42 (May 2003): 169–95. In addition to the three colonial styles already mentioned, Heehs identifies three postcolonial styles of orientalism, including "critical," "reductive," and "reactionary."

74. See Gayatri Chakravorty Spivak, "Resident Alien," in *Relocating Postcolonialism*, ed. David Theo Goldberg and Ato Quayson (Oxford: Blackwell, 2002), 58; and Meenakshi Mukherjee, Introduction to Rabindranath Tagore, *Gora*, trans. Sujit Mukherjee (New Delhi: Sahitya Akademi, 1998), ix–xxiv.

75. Ashis Nandy, *The Intimate Enemy: Loss and Recovery of Self under Colonialism* (Delhi: Oxford University Press, 1983), 97.

76. Sri Aurobindo, *On Himself Compiled from Notes and Letters*, Birth Centenary Library (Pondicherry: Sri Aurobindo Ashram Trust, 1972), 26:1. All quotations and references to Aurobindo's writings are from this thirty-volume Birth Centenary Library edition, by volume and page number, unless cited otherwise.

77. I inflect some of these terms with interpretations derived from Michael Löwy and Robert Sayre's helpful typology of Romanticism into six broad categories: (1) restitutionist, (2) conservative, (3) fascistic, (4) resigned, (5) reformist, and (6) revolutionary/utopian. They further divide revolutionary/utopian into five sub categories: (1) Jacobin-democratic, (2) populist, (3) utopian-humanist socialist, (4) libertarian, and (5) Marxist. See Michael Löwy and Robert Sayre, *Romanticism against the Tide of Modernity*, trans. Catherine Porter (Durham, NC: Duke University Press, 2001), 57–87.

78. Aurobindo, *"Bande Mataram": Early Political Writings*, 1:65, 51; ibid., 1:73, 74; letter to Barindra cited in Peter Heehs, *Sri Aurobindo: A Brief Biography* (Delhi: Oxford University Press, 1989), 132.

79. K. R. Srinivasa Iyengar, *Sri Aurobindo: A Biography and a History*, 2 vols. (Pondicherry: Aurobindo Ashram Trust, 1972), 1:26.

80. Aurobindo, *Karmayogin: Early Political Writings*, 2:11, 19.

81. Iyengar, *Aurobindo*, 1:328.

82. Aurobindo, "Uttarpara Speech," in *Karmayogin: Early Political Writings*, 2:4.

83. Aurobindo, *On Himself*, 26:57.

84. James H. Cousins, *The Kingdom of Youth: Essays towards National Education* (Madras: Ganesh, 1917), 45.

85. Cited in Iyengar, *Aurobindo*, 1:424.

86. Heehs, *Sri Aurobindo*, 48.

87. Aurobindo, "The Life of Nationalism," in *On Nationalism, First Series* (Pondicherry: Sri Aurobindo Ashram, 1965), 39.

88. Sri Aurobindo, *The Human Cycle in Social and Political Thought*, vol. 15; for the letter to Barindra, see Heehs, *Sri Aurobindo*, 134.

89. Nandy, *Intimate Enemy*, 97, 85.

90. Nandy's book is itself caught up in the dubious project of justifying an alternative cultural universalism with an Indian origin that somehow goes beyond the psychic damage created by colonialism. Even though Nandy attempts to separate his notion of culture from religious essentialism, this universalism in his treatment is ultimately one that updates Gandhi's synthesis of Hindu Brahmanical tendencies with a Christian ethics of martyrdom and self-sacrifice.

91. Nandy, *Intimate Enemy*, 83. Similarly, Nandy is not entirely persuasive when he suggests that Kipling saw India only in terms of Kshatriyahood. While martial values are clearly of great importance within Kipling's imperialist ethics, it would be more accurate to suggest that Kipling perceives Indian religions (with Brahmanism being one strain within this vast spectrum) as esoteric oddities that he occasionally incorporates but cannot quite fully define. The residual orientalism in Kipling makes him overvalue the highly elaborated religious character of India and at the same time dismiss what he sees as its irrational effects.

92. See Aurobindo, *Collected Poems: The Complete Poetical Works*, and *Collected Plays and Short Stories: Parts One and Two*, vols. 5, 6, 7.

93. Aurobindo, *On Quantitative Metre*, 5:339–87.

94. Aurobindo, *"Poems in New Metres" and "Metrical Experiments,"* 5:582.

95. Aurobindo, *On Himself*, 26:229; Aurobindo, *Savitri: A Legend and a Symbol*, vols. 27 and 28.

96. Aurobindo, *Savitri*, 27:preface.

97. Aurobindo, *Savitri*, 28:138.

98. Aurobindo, *Savitri*, 27:1.

99. Aurobindo, *Savitri*, 29:724. For full-length expositions of *Savitri*, see *Aurobindo's Letters on Savitri*, 29:725–816; Iyengar, *Aurobindo*; A. B. Purani, *Sri Aurobindo's* Savitri: *An Approach and a Study* (Pondicherry: Sri Aurobindo Ashram Trust, 1956); Prema Nandakumar, *A Study of* Savitri (Pondicherry: Sri Aurobindo Ashram, 1962); Nandakumar, *Dante and Sri Aurobindo: A Comparative Study of* The Divine Comedy *and* Savitri (Madras: Affiliated East-West Press, 1981); K. D. Sethna, *The Poetic Genius of Aurobindo* (Pondicherry: Sri Aurobindo Ashram Trust, 1974); V. Madhusudan Reddy, Savitri: *Epic of the Eternal* (Hyderabad: Aurodarshan Trust, 1984); R. K. Singh, Savitri: *A Spiritual Epic* (Bareilly: Prakash Book Depot, 1984); and D. S. Mishra, *Poetry and Philosophy in Sri Aurobindo's* Savitri (New Delhi: Harman Publishing House, 1989).

100. See Stephen H. Phillips, "*Savitri* and Aurobindo's Criterion of 'Spiritual Objectivity,'" *Journal of South Asian Literature* 24, no. 1 (Winter–Spring 1989): 37–49.

101. Aurobindo, *Savitri*, 28:22.

102. "We in India, or at any rate those races among us which are in the vanguard of every forward movement, are far more nearly allied to the French and Athenian than to the Anglo-Saxon, but owing to the accident of British domination, our intellects have been carefully nurtured on a purely English diet." See Aurobindo, "New Lamps for Old-5," (*Indu Prakash*, October 30, 1893) in *"Bande Mataram": Early Political Writings*, 1:32.

103. Aurobindo, *On Himself*, 26:69, 245, 393, 403. The five levels are inanimate matter, life, consciousness, overmind, and supermind.

104. See Nicholas Goodrick-Clarke, *Hitler's Priestess: Savitri Devi, the Hindu-Aryan Myth, and Neo-Nazism* (New York: New York University Press, 1998); and Savitri Devi Mukherjee, *The Lightning and the Sun* (Calcutta: Savitri Devi Mukherjee, 1958).

105. James H. Cousins, *New Ways in English Literature* (Madras: Ganesh, 1917), 27, 15.

106. Sri Aurobindo, *The Future Poetry and Letters on Poetry, Literature and Art*, 9:8. See also, Dilip Kumar Chatterjee, "Cousins and Sri Aurobindo: A Study in Literary Influence," *Journal of South Asian Literature* 24, no. 1 (Winter–Spring 1989): 114–23.

107. Aurobindo, *Future Poetry*, 9:42.

108. Aurobindo, "The New Mantra" (August 22, 1920), in *Karmayogin: Early Political Writings*, 2:431.

109. See K. D. Verma, "Observations," in *Sri Aurobindo*, a special issue of *Journal of South Asian Literature* 24, no. 1 (Winter–Spring 1989): 1–9.

110. Aurobindo, *The Future Poetry*, 9:126.

111. Aurobindo, *The Future Poetry*, 9:203.

112. Aurobindo, *The Future Poetry*, 9:279, 281, 288.

CHAPTER THREE
THEOSOPHISTRIES

1. Gauri Viswanathan, *Outside the Fold: Conversion, Modernity, and Belief* (Princeton, NJ: Princeton University Press, 1998), 177–207; Gauri Viswanathan, "The Ordinary Business of Occultism," *Critical Inquiry* 27 (Fall 2000): 1–20. The coinage *theosophistry* can be found in Edmund Garrett, *Isis Very Much Unveiled, Being the Story of the Great Mahatma Hoax* (London: Westminster Gazette Office, n.d.). It is my intention to use this term not just pejoratively (as does Garrett) but as shorthand for Theosophy's linguistic potential and literary outreach.

2. Hent de Vries, *Philosophy and the Turn to Religion* (Baltimore: Johns Hopkins University Press, 1999), 11.

3. See John Algeo, *Blavatsky, Freemasonry, and the Western Mystery Tradition* (London: Theosophical Society, 1996).

4. J. N. Farquhar, *Modern Religious Movements in India* (New York: Macmillan, 1915), 224.

5. For a full-fledged account of Theosophy's transition from Western Gnosticism to Indian philosophy, see Joscelyn Godwin, *The Theosophical Enlightenment* (Albany: State University of New York Press, 1994).

6. See Christmas Humphreys and Elsie Benjamin, eds., *The Mahatma Letters to A. P. Sinnett*, 3rd ed., comp. A. T. Barker (Adyar: Theosophical Publishing House, 1962), 1, 4, 22; C. Jinarajadasa, ed., *Early Teachings of the Masters, 1881–1883* (Adyar: Theosophical Publishing House, 1923).

7. See also Geoffrey A. Barborka, *The Mahatmas and Their Letters* (Adyar: Theosophical Publishing House, 1973); George E. Linton and Virginia Hanson, *Reader's Guide to the Mahatma Letters to A. P. Sinnett* (Adyar: Theosophical Publishing House, 1972); Margaret Conger, *Combined Chronology for Use with the Mahatma Letters to A. P. Sinnett and the Letters of H. P. Blavatsky to A. P. Sinnett* (Pasadena, CA: Theosophical University Press, 1973); Mary K. Neff, *The "Brothers" of Madame Blavatsky* (Adyar: Theosophical Publishing House, 1932); and John Algeo, *Senzar: The Mystery of the Mystery Language* (London: Theosophical History Center, 1988).

8. Richard Hodgson, "Report of the Committee Appointed to Investigate Phenomena Connected with the Theosophical Society," *Proceedings of the Society for Psychical Research* 3 (1885): 201–400; Hodgson, "The Defence of the Theosophists," *Proceedings of the Society for Psychical Research* 9 (1894): 129–59.

9. See for instance, K. R. Sitaraman, *Isis Further Unveiled* (Madras: Addison, 1894). For a definitive refutation of *The Mahatma Letters*, see Harold Edward Hare and William Loftus Hare, *Who Wrote the Mahatma Letters?* (London: Williams and Norgate, 1936). For a defense, see H.R.W. Cox, *Who Wrote the March-Hare Attack on the Mahatma Letters?* (Victoria, BC: H. P. Blavatsky Library, n.d.).

10. *Mahatma Letters*, 4.

11. K. Paul Johnson, *The Masters Revealed: Madame Blavatsky and the Myth of the Great White Lodge* (Albany: State University of New York Press, 1994), 116–75; an earlier version was published as *In Search of the Masters: Behind the Occult Myth* (South Boston, VA: Hedderly Benton, 1990).

12. Vernon Harrison, *H. P. Blavatsky and the SPR: An Examination of the Hodgson Report of 1885* (Pasadena, CA: Theosophical University Press, 1997). See also British Library, Additional Manuscripts 45284, 45285, 45286.

13. *Mahatma Letters*, 22, 23; *The Secret Doctrine: The Synthesis of Science, Religion, and Philosophy* (London: The Theosophical Publishing Company, 1888), 1.579.

14. For this argument about the miracle and the special effect, I rely on the discussion by Hent de Vries, "In Media Res: Global Religion, Public Spheres, and the Task of Contemporary Comparative Religious Studies," in *Religion and Media*, ed. Hent de Vries and Samuel Weber (Stanford, CA: Stanford University Press, 2001), 23.

15. Geoffrey Barborka, *The Peopling of the Earth: A Commentary on Archaic Records in "The Secret Doctrine"* (Wheaton, IL: Theosophical Publishing House, 1975).

16. Godwin, *Theosophical Enlightenment*, 319.

17. For a succinct exposition of the racial categories, see Carla Risseuw, "Thinking Culture through Counter-Culture: The Case of Theosophists in India and Ceylon and Their Ideas on Race and Hierarchy," in *Gurus and Their Followers: New Religious Reform Movements in Colonial India*, ed. Antony Copley (Oxford and Delhi: Oxford University Press, 2000), 180–205, 199. The quote about the Teutons is from Annie Besant's exposition of HPB in *The Pedigree of Man* (Adyar: Theosophical Publishing House, 1905), 151.

18. Viswanathan, *Outside the Fold*, 205.

19. For a sense of the vast literature spawned around Theosophy, see Michael Gomes, *Theosophy in the Nineteenth Century: An Annotated Bibliography* (New York: Garland Press, 1994).

20. See J. Krishnamurti, *The First and Last Freedom*, foreword by Aldous Huxley (London: Victor Gollancz, 1954); J. Krishnamurti, *Krishnamurti's Journal* (London: Victor Gollancz, 1982); J. Krishnamurti, *Krishnamurti on Education* (New Delhi: Orient Longman, 1974); J. Krishnamurti, *Commentaries on Living*, 1st, 2nd and 3rd ser., ed. D. Rajagopal (London: Victor Gollancz, 1956, 1958, 1960); J. Krishnamurti, *Truth and Actuality* (San Francisco: Harper and Row, 1978); Mary Lutyens, *The Years of Awakening* (London: J. Murray, 1975); Pupul Jayakar, *Krishnamurti: A Biography* (San Francisco: Harper and Row, 1986); and Radha Rajagopal Sloss, *Lives in the Shadow with J. Krishnamurti* (Reading, MA: Addison-Wesley, 1991).

21. Krishnamurti, *Commentaries on Living*, 1st ser., 23; Krishnamurti, *Truth and Actuality*, 87–88.

22. Fernando Ortiz, *Cuban Counterpoint: Tobacco and Sugar*, trans. Harriet de Onis (New York: Knopf, 1947), 102–3.

23. "We, therefore, need a new literary and cultural internationalism which involves risks and dangers, which calls us into question fully as much as it acknowledges the Other, thereby also serving as a more adequate and chastening form of self-knowledge. This 'internationalism of the national situations' neither reduces the 'Third World' to some homogeneous Other of the West, nor does it vacuously celebrate the 'astonishing' pluralism of human cultures; rather, by isolating the common *situation* (capitalism, imperialism, colonialism)

shared by very different kinds of societies, it allows their differences to be measured against each other as well as against ourselves." See Fredric Jameson, foreword to *Caliban and Other Essays*, by Roberto Fernandez Retamar, trans. Edward Baker (Minneapolis: University of Minnesota Press, 1989), xi–xii.

24. James Joyce, *Ulysses: The Corrected Text*, ed. Hans Walter Gabler with Wolthard Steppe and Claus Melchior (New York: Vintage, 1986), 7.783–87. All further references are to chapter and line numbers in this edition.

25. Ernest Boyd, *Ireland's Literary Renaissance* (New York: Knopf, 1922), 214–15. See also Standish O'Grady, *History of Ireland*, 2 vols. (New York: Lemma, 1970); and the recently published book by Joseph Allen, *Irish Orientalism: A Literary and Intellectual History* (Syracuse, NY: Syracuse University Press, 2004).

26. I disagree here with Richard Kearney, who overstates the case when he says that Joyce "treats myth as an agency for iconoclasm rather than conformism, of difference rather than integration, of subversion rather than restoration." I think Joyce's use of myth is far more ambivalent than Kearney suggests. See Richard Kearney, "Utopian and Ideological Myths in Joyce," *James Joyce Quarterly* 28, no. 4 (1991): 873. For a fuller account of the references to Theosophy, see Stuart Gilbert, *James Joyce's* Ulysses (New York: Vintage, 1955), 41–50; Thornton Weldon, *Allusions in* Ulysses (Chapel Hill: University of North Carolina Press, 1968); and Don Gifford, Ulysses *Annotated* (Berkeley University of California Press, 1988).

27. See James McMichael, *"Ulysses" and Justice* (Princeton, NJ: Princeton University Press, 1991), 10. Blavatsky defines *ākāśa* as "a vast repository where the records of every man's life as well as every pulsation of the visible Cosmos are stored up for all Eternity." See H. P. Blavatsky, *Isis Unveiled* (Pasadena, CA: Theosophical University Press, 1972), 179. Slightly later in the episode, Stephen will repeat the phrase "Akasic records" (7.928).

28. Blavatsky, *The Secret Doctrine*, 1.104.

29. Karen Lawrence, *The Odyssey of Style in* Ulysses (Princeton, NJ: Princeton University Press, 1981), 67.

30. In 1885, Richard Hodgson's report for the Society for Psychical Research denounced Blavatsky, as discussed earlier. See Peter Washington, *Madame Blavatsky's Baboon: Theosophy and the Emergence of the Western Guru* (London: Secker and Warburg, 1993), 83. The Society for Psychical Research included noted members such as Gladstone, Ruskin, Tennyson, Balfour, and William James. See also A. Gauld, *The Founders of Psychical Research* (London: Routledge and Kegan Paul, 1968).

31. See, for instance, Vivian Mercier, "John Eglinton as Socrates: A Study of 'Scylla and Charybdis,'" in *James Joyce: An International Perspective*, ed. Suheil Badi Bushrui and Bernard Benstock (Totowa, NJ: Barnes and Noble, 1982), 65–81.

32. See Arthur H. Nethercot, *The First Five Lives of Annie Besant* (Chicago: University of Chicago Press, 1960), 183–200.

33. See Michael Seidel, *Epic Geography: James Joyce's* Ulysses (Princeton, NJ: Princeton University Press, 1976), 61.

34. See Anne Taylor, *Annie Besant: A Biography* (New York: Oxford University Press, 1992), 248.

35. So, Joyce's rendering of Irish cultural politics resembles Partha Chatterjee's recent depiction of Indian anticolonial nationalism that has already been discussed in earlier chapters. Partha Chatterjee, *The Nation and Its Fragments: Colonial and Postcolonial Histories* (Princeton, NJ: Princeton University Press, 1993).

36. I use *parasitical* in the complex sense that Michel Serres has defined it, indicating a digressive, supplementary, and cacophonic structure to the harmonic notion of organic unity. See Michel Serres, *The Parasite*, trans. Lawrence R. Schehr (Baltimore: Johns Hopkins University Press, 1982).

37. W[illiam] B[utler] Yeats, "Occult Notes and Diary, Etc.," transcription of copy-book journal dated October 1889, referenced as National Library of Ireland Manuscript 13570; published as appendix A in *W. B. Yeats, Memoirs: Autobiography, First Draft, Journal*, transcribed and ed. Denis Donoghue (London: Macmillan, 1972), 281; see also Harbans Rai Bachchan, *W. B. Yeats and Occultism* (London: Books from India, 1976).

38. See Julia Wasserman, "'All the Butter to Worship You with My Dear': Hindu Sexual Language and Ritual in *Ulysses*," *Publications of the Arkansas Philological Association* 3, no. 2 (1977): 53–59.

39. See Sylvester Tomkyns, Jr., *The Ghost-Mystery at Knotty Ash, Liverpool! Or The Mysterious Midnight Funeral!* (London, 1891). References to mystical chanting can be found in Æ's *The Candle of Vision* (London: Macmillan, 1918), and his three-act verse play *Deirdre* (performed 1902, published 1907), that features Mananaun MacLir, also referred to in *Ulysses*, 9.191. For the spiritual androgyny, see also Don Gifford's note for the reference to "new paganism" (1.176) that glosses William Sharp's short-lived *Pagan Review* and its promotion of "co-partnery" and "sexual emotion." Gifford, *"Ulysses" Annotated*, 17.

40. At the same time, it should be remembered that the young Joyce was not unsusceptible to the influences of Theosophy from literary mentors such as Yeats, Æ and Lady Gregory. Ellmann writes of the late night visit that Joyce paid Æ: "Joyce finally said shyly what he had prepared as part of his bold offensive in advance, that he thought it possible that an avatar might be born in Ireland. He may have been referring to himself but his implication, as Russell understood it, was that the sight of his host comfortably smoking his pipe in an armchair had made Joyce think that the avatar was not in front of him. He remained, nevertheless, for hours, talking." See Richard Ellmann, *James Joyce* (New York: Oxford University Press, 1959; rev. ed., 1983), 102–3.

41. See Homi Bhabha, "Articulating the Archaic," in *Literary Theory Today*, ed. Peter Collier and Helga Geyer-Ryan (Ithaca, NY: Cornell University Press, 1990), 206.

42. Theosophical doctrine located the astral soul at the *omphalos*. For an exposition of the Joycean pun of *omphalos/om-phallus*, see Julian Wasserman, "James Joyce and the Left Hand of God: Hinduism in Ulysses," *Ball State University Forum* 27, no. 3 (1986): 56.

43. G. V. Desani, *All about H. Hatterr*, introduction by Anthony Burgess (New York: McPherson, 1986), 27; see also *All about H. Hatterr: A Gesture* (New York: Farrar, Straus, and Young, 1951; reissued as *All about H. Hatterr*, 1970). All further

references are to page numbers in the 1986 McPherson edition and are cited parenthetically in the text. First published in 1948, the novel's "Joycean" sensibility was especially recognized by reviewers. Desani also received lavish praise from T. S. Eliot and E. M. Forster. The 1970 reissue was called "a new and Oriental H. C. Earwicker" by the *Statesman* of Calcutta, and "a hotch-pot of *Panchatantra, Kamasutra,* and Joyce" by the *Indian Review* in Madras. American reviews concurred. The *Washington Post* had a full-page complimentary review, and *Newsweek* placed Desani's use of English as lying "somewhere between that of such disparate experimentalists as Joyce and Danny Kaye," especially drawing attention to "the calculated mishandling of French, German, Spanish, Russian, plus serenely witty baboo." And to round things off, the *Nation* said, "[O]ne might think of this guffawing Indian as a lunatic hybrid by S. J. Perelman out of James Joyce. Incredible profusion—puns in half a dozen languages." I rely on the following articles for some of this information. See D. M. Burjonjee, "The Dialogue in G. V. Desani's *All about H. Hatterr,"* *World Literature Written in English* 13, no. 2 (1974): 191–224; S. C. Harrex, "G. V. Desani: Mad Hatterr Sage," *Miscellany* 92 (1979): 11–48; M. K. Naik, "The Method in the Madness: All about *All about H. Hatterr,"* in *Studies in Indian English Literature* (New Delhi: Sterling, 1987), 1–33; Dieter Riemenschneider, "G. V. Desani's *All about H. Hatterr* and the Problem of Cultural Alienation," *Literary Criterion* 20, no. 2 (1985): 23–35.

44. Richard Ellmann, *The Consciousness of Joyce* (New York: Oxford University Press, 1977), 93.

45. Colin MacCabe, *"Finnegans Wake* at Fifty," *Critical Quarterly* 31, no. 4 (1989): 4.

46. Jack Vespa, "Another Book at the Wake: Indian Mysticism and the *Bhagavad-Gita* in 1.4 of *Finnegans Wake,"* *James Joyce Quarterly* 31, no. 2 (1994): 81–87.

47. J. Krishnamurti, *Commentaries on Living,* 1st ser., 116–17.

48. This has nonetheless been a theme in recent criticism of *Ulysses* that takes its Irish contexts seriously, unlike humanist applications of it in terms of generalized European allegory. For instance, a generally perspicacious critic, such as Franco Moretti, unfairly dismisses the Irishness of the novel as a provincial distraction: "if Joyce were an Irish writer comprehensible and containable without any loose threads within Irish culture he would no longer be Joyce; if the city of *Ulysses* were the real Dublin of the turn of the century, it would not be the literary image par excellence of the modern metropolis. . . . *Ulysses* fully belongs to a critical turning point of international bourgeois culture—a status it would not have achieved in the investigation of Ireland's peripheral and backward form of capitalism." Forcing a choice between cultural particularism and cosmopolitan generalism in Joyce studies, Moretti's bizarre exclusion of the "peripheral" indicates a symptomatic continuation of the initial problem of syncretism as it was posed within *Ulysses,* but for that matter, not adequately. See Franco Moretti, "The Long Goodbye: *Ulysses* and the End of Liberal Capitalism," in *Signs Taken for Wonders: Essays in the Sociology of Literary Forms,* trans. and ed. Susan Fischer, David Forgacs, and David Miller (New York: Verso, 1983; rev. ed., 1988), 189–90.

49. David Lloyd, *Anomalous States: Irish Writing and the Post-Colonial Moment* (Durham, NC: Duke University Press, 1993), 110.

50. See Washington, *Madame Blavatsky's Baboon*, 44–45. Blavatsky got rid of her baboon by the time she was entertaining in London in the 1880s.

51. See Declan Kiberd, *Inventing Ireland: The Literature of the Modern Nation* (Cambridge, MA: Harvard University Press, 1995), 253.

52. See Gilbert, *James Joyce's Ulysses*.

53. See Christine Froula, "History's Nightmare, Fiction's Dream: Joyce and the Psychohistory of *Ulysses*," *James Joyce Quarterly* 28, no. 4 (1991): 865.

54. For an exploratory reading of Joyce through Deleuze and Guattari, see Vicki Mahaffey, " 'Minxing Marrage and Making Loof ': Anti-Oedipal Reading," *James Joyce Quarterly* 30, no. 2 (1993): 219–37.

55. Salman Rushdie, *The Moor's Last Sigh* (London: Jonathan Cape, 1995), 20.

56. Rushdie, *The Moor's Last Sigh*, 20.

57. See John Banville, "An Interview with Salman Rushdie," *New York Review of Books*, March 4, 1993, 34–36.

CHAPTER FOUR
THE HINDU SUBLIME, OR NUCLEARISM RENDERED CULTURAL

1. Robert Jay Lifton and Richard Falk, *Indefensible Weapons: The Political and Psychological Case against Nuclearism* (New York: Basic Books, 1982), ix.

2. See Ashis Nandy, "The Epidemic of Nuclearism: Clinical Profile of the Genocidal Mentality," in *The Nuclear Debate: Ironies and Immoralities*, ed. Zia Mian and Ashis Nandy (Colombo, Sri Lanka: Regional Centre for Strategic Studies, 1998), 1; and Piyush Mathur, "Nuclearism: Contours of a Political Ecology," *Social Text* 66 (Spring 2001): 1–18.

3. Ashis Nandy, "Introduction: Science as a Reason of State," in *Science, Hegemony and Violence: A Requiem for Modernity*, ed. Ashis Nandy (Delhi: Oxford University Press, 1988), 8; Nandy, *Alternative Sciences: Creativity and Authenticity in Two Indian Scientists* (Delhi: Allied Publishers, 1978), 11.

4. See Jonathan Schell, *The Unfinished Twentieth Century* (New York: Verso, 2001), 72–73.

5. Jacques Derrida, "No Apocalypse, Not Now (full speed ahead, seven missiles, seven missives)," *Diacritics* 14, no. 2 (1984): 24.

6. For those interested in informing themselves about these larger goals, they can be best accomplished by reading Praful Bidwai and Achin Vanaik's *New Nukes: India, Pakistan and Global Nuclear Disarmament* (New York: Olive Branch Press, 2000). *New Nukes* is a comprehensive and brilliant scholarly manifesto that covers several technical and strategic aspects of South Asian nuclearization and that also offers a full-fledged critique of international relations discourse in relation to the event, something that is beyond the scope and expertise of this chapter.

7. http://www.newscum.org/century/finalresults.htm.

8. James A. Hijiya, "The *Gita* of J. Robert Oppenheimer," *Proceedings of the American Philosophical Society* 144, no. 2 (June 2000): 123. For comparison, this is

Charles Wilkins's translation, the first into any European language: "I am Time, the destroyer of mankind, matured, come hither to seize at once all those who stand before us." Charles Wilkins, *The Bhăgvăt-Gēētā or Dialogues of Krĕĕshnă and Ărjōōn in Eighteen Lectures* (London, 1785), 93.

9. See Lansing Lamont, *Day of Trinity* (London: Hutchinson, 1965), 70.

10. William Laurence, *Men and Atoms* (New York: Simon and Schuster, 1959), 120; see also James A. Aho, "'I Am Death . . . Who Shatters Worlds': The Emerging Nuclear Death Cult," in *A Shuddering Dawn: Religious Studies and the Nuclear Age,* ed. Ira Chernus and Edward Tabor Linenthal (Albany: State University of New York Press, 1989), 49–68.

11. Although, Oppenheimer is also said to have self-deprecatingly remarked later that the best thing anyone said after the test was Kenneth Bainbridge's comment, "[N]ow we are all sons of bitches." See Aho, "'I Am Death . . . Who Shatters Worlds,'" 53.

12. Alexander Piatigorsky, Introduction to *The* Bhagavad Gita, trans. J.A.B. van Buitenen (Rockport, MA: Element, 1997), 19. This passage will be discussed at greater length below.

13. Hijiya, "The *Gita* of Oppenheimer," 125, 126, 129.

14. Paul Strathern, *Oppenheimer and the Bomb* (London: Arrow Books, 1998), 15.

15. A footnote in Hijiya's article is especially revealing of this interpretation of Oppenheimer's Vedanta as a form of personal solipsism: "Besides Oppenheimer's general reluctance to discuss personal motives, there was a particular reason why he might not talk about the Gita—his associates' ignorance of it. Talking to most Western scientists, journalists, or government officials about Hinduism would be like speaking to them in a foreign language. At best they would be bewildered. At worst they would think he was a kook. Under the circumstances, Oppenheimer probably thought it best to keep his philosophy to himself." Hijiya, "The *Gita* of Oppenheimer," 127n.16, 139, 140, 143, 145. Hijiya's attempts to translate Oppenheimer's Hinduism in terms of "duty, fate, and faith" are also inadequate misconceptions.

16. Thomas Weiskel, *The Romantic Sublime* (Baltimore: Johns Hopkins University Press, 1976), 97.

17. Vijay Mishra, *The Gothic Sublime* (Albany: State University of New York Press, 1994), 36.

18. See Lamont, *Day of Trinity,* 176; see also Peter Schwenger, *Letter Bomb: Nuclear Holocaust and the Exploding World* (Baltimore: Johns Hopkins University Press, 1992).

19. Derrida, "No Apocalypse, Not Now," 26.

20. But, as is frequently pointed out, the *Mahābhārata* demonstrates the lowly origins of the Kaurava line. By birth a fisherwoman who smelled of fish (*matsyagandhī*), Satyavati agrees to marry her lovestruck suitor King Santanu only if her progeny can inherit the kingdom, whereupon Santanu's heir-apparent Bhishma renounces both marriage and the throne. When Satyavati's sons Chitrangada and Vichitraveerya die heirless, the epic features the necessary insemination of Vichitraveerya's wives by the sage Vyasa, who was himself the natural son of Satyavati.

21. See Bal Gangadhar Tilak, *The Hindu Philosophy of Life, Ethics and Religion.*

Om-tat-sat, Śrimad Bhagavadgita Rahasya; or, Karma-Yoga-Śastra, Including an External Examination of the Gita, the Original Sanskrit Stanzas, Their English Translation, Commentaries on the Stanzas, and a Comparison of Eastern with Western Doctrines (Poona: R. B. Tilak, 1935–36).

22. See V. M. Joshi, *A Gist of the Gita-Rahasya* (Poona: Arya Bhushan Press, 1917), 2.

23. B[al] G[angadhar] Tilak, *The Orion, or Researches into the Antiquity of the Vedas* (Bombay: Radhabai Atmaram Sagoon, 1893).

24. Vasant Kaiwar, "The Aryan Model of History and the Oriental Renaissance: The Politics of Identity in an Age of Revolutions, Colonialism, and Nationalism," in *Antinomies of Modernity: Essays on Race, Orient, Nation,* ed. Vasant Kaiwar and Sucheta Mazumdar (Durham, NC: Duke University Press, 2003), 45–46.

25. Mohandas Karamchand Gandhi, *Gita—My Mother,* ed. Anand T. Hingorani (Bombay: Bharatiya Vidya Bhavan, 1965), 12, 15, 16, 29, 54.

26. Gandhi, *Gita—My Mother,* 29.

27. Gandhi, *Gita—My Mother,* 62.

28. Sri Aurobindo, *Essays on the Gita* (New York: E. P. Dutton, 1953), 123.

29. Purushottam Billimoria, "Metadialectics of the *Bhagavadgītā,*" in *The Contemporary Essays on the Bhagavadgītā* ed. Braj M. Sinha (New Delhi: Siddharth Publications, 1995), 56.

30. Schlegel's Latin appreciation is as follows: "Magistrorum reverentia a Brachmanis inter sanctissima pietatis officia refertur. Ergo te primum, Vates sanctissime, Numinisque hypopheta! quisquis tandem inter mortales dictus tu fueris, carminis bujus auctor, cujus oraculis mens ad excelsa quaeque, quaeque, aeterna atque divina, cum inenarraoih quddam delectatione rapitur-te primum, inquam, salvere jubeo, et vestigia tua semper adore." Cited in Sir Edwin Arnold, *The Song Celestial* (London: Trübner, 1885), preface, n.p.

31. In Blake's own words, "[T]he subject is Mr. Wilkin [*sic*] translating the Geeta; an ideal design, suggested by the first publication of that part of the Hindoo Scriptures translated by Mr. Wilkin. I understand that my Costume is incorrect; but in this I plead the authority of the ancients, who often deviated from the Habits, to preserve the Manners." See George Hendrick, Introduction to Charles Wilkins, *The Bhăgvăt-Gēētā* (facsimile rpt., Gainesville, FL: Scholars' Facsimiles and Reprints, 1959), viii; and Mary Lloyd, *Sir Charles Wilkins, 1749–1836* (London: India Office Library and Records Report, 1978), 19. Unfortunately, the etching was subsequently lost.

32. Warren Hastings, Preface to Charles Wilkins, *The Bhăgvăt-Gēētā,* 10–13, 10, 6.

33. Charles Wilkins, *The Bhăgvăt-Gēētā,* 24.

34. T[homas] S[tearns] Eliot, *The Complete Poems and Plays of T. S. Eliot* (London: Faber and Faber, 1969), 187–88. See also Eric J. Sharpe, *The Universal Gītā: Western Images of the Bhagavad Gītā* (LaSalle, IL: Open Court Press, 1985).

35. Cited in Arnold, *The Song Celestial,* n.p.

36. See Rabindranath Tagore, *In Persia,* in *Tagore Rachanabali,* 23:433, cited in Dilip Bose, *Bhagavad-Gita and Our National Movement* (New Delhi: People's Publishing House, 1981), 28–29.

37. If the red slayer think he slays,
   Or if the slain think he is slain,
   They know not well the subtle ways
   I keep, and pass, and turn again.

   Far or forgot to me is near;
   Shadow and sunlight are the same;
   The vanished gods to me appear;
   And one to me are shame and fame.

   They reckon ill who leave me out;
   When me they fly, I am the wings;
   I am the doubter and the doubt;
   And I the hymn the Brahmin sings.

   The strong gods pine for my abode,
   And pine in vain the sacred Seven;
   But thou, meek lover of the good!
   Find me, and turn thy back on heaven.

Ralph Waldo Emerson, "Brahma," in *Emerson: Collected Poems and Translations*, ed. Harold Bloom and Paul Kane (New York: Library of America, 1994), 159–60.

38. See Henry David Thoreau, *Walden, or Life in the Woods* (New York: Library of America, 1985), 559; and Thoreau, *A Week on the Concord and Merrimack Rivers* (New York: Library of America, 1985), 116, 114. Wai Chee Dimock has discussed the circulation of the Bhagavadgītā as a pacifist and dissenting text from India to Europe and North America via Wilkins's translation and back again to India via South Africa from Gandhi's reading of Thoreau. See Wai Chee Dimock, "Planetary Time and Global Translation: 'Context' in Literary Studies," *Common Knowledge* 9, no. 3 (2003): 488–507. Also see her *Five Continents and Four Millennia* (Princeton, NJ: Princeton University Press, forthcoming).

39. J. S. Bright, *Gandhian Thought: Including a Comparative Study of Thoreau's Philosophy* (New Delhi: Pankaj Publishers, 1976), 5–6.

40. Gandhi, *Gita—My Mother*, 65.

41. Gandhi, *Gita—My Mother*, 64.

42. Giorgio Agamben, *Homo Sacer: Sovereign Power and Bare Life*, trans. Daniel Heller-Roazen (Stanford, CA: Stanford University Press, 1998).

43. See Edward. P. Thompson, "Notes on Exterminism, the Last Stage of Civilization," in *Exterminism and Cold War*, ed. E. P. Thompson (London: New Left Books, 1982).

44. John Whittier Treat, "Hiroshima and the Place of the Narrator," *Journal of Asian Studies* 48, no. 1 (February 1989): 29–49; see also Treat, *Writing Ground Zero: Japanese Literature and the Atomic Bomb* (Chicago: University of Chicago Press, 1995).

45. Michael Ondaatje, *The English Patient* (New York: Vintage International, 1992), 287.

46. Ondaatje, *The English Patient*, 286.

47. Georges Bataille, "Concerning the Accounts Given by the Residents of Hiroshima," in *Trauma: Explorations in Memory*, ed. Cathy Caruth (Baltimore: Johns Hopkins University Press, 1995), 225.

48. See Thomas Pynchon, *Gravity's Rainbow* (New York: Penguin, 1973), 733, 747; and Aimé Césaire, *Discourse on Colonialism*, trans. Joan Pinkham (1955; rpt., New York: Monthly Review Press, 1972).

49. Jasjit Singh, "Why Nuclear Weapons?" in *Nuclear India*, ed. Jasjit Singh (Delhi: Institute for Defence Studies Analysis, 1998), 11; Dietmar Rothermund, *Mahatma Gandhi: An Essay in Political Biography* (New Delhi: Manohar, 1991), 107–17. Bidwai and Vanaik disagree with Rothermund's speculations regarding Gandhi's ambivalence, *New Nukes*, 142. For a bizarre reading that parallels various Gandhian ideas to nuclear actions even as it makes an antinuclear argument, see James W. Douglass, *Lightning East to West: Gandhi, Jesus, and the Nuclear Age* (New York: Crossroad, 1983).

50. The violence suffered by the Sikhs at the hand of the Mughals is also referred to in Panjabi as a *dharam yuddh*.

51. Frances Ferguson, "The Nuclear Sublime," *Diacritics* 14, no. 2 (Summer 1984): 7; Ira Chernus, *Dr. Strangegod: On the Symbolic Meaning of Nuclear Weapons* (Columbia: University of South Carolina Press, 1986), 106–18; James A. Aho, "'I Am Death . . . Who Shatters Worlds,'" 49–68; and Rudolph Otto, *The Idea of the Holy* (New York: Oxford University Press, 1973).

52. Constituent Assembly of India (Legislative) Debates, 2nd sess. (1948), 5:320, cited in Itty Abraham, *The Making of the Indian Atomic Bomb: Science, Secrecy and the Postcolonial State* (London: Zed Books, 1998), 28.

53. See C. Rajagopalachari, *The Voice of the Uninvolved: Speeches and Statements on Atomic Warfare and Test Explosions* (New Delhi: National Book Trust India, 1960), 2, 21, 65, 86.

54. Freeman Dyson, *Weapons and Hope* (New York: Harper and Row, 1984), 27.

55. James M. Gustafson, in *The Bhagavad Gita and Nuclear Policy: The Chicago Colloquium*, ed. Puracu Palakirusnan (Bombay: Bharatiya Vidya Bhavan, 1993), 56.

56. Hannah Arendt, *The Human Condition* (Chicago: University of Chicago Press, 1958), 241.

57. Here, Hijiya's idea that the notion of *dharma* derived from the Bhagavadgītā allowed the rationalization that "Oppenheimer believed it was the duty of the scientist to build the bomb, but it was the duty of the statesman to decide whether or how to use it," seems spurious to apply to him alone, as that principle seems standard for all modernized state-centered bureaucracy. If put in that manner, surely isn't the entirety of Western civilization based on the Bhagavadgītā's notion of professional ethics? Hijiya, "The *Gita* of Oppenheimer," 137.

58. Georges Bataille, "Residents of Hiroshima," 229, 232.

59. Bataille, "Residents of Hiroshima," 231, 233.

60. J.A.B. van Buitinen, *The Bhagavad Gita*, 11.27–30.

61. See Srinivas Aravamudan, "The Return of Anachronism," in *Periodization: Cutting Up the Past*, special issue of *Modern Language Quarterly* 62, no. 4 (December 2001): 331–53.

62. A survey of postmodern and postnuclear "surviving fictions" reveals one strain of postnuclear writing that interprets literature itself as explosion, dispersal, and disappearance (in writings by Sartre, Beckett, Blanchot, and Derrida) even as feminist fiction attempts to transcend postnuclear repetition. See Mária Minich Brewer, "Surviving Fictions: Gender and Difference in Postmodern and Postnuclear Narrative," *Discourse: Journal for Theoretical Studies in Media and Culture* (Spring–Summer 1987); and Brewer, "Samuel Beckett: Postmodern Narrative and the Nuclear Telos," *boundary 2* (Fall–Winter 1987): 153–70.

63. Lamont, *Day of Trinity*, 285.

64. Shiv Visvanathan, "Atomic Physics: The Career of an Imagination," in *Science, Hegemony and Violence*, ed. Ashis Nandy, 126. Even if not very well explained in the article, this impossible mixture of myths is not arbitrary. Prometheus defied the gods by bringing knowledge of fire to mankind and is punished as a result. Hamlet's moral indecision ultimately leads to the carnage of the revenge tragedy at the play's conclusion once his mind is tardily made up; *Hamlet* was one of Oppenheimer's favorite texts. Raskolnikov, the hero of Dostoevsky's *Crime and Punishment*, who kills without sufficient motive and hence enshrines modern existentialism, fascinated Oppenheimer in his youth at Cambridge when he was suffering from severe depression. All three examples involve asymmetries of violence, revenge, and the open-ended relationship between the human and the divine. For another assessment of Oppenheimer as nuclear scientist, see S. S. Schwebe, *In the Shadow of the Bomb: Oppenheimer, Bethe, and the Moral Responsibility of the Scientist* (Princeton, NJ: Princeton University Press, 2000).

65. Edward R. Murrow, "See It Now: A Conversation with J. Robert Oppenheimer," CBS Studios archive, New York, 1955; Len Giovannitti and Fred Freed, *The Decision to Drop the Bomb* (New York: Coward McCann, 1965); Nitin Sawhney, "Broken Skin," "The Conference," and "Beyond Skin," in the compact disc, *Beyond Skin* (London: Outcaste Records, 1999).

66. See George Perkovich, *India's Nuclear Bomb: The Impact on Global Proliferation* (Berkeley: University of California Press, 1999), 14.

67. See Zulfikar Ali Bhutto, *If I Am Assassinated* (New Delhi: Vikas, 1979), 138.

68. See A.P.J. Abdul Kalam (with Arun Tiwari), *Wings of Fire: An Autobiography* (Hyderabad, India: Universities Press India, 1999), xv, 97, 147.

69. Bidwai and Vanaik, *New Nukes*, xiii.

70. "72.8% Oppose Use of N-weapons, Says Survey," *Economic Times* (New Delhi) June 24, 1998.

71. Bidwai and Vanaik, *New Nukes*, xii; Singh, "Nuclear India," 14.

72. Robert Jungk, *The New Tyranny: How Nuclear Power Enslaves Us*, trans. Christopher Trump (New York: F. Jordan Books/Grosset and Dunlap, 1979); Elaine Scarry, *The Body in Pain: The Making and Unmaking of the World* (New York: Oxford University Press, 1985).

73. Gabrielle Hecht, "Peasants, Engineers, and Atomic Cathedrals: Narrating Modernization in Postwar Provincial France," *French Historical Studies* 20,

no. 3 (1997): 381–418; also cited in Abraham, *Making of the Indian Atomic Bomb*, 9.

74. Lifton and Falk, *Indefensible Weapons*, 13–22, 83–89, 11.

75. See Varun Sahni, "Going Nuclear: Establishing an Overt Nuclear Weapons Capability," in *India and the Bomb: Public Opinion and Nuclear Options*, ed. David Cortright and Amitabh Mattoo (Notre Dame, IN: University of Notre Dame Press, 1996), 85–108; Samina Ahmed and David Cortright, eds., *Pakistan and the Bomb: Public Opinion and Nuclear Options* (Notre Dame, IN: University of Notre Dame Press, 1998); and Moonis Ahmar, *The CTBT Controversy: Different Perceptions in South Asia* (Karachi: Department of International Relations, University of Karachi, 2000).

76. Romila Thapar, *Somanatha: The Many Voices of a History* (New Delhi: Penguin Viking, 2004).

77. See Z. Mian, A. H. Nayyar, and M. V. Ramanna, "Bringing Prithvi down to Earth: The Capabilities and Potential Effectiveness of India's Prithvi Missile," *Science and Global Security* 7, no. 3 (1998): 333–60. See also the work done by the International Network of Engineers and Scientists against Proliferation.

78. "Partition" is, of course, an inexact word, as it assumes that there was an unified India before it, an assumption that Indian nationalists are much more likely to make than Pakistanis or Bangladeshis. For a discussion of the philosophical and historical issues concerning partition, see Gyanendra Pandey, *The Construction of Communalism in Colonial North India* (Delhi: Oxford University Press, 1990).

79. See Royce J. Ammon, *Global Television and the Shaping of World Politics: CNN, Telediplomacy, and Foreign Policy* (Jefferson, NC: McFarland, 2001).

80. Arundhati Roy, *The End of Imagination* (Kottayam: D C Books, 1998); also published in various newspapers and global media, and as the "Introduction" to Bidwai and Vanaik, *New Nukes*.

81. Srinivas Aravamudan, "Fables of Censorship: Salman Rushdie's *Haroun and the Sea of Stories*," *Western Humanities Review*, 49, no. 4 (Winter 1995): 323–29.

82. Scott D. Sagan and Kenneth N. Waltz, *The Spread of Nuclear Weapons: A Debate* (New York: W. W. Norton, 1995).

83. See Kenneth Waltz, "Nuclear Myths and Political Realities," *American Political Science Review* 84, no. 3 (September 1990): 731–45; Sagan and Waltz, *Spread of Nuclear Weapons*; and John Mearsheimer, "Why We Will Soon Miss the Cold War," *The Atlantic Monthly* 266, no. 2 (August 1990): 35–42.

84. For a critique of nuclearist neorealism, see Abraham, *Making of the Indian Atomic Bomb*, 15–21; and Bidwai and Vanaik, *New Nukes*, 156–85.

85. See Kumkum Sangari, Neeraj Malik, Sheba Chhachhi, and Tanika Sarkar, "Why Women Must Reject Nuclearisation," in *Out of Nuclear Darkness: The Indian Case for Disarmament* (New Delhi: Movement in India for Nuclear Disarmament, 1998), 47–56.

86. See Bidwai and Vanaik, "Ramshackle Deterrence," in *New Nukes*, 175–78.

87. Brigadier S. K. Malik, *The Quranic Concept of War* (New Delhi: Himalaya Books, 1986), 58–59.

88. Derrida, "No Apocalypse, Not Now," 20–31.
89. Mathur, "Nuclearism," 9, 2–3, 5.

CHAPTER FIVE
BLASPHEMY, SATIRE, AND SECULARISM

1. See Talal Asad, *Formations of the Secular: Christianity, Islam, Modernity* (Stanford, CA: Stanford University Press, 2003), 25. Asad also radicalizes the challenge already posed to the secularization thesis by José Casanova in his account of the late modern deprivatization of religion. See José Casanova, *Public Religions in the Modern World* (Chicago: University of Chicago Press, 1994).

2. See, for instance, Bruce B. Lawrence, *Shattering the Myth: Islam beyond Violence* (Princeton, NJ: Princeton University Press, 1998); and A. G. Noorani, *Islam and Jihad: Prejudice versus Reality* (London: Zed Books, 2002).

3. Hent de Vries, *Philosophy and the Turn to Religion* (Baltimore: Johns Hopkins University Press, 1999), 11.

4. Sadik Jalal 'Al-Azm, "The Importance of Being Earnest about Salman Rushdie," in *Reading Rushdie: Perspectives on the Fiction of Salman Rushdie*, ed. M. D. Fletcher (Amsterdam: Rodopi, 1994), 255–92.

5. Asad, *Formations of the Secular*, 197.

6. Mehdi Mozaffari, *Fatwa: Violence and Discourtesy* (Aarhus, Denmark: Aarhus University Press, 1998), 48–49; Sadik J[alal] 'Al-Azm, "The Satanic Verses Post Festum: The Global, The Local, The Literary," *Comparative Studies of South Asia, Africa, and the Middle East* 20, nos. 1–2 (2000): 57.

7. See Salman Rushdie, "The Book Burning," *New York Review of Books* 36, no. 3, March 2, 1989, 26.

8. See Ashis Nandy, "An Anti-Secularist Manifesto," in *The Romance of the State and the Fate of Dissent in the Tropics* (New Delhi: Oxford University Press, 2003), 34–60; and Nandy, "The Politics of Secularism and the Recovery of Religious Tolerance," in *Time Warps: The Insistent Politics of Silent and Evasive Pasts* (New Delhi: Permanent Black, 2002), 61–88.

9. Homi Bhabha, untitled, *New Statesman*, March 3, 1984, in *The Rushdie File*, ed. Lisa Appignanesi and Sara Maitland (London: ICA/Fourth Estate, 1989), 139–40.

10. See Pnina Werbner, "Allegories of Sacred Imperfection: Magic, Hermeneutics, and Passion in *The Satanic Verses*," in *Current Anthropology: A World Journal of the Human Sciences* (February 1996): supplement, 55–86. A number of respondents to Werbner's article reveal the difficulties at stake in her gambit for those interested in speaking for a Muslim position—namely, responses by Akbar Ahmad, Talal Asad, and A. R. Kidwai.

11. See Gayatri Chakravorty Spivak, "Reading *The Satanic Verses*," in *Outside in the Teaching Machine* (New York: Routledge, 1993), 217–41. The cynicism and opportunism involved in justifying the invasion of Afghanistan on behalf of Afghani women is no less culpable than the imprisonment of Muslim women by the Taliban, especially as the precursor *mujahiddin* who ushered Islamism into the area were the surrogate armies of Western intelligence agencies seek-

ing to combat the Soviet invasion. So-called fundamentalism is not so much a "medieval" throwback as an alternative modernity that matches the Christian Religious Right's notion of theodemocracy in equal measure. No doubt, there would be many, including myself, who would want to oppose these rightist attitudes as well as the patronizing gestures made to Muslims others by Eurocentric liberals, but it is important not to lose sight of the mutual complicity of the clashing fundamentalisms propounded between the Bushes and the Bin Ladens of the world, as Tariq Ali has suggested. See Tariq Ali, *The Clash of Fundamentalisms: Crusades, Jihads and Modernity* (London: Verso, 2002); and Ali, *Bush in Babylon: The Recolonisation of Iraq* (New York: Verso, 2003).

12. For more contextual information and discussion about South Asian Islam, see Bruce Lawrence and David Gilmartin, eds., *Beyond Turk and Hindu: Rethinking Religious Identities in Islamicate South Asia* (Gainesville: University Press of Florida, 2000); Ayesha Jalal, *Self and Sovereignty: Individual and Community in South Asian Islam since 1850* (New York: Routledge, 2000); Asim Roy, *Islam in South Asia: A Regional Perspective* (New Delhi: South Asian Publishers, 1996); Annemarie Schimmel, *Islam in the Indian Subcontinent* (Leiden: E. J. Brill, 1980); Aziz Ahmad, *An Intellectual History of Islam in India* (Edinburgh: Edinburgh University Press, 1969); and Mushirul Hasan, *Islam in the Subcontinent: Muslims in a Plural Society* (New Delhi: Manohar, 2002).

13. Salman Rushdie, *The Satanic Verses* (London: Viking, 1988), 5. Subsequent citations to this edition will be parenthetical page references in the main text.

14. D. V. Chitaley and S. Appu Rao, *The Code of Criminal Procedure 1973 (2 of 1974) with Exhaustive, Analytical and Critical Commentaries* (Bombay: All-India Reporter, 1974–76), vol. 4. See also Ratanlal Ranchoddas and Dhirajlal Keshavlal Thakore, *Indian Penal Code: Act 45 of 1860, Promulgated October 6, 1860*, 20th ed., (Bombay: Bombay Law Reporters Office, 1951).

15. Some of the newly created legislation with ominous titles foreshadows current realities such as the PATRIOT Act in the United States or POTA (Prevention of Terrorism Act) in India. The acronyms produced in the emergency for surveillance legislation were MISA (Maintenance of Internal Security Act) and COFEPOSA (Conservation of Foreign Exchange and Prevention of Smuggling Activities).

16. Syed Shahabuddin, "You did this with satanic forethought, Mr Rushdie," *Times of India*, October 13, 1988, cited in Lisa Appignanesi and Sara Maitland, eds., *The Rushdie File* (London: ICA/Fourth Estate, 1989), 48.

17. Article 416:

A person is said to "cheat by personation" if he cheats by pretending to be some other person, or by knowingly substituting one person for another, or representing that he or any other person is a person other than he or such other person really is.

Explanation: The offence is committed whether the individual personated is a real or imaginary person.

COMMENT: To "personate" means to pretend to be a particular person. . . . If a person at Oxford, who is not a member of the university, go to a shop for the purpose of fraud, wearing a commoner's cap and gown, and obtain goods, this appearing in a cap and gown is a sufficient false pretence although nothing passed in words.

The person personated may be a real or an imaginary person.

See Ranchoddas and Thakore, *Indian Penal Code*, 337–38.

18. The Indian film industry is often associated just with Bollywood (Bombay's Hollywood as it were) but the "theological" is an especially important genre in Indian regional cinema, reaching its acme with the NTR films in Telugu. The main studios for the production of southern Indian cinema (in the southern Indian languages of Tamil, Telugu, Malayalam, and Kannada) are in Madras, Hyderabad, and Bangalore. The film studios in Chennai (Madras) are in Kodambakkam, and hence the sobriquet of "Kollywood" has developed as a parody of a parody.

19. Robert C. Elliott, *The Power of Satire: Magic, Ritual, Art* (Princeton, NJ: Princeton University Press, 1960), 15–17.

20. Elliott, *Power of Satire*, 281.

21. Elliott, *Power of Satire*, 17.

22. Salman Rushdie, interview on the British television program *Channel 4*, "The Bandung File," February 14, 1989, cited in Appignanesi and Maitland, *Rushdie File*, 29.

23. Elliott, *Power of Satire*, 15.

24. See Lee Siegel, *Laughing Matters: Comic Tradition in India* (Chicago: University of Chicago Press, 1987), 70.

25. T. B. Irving, "The Rushdie Confrontation: A Clash in Values," *Iowa Review* 20, no. 1 (1990): 176; Beert C. Verstraete, "Classical References and Themes in Salman Rushdie's *The Satanic Verses*," *Classical and Modern Literature* 10 (1990): 329.

26. For some more discussion of these genres, see Ashish Rajadhyaksha and Paul Willemen, *Encyclopaedia of Indian Cinema*, rev. ed. (New Delhi: Oxford University Press, 1999), 13, 155, 204. For the visuality of the sacred in India, see Diana L. Eck, *Darsan: Seeing the Divine Image in India* (Chambersburg, PA: Anima Books, 1985).

27. For an excellent study exploring the contours of postcolonial satire, see John Clement Ball, *Satire and the Postcolonial Novel: V. S. Naipaul, Chinua Achebe, Salman Rushdie* (New York: Routledge, 2003).

28. Salman Rushdie, "The Empire Writes Back with a Vengeance," *The Times*, July 3, 1982, 8.

29. William Shakespeare, *The Tempest*, in *The Riverside Shakespeare* (Boston: Houghton Mifflin, 1974), 4.1. 188–89.

30. Daniel Defoe, *The History of the Devil, as Well Ancient as Modern* (London: Warner, 1727), 81.

31. Luisa da Urtubey, *Freud et le diable* (Paris: Presses Universitaires de France, 1983).

32. Sara Suleri, *The Rhetoric of English India* (Chicago: University of Chicago Press, 1992), 191, 206.

33. See Rajadhyaksha and Willemen, *Encyclopaedia of Indian Cinema*, 257, 304.

34. Spivak, "Reading *The Satanic Verses*," 223, 241.

35. Purnima Mankekar, *Screening Culture, Viewing Politics: An Ethnography of Television, Womanhood, and Nation in Postcolonial India* (Durham, NC: Duke University Press, 1999), 165–66.

36. Jacques Derrida, "No Apocalypse, Not Now (full speed ahead, seven missiles, seven missives)," *Diacritics* 14, no. 2 (1984): 24, 25.

37. Walter Benjamin, "Critique of Violence," in *Reflections, Essays, Aphorisms, Autobiographical Writings*, trans. Edmund Jephcott, ed. Peter Demetz (New York: Harcourt Brace Jovanovich, 1978), 283.

38. Alexander Pope, *The Dunciad*, in *The Poems of Alexander Pope: A Reduced Version of the Twickenham Text*, ed. John Butt (New Haven, CT: Yale University Press, 1963), 4: 655–56.

39. See William E. Smith, "The New Satans," *Time*, March 6, 1989, 37; and Michael M. J. Fischer and Mehdi Abedi, *Debating Muslims: Cultural Dialogues in Postmodernity and Tradition* (Madison: University of Wisconsin Press, 1990), 388.

40. Sir Philip Goodhart, "What Is Safety Worth to Salman Rushdie?" *Sunday Telegraph*, March 12, 1989, 26.

41. Derrida, "No Apocalypse, Not Now," 29.

CHAPTER SIX
NEW AGE ENCHANTMENTS

1. See Benedict Anderson, "Replica, Aura, and Late Nationalist Imaginings," *Qui Parle* 7, no. 1 (Fall–Winter 1993): 1–21; and Chetan Bhatt, *Liberation and Purity: Race, New Religious Movements, and the Ethics of Postmodernity* (London: University College London Press, 1997); Sucheta Mazumdar, "The Politics of Religion and National Origin: Rediscovering Hindu Indian Identity in the United States," in *Antinomies of Modernity: Race, Orient, Nation*, ed. Vasant Kaiwar and Sucheta Mazumdar (Durham, NC: Duke University Press, 2003), 223–60; and Vijay Prashad, *The Karma of Brown Folk* (Minneapolis: University of Minnesota Press, 2000).

2. See Wilfred Cantwell Smith, *The Meaning and End of Religion: A New Approach to the Religious Traditions of Mankind* (Minneapolis: Fortress Press, 1991); Talal Asad, *Genealogies of Religion* (Baltimore: Johns Hopkins University Press, 1993); and Peter van der Veer, *Imperial Encounters: Religion and Modernity in India and Britain* (Princeton, NJ: Princeton University Press, 2001).

3. This synthesis will begin to fail rapidly once New Age monisms are felt as inadequate when compared with fundamentalist ideas of religious transcendence.

4. Paul Heelas, *The New Age Movement: The Celebration of the Self and the Sacralization of Modernity* (Oxford: Blackwell, 1996), 22.

5. See Wouter J. Hanegraaff, "Prospects for the Globalization of New Age: Spiritual Imperialism versus Cultural Diversity," and Liselotte Frisk, "Globalization or Westernization? New Age as a Contemporary Transnational Culture," in *New Age Religion and Globalization*, ed. Mikael Rothstein (Aarhus, Denmark: Aarhus University Press, 2001), 15–30, 31–41; Andrea Grace Diem and James R. Lewis, "Imagining India: The Influence of Hinduism on the New Age

Movement," in *Perspectives on the New Age,* ed. James R. Lewis and J. Gordon Melton (Albany: State University of New York Press, 1992), 48–58; Robert Basil, ed., *Not Necessarily the New Age* (Buffalo, NY: Prometheus Books, 1988); and J. Gordon Melton, Jerome Clark, and Aidan A. Kelly, eds., *New Age Encyclopedia: A Guide to the Beliefs, Concepts, Terms, People, and Organizations That Make Up the New Global Movement toward Spiritual Development, Health and Healing, Higher Consciousness, and Related Subjects* (Detroit: Gale Research, 1990). For histories of Buddhism in the United States, see Rick Fields, *How the Swans Came to the Lake: A Narrative History of Buddhism in America* (Boulder, CO: Shambhala, 1981); Richard Hughes Seager, *Buddhism in America* (New York: Columbia University Press, 1999); and Charles Prebish, *Luminous Passage: The Practice and Study of Buddhism in America* (Berkeley: University of California Press, 1999).

6. Wendell Thomas, *Hinduism Invades America* (Boston: Beacon Press, 1930), 208.

7. See Carl T. Jackson, *Oriental Religions in American Thought* (Westport, CT: Greenwood Press, 1981); and Olav Hammer, *Claiming Knowledge: Strategies of Epistemology from Theosophy to the New Age* (Leiden: Brill, 2001).

8. See Steven Vertovec, *The Hindu Diaspora: Comparative Patterns* (London: Routledge, 2000), 14; Steven Vertovec, Colin Clark, and Ceri Peach, eds., *South Asians Overseas: Migration and Ethnicity* (Cambridge: Cambridge University Press, 1990); Roger Ballard, ed. *Desh Pardesh: The South Asian Presence in Britain* (London: C. Hurst, 1994); Crispin Bates, ed., *Community, Empire and Migration: South Asians in Diaspora* (New York: Palgrave, 2001); Richard Burghart, ed., *Hinduism in Great Britain* (London, Tavistock, 1987); Harold Coward, John R. Hinnells, and Raymond Brady Williams, eds., *The South Asian Religious Diaspora in Britain, Canada and the United States* (Albany: State University Press of New York, 2000); Sunaina Maira, *Desis in the House: Indian American Youth Culture in New York City* (Philadelphia: Temple University Press, 2002); Carla Petievich, ed., *The Expanding Landscape: South Asians and the Diaspora* (New Delhi: Manohar, 1999); Sandhya Shukla, *India Abroad: Diasporic Cultures of Postwar America and England* (Princeton, NJ: Princeton University Press, 2003); Peter van der Veer, *Nation and Migration: The Politics of Space in the South Asian Diaspora* (Philadelphia: University of Pennsylvania Press, 1995); and Raymond Brady Williams, *Religions of Immigrants from India and Pakistan: New Threads in the American Tapestry* (Cambridge: Cambridge University Press, 1988).

9. For an interesting article on the New Age literary system, see Lisbeth Mikaelsson, "*Homo accumulans* and the Spiritualization of Money," in Lewis and Melton, eds., *Perspectives on the New Age,* 94–112.

10. Walter Benjamin, "The Work of Art in the Age of Mechanical Reproduction," in *Illuminations,* ed. Hannah Arendt, trans. Harry Zohn (New York: Schocken Books, 1969).

11. Herbert V. Guenther and Chögyam Trungpa, *The Dawn of Tantra* (Berkeley, CA: Shambhala, 1975), 42.

12. Jacques Derrida, "Above All, No Journalists!" in *Religion and Media,* ed. Hent de Vries and Samuel Weber (Stanford, CA: Stanford University Press, 2000), 56–93.

13. Romain Rolland, *Prophets of the New India* (London: Cassell, 1930), 520–48.

14. See Diana L. Eck, " 'New Age' Hinduism in America," in *Conflicting Images: India and the United States*, ed. Sulochana Raghavan Glazer and Nathan Glazer (Glenn Dale, MD: Riverdale, 1990), 111–42.

15. Michel Foucault, "Of Other Spaces," *Diacritics* 16, no. 1 (Spring 1986): 23–24.

16. Erik H. Erikson, *Gandhi's Truth: On the Origins of Militant Nonviolence* (New York: Norton, 1969), 396, 403, 407.

17. Akeel Bilgrami, "Gandhi's Integrity: The Philosophy behind the Politics," *Postcolonial Studies* 5, no. 1 (2002): 79–93.

18. I cannot put this better than Gayatri Chakravorty Spivak, who speaks of a secularity that does not play into the Christianized agenda of secularism as one that "detranscendentalizes the radical other [of the divine] into figurative instrumentality." Gayatri Chakravorty Spivak, "The Secular University Today," public lecture, annual convention of the Modern Language Association, San Diego, CA, December 27, 2003.

19. For a much more detailed account of Gandhi's "Theosophical Connection," see Margaret Chatterjee, *Gandhi and His Jewish Friends* (Delhi: Macmillan, 1992), 1–22; 172–75.

20. Raja Rao, *Kanthapura* (New York: New Directions Paperback, 1967), 10, 11–12.

21. Rao, *Kanthapura*, 34.

22. Rao, *Kanthapura*, 62–63.

23. Rao, *Kanthapura*, 180–81; see also Rumina Sethi, *Myths of the Nation: National Identity and Literary Representation* (Oxford: Clarendon Press, 1999), 23, 44; C. D. Narasimhaiah, *The Writer's Gandhi* (Patiala: Punjabi University, 1967), 75–79; and Chitra Sankaran, *The Myth Connection: The Use of Hindu Mythology in Some Novels of Raja Rao and R. K. Narayan* (New Delhi: Allied Publishers, 1993), 30–66.

24. R. K. Narayan, *Waiting for the Mahatma* (Lansing: Michigan State University Press, 1955), 24.

25. For criticism of Narayan's portrait of Gandhi, see C. D. Narasimhaiah, *The Writer's Gandhi* (Patiala: Punjab University, 1967); and A. N. Kaul, "R. K. Narayan and the East-West Theme," in *Indian Literature*, ed. A. Poddar (Simla: Indian Institute of Advanced Study, 1972).

26. V. S. Naipaul, *The Mystic Masseur* (London: Andre Deutsch, 1969), 20.

27. Naipaul, *Mystic Masseur*, 37, 61, 138.

28. Naipaul, *Mystic Masseur*, 106, 14.

29. Naipaul, *Mystic Masseur*, 112.

30. Naipaul's cutting satire of the Trinidadian Indians involves the incident during which Ganesh's group floats the idea of a rival newspaper to counter Narayan's the *Hindu*. The idea of the *Sanatanist* (based on the Arya Samaj's idea of *sanātana dharma* as reform Hinduism) is vetoed by the printer as too close to the *Satanist*, "and too besides, my father ain't a Sanatanist. We is Aryans." However, the sole number of the *Dharma* features well-known staples

of Guru English, such as that ancient Indians knew how to fly. See Naipaul, *Mystic Masseur*, 173, 178.

31. Naipaul, *Mystic Masseur*, 207. Selywn R. Cudjoe makes an interesting (if overly schematic) case for the novel as representing a Trinidadian transition from feudalism to capitalism, from Hinduism to Christianity, from metaphysics to empiricism, and from religion to politics. See Selwyn R. Cudjoe, *V. S. Naipaul: A Materialist Reading* (Amherst: University of Massachusetts Press, 1988), 37–45.

32. Seepersad Naipaul, *The Adventures of Gurudeva*, foreword by V. S. Naipaul (London: Heinemann, 1995).

33. V. S. Naipaul, "Foreword," to Seepersad Naipaul, *Gurudeva*, 8.

34. Naipaul, *Mystic Masseur*, 206, 70.

35. See R. K. Narayan, *The Guide* (New York: Viking, 1958). It is possible that the novel alludes to the fast unto death by Potti Sriramulu in 1952, an event that accelerated the creation of the linguistically based state of Andhra Pradesh out of the former Madras Presidency.

36. Peter Hazlehurst, "Beatles Begin Their Career as 'Sages,' " *The Times*, February 21, 1968.

37. See The Beatles, *The Beatles Anthology* (San Francisco: Chronicle Books, 2000), 260–63, 281–86.

38. See Robert McCutchan, "The Social and the Celestial: Mary Douglas and Transcendental Meditation," *Princeton Journal of the Arts and Sciences* 1, no. 2 (1977): 70; Maharishi Mahesh Yogi, *Science of Being and Art of Living* (New York: NAL Dutton, 1968).

39. See Anthony Campbell, *Seven States of Consciousness: A Vision of Possibilities Suggested by the Teachings of Maharishi Mahesh Yogi* (New York: Harper and Row, 1974); Peter Russell, *The TM Technique: An Introduction to Transcendental Meditation and the Teachings of Maharishi Mahesh Yogi* (New York: VikingPenguin, 1989).

40. See Mikael Rothstein, *Belief Transformations: Some Aspects of the Relation between Science and Religion in TM and ISKCON* (Aarhus, Denmark: Aarhus University Press, 1996), 85; Dev Samaj, *The Basic Principles of the One, True, Science-Grounded Religion* (Lahore: Jiwan Press, 1920).

41. W. K. Coors, foreword to Jay B. Marcus, *TM and Business: Personal and Corporate Benefits of Inner Development* (New York: McGraw-Hill, 1977), xvi–xvii.

42. http://160.149.101.23/chap/relpractice/indian/tm.htm.

43. Somerset Maugham, *The Razor's Edge* (London: Penguin, 1963), 153, 261, 273.

44. For a mere sampling, see Bhagwan Shree Rajneesh, *The Mustard Seed* (1975); *I Am the Gate* (1977); and *The Psychology of the Esoteric* (1979), all published in New York by Harper and Row; for a posthumously crafted autobiography using his own words, see Osho, *Autobiography of a Spiritually Incorrect Mystic* (New York: St. Martin's Press, 2000). Several books about Rajneesh contain extensive bibliographies of many of his voluminous publications and transcribed lectures.

45. Arjun Appadurai, *Modernity at Large: Cultural Dimensions of Globalization* (Minneapolis: University of Minnesota Press, 1996), 139–57.

46. See Lewis F. Carter, *Charisma and Control in Rajneeshpuram: The Role of Shared Values in the Creation of a Community* (New York: Cambridge University Press, 1990), 40; and W. E. Mann, *The Quest for Total Bliss: A Psycho-Sociological Perspective on the Rajneesh Movement* (Toronto: Canadian Scholars Press, 1991).

47. Carter, *Charisma and Control*, 158–200.

48. Aubrey Menen, *The New Mystics* (London: Thames and Hudson, 1974); Gita Mehta, *Karma Cola: Marketing the Mystic East* (New York: Simon and Schuster, 1979).

49. Frances FitzGerald, *Cities on a Hill: A Journey through Contemporary American Cultures* (New York: Simon and Schuster, 1986), 247–381.

50. Marion S. Goldman, *Passionate Journeys: Why Successful Women Joined a Cult* (Ann Arbor: University of Michigan Press, 1999), 41.

51. Osho, *Love, Freedom, and Aloneness: A New Vision of Relating* (New York: St. Martin's Press, 2001), 1.

52. Carter, *Charisma and Control*, 97.

53. John Updike, *S.* (New York: Knopf, 1988), 228, 219, 86.

54. Updike, *S.*, 47, 51, 51–52, 106–7, 98, 258, 265–79; John Updike, "Unsolicited Thoughts on *S.*," in Updike, *Odd Jobs* (New York: Knopf, 1991), 858–59, cited in James A. Schiff, *Updike's Version: Rewriting* The Scarlet Letter (Columbia: University of Missouri Press, 1992), 110. See also Fitzgerald, *Cities on a Hill*; Mircea Eliade, *Yoga: Immortality and Freedom*, trans. Willard R. Trask (Princeton, NJ: Princeton University Press, 1970); Eliade, *A History of Religious Ideas*, trans. Willard R. Trask, 3 vols. (Chicago: University of Chicago Press, 1978); Joseph Campbell, *The Masks of God Volume Two: Oriental Mythology* (New York: Penguin, 1978); and Ajit Mookerjee, *Kundalini: The Arousal of the Inner Energy* (New York: Destiny Books, 1982).

55. See Bhagwan Shree Rajneesh, "Zorba and Buddha: Their Split Is Your Social Disease," in *Beyond Enlightenment* (Boulder, CO: Rajneesh Foundation Europe, 1986), 156–79.

56. Updike, *S.*, 115, 32, 33. For a compelling reading of the modern function of secrecy in *S.*, see Judie Newman, "Guru Industries, Ltd.: Red-Letter Religion in Updike's *S.*," in *John Updike and Religion: The Sense of the Sacred and the Motions of Grace*, ed. James Yerkes (Grand Rapids, MI: William B. Erdmans Publishing, 1999), 228–41; see also Matei Calinescu, "Secrecy in Fiction: Textual and Intertextual Secrets in Hawthorne and Updike," *Poetics Today* 15, no. 3 (1994): 444–65. See Hugh B. Urban, "Zorba the Buddha: Capitalism, Charisma, and the Cult of Bhagwan Shree Rajneesh," *Religion* 26 (1996): 161–82; and Hugh Milne, *Bhagwan: The God That Failed* (New York: Caliban Books, 1986), 56; see also James S. Gordon, *The Golden Guru: The Strange Journey of Bhagwan Shree Rajneesh* (Lexington, MA: Stephen Greene Press, 1987).

57. Milne, *Bhagwan*, 65.

58. Hanif Kureishi, *The Buddha of Suburbia* (Harmondsworth: Penguin, 1990), 16, 5, 21, 25, 32, 31, 115.

59. Kureishi, *Buddha of Suburbia*, 48, 102.

60. Kureishi, *Buddha of Suburbia*, 263.

61. Berthold Schoene, "Herald of Hybridity: The Emancipation of Difference in Hanif Kureishi's *The Buddha of Suburbia*," *International Journal of Cultural*

Studies 1, no. 1 (1998): 120. For a convincing account of "the intertextual and intercultural correlation between Kureishi's novel and the oeuvre of the Beatles," see Jörg Helbig, "'Get Back to Where You Once Belonged': Hanif Kureishi's Use of the Beatles-Myth in *The Buddha of Suburbia*," in *Across the Lines: Intertextuality and Transcultural Communication in the New Literatures in English*, ed. Wolfgang Klooss (Amsterdam: Rodopi, 1998), 78, 77–82.

62. Kureishi, *Buddha of Suburbia*, 279.

63. Deepak Chopra, *Ageless Body, Timeless Mind: The Quantum Alternative to Growing Old* (New York: Crown Publishing, 1995); *The Seven Spiritual Laws of Success: A Practical Guide to the Fulfillment of Your Dreams* (New York: Amber Allen Publishing, 1995); see also, *Quantum Healing: Exploring the Frontiers of Mind/Body Medicine* (New York: Bantam Books, 1989).

64. Pat Jordan, "In Deepak We Trust," *Sales and Marketing Management*, August 1997, 58–65; Stephen Alter, "Dr. Feelgood," *Far Eastern Economic Review*, June 26, 1997, 78.

65. Deepak Chopra, *Return of the Rishi: A Doctor's Search for the Ultimate Healer* (Boston: Houghton Mifflin, 1988).

66. Mary Elizabeth Cronin, "A Spiritual Empire: Deepak Chopra's Metaphysical Message Is Resonating Globally," *Seattle Times*, February 12, 1997, E1.

67. "From Here and Now to Eternity: An Interview with Deepak Chopra, M.D.," *Psychology Today*, November–December 1993, 36–37.

68. See Chopra, *Quantum Healing; Return of the Rishi: A Doctor's Story of Spiritual Transformation and Ayurvedic Healing* (Boston: Houghton Mifflin, 1991); *The Path to Love: Renewing the Power of Spirit in Your Life* (New York: Random House, 1997).

69. Chopra, *Ageless Body, Timeless Mind*.

70. *New York Times*, September 23, 2001, A4.

71. *New York Times*, September 25, 2001, A5, A6, A23.

72. François Gautier, *The Guru of Joy: Sri Sri Ravi Shankar and the Art of Living* (New Delhi: Books Today, 2002); see also http://www.artofliving.org/.

73. Alex Kuczynski, "Spiritual Balm, at Only $23.95," *New York Times*, October 21, 2001, Sunday Styles, sec. 9, pp. 1, 10.

74. Cited in Jordan, "In Deepak We Trust," 61.

AFTERWORD

1. Take, for instance, the two brilliant books by Gauri Viswanathan, *Masks of Conquest: Literary Study and British Rule in India* (New York: Columbia University Press, 1989) and *Outside the Fold: Conversion, Modernity, and Belief* (Princeton, NJ: Princeton University Press, 1998).

2. Tabish Khair, *Babu Fictions: Alienation in Contemporary Indian English Novels* (Delhi: Oxford University Press, 2001), 86.

3. Khair, *Babu Fictions*, ix, 123. Furthermore, when conflicts erupt within the field, they are between Brahmanized, colonial, and cosmopolitan baboos; these positions represented by Raja Rao, V. S. Naipaul, and Salman Rushdie, respectively (xiv).

4. Martin Heidegger, "The Question Concerning Technology," in *Basic Writings,* ed. David F. Krell (New York: Harper and Row, 1977), 298.

5. See Gayatri Chakravorty Spivak, *The Death of a Discipline: The Wellek Library Lectures in Literary Theory* (New York: Columbia University Press, 2003), 72, 84. Here, I think it is important to register that while I endorse Spivak's call to shift away from globalizing new immigrant literature and instead engage in a planetary comparative literature, the topic of Guru English is an exception to the extent that it can only be cogently analyzed by paying close attention to the metropolitan circuit of a globally dominant language. So, while appreciating the spirit of the call, I do not heed it in this particular project.

Index

Abe, Stanley K., 85, 287n60
Abraham, 34, 191
Abraham, Itty, 163
acrolect, 3, 271n2
Adam, William, 43
Adam and Eve, 60, 61
Adler, Felix, 147
advaita, 54, 62, 64, 150, 151, 154, 155, 243, 247, 259; neo-, 27, 57–58, 276n9. *See also* Vedanta
Advani, Lal Krishna, 172
advertising, 123, 196, 203, 205, 209, 225, 239, 260, 261, 262
Æ (George Russell), 34, 101, 116, 118, 120, 121, 124, 125, 293n40
aesthetics, 48, 72, 103, 136, 138, 148, 161, 162, 169, 183, 198, 211
Africa, 1, 2, 111, 158, 222, 224
Aga Khan, 201, 227, 229
Agamben, Giorgio, 158
Agnihotri, Sattyanand (Shri Dev Guru Bhagwan), 245
ākāśa, 117, 118, 140
Akbar I (Mughal emperor), 199
Akbar II (Mughal emperor), 42
Akhnaton, 100
al-'Afghani, Jamal ad-din, 109
al-'Azm, Sadik Jalal, 187
al-Ṭabarī, Ibn Jarīr, 202
Alexander, 34
Ali (Khalifa), 210, 211, 213
Almond, Philip, 82
Althusser, Louis, 188
America, United States of. *See* United States of America
Americas, 2, 17, 91, 108
Amherst, Governor General, 41
Amin, Idi, 194
Amritanandamayee Ma, 229
anachronism, 63, 169, 281n1
Anand, Mulk Raj, 134, 239
Anderson, Benedict, 20, 31, 80, 221
androgyny, 65, 125, 263, 293n39
Anglicanism. *See* Christianity
anglicists, 17, 27–28, 34, 41, 63, 64, 65, 192,

285n48. *See also* English education; orientalists
Anstey, F., 133
anthropology, 22, 29, 184, 197, 213, 221, 225, 263, 265
apocalypse, 145, 169, 185, 217, 218, 249, 267
Appadurai, Arjun, 21, 248
Arabic (language), 1, 39, 176, 182, 196, 197, 207
Aravamudan, Srinivas, 281n1, 282n2
Archer, Mildred, 15
archetypes (of gurus), 229, 239, 262
Archilochus, 197
Arendt, Hannah, 165, 166
Aristotle, 118
Arjuna (character in Mahābhārata), 146, 147, 149, 150, 155, 156, 157, 162, 165, 166, 167, 168, 169, 178, 269. *See also* Bhagavadgītā
Arnold, Edwin, 18, 84, 153, 154
Arunachalam, V. S., 173
Arundale, Rukmini, 37
Arya Samaj, 75, 89, 105, 107, 110, 240, 244, 307n30
Aryans, 34, 64, 100–101, 111, 129, 151, 307n30; and Nazism, 100–101
Asad, Talal, 19, 184, 221, 302n1, 302n10
ashram, 95, 99, 100, 224, 230, 241, 242, 252, 254, 255
associationism, 111, 253
atheism, 19, 42, 111, 120, 225
Atkinson, William Walker (Yogi Ramacharaka), 223
atomic bomb, 23, 60, 143, 146, 147, 148, 158, 160–64, 166, 167, 170, 172, 173, 175, 182, 217, 296n11, 299n57. *See also* nuclearism
Augustine, Saint, 234
aum (Hindu sacred syllable), 41, 125, 126, 129, 136, 137, 141, 253, 293n42
Aum Shinrikyo, 248
aura, 225, 226, 227, 242, 255, 264
Aurobindo, Sri, 22, 28, 45, 67, 69, 91, 94, 95, 96, 97, 98, 99, 100, 101, 102, 103, 134,

265–70, 311n5; as discourse, 6, 8–9,
60–62, 90, 128, 206, 225; as Hindu
English, 184, 272n13; humorous aspects
of, 34–35, 307n30; Islam as part of, 24,
143, 272n13; as register, 6, 7–8, 31–37,
60, 90, 128, 252; as soporific of, 35; as
symptom of secularism, 184; as theory
of excess, 220, 225. *See also* transidiomaticity; cosmopolitanism
guru literature, 60–62, 67, 91–104, 137,
225, 250, 257, 259, 263
Gustafson, James, 165

Haeckel, Ernst, 151
Hagelin, John, 246
Haggard, H. Rider, 211
Halhed, Nathaniel Brassy, 27, 36, 37, 64
Halliday, Michael, 6
Hallisey, Charles, 83, 286n55
Ham, 34
Hamilton, Elizabeth, 221
Ha'nish, Rev. Dr. Otman Zar-Adusht, 223
Hare Krishnas, 18
Hari Rama (Yogi), 223
Harrison, George, 242, 243, 255, 257
Harrison, Vernon, 108
Harvard University, 40, 223
Hastie, William, 74
Hastings, Warren, 36, 69, 154, 155
Hawthorne, Nathaniel, 252, 254
Heard, Gerald, 57
Heaven's Gate, 248
Hebrew, 35
Heelas, Paul, 222
Hegel, 64, 151, 155
Heidegger, Martin, 89, 268
Herder, Johann Gottfried, 64
hermeticism, 107, 118, 119
Herodotus, 34
Herrnstein Smith, Barbara, 30
heterotopia, 230, 231, 247
Hijiya, James, 146, 147, 148, 296n15,
299n57
Hindi (language), 2, 14, 45, 95, 196,
212, 239
Hindu gods and goddesses: Brahma, 34,
156; Durga (Bhawani), 49, 71, 93; Gane-
sha (Vinayaka), 15, 35, 199, 240; Hanu-
man, 88, 199; Indra, 35; Jagaddhatri, 71;
Kali, 71; Kalki, 100; Krishna, 35, 51, 57,
74, 75, 88, 90, 94, 100, 142, 146, 147, 149,

150, 153, 155, 156, 157, 162, 165, 167–69,
178, 195, 199, 211, 212, 232, 236, 242, 269;
Lakshmi, 71; Mariamman, 15; Muruga
(Skanda), 15, 34; Saraswati, 71; Shakti,
56, 92, 93, 99, 124, 125, 163, 171, 253;
Shiva, 34, 50, 84, 124, 125, 179, 236, 237,
252, 253, 255; Vishnu (Narayana), 35, 68,
71, 94, 100, 149, 156; Viswacarman, 35.
See also Hinduism
Hindu Right, 19, 34–36, 71, 91, 151–52,
171, 173, 179, 185, 212, 216, 220–21,
224, 265
Hinduism, *passim*; attacks on, 40; Christianized, 18, 24, 52, 288n90; cyclical time
in, 37; and deism, 6, 26, 38, 43, 67; devotional, 45, 49, 149, 150, 153, 226; diasporic, 191, 224–25; as English nominalization, 41; English-language
proselytization of, 8, 38, 40–41, 45, 46,
52, 54–55; and geography, 34–36; as majoritarian religion, 21, 26; and maternal
notions of deity, 51, 71, 87, 99; mentality
created by, 171, 177; modern, 38, 105,
142, 274n30; modernization of, 16–19;
muscular, 56, 75; myths of, 97, 179, 192,
236; neo-, 64, 143, 179, 222, 224, 225;
New Age, 220–64; as pantheism, 43, 64;
"Protestant," 152–53; rishis as ancient
exponents of, 8, 34, 49, 54, 56, 102, 156,
258; semitized, 64; as "socialinduism,"
240; "syndicated," 27, 64, 82, 91; and
transmigration of the soul, 54, 60, 88, 99,
121, 124, 192, 199, 200, 203, 206; universality of, 50, 64, 75; Vedic, 31, 33–36, 47,
50, 52, 54, 75, 76, 88, 96, 101, 153, 173,
174, 223, 235, 243, 245, 246. *See also* Arya
Samaj; Brahmo Samaj; Hindu gods and
goddesses; Hindu Right; Theosophy;
Vedanta; Yoga
Hiroshima, 146, 158, 159, 160, 161, 162,
166, 170, 181
Hitler, Adolf, 100
Hodges, William, 16
Hodgson, Brian, 82
Hodgson, Richard, 108, 109, 127, 292n30
Hollywood, 29, 57, 113, 195, 199, 220, 257,
260, 262; Hindus in, 220, 239
holocaust, 157, 161, 162, 164, 183, 267
Holwell, John Zephaniah, 33, 52
Home Rule, Indian, 69, 120, 139, 151, 153,
161, 234, 236

61660410R00209

Made in the USA
Lexington, KY
16 March 2017